THE CONSUMING BODY

Theory, Culture & Society

Theory, Culture & Society caters for the resurgence of interest in culture within contemporary social science and the humanities. Building on the heritage of classical social theory, the book series examines ways in which this tradition has been reshaped by a new generation of theorists. It will also publish theoretically informed analyses of everyday life, popular culture and new intellectual movements.

EDITOR: Mike Featherstone, *University of Teesside*

SERIES EDITORIAL BOARD
Roy Boyne, *University of Northumbria at Newcastle*
Mike Hepworth, *University of Aberdeen*
Scott Lash, *University of Lancaster*
Roland Robertson, *University of Pittsburgh*
Bryan S. Turner, *Deakin University*

Recent volumes include:

Risk Society
Towards a New Modernity
Ulrich Beck

Max Weber and the Sociology of Culture
Ralph Schroeder

Postmodernity USA
The Crisis of Social Modernism in Postwar America
Anthony Woodiwiss

The New Politics of Class
Social Movements and Cultural Dynamics in Advanced Societies
Klaus Eder

The Body and Social Theory
Chris Shilling

Symbolic Exchange and Death
Jean Baudrillard

Sociology in Question
Pierre Bourdieu

Economies of Signs and Space
Scott Lash and John Urry

Religion and Globalization
Peter Beyer

Baroque Reason
The Aesthetics of Modernity
Christine Buci-Glucksmann

THE CONSUMING BODY

Pasi Falk

SAGE Publications
London • Thousand Oaks • New Delhi

To my beloved wife, Liisa

SAGE Publications Ltd
6 Bonhill Street
London EC2A 4PU

SAGE Publications Inc
2455 Teller Road
Thousand Oaks, California 91320

SAGE Publications India Pvt Ltd
32, M-Block Market
Greater Kailash – I
New Delhi 110 048

British Library Cataloguing in Publication data

Falk, Pasi
  Consuming Body. – [Theory, Culture &
Society Series)
I. Title II. Series
306.3

ISBN 0–8039–8973–3
ISBN 0–8039–8974–1 (pbk)

Library of Congress catalog card number 94–066633

Typeset by Photoprint, Torquay, Devon.
Printed in Great Britain by The Cromwell Press Ltd,
Broughton Gifford, Melksham, Wiltshire

CONTENTS

ACKNOWLEDGEMENTS

I would like to thank all my colleagues and friends at the University of Helsinki for inspiring discussions around the themes of body and consumption. Special thanks for Bryan Turner, Jukka Siikala and J.P. Roos for their valuable comments during the creation of this book. I am also indebted to the editors of Sage, Stephen Barr, Louise Murray and Rosemary Campbell, whose professional skills turned this book-project into reality.

The publication details of the original versions of the chapters in this book are as follows:
Chapter 2 (Body, Self and Culture) is elaborated from the original version published with the title 'Modern Oralities – a cultural topology of the consuming body' in *Research Reports of the Department of Sociology*, University of Helsinki, No. 227, 1992. Chapter 3 (Corporeality and History) was originally published in *Acta Sociologica*, Vol. 28, No. 2, 1985: 115–36 with the title 'Corporeality and Its Fates in History'. Reprinted with the permission of Scandinavian University Press. Chapter 4 (Towards an Historical Anthropology of Taste) was originally published in *Social Science Information*, Vol. 30, No. 4, 1991: 758–90 with the title 'Homo Culinarius – towards an historical anthropology of taste'. Chapter 5 (Consuming Desire) was originally published with the title 'Consuming Supplements – paradoxes of modern hedonism' in *Research Reports of the Department of Sociology*, University of Helsinki, No. 226, 1992. Chapter 7 (Pornography and the Representation of Presence) was originally published with the title 'The Representation of Presence: Outlining the Anti-aesthetics of Pornography' in *Theory, Culture and Society*, Vol. 10, No. 2, 1993: 1–42.
I would like to thank the publishers for their permission to reprint this work.

Copies of Aspirin advertisments (Chapter 6) courtesy of Bayer.

PREFACE

Bryan S. Turner

Ten or 15 years ago it was possible to argue that the body was a topic which had been systematically and seriously neglected in the social sciences, particularly in the sociology of modern culture. However, in the 1980s a small trickle of books began to appear which both problematized the body as a topic in social theory and also recognized the body as a major issue in modern culture and politics. The social background to the emerging interest in the sociology of the body included the political and social impact of feminism and the women's movement in the academy and broader society, the complex legal and ethical questions surrounding the new medical technologies of in vitro fertilization, the development of the techniques of virtual reality, the increasing use of cyborgs for both military and industrial purposes, and the development of an aesthetics of the body in consumer culture. The evolving interest in the body on the part of sociologists was signalled by such publications as John O'Neill's *Five Bodies* (1985) and *The Communicative Body* (1989), Francis Barker's *The Tremulous Private Body* (1984), David Armstrong's *The Political Anatomy of the Body* (1983), Don Johnson's *Body* (1983) and *The Body and Society* (Turner, 1984). These studies were influenced by a variety of theoretical and philosophical traditions, but the work of Michel Foucault (1981, 1987 and 1988) was clearly of major significance in the development of a general analysis of the body. In addition to the perspective of Foucault on the discipline of the body in a carceral society, social theories also drew heavily on the phenomenological perspective of Maurice Merleau-Ponty (1962), but the interest in the phenomenology of the body should be seen as an effect of a broader concern with the understanding of the everyday life-world and the life-nexus, the study of which had been profoundly shaped by both Martin Heidegger's critique of the metaphysics of being (Dreyfus, 1991), by Edmund Husserl's commentary on the philosophy of Descartes (Husserl, 1991) and by the parallel development of the concept of the 'life-nexus' (*Lebenszusammenhang*) in Wilhelm Dilthey's philosophy. The complex inter-relationship between Husserl, Heideggar, Foucault and the growth of the sociology of the body has yet to be fully explored and understood. However, this critical response to the rationalism of Descartes and the Cartesian view of the subject led eventually into a post-structuralist orientation to the importance of emotions, desire and the affective life, the modern self is seen as charged by sensibility and emotions, and by the need for coporeal intimacies.

It is now no longer possible to talk about the absence of the body in social theory. In a variety of subfields within the social sciences there has been a plethora of publications relating to the body; one indication of the quality of this recent scholarship is the work edited by Michel Feher, *Fragments for a History of the Human Body* (1989). None the less we do not possess a coherent and comprehensive theory of the body which would address the huge range of problems relating to the issue of human embodiment, the body and the body-image. This Preface provides a pretext for developing a sketch of what such a comprehensive theory might entail.

At present the sociology of the body is highly developed in three areas. Firstly the bulk of research on the body has been into representational issues, examining the symbolic significance of the body as a metaphor of social relationships. Research on the representational aspect of the body has dominated much of the anthropological tradition, and the research of Mary Douglas on *Purity and Danger* (1966) and *Natural Symbols* (1970) created a tradition of scholarly enquiry into the problems of danger and risk surrounding the orifices of the body as representations of the dangers surrounding transitional points in social life. In medieval Christian culture the five senses were doors or windows on the soul, through which dangers could enter and threaten the spiritual life of the individual; it was important to guard these openings. The mouth was a door through which the Devil could enter the castle of the body (Pouchelle, 1990). Douglas' work was therefore a stimulating and original contribution to the traditional notion of taboo and pollution in anthropological work. Douglas' analysis of cosmology can be seen to be an extension of the work of writers like Emile Durkheim, Marcel Mauss and Robert Hertz who explored the problem of the sacred and profane distinction as it related to the construction of the body as a representation of social divisions. Hertz's study of the sacred nature of the right hand in his *Death and the Right Hand* (1960) pointed to the importance of the body in a range of dichotomies and conceptual schema, including the notion of the inside and the outside. Hertz's work on handedness in relation to the sacred (right)/profane (left) distinction has been generally important for work on the asymmetry of the human body, where sidedness is fundamental to the cultural preference for the right side and right hand (Coren, 1992; Turner, 1992). These representational studies have also been highly developed in the history of art and in the historical analysis of the nature of political sovereignty. Here again the historical research of E.H. Kantorowicz (1957) on the nature of the sacred and profane body of the king was a major development in understanding the symbolic role of the body in political discourse. Louis Marin's analysis (1988) of the king's narrative and the power of the king's body in France might also be taken as a paradigmatic illustration of this approach to sovereignty. The representational issues surrounding the human body typically hinge on the anatomical differences between men and women. Representations of women's bodies therefore often indicate the paradoxical role of women in society as creative agents through reproduction and subordinates through the patriarchal power of men. These contradictory images of women have often been exaggerated within a religious framework where the masculinity of God conflicts with the universality of the divine. This problem was focused in Christianity on the figure of Mary who was both subordinate to God's will but who also reproduced Christ as a man. The idea of immaculate conception was important to suggest that Mary's earthly existence as a woman did not contaminate Christ as a divine figure. In Mariology there was therefore a strong temptation to see Mary as co-redemptrix with Christ. This ambiguity in the power and status of Mary presented a variety of representational problems for medieval art which were resolved by various symbolic presentations of Mary as virgin and Mary as mother (Miles, 1986).

The second major focus of the recent development of sociology of the body has been around the question of gender, sex and sexuality. The questions about the gendered nature of power have been facilitated by feminist and gay writing on the body. Much of the development of feminist writing in this area has depended upon the creative work of writers like Julia Kristeva (Crownfield, 1992), Donna Haraway (1989) and Arlie Hochschild (1983). The general drift of much of this debate can be summarized in the notion that, while we are born either male or female, masculinity and femininity are social and cultural products. There has been considerable interest therefore in how costume and fashion help to fabricate the female body (Gaines and Herzog, 1990). In this sense, sex has a history of being constructed by the powerful discourses of religion, medicine and the law. The work of Foucault on the historical construction of sexuality has once more played a major role in this area. Foucault's work was initially directed towards the various institutions, practices and techniques by which the body is disciplined, but his later work moved more in the area of how the self is produced through the production of the body, that is, through the technologies of the self (Martin et al., 1988). The work of Foucault has inspired a number of major historical enquiries into the complex relationship between the body, gender and sexuality. One might mention in particular the work of Thomas Lacqueur (1990). In his *Making Sex, Body and Gender from the Greeks to Freud*, Lacqueur has shown how medieval theories of sexuality held to the doctrine of a single sex with dichotomous genders in which the female body was simply a weakened or inverted form of the male body. Anatomical investigation was unable to transform this rigid ideological notion into an alternative discourse until the emergence of Freudian psychoanalysis. A considerable amount of contemporary scholarship therefore has gone into the historical analysis of the impact of Christian ideology on the presentation of gender differences as differences of a moral order (Aries and Bejin, 1985; Cadden, 1993; Rousselle, 1988). Although much of this analysis is concerned with the historical shaping of the difference between men and women, gender differences continue to play a major role in the representation of power and authority in contemporary industrial societies. For example, Emily Martin (1987) in her *The Woman in the Body* has presented a fascinating analysis of the relationship between industrial production and reproduction in which for example, the reproduction of children is still referred to as 'labour'.

The third arena within which the sociology of the body has played a major theoretical role in recent debates in the social sciences is in the area of medical issues. The sociology of the body has been important in providing a sociological view in such categories as sickness, disease and illness (Turner, 1987). The body is crucial to the whole debate about the social construction of medical categories where the naive empiricism of conventional medicine has been challenged by the notion that diseases have a history, are culturally shaped by current scientific discourses and owe their existence to relations of power. Of course, the social constructionist debate is highly provocative and to some extent unresolved and unsettled, but it has provided a powerful paradigm for challenging much of the taken-for-granted wisdom of conventional medicine. David Armstrong's *The Political Anatomy of the Body* (1983) provides a useful illustration of the impact of the new sociology of knowledge on the historical analysis of medicine via a focus on the spatial and temporal dispersion of the human body. Once again much of this historical critique of the taken-for-granted paradigm of medicine has been promoted by feminist analysis and feminist theory, particularly in relation to conditions like anorexia nervosa (Bell, 1985; Brumberg, 1988).

There is therefore in contemporary social theory a strong movement towards an elaboration of the sociology of the body ranging from the postmodern debate (Boyne, 1988), to calls for 'rematerializing the human in the social sciences of religion' (McGuire, 1990), and to the reappraisal of major literary figures in terms of the metaphor of the body as in the case of *Jane Austen and the Body* (Wiltshire, 1992). Despite this effervescence of activity in the field, the body remains illusive and ill-defined; we still lack a general theory of the body in society and of society in the body. The great importance, indeed the joy, of reading Pasi Falk's *The Consuming Body* is the realization that a general perspective on the body is, to use a body metaphor, 'near at hand'. Falk's book shows how we can move from the analysis of corporeality to an analysis of the organs of the body and, via this brilliant study of the mouth, to an analysis of social reciprocity and social solidarity, concluding, through an analysis of taste and disgust, with a theory of modern consumption and the self as realized through self expression in consumption. In this Preface I propose to identify a number of core features which are necessary to constitute, from a theoretical stand point, a coherent outline of the body following the lead of Falk in his historical account of the orders of society, which bind the body to society, and the way in which the body shapes social relations. My anxiety with the existing social theory of the body is that it fails to move beyond the notion of representation and social construction to a genuine understanding of social reciprocity which is the core issue in any sociological perspective. Falk's superb and sustained analysis of orality seems to me to provide exactly the link which is necessary to pull together an implicitly individualistic approach to the body in much contemporary writing to a genuinely social view of the nature of human embodiment.

A general outline of the theory of the body requires the following:

(a)   a sophisticated understanding of the very notion of embodiment which would be a method of exploring the systematic ambiguity of the body as corporality, sensibility and objectivity;

(b)   an embodied notion of the social actor and a comprehensive view of how the body-image functions in social space;

(c)   a genuinely sociological appreciation of the reciprocity of social bodies over time, that is an understanding of the communal nature of embodiment and;

(d)   a thoroughly historical sense of the body and its cultural formation.

These elements are implicit in Falk's study of the body and modern consumption, and in the Preface I merely offer some slight emphasis to his general approach. I conceive of these areas of analysis in terms of a hierarchy: from the nature of embodiment, which addresses the whole question of social existence; to the nature of the social actor; to the social level of exchange and reciprocity, and to the most general level of historical, cultural formations.

The debate about embodiment has emerged out of a general dissatisfaction with the legacy of Descartes' rational actor which was the foundation of nineteenth-century social sciences models of reality and which survived into contemporary theory via Max Weber's sociology of action and Talcott Parsons' general theory of voluntaristic social action in the 1950s. The phenomenological tradition has attempted to provide a more sustained notion of the relationship between the objective instrumental body and the subjective living body, which is captured in the distinction in the German between *Korper* and *Leib* (Honneth and Joas, 1988). The notion of embodiment suggests that all of the fundamental processes of conception, perception, evaluation and judgement are connected to the fact that human beings are embodied social agents. It is not the case simply that human beings have a body but they are involved in the development of their bodies over their own life-cycle; in this respect, they are bodies. In this regard, the notion of the sociology of the body may be somewhat misleading in suggesting a special area of sociological enquiry. It might be more appropriate to talk about a sociology of embodiment indicating that the question of the human body and embodied experience cannot be isolated to a particular field subdiscipline or area of study. In the development of this approach, an implicit philosophy anthropology has been profoundly important especially in the work of writers like Arnold

Gehlen (1988). I believe that Falk has incorporated this notion of the body and embodiment into his whole approach to consumption, because he realizes that, while one can talk about an objective body, as sociologists we need to concentrate on corporeality or bodiliness as the experientiality of the body. As he says in the introduction to his book 'the body has to be understood as a sensory and sensual being'.

The nature of corporeality and embodiment leads directly into the question of the self and the social actor. The characterization of the social actor has been an issue which has dominated the entire development of the social sciences, involving as it does questions about the rationality of social action, the importance or otherwise of affective and emotional elements, and the role of symbol and culture in the constitution of the social self. By and large the corporeality of the social actor has been, until recent years, neglected in the analysis of social action. The brilliance of Falk's approach to this question is to cast it in a distinctively historical context, that is we do not have to decide on an essentialist definition of the social actor but rather we are obliged to explore the historical setting of the corporeality of the social self. Recent writing on the body has indeed associated the emergence of the debate about the body with the growing importance of the postmodern or reflexive self in high modernity. For example, Anthony Synnott has stated somewhat baldly that 'the body is also, and primarily, the self. We are all embodied' (1993:1). In a similar fashion, Chris Shilling, following the approach of Anthony Giddens to contemporary forms of intimacy, also argues that the project of the self in modern society is in fact the project of the body; 'there is a tendency for the body to become increasingly central to the modern person's sense of self-identity' (Shilling, 1993:1). The transformation of medical technology in recent years has made possible the construction of the human body as a personal project through cosmetic surgery, organ transplants, and transsexual surgery. In addition there is the whole panoply of dieting regimes, health farms, sports science and nutritional science which are focused on the development of the aesthetic, thin body. Both Synnott and Shilling have noted that modern sensibility and subjectivity are focused on the body as a representation of the self, such that the body is in contemporary society a mirror of the soul. I have argued (Turner, 1984) that this involves a profound process of secularization whereby the diet is transformed from a discipline of the soul into a mechanism for the expression of sexuality which is in turn the focus of modern self-hood. Whereas traditional forms of diet subordinated desire in the interests of the salvation of the soul, in contemporary consumer society the diet assumes an entirely different meaning and focus, namely as an elaboration or amplification of sexuality. The project of the self therefore is intimately bound up with these historical transformations of the nature of the body, its role in culture and its location in the public sphere.

However, the claim made by Giddens and adopted by Shilling that high modernity is marked by the development of self-reflexivity is a problematic historical claim. It can be argued by contrast that the history of self-reflexivity has to be traced to the transformation of confessional practice in the twelfth century (Morris, 1987), through the growth of Christian disciplines and spiritual manuals in the Reformation, to the Protestant tradition of piety and to the Protestant diary, and to the Counter-Reformation's elaboration of baroque mentalities. In particular the seventeenth century had a very distinctive conception of the person as a construct or artifice, as the product of social intervention and cultural organization. The individual, as a creation of social and historical arrangements, was revizable. The idea that the world is a stage and all the people merely players perfectly expressed this view. What is significant about contemporary society is the fact that the possibility of the body/self as a project is now open to a mass audience, being no longer the goal or ideal of an elite court group or high bourgeois culture. Dieting, jogging, the work-out, mass sport, and physical education have all brought the idea of the perfect body to a mass audience. In this sense, Giddens' claims about self-reflexivity and the democratization of love are certainly plausible in that the quest for personal satisfaction through the body beautiful is now a mass ideal. The significance of Pasi Falk's approach to the body is to connect the emergence of the modern self with the idea of consumption. Following the work of Colin Campbell (1987) on the relationship between romanticism and consumerism, Pasi Falk argues that the sense of the self in contemporary society is profoundly connected with the idea of unlimited personal consumption (of food, signs and goods). I consume, therefore I am. The modern advertising industry has of course elaborated the whole idea of the consuming self as the ideal form of the modern person. In the process of developing this argument, Pasi Falk also provides us with a profoundly important critique of Foucault's treatment of the self as merely the effect of discipline and technologies of the self. Foucault's continuing commitment to structuralist forms of analysis subordinated not only the phenomenology of experience and the sensual body, but also removed any possibility of resistance or opposition to disciplinary practices. Perhaps to Pasi Falk's analysis of the consuming self, we might add the notion that for the self in a consumer society, it is the body-image that plays the determining role in the evaluation of the self in the public arena (Schilder, 1964). It is the surface of the body which is the target of advertising and self-promotion, just as it is the body surfaces which are the site of stigmatization. The modern consuming self is a representational being.

Sociology is ultimately not an analysis of representational meanings, but a science or discipline of action and interaction. We need to understand the body in the processes of action and interaction at the level of everyday reciprocities and exchange. Pasi Falk's approach to eating and consumption provides him with an important way of developing the notion of social solidarity from an analysis of the consuming body. One might note that the very word sociology comes from the Latin *socius* meaning friendship or companionship; sociology is a science of friendship and companionship.

Companionship is in literal terms a community based upon the sharing of bread and we might therefore suggest that sociology is an analysis of the eucharistic community, that is an enquiry into forms of solidarity based upon the reciprocity of (already always social) bodies in a context of shared eating. While sociologists have typically grounded social solidarity in the idea of shared values, there may be a more primitive notion of community, that is an eating community. Here again the mouth is a particularly interesting feature of the human body, being the site of an ambiguous set of practices which include eating and biting, kissing and shouting, sucking and talking. Pasi Falk draws our attention to an important relationship between words and food, because words and food are crucial means of reciprocity and exchange. The argument about self formation is now connected, through a discussion of eating, with the formation of society itself as an eating community.

In an argument which is highly connected to Emile Durkheim's analysis of the sacred profane dichotomy in *The Elementary Forms of Religious Life* (1961) Pasi Falk draws an historical contrast between the ritual meal of primitive society and the individuated forms of eating and consumption in modern society in an analysis which contrasts communion with exchange. It is important to note that Fustel de Coulanges, who influenced Durkheim's view of religion and society, argued in *The Ancient City* in 1864 (Fustel de Coulanges, n.d.) that the hearth was the institution which created the foundation of classical Roman society; the hearth was the focal point where the family was gathered in ritualistic activities, which created fundamental social bonds. The gods of the family hearth were particularistic deities of the social group. In Pasi Falk's version of the elementary forms of society, it is the eating community and the ritual meal which provide the ground-work for the formation of society as such. One might also note that this is a line of argument which follows the earlier work of William Robertson Smith (1927), who in his lectures of 1889 on the primitive semitic society also drew attention to the social functions of the ritual meal of sacrifice in the formation of Abrahamic religions. In Christianity this ritual meal had been converted into a formal communion with God through the ritual consumption of the body and blood of Christ. Just as the affective bond between mother and child is formed through female lactation, so the intimate emotional bond at the base of society is formed by shared consumption of food around a ritualized pattern of eating. For Pasi Falk the transformation taking place in modern society is thus away from the collective rituals of eating to the privatized meal. Here again the history of society is linked to the history of the body, that is to the transformations of taste taking place in the reorganization of eating.

One might argue that one of the most profound dichotomies in the study of society which has been developed by sociology has been the contrast between community and association which follows from the work of Ferdinand Tönnies (1957). The *Gemeinschaft/Gesellschaft* distinction has influenced much of subsequent sociology; wherever there is a distinction between universalism and particularism, between neutrality and affectivity, between the local and global, between the rational and the non-rational as in for example Talcott Parsons' concept of the pattern variables, one can detect the legacy of Tönnies. In Pasi Falk's hands, this *Gemeinschaft/Gesellschaft* distinction is transformed into a theory of the body/self/society such that the communal bonds of the ritual meal are eventually replaced by the privatized forms of consumption in modern society, but this historical transformation is also one from the open body/closed self to the closed body/open self of modern society. Pasi Falk's notion, which again follows Durkheim's views on individualism and individualation, is that in primitive society the self is underdeveloped but by constrast the body is open, whereas in contemporary society the self is overdeveloped and correspondingly the body is closed. This open/closed body distinction is thus mapped onto a notion of collective and individualized patterns of eating. One might add to Pasi Falk's view of the transformation of the ritualized meal into restaurant snack, the Weberian notion of the rationalization of the distribution and consumption of food. The modern consumption of food is not only shaped by commercial transformations of eating in the restaurant but also by the application of science through dietetics and nutrition to the production of effective and efficient means of eating. One could imagine a research programme which would trace the impact of home economics, nutritional science and dietetics on the rationalization of the consumption of food as an illustration of the secularization and rationalization of food-consumption. In a recent study of the impact of Fordism and Taylorism on the food industry, George Ritzer (1993) has analysed McDonaldization as an illustration of Weber's theory of rationalization and disenchantment. McDonalds operates with a limited menu, precise measurements of food and standardized systems of delivery in order to achieve efficiency, profitability and reliability. McDonaldization removes all surprises from life; its production methods remove the unpredictable from eating, including the risk of food poisoning. The short hasty lunch undertaken at McDonalds is thus the opposite of the orgiastic ritual meal of the primitive hoard. The gap between the traditional family meal with its bourgeois civility and conviviality and the privatized lunch time bite at McDonalds perhaps beautifully captures the distinction between the life world and the rational system of modern industrial society.

It is probably appropriate to regard sociology as an alternative commentary on the limitations and failures of classical economic theories of economic action, need and rational behaviour. Sociology developed as an alternative to the notion of economizing actions by considering the non-utilitarian significance of consumption, the role of non-rational and affective issues in consumer choice, the political regulation of knowledge, and the constraints on the sovereignty of the consumer. Sociology functioned as a critique of the underlying moral and political assumptions of the operation of markets in civil society. Pasi Falk's superb study of the mouth, consumption, the body and society could be seen as a continuation of that classical theme, namely as a critique of the disembodied actor of classical economic theory. His analysis of luxury, conspicuous consumption and the social implications of modern patterns of eating is a genuine sociological contribution to economic theory, again very much in the tradition of Durkheim's critique of Manchester economics and its utilitarian assumptions. Pasi Falk takes us a long way towards a comprehensive sociology of the body, but there is clearly much work still to be done especially around the idea of the postmodern body, the relation between the body and risk society, the continuation of the gender division and the sexual division of labour and the implications of virtual reality for social embodiment. Although there is much terrain to cover, Pasi Falk's path-breaking study points us clearly in the right direction through this stimulating analysis of the sensuality of orality and corporeality.

References

Aries, P. and Bejin, A. (eds) (1985) *Western Sexuality: Practice and Precept in Past and Present Times*. Oxford: Basil Blackwell.

Armstrong, D. (1983) *The Political Anatomy of the Body: Medical Knowledge in Britain in the Twentieth Century*. Cambridge: Cambridge University Press.

Barker, F. (1984) *The Tremulous Private Body: Essay on Subjection*. London and New York: Methuen.

Baudrillard, J. (1993) *Symbolic Exchange and Death*. London: Sage.

Bell, R.M. (1985) *Holy Anorexia*. Chicago and London: University of Chicago Press.

Boyne, R. (1988) 'The Art of the Body in the Discourse of Postmodernity, *Theory Culture and Society*. 5 (2/3): 527–42.

Bourdieu, P. (1990) *The Logic of Practice*. Cambridge: Polity Press.

Brumberg, J.J. (1988) *Fasting Girls: the Emergence of Anorexia Nervosa as a Modern Disease*. Cambridge, MA: Harvard University Press.

Cadden, J. (1993) *Meanings of Sex Difference in the Middle Ages: Medicine, Science and Culture*. Cambridge: Cambridge University Press.

Campbell, C. (1987) *The Romantic Ethic and the Spirit of Modern Consumerism*. Oxford: Basil Blackwell.

Coren, S. (1992) *Lefthander: Everything you Need to Know about Left-handedness*. London: John Murray.

Crownfield, D. (ed.) (1992) *Body/Text in Julia Kristeva: Religion, Women and Psychoanalysis*. New York: State University of New York Press.

Douglas, M. (1986) *Purity and Danger: An Analysis of Concepts of Pollution and Taboo*. Harmondsworth: Penguin.

Douglas, M. (1970) *Natural Symbols: Explorations in Cosmology*. London: Barrie and Rockliff.

Dreyfus, H.L. (1991) *Being-in-the-World*. Cambridge, MA: The MIT Press.

Durkheim, E. (1961) *The Elementary Forms of the Religious Life*. New York: Colliert Books.

Elias, N. (1978) *The Civilising Process*. Vol. 1. Oxford: Basil Blackwell.

Feher, M. (ed.) with Naddaf, R. and Tazi, N. (1989) *Fragments for a History of the Human Body*. New York: Zone (3 vols).

Foucault, M. (1981) *The History of Sexuality, Vol. 1 An Introduction*. Harmondsworth: Penguin.

Foucault, M. (1987) *The Use of Pleasure. The History of Sexuality, Vol. 2*. Harmondsworth: Penguin.

Foucault, M. (1988) *The Care of the Self. The History of Sexuality, Vol. 3*. Harmondsworth: Penguin.

Fustel de Coulanges, N. (n.d.) *The Ancient City*. Garden City: Doubleday, Anchor Books.

Gaines, J. and Herzog, C. (eds) (1990) *Fabrications: Costume and the Female Body*. New York and London: Routledge.

Gehlen, A. (1988) *Man: his Nature and Place in the World*. New York: Columbia University Press.

Haraway, D.J. (1989) *Primate Visions: Gender, Race and Nature in a World of Modern Science*. London: Verso.

Hertz, R. (1960) *Death and the Right Hand*. London: Cohen and West.

Hochschild, A. (1983) *The Managed Heart: Commercialisation of Human Feeling*. Berkeley: University of California Press.

Honneth, A. and Joas, H. (1988) *Social Action and Human Nature*. Cambridge: Cambridge University Press.

Husserl, E. (1991) *Cartesian Meditations: an Introduction to Phenomenology*. Dordrecht: Kluwer.

Johnson, D. (1983) *Body*. Boston: Beacon Press.

Kantorowicz, E.H. (1957) *The King's Two Bodies*. Princeton, NJ. University of Princeton Press.

Lacqueur, T. (1990) *Making Sex, Body and Gender from the Greeks to Freud*. Cambridge, MA: Harvard University Press.

Leder, D. (1990) *The Absent Body*. Chicago: University of Chicago Press.

Levidow, L. and Robins, K. (1989) *Cyborgs Worlds: The Military Information Society*. London: Free Association Books.

McGuire, M.B. (1990) 'Religion and the Body: Rematerializing the Human Body in the Social Sciences of Religion', *The Journal for the Scientific Study of Religion*. 29 (3): 283–96.

Marin, L. (1988) *Portrait of the King*. London: Macmillan.

Martin, E. (1987) *The Woman in the Body: A Cultural Analysis of Reproduction*. Milton Keynes. Open University Press.

Martin, L.H., Gutman, H. and Hutton, P.H. (eds) (1988) *Technologies of the Self: a Seminar with Michel Foucault*. London: Tavistock.

Merleau-Ponty, M. (1962) *Phenomenology of Perception*. London: Routledge & Kegan Paul.

Miles, M.R. (1986) 'The Virgin's One Bare Breast: Female Nudity and Religious Meaning In Tuscan Early Renaissance Culture', in S.R. Suleiman (ed.), *The Female Body in Western Culture: Contemporary Perspectives*. Cambridge, MA: Harvard University Press: 193–208.

Morris, C. (1987) *The Discovery of the Individual 1050–1200*. Toronto: University of Toronto Press.

O'Neill, J. (1985) *Five Bodies: the Human Shape of Modern Society*. Ithaca and London: Cornell University Press.

O'Neill, J. (1989) *The Communicative Body*. Evanston, IL: Northwestern University Press.

Pouchelle, M.-C. (1990) *The Body and Surgery in the Middle Ages*. New Brunswick, NJ: Rutgers University Press.

Ritzer, G. (1993) *The McDonaldization of Society*. London: Sage.

Rousselle, A. (1988) *Porneia: on Desire and the Body in Antiquity*. Oxford: Basil Blackwell.

Schilder, P. (1964) *The Image and Appearance of the Human Body*. New York: John Wiley.

Shilling, C. (1993) *The Body and Social Theory*. London: Sage.

Smith, W.R. (1927) 'Lectures on the Religion of the Semites' (unpublished).

Synnott, A. (1993) *The Body Social: Symbolism, Self and Society*. London: Routledge

Tönnies, F. (1957) *Community and Association*. Michigan: Michigan State University Press.

Turner, B.S. (1984) *The Body and Society: Explorations in Social Theory*. Oxford: Basil Blackwell.

Turner, B.S. (1987) *Medical Power and Social Knowledge*. London: Sage.

Turner B.S. (1992) *Regulating Bodies: Essays in Medical Sociology*. London: Routledge.

Wiltshire, J. (1992) *Jane Austen and the Body*. Cambridge: Cambridge University Press.

1

INTRODUCTION

The human body occupies an ambiguous, even a paradoxical role in cultural categorizations – from the cosmologies of the archaic societies to the discursive and non-discursive practices of modern Western civilization. It is the most obvious and familiar visible 'thing' perceived and yet a blind-spot which tends to disappear in the very act of perception or, more generally, in the relatedness to the outside world. The ambiguous nature of the body may be formulated by means of a number of binary oppositions which all posit the body in a double role. The body is both the Same and the Other; a subject and an object, of practices and knowledge; it is both a tool and raw material to be worked upon. Or, regarded from an experiential viewpoint, the body appears to oscillate between presence and absence (Leder, 1990), most paradoxically in the intense 'feelings' – both as sensations and emotions, the latter of which also are, in the (first and) last instance, bodily modes of 'being in the world' (Merleau-Ponty, 1981) – the body seems to be simultaneously highly articulated and yet in a state of disappearance.

The mystery of the body is not solved by any biological or physiological knowledge – which is in fact only one mode of objectivizing the body in a certain epistemic discourse. Then again, my focus on the body in the present context is not one of reducing it to a biological organism, rather, my aim is to detect its historically changing position in various cultural categorizations and its various manifestations as an entity embedded in or subsumed to the Order – be it practical or discursive, or both simul-taneously, as Foucault would have it – but also acting as a site of transgression which resists Order.

As an element in cultural categorizations, the role of the human body goes far beyond its concrete physical boundaries. It acts as the basic model for cosmological schemes and not just the mere anthropomorphism of the so-called primitive cosmologies but also as a less obvious basic scheme rendering conceptual means to conceive of the Order of the outside world and its relation to the inside – as exemplified aptly in the cosmological model which has been so central in our (Western) cultural tradition, that is, the model of macrocosmos–microcosmos continuity (and analogy) deriving from Greek Antiquity (Couliano, 1987: 111–17).

But beyond this, the body occupies a much more central role 'in the mind' acting as the basis for signification and thus for the use of language in ordering both the world and action in it – even in its everyday use, as Mark

Johnson has stated in his study of the 'bodily basis of meaning, imagination and reason' (Johnson, 1987). Actually all the basic spatial and temporal categorizations – starting from the distinction 'of inside and outside to the distinction of left and right and all the active (temporal) functions between them – are based on the bodily organization. The body functions as a scheme which is then projected and unnoticeably metaphorized into neutral linguistic categories and instruments of thought.

This, in itself a fascinating topic, is not, however, the path I have taken. My focus is in the *historicity* of the body, specified, on the one hand, into the changing modes of thematization, as something subsumed to the Order, and, on the other hand, to the fates of *corporeality* or bodiliness as the *experientiality* of the body which is always related to the former. Thus, the distinction between body and corporeality, and consequently, the focusing on the latter does not only imply an emphasis on the relational and dynamic role of the human body' (and a distancing from the biological body conception) in the web of social and cultural liaisons;[1] it concerns more specifically the effects of these liaisons on the experiential aspect of the body – the body as a *sensory* and *sensual* being.

But, as I try to explicate further below (Chapters 3 and 4), the human body as a sensory and sensual being presupposes always (already) its counterpart, the 'sensible' body, that is, a body subsumed to a cultural Order – both symbolic and practical – defining its boundaries and its position in the larger whole (community or society). Even the transgressive manifestations of corporeality which momentarily collapse the Order – such as the *carni*valistic inversion of social hierarchies or the laughter breaking the order of meaning and language – are still conditioned by and related to those culturally constituted boundaries which are trespassed.

Accordingly, while dealing with the historically changing cultural and social orders and the role of the subject in relation to these, the human body should be kept within focus instead of replacing it by an abstracted model of human being as agent or actor. The latter stance, turning the body into a blind-spot, is characteristic of the sociological tradition, from the classics onwards. On the other hand, the human body has a much more integral position in the anthropological tradition, even though there have also been strong tendencies (especially evolutionism) to reduce the body to mere biology (Featherstone, 1991; B.S. Turner, 1991) – a line of thought which is driven to its extreme in the interpretations categorized under the title of sociobiology.

The pursuit of putting the body in its proper and unambiguous 'place' only repeats in new forms the basic ambivalence of the human body which is 'both "thou" and "it" – at once a distinctive animate, socially aware subject and an object painted, broken, adored, abused, and examined' (Grimes, 1982: 87); as a being both *seeing* and *seen* (Merleau-Ponty, 1964); both *being* and *having* a body (Starobinski, 1982). The expression 'me and my body' does not only manifest an historical specific body-sovereignty but also a distinction in which the body is defined as something outside 'my self' – as an out-look and/or an object to be moulded, disciplined, cultivated, etc. and as an instrument used in material or symbolic (expressive) 'labour'.

The centrality of the human body becomes most evident when thematizing the constitution of the subject, or more precisely, the formation of the self corresponding to the culturally and historically specific Order binding, moulding and 'disciplining' (Foucault) the body. The idea of the close relationship between body and self is essential in the psychoanalytical discourse, from Freud's classic formulation onwards, according to which 'the ego is first and foremost a bodily ego' being 'not merely a surface entity, but [being] itself the projection of a surface' (Freud, 1984: 364 [1923]).[2] Leo Bersani explicates the idea in more detail:

> the ego is not only, in Freud's mental topography, that part of the mental apparatus most directly influenced by the body's contact with the world, it is also a mental projection of bodily surfaces. [. . .] It fantasmatically repeats the body's contact with the world in something, perhaps, like metaperceptual structures. The ego is not a surface; it is a *psychic imitation* of surfaces. (Bersani, 1990: 95)

As the scope is expanded from 'ego' to 'self',[3] the constitution of the subject is conceived of as a dynamics which covers all the modes of interaction mediated by the apertures of the (body)surface and which ends up in an experienced continuity of 'me being in the world' distinguished from the experience of 'me being (identical with) the world', in other words, a mode of existence which defines the subject – in a more or less articulated manner – as a *separate* being.

This is where the paradoxical role of the body as 'contained and container at once' (Stewart, 1984: 104) is actualized. The boundaries or limits of the body are thematized both from outside-in and inside-out: 'known from an exterior, the limits of the body as object; known from an interior, the limits of its physical extension into space' (Stewart, 1984: 104). And furthermore, this is where the sensory apertures – or in Lacan's terms 'erotogenic zones' (Lacan, 1977: 314–15) – transmitting the inside/outside in both directions gain a central meaning: 'these apertures of ingestion and emission work to constitute the notion of the subject, of the individual body and ultimately the self', as Susan Stewart (1984) notes. That which the body lets or takes in and out is crucial both from the exterior and interior point of view, or alternatively formulated, both from the vantage point of the cultural categorizations defining the subject's 'place' within the Order and from the subject's vantage point defining his or her (bodily) boundaries and the relationship to the 'not-me'.

The dynamized model of subject constitution – as self-formation – is essentially something other and more than the biological organism–environment interaction (metabolism), it is not an interaction in merely material or energetic terms but an interaction in terms of sensory experience which is necessarily linked to the realm of *representations*. The link to representations is unavoidable regardless of whether we view the constitution of the subject from an ontogenic or from a cultural perspective. From an ontogenic perspective, the sensory interaction articulating the bodily boundaries and the distinction of inside and outside is right from the start also a mental process which defines the 'me' in relation to the 'not-me' in terms of *mental* representations. From a cultural and social perspective the bodily boundaries and the flows through its orifices are defined from the 'outside', by a symbolic and practical Order which exists for the subject primarily as *cultural* representations or as cultural categorizations which structure the world into a system of differences into which the body and self is placed.

Thus we arrive at the site where both perspectives on subject constitution intersect and where the mediation between mental and cultural representations takes place – the common ground that cannot be detected unless the constitution of the subject is brought back to its bodily basis. As noted above, this does not imply a reduction to 'biology' but rather an opening up of a perspective which aims at overcoming the unsolvable duality of psychology and sociology – the two mutually incompatible approaches both of which tend to by-pass the human body.

Keeping the body and corporeality within focus requires, it seems, a return to the Nietzschean programme which systematically relates the constitution of Orders – from political and moral to aesthetic ones – to the bodily basis they both build on and aim to mould. And this is in fact the perspective to be found, in different variations, among the representatives of post-structuralism (Lyotard, Deleuze and Guattari, Foucault, Kristeva and Derrida – each of them with different points of emphasis). Being aware of the ambiguous use of the term 'post-structuralism' – and of the fact that most of those labelled as such reject such an identity themselves – I shall venture to characterize the common ground of these thinkers in rather general terms.

The post-structuralist stance is characterized by a systematic questioning of postulated (and reductionistic) dualisms. First, the Order is conceived of as a continuum from social hierarchies to language and psychic structures. Or, to use Lyotard's earlier formulation (from the early 1970s): the 'political economy', the 'economy of the language' and the 'libidinal economy' are not only intertwined but are all parts of the same network producing one another (Lyotard, 1978 [1971]).

Second, the post-structuralists aim at overcoming the distinction between 'structure and action' or 'language and speech' (de Saussure) by means of a conceptual apparatus which focuses on the irreducible in-between. Consequently, for example, Foucault has operated with the reciprocal productivity of discursive and non-discursive formations and practices, and of power/knowledge, or with the concept of 'enunciation' (*enoncé*) conceived of both as an act and a linguistic unit. In its most elaborated form the principle of irreducibility is found by Derrida, in his concept of '*différance*', being simultaneously both structural (spatial) and actional (temporal), referring both to difference and the act of 'deferring'.

Both of these principles express a stance critical of structuralistic orthodoxy while the third one, the rejection of the philosophy of the subject, may rather be conceived of as a critical elaboration of the structuralist position. This is precisely where post-structuralist thought thematizes the human body, primarily drawing on the psychoanalytical discourse, even if in a critical manner (Deleuze and Guattari, 1983 [1972]; Foucault, 1981 [1976]). The concept of the subject is not simply eliminated but replaced by the concept of the body – a transformation which, in David Wellbery's words, 'disperses (bodies are multiple), complexifies (bodies are layered systems), and historicizes (bodies are finite and contingent products) subjectivity rather than exchanging it for a simple absence' (Wellbery, 1990: xv).

The post-structuralist approach involves, however, a range of different paths to the centrality of the human body. This is aptly exemplified in the auto-critique Michel Foucault presents when redefining his project on the 'History of Sexuality'.

The most extensively articulated treatment of the problem of the subject resolved by the thematization of the body is to be found in Michel Foucault's writing, especially in the texts from the 1970s. Here the body is the ultimate object of all intervention (from the outside) involving all the practices of power and knowledge which aim at a 'disciplined' body and even including the Order of subjectivity – structuration of the psyche – in its individualized form as a mere effect of the power-technological intervention: the soul is the prison of the body and not the other way around (Foucault, 1979). Thus, Foucault takes the Nietzschean programme to its extreme where everything 'supplementing' the body is part of the continuous Order, which is nothing else than 'the regimen that bodies pass through; the reduction of randomness, impulse, forgetfulness; the domestication of an animal, as Nietzsche claimed, to the point where it can make, and hold to, a promise' (Wellbery, 1990: xv).

Nevertheless, the pursuit of avoiding the subject philosophical stance (Foucault, 1982a: 9) leads Foucault into a problematic situation in which every characterization of the human body is turned into an ordering (discursive) intervention, that is, into part of the 'soul'. The dilemma is crystallized in the statement Foucault makes at the end of the introductory part of the *History of Sexuality* (1981: 157) according to which the fight against all definitions of sexuality should not draw on 'sex-desire' but on '*bodies and pleasures*', and that is all that can be said, because every positive characterization beyond this supplements the body with the construction of the soul, being itself part of the power/knowledge intervention from without.

Foucault's power-technological approach proved to be efficient when analysing the genealogy of the modern subject as a process of objectivization, that is, how the subject is produced as an object both of domination and knowledge (in asylums, prisons, etc.). The interpretation, so it seemed, did away with the problematic dualism in which the external (cultural/societal) Order defining the 'site' and conditions for subject

constitution still presupposed a separate thematization of subject constitution itself and so a philosophy of the subject. In other words, if the
structuration of subjectivity is located in the same continuum with the
interventionist strategies (targeted on the body), there is no need to define
a 'site' for subject constitution (a 'site' which actually presupposes a break
in the continuum).

Then again, this implies a reduction wherein the body as object is
thematized only as the body of the *other* – even when it appears as the
other's *own* body – thus excluding the possibility of dealing with both the
interactive and self-reflective dimensions of subject constitution. In other
words, the subject is reduced to a mere product surrounding the indefin-
able body, lacking the autonomy that would allow a 'producing' relationship with the outside and with itself. These other dimensions of subject
constitution presuppose the very 'site' (which Foucault had eliminated)
redefining it as a – more or less narrow – room for manoeuvre, to certain
degrees of freedom.

These are precisely the missing elements that Foucault discovers in the
early 1980s complementing the 'technologies of domination' with 'another
type of technique', the 'technologies of the self', and focusing on 'the
interaction between these two of self' (Foucault, 1982a: 10) – that
produced as an object from without and that producing itself.[4] In effect
Foucault restructured his project on the 'History of Sexuality' by outlining
the genealogy of the moral subject from a perspective which gave a
primary position to the technologies of the self with the aim of following
their changing relationship to power relations – a task which unfortunately
was never completed.

Yet Foucault's focus is on the constitution of the *moral* subject,
narrowing the concept of the self to those 'techniques' in which the subject
occupies an active and reflective role in relation to his own body – as the
subject of desire. Thus the 'technologies of the self' refer merely to a
certain aspect of self-formation without explicating its contextual meaning,
that is, its relationship to the other aspects of self-formation. This could be
interpreted as an indication of Foucault's persistent suspicion of the
psychoanalytic discourse, but it could also be regarded simply as an
elaboration of his 'original' programme which thematizes the genealogy of
the modern subject with an emphasis on its possible subversive or
oppositional potentials.

These programmatic principles do not figure in the present context and
consequently the mode of thematizing the relationship between corporeality and self-formation is closer to the thinking of those post-structuralists
who proceed, though critically, from the basic psychoanalytical formulations; from Lacan for whom subject-formation takes place at the
intersection of the body and the signifier (Wellbery, 1990: xv) to Derrida
and Kristeva, both of whom focus on the intersections of body, self and
culture.

However, my focus in the present context is more specific than the demarcations between body, self and culture. My specific theme is modern consumption, a theme which is approached by means of an interpretative scheme linking these three figures – body, self and culture (or society) – together. Thus the overall theme, reaching from corporeality to consumption, could be summarized as follows: first, human bodily existence is thematized both as the basis and – in topological terms – as the 'model' of the constitution of the subject, or more precisely, the psycho-somatic entity called the self. And, second, modern consumption is thematized as the primary realm of self-construction, offering material for both its social and personal dimensions, and for both sides of individuation – as separation and as self-completion.

The story takes off from the sensory and sensual body (Chapter 2) moving then to a topological characterization of the role of the interactive body openings which allows us to build a bridge from the body to the self and finally contextualize both of these to culturally and historically specific Orders. The *mouth* is the central character in the story outlining the corporeality of (modern) consumption – as I shall try to explicate in the following – not only due to its role as the primal organ of consumption (eating) but also due to its expressive functions, as an organ of speech.

Chapter 3 ('Corporeality and History') delineates an historical process transforming the relatively 'open' pre-modern body, allowing a wider range of bodily and affective *ex*-pressions, into a relatively 'closed' body controlling the boundaries and the flows passing through its sensory openings.

Chapter 4 ('Towards an Historical Anthropology of Taste') thematizes in more detail the relationship between 'sensations and representations' in the primal scene of consumption, that is, eating, with a specific focus on 'the anthropology of taste'. The article scrutinizes the role of ambivalences at work in the cultural definitions of the edible versus inedible – that which can be accepted *into* the body and that which must be kept *outside* it – in relation to corresponding bodily (sensory) reactions.

Chapter 5 ('Consuming Desire') traces the discursive genealogy of modern consumption in a mode inspired by the Derridean scheme of 'supplementarity'. Departing from the naturalistic (need satisfaction) and productionistic (consumption as an effect of production) model, the argumentation proceeds to an analysis of the irreducible character of the *desire–(object) desired* dynamics which is shown to acquire a specific form in the 'self-building' project of the modern individual characterized by both a pursuit of completion and of separation. The former moment may be interpreted as an introjective mode of self-construction aiming at 'eating in' to one's self the 'good objects' (Klein) of the outside world, while the latter is the very prerequisite of individual existence, a maintenance and articulation of the boundaries of the body and self distinguishing the inside from the outside world – or, in social terms, from the others.

Chapter 6 ('Selling Good(s)') shifts the focus to the modes in which products have been transformed into representations of 'good objects' in the history of modern advertising. It appears that the 'evolution' of modern advertising makes it possible to locate the phases in which the whole modern world of goods is completed – turning goods into representations and consumption into (self-related) experience. The emphasis in the language of advertising shifts towards a 'rhetoric' which does not (have to) make (falsifiable) promises or give (falsifiable) evidence but instead creates representations which are *experienced* as convincing, effective and/or merely 'pleasing' due to a mode of representation which constitutes a link between the product and an undefined 'good' primarily by connotative and associative means.

Finally, the last chapter ('Pornography and the Representation of Presence') focuses on the changing role of iconic representation in the Western tradition and specifically on the ambivalences of 'ocular introjection' (N.O. Brown) which are manifested as a pursuit of distanced and (aesthetic) reflective reception of literary and iconic representations, on the one hand, and in the pursuit of bringing back the representation to its 'authentic' presence (or realness). This topic is analysed through the specific case of pornography where the demarcation of representation and 'presence', or that which may be represented and that which may not, is manifested in a paradigmatic way. The special case of pornography opens up a perspective on the fates of representations in modern society in more general terms. Paradoxically, the pursuit of evidential explicitness, which is also found in other 'documentary' genres of media-publicity outside pornography, seems to promote what Jean Baudrillard has called 'hyperreality'.

Notes

1. This is the basis for the distinction presented by Francis Barker, a distinction of 'body' and 'bodiliness' which he argues for as follows:

> however necessary it may be to isolate the body for analytic purposes, the body in question is not a hypostatized object, still less a simple biological mechanism of given desires and needs acted on externally by controls and enticements, but a relation in a system of liaisons which are material, discursive, psychic, sexual, but without stop or centre. (Barker, 1984: 12)

My concept of 'corporeality' follows, by and large, the same Foucauldian lines but with a specific emphasis on the communicative aspect (O'Neill, 1989), on the one hand, and on the experiential aspect, on the other. Furthermore, I am focusing on the role of corporeality in the constitution of the subject in a way to be explicated below.

2. In the English translation (1927) a footnote, authorized by Freud himself, has been added here noting that 'the ego is ultimately derived from bodily sensations, chiefly from those springing from the surface of the body', followed by a statement, 'it may thus be regarded as a mental projection of the surface of the body, besides, as we have seen above, representing the superficies of the mental apparatus' (Freud, 1984: 364).

3. The terms 'ego' and 'self' are quite often used as synonyms mainly due to an indeterminate notion of the latter. In the mental 'topography' outlined by Freud (in different versions) 'ego' refers, however, to a more limited aspect of the whole personality, the latter being rather close to the notion of 'self'. 'Self' may be conceived of as 'a descriptor of the

whole personality, including areas both of conscious and unconscious functioning, with the particular connotation of a relatively permanent structure' (Frosh, 1991: 68).

4. Foucault describes the necessary complement, the other type of technique in his auto-critical note as follows:

> Techniques that permit individuals to affect, by their own means, a certain number of operations on their own bodies, their own souls, their own thoughts, their own conduct, and this in a manner so as to transform themselves, modify themselves, and attain a certain state of perfection, happiness, purity, supernatural power. Let us call this kind of technique technologies of the self. (Foucault, 1982a: 10)

2

BODY, SELF AND CULTURE

The first perspective on the topic of the consuming body will be opened by means of a 'topological' scheme linking body, self and culture together. Here the line from human corporeality to consumption could be summarized in the following two theses. First, human bodily existence is thematized both as the basis and as the 'model' of the constitution of the subject or, more precisely, the psycho-somatic entity called the self. And, second, modern consumption is thematized as the primary realm of self-construction, offering material for both its social and personal dimensions, and for both sides of individuation – as separation and as self-completion.

Beginning with the sensory and sensual body I shall proceed into the 'topology' of body openings which allows us to build a bridge from the body to the self and finally contextualize both of these to culturally and historically specific Orders. The *mouth* is the central character in the story outlining the corporeality of (modern) consumption – as I shall try to explicate in the following – not only due to its role as the primal organ of consumption (eating) but also due to its expressive functions, as an organ of speech.

Sensory organization

The role of the different senses, or in topological terms, different sensory bodily openings – conventionally categorized as the close or contact senses (touch, smell, taste) and the distant ones (sight, hearing)[1] – is by no means a biological constant. Sensory organization is, in a fundamental way, dependent on the cultural and social Order. The changes in the sensory organization are always, in one way or another, conditioned by the changes in the Order – defined in general terms, from practices to discourses.

The link between sensory organization and the Order is also the basis on which the senses are hierarchized into 'higher' and 'lower' ones. In the Western tradition, from Plato to Kant and after, the higher position is granted to the distant senses, especially the eye, while the contact senses are defined as the lower ones. The principle for the evaluative distinction changes in the course of history – from the praise of contemplative reflection to the negativization of bodiliness and purification of aesthetic experience – nevertheless, the common denominator remains: the prioritization of *distance* as a necessary precondition for reflection and/or *represen-tation* (see Chapter 7).

Thus it would seem that the historical change of sensory organization – conventionally conceived as a shift of emphasis from the close senses to the distant ones, or 'from the primacy of hearing and touching to the primacy of seeing' (Ginzburg, 1990: 93; Lowe, 1982: 95) – actually realizes these ideals in a civilizing process of sense refinement.

This is, however, too hasty a conclusion which disregards the change in the *functions* of the different senses. Undoubtedly, sensory stimulation in the modern condition is dominated especially by the visual (Bell, 1976: 105–8) giving primacy to the eye over, say, the mouth (taste/smell). Then again, if the eye simultaneously gains 'mouth-like' functions, turns into a 'voracious' organ engaged in 'iconophagy' (Mattenklott, 1982: 78–102) or functions as a channel for 'ocular introjection' modelled by the oral one (N.O. Brown, 1966: 122), the interpretation becomes problematic. Or, in another formulation, if the eye functions as a 'contact at distance' (Blanchot, 1977), the very distinction between distance and contact senses must be reconsidered.

The problematization of the distinction between close and distant senses as channels of (sensory) 'influx' is the first step which calls for a more detailed view of the topological aspects of the body and its sensory openings.

Undoubtedly, there is a difference in the form of the 'sensory stimulus', that is, between the material incorporation of eating and the optical reception of seeing but, when regarded as flows which are conditioned by representations, the situation looks quite different. Eating constitutes a receptive relationship to the outside world in terms of representations,[2] and so does seeing – though in different ways. The sensory aspect of eating – the sense of taste (broadly understood) – is not transformed into a *mental* representation in the manner visual perception turns into mental 'images' (of memory and imagination),[3] but nevertheless, both are still moulded by the *cultural* representations. The latter outline the coordinates both to that which is eaten (and what it tastes like) and to that which is seen, and how.

The physiological fact according to which the sensory apparatus is able to make distinctions is only a prerequisite for the practically endless variation of cultural categorizations, turning specific registers into mean-ingful ones, as representations. However, all this requires one basic condition: there must be a distinction between the *outside* and *inside*, a distinction which appears to be nothing else than a logical truism. Of course the distinction is the condition for something to be allowed or taken in – or given out, for that matter. But if we refuse to reduce the constellation to biology, that is, to the interaction of the organism (the 'open system') with its environment,[4] the situation looks, again, much more complicated. And this is where we have to expand the scope into the cultural topology of the (consuming) body.

Anthro(to)pology

Insofar as the inside/outside difference and the mediation between these
are conceived of in representational terms, the distinction involves already
a notion of a subject which relates itself to the environment as culture
(Order). In other words, the human body as a cultural entity is always
already a subject interacting with the 'outside' in terms of representations.
This is the first bridge, that from the body to the self, but it also actualizes
the second one, that from the body/self to culture (Order) revealing the
complicated character of the inside/outside distinction.

Surely the sensory receptors are located on the body surface. Nevertheless, the mode in which the subject is defined within the cultural Order (or
social structure) has crucial implications for the way the inside/outside
distinction is structured. This may be explicated schematically by the
following theses. First, the stronger the cultural Order and the community
bonds in which the subject is constituted, the more 'open' is the body both
to outside intervention and to a reciprocal relationship with its cultural/
social context. In general terms, this is the situation in a 'primitive' society
in which the constitution of the subject acquires the form of a 'group-ego'
(Parin, 1978) or 'group-self' (Roland, 1988)[5] defining the boundaries
between inside and outside primarily in collective terms. And, second, the
less rigid the cultural Order and the weaker the community bonds, the
more intertwined are the boundaries of the self with those of the individual
body. In other words, the constitution of the subject takes the form of an
individual self – especially characteristic of modern society – articulating
the inside/outside distinction primarily at the boundaries of the individual
self, and thus the body surface.

In the former (primitive) case the environment (of the body) is rather
conceivable as a second 'inside' which confronts the outer realms of the
'others' (not-us, non-humans, etc.) located in the 'nature' beyond (our)
culture. In the modern configuration the inside/outside distinction is more
articulated at the boundaries of the individual self and body implying that
the 'society' (*Gesellschaft*) is characterizable rather as an 'outside' – a
'second nature' – in distinction to the 'inwardness' of the archaic community (*Gemeinschaft*).

I am not, of course, claiming that primitive society is an entropic
homogeneous mass or that the modern society is a collection of atomistic
units. The historical reality and cultural variety looks quite different.
Nevertheless, what I am proposing is that the schematically formulated
duality delineates a structural characteristic in the genealogy of the modern
individual self – further specified as a 'consuming body' – as it is manifested
in Western culture (the theme which will be substantiated further below).
However, in the present context the scheme serves as a demonstration of
the *historicity* of sensory organization. It is precisely the restructuring of
the inside/outside distinction(s) – shifting the emphasis from the collective
level to the individual one – that transforms sensory organization; turning

the eye into an organ which both keeps the objects at a distance (outside) and 'eats' them inside, or, defines the mouth as the sensory site for *individual* 'judgement of taste'.

The latter may be illustrated in the following way. A cultural order in which an alimentary code (food taboos, ritual rules) defines that which may be eaten, by whom, how and when, does not leave much room for individual matters of taste. The sense of taste is surely there, but the 'judgement' is located primarily at the boundaries of the culture, in the 'mouth' of the community, as it were. Only when these boundaries grow weaker, is the judgement of taste transposed into the level of the individual self, body and mouth – still, however, related and conditioned by cultural representations.

Here we can give the well known slogan of the old scholastics – *de gustibus non disputandum* (one cannot dispute about taste) – two quite opposite meanings. In the (primitive) case of the strong alimentary code – to which it was never applied – it would refer to the fact that the judgement of what to eat and what not is made by the 'mouth' of the community according to the rules that are beyond doubt. In the modern case of individualized judgement the slogan may be conceived of in a way closer to the scholastic stance: taste cannot be disputed because it is based on the 'nature' of the individual being (body) and not in culture. Even if we do not accept the scholastic naturalization of the sense of taste,[6] referring to the fact that taste sensations never exist divorced from the realm of representations, we may still see the relevance of the idea according to which the judgement of taste is made individual, implying that the inside/outside distinction becomes more articulated on the boundaries of the individual self, the bodily surface and its sensory openings.

When considering the historicity of sensory organization, it is not enough to point to the changes in the 'stimulative' environment – to the expanding flows of images looked upon, texts to be read and new (gustatory) tastes to be experienced – which take place especially from the nineteenth century onwards in the Western world. The changing modes of reception are not only about a 'learned' ability to incorporate new modes of stimuli (mainly as representations) but essentially about the intermediating boundaries reduced to the individual (bodily) level.

Let us take an example. In the interpretation presented by Howes and Lalonde (1991) the matters of taste (judgement) are actualized in the Western history from the eighteenth century onwards primarily due to the diversification of culinary culture ('the influx of exotic foods from other continents', etc.; Howes and Lalonde, 1991: 127) and thus also of (gustatory) tastes – then expanded to other realms of individual choice, especially the aesthetic. However, the situation described builds on the preconditions that turn matters of taste into individual ones, that is, the process which actualizes the 'freedom' of individual choice and bodily sovereignty implying the possibility to *control* the flows from outside in – at least in principle. This is precisely the other dimension of the bodily control which Norbert Elias (1982) fails to thematize when he narrows the scope of the 'civilizing process' to an increased (internalized) control of the bodily and/or affective *ex*-pressions.

The mouth

The perspective outlined above allows us to focus on one of the central aspects which grants the *mouth* a particular role as a sensory body opening, especially as the site of judgement. It is not due to the discriminating powers of the sense of taste as such (Howes and Lalonde, 1991: 132) but primarily due to the fact that the mouth is the most *controlled* sensory opening of the body – with regard to the influx (eating), but also concerning the 'sublimated' outflux of speech (which will be dealt with further below). In topological terms, the mouth is a curious in-between of the outside and inside (Derrida, 1986: xxxviii), as illustrated by Figure 2.1.

The mouth is a 'vestibule' – of the larynx, as the anatomical terminology goes – functioning as an instance of a threefold choice or judgement. The first gate (a) controls that which is allowed into the mouth in the first place and in fact this is the function which may be regarded as a derivative of the 'judgement' taking place outside the individual (body), in the cultural state of strong alimentary rules: one does not put in the mouth forbidden 'polluting' things. But this is the first decision to be made in an individualized situation, too, exemplifying the subject's separateness from the outside.[7]

The second gate (c) has a more crucial role in the individualized setting. It involves the decision to take that something irreversibly into one's body and self, thus making that something part of 'me' (*Der Mensch ist was er isst*). But the actual judgement – of taste – takes place between these two gates, in the intermediate site between inside and outside (b). This is what gives the mouth and its sensory function, taste (linked to other sensory registers, especially the sense of smell), a particular position. In Walter Ong's words, 'taste is a yes-or-no sense, a take-it-or-don't-take-it sense

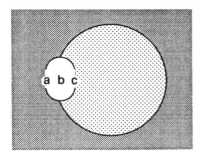

Figure 2.1 *The topology of the mouth*

letting us know what is good and what is bad for us in the most crucial physical way' (Ong, 1967: 5).

The in-between site of judgement, the mouth (b), is surely not independent of the cultural representations extending from the binary opposition of edible versus inedible to more subtle evaluative distinctions. Nevertheless, the weakening of strong alimentary codes, and rigid cultural categorizations in general (Order), not only grants the boundaries of the individual body and self a stronger role in the inside/outside distinction, but also stresses the role of the individualized mouth as an intermediary channel to be controlled and thus as the site of judgement. This may be conceived of as a step towards individual 'freedom' (of choice) and body sovereignty, but it also implies a less apparent yet more fundamental change in the role of 'eating' or, formulated in general terms, a change in the mode in which (the objects of) the outside world are taken in into the body and the self and, furthermore, a change in the mode in which the influx relates to the outflux, as it were.

The last point takes us to another important topological characteristic of the mouth. Mouth is a body opening which intermediates flows in both directions; a *bidirectional* sensory opening.[8] I am not referring here to the mouth's role in the bidirectional flows of respiration, which is a simple necessity and as such lies out of control.[9] Neither am I dealing with the concrete physiological reverse of eating, that is, vomiting (in spite of its cultural significance). What I am concerned with here is a two-way-ness which relates people to each other and to the social whole in a reciprocal and/or interactive mode, as sharing, giving and taking or exchanging – in representational terms. Actually, this is a characteristic not only of the mouth but also of the eyes, in the 'chiasm of looks' as Maurice Merleau-Ponty (1964) puts it.[10] But, as we shall find out, even the bidirectional function of the eyes is modelled by the mouth.

The first bidirectional dimension of the mouth may be characterized as follows: eating itself involves a culturally structured activity in form of a shared (ritual) *meal*, a certain kind of bidirectionality moulded by the principle of 'to eat and be eaten by' (Chapter 4). This is characteristic of so-called primitive society, in which the ritual sharing of food and its physical incorporation functions simultaneously as an act in which the partaker is incorporated or 'eaten' into the community. Eating together (*com*) the same bread (*panis*) transform the eaters into companions, according to the etymological roots. The same applies also to the reciprocal (gift) exchange, which may be conceived of as a temporalized and serialized mode of sharing; transactions between 'dividuals' (cf. Marriott, 1976: 111). This is certainly something other than the money-mediated exchange of equivalents in which the symbolic 'third' (money) intervenes, transforming the relationship between 'persons' (primarily as groups) into an in-dividualized relationship between the subject and the (material) object (Goux, 1990: 122–33).

The other bidirectional dimension of the mouth – the relationship between eating (in) and speaking (out), food and words – is actualized when outlining the historical and cultural change characterized by the erosion of rigid community structures and the coming of the individual self as these are manifested in Western history, culminating in what may loosely be called the 'modern society'. It should be noted, however, that when I operate with such generalizing concepts as 'primitive society' and 'modern society', my aim is not to delineate historical and/or evolutionary processes leading possibly from the former to the latter (Elias, 1982; Kleinspehn, 1987).

The problem on which I am focusing is those specific characteristics of modern society which may be conceived of as crucial for the understanding of the modern individual and his/her foodways. This is the vantage point for the reconstructive aim which explicates the selective genealogy of the basic dimension in which the change manifests itself in its most articulated manner, that is, the dimension of orality. So, in making generalizations where the primitive society or the 'other' (non-Western) culture is extended on an historical scale to cover the whole pre-modern condition as opposed to the modern one, I am not describing actual societies but explicating the differences in that basic dimension when compared with the modern condition and from its vantage point. Thus, the procession from pre-modern to modern orality should be understood as an *illustration* of the latter, literally, 'lighting up' its contours against the background, the cultural and historical Other.

The basic model is, however, the mouth, which in the following is first dealt with on the 'ontogenic scene' then proceeding to pre-modern orality and finally to modern orality.

The ontogenic scene

The first difference experienced by the child, the difference which is constituted on the basis of the first symptoms of erosion of the complete mother–child symbiosis, identifies the binary opposition of inside/outside with that of good/bad and that of edible/inedible. This is the situation preceding actual object-relations, in a representational sense, and thus the difference is experienced only as (unrepresentable) deviations or fluctuations in the continuous state of satiety, the symbiotic well-being. So, what the identity of the binary opposition in the child's experience actually means is that the components cannot yet be distinguished as separate. They are just temporary deviations in the state of mere 'insideness'.

There is no experience of the difference (whatever one might want to call it) in terms of objectification until the deviations are turned into a structured movement between *presence* and *absence*. Thus the distinction between outside and inside is not constituted until the symbiotic state of

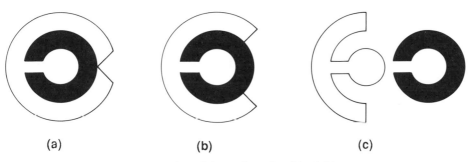

      (a)   (b)   (c)

Figure 2.2 *The constitution of inside/outside and subject/object*

existence is turned into an object (source) through its (relative) absence. In Lacanian terms, it is the absence or the *lack* which constitutes the object and thus the distinction of outside and inside, and finally, the first step in the process of separation which is also to be conceived of as the primary form of subject–object relationship – the relation of me to not-me, which is simultaneously defined as lacking (from me) and 'good', the object of desire to be incorporated into 'me' (body/self). In other words, the good as an object – the 'good object' (Klein, 1932) – is not inside, but something which is desired to be incorporated, to be taken into the inside. The first steps in the process of separation and individuation are illustrated in Figure 2.2.

The first topological scheme (a) depicts a state of (mother–child) symbiosis, which is a biological reality in the pre-natal condition but which is continued in the early post-natal phase as a mental and cultural reality. In the symbiotic situation the outside simply does not exist for the neonate: that which surrounds is also inside, as the continuum of mother–breast–milk. The second scheme (b) describes the situation of symbiosis in the process of erosion producing an elementary experience of the outside in the oscillation of presence and absence (of the mother–breast–milk), then leading to a preliminary state and experience of separateness, illustrated by the third scheme (c). At this point the outside appears, not only the outside as distinct from the inside but also in relation to the object outside – that which was mere insideness (a) but is transformed into an object through its *lack*. So, the primary relationship to the outside is simultaneously a relationship to the object outside – as the lacking, good and desired object, all boiled down to one and the same thing.

The oral phase, depicted schematically above, will be sufficient for the development of my argument concerning the basic oral mode of self-formation, which already links the mouth and eye together. The Freudian concept of 'primary identification' refers to two parallel modes of incorporation, that of *introjection* (first introduced by Ferenczi) and that of *imitation*, which are actually structured according to the mouth/eye distinction (cf. Fenichel, 1982: 36–9 [1946]). Introjection is the oral mode of self-formation in which the self (inside) is filled up with the good/lacking objects. Imitation follows the same oral principle only now realized within the realm of the visible, through the eating eyes.[11] In Otto Fenichel's words,

> The primitive reactions of imitating what is perceived and the oral introjection of what is perceived belong close together. [. . .] The concept of a primary identification denotes that actually 'putting into the mouth' and 'imitation for perception's sake' are one and the same and represent the very first relation to objects. (Fenichel, 1982: 37)

Yet, it is the mouth that acts as a model for all sensory reception and for the reciprocal relationship to the outside as object(s): 'Taking-into-the-mouth or spitting-out is the basis for all perception, and in conditions of regression one can observe that in the unconscious all sense organs are conceived as mouth-like' (Fenichel, 1982: 37). The parallel of the oral and visual explicated above may now be related to Gert Mattenklott's somewhat extreme inversion according to which the 'original drive for incorporation' is not an oral one but a visual one, that is, it can be satisfied only by 'images' (Mattenklott, 1982: 84–5). Even if the mere inversion is rather questionable (Derrida, 1986; Lehmann, 1983) the interpretation points, however, implicitly to an important aspect: whether the incorporation is mediated by mouth or eyes, the object of introjection exists for the introjector necessarily as a *representation*.

From an ontogenic point of view, the basis for representation emerges with the very *difference* – as a fact or act (cf. Derrida's *différance*)[12] – which stabilizes the oscillation of presence and absence into the distinctions of inside/outside and subject/object. This is also where the *distance* is created which activates the distance senses. Thus the notion of representation may be related to its literal meaning, as something which returns to presence. When the oscillation is experienced merely as a difference in the bodily state – between satiety and hunger, comfort and discomfort – there is no room for representation. But as soon as the oscillation is turned into an object now present, next absent and then reappearing again, a 'place' for a representation is opened – in that empty place which is created by the absence of the object (the lack), as a desire for the object preceding its re-appearance.[13]

However, the primal representation remains – paradoxically enough – unrepresentable, not only because it precedes entering into the Symbolic (Lacan), into language, but because the object, constituted through the loss (of insideness) cannot be anything else than a lacking, that is, desired, that is, good object.

Nevertheless, precisely because of its 'nameless' origin it is (re)named endlessly as whatever 'good things' that may be coded into cultural representations and thus also to individual dreams – from myths of the primitive society to modern consumer goods – as representations (see Chapter 6). So, from the subject's point of view the identity of the distinctions inside/outside and good/bad is broken, structuring the outside as a world of objects at least into two parts: that which is good and that which is not or, in alternative formulation, that which is desired into (inside) the body and self and that which is not.

But how is the difference transformed into a meaningful distinction? This is where the structured cultural representations – cultural categorizations – reveal their determining character.

The cultural scene

A cultural categorization in its elementary form *is* the very *naming* of the unrepresentable 'good' structured in a binary mode and thus defining its opposite, the 'bad', or, in other words, what is desired or allowed to enter inside (introjection) and what should be kept outside or must be expelled if it has managed to get inside (projection). In bodily (oral) terms, the binary opposition acquires the form edible versus inedible (see above pp. 16–17).

But, of course, cultural representations and categorizations are much more than just the cosmos divided into two parts. The categorization grows both in extensive and intensive dimensions to ever more subtle distinctions, as a system of differences called language. But as Derrida has pointed out, the difference can never exist in a pure neutral mode. It always involves an evaluative aspect which grants the first term a defining, and hence, an excluding power over the second, the 'other' (Derrida, 1981a). This is what difference is about, a difference which is necessarily structured in binary form, related to the third (cf. Lévi-Strauss' [1965] 'culinary triangle') and built into colossal complexes. What we find, in the last instance, within every possible binary opposition, is the opposition of *inside* and *outside* – as Derrida notes when deconstructing Plato's ideas on writing (or '*pharmakon*'):

> In order for these contrary values (good/evil, true/false, essence/appearance, inside/outside) to be in opposition, each of the terms must be simply *external* to the other, which means that one of these oppositions (the opposition between inside and outside) must already be accredited as matrix of all possible oppositions. (Derrida, 1981a: 103)

Thus, when moving around either on the ontogenic or the cultural scene we are using topological tools, whether consciously or not (I prefer the former). Yet, we still need some additional bricks to build the bridge from the ontogenic to the cultural scene. To start with, it is evident that every culture must supply a basis for the constitution of the subject – in the general terms formulated above – in order to produce human beings, which are capable of – more or less – separate existence and autonomous conduct. This is almost a tautological formulation: the original symbiosis must be broken, that is, there must be an ontogenesis, referring to the birth of a human being not only in biological (neonate) but also in mental (self) and cultural (subject) terms – whatever culturally specific form this process acquires.

The missing bricks for the bridge are found precisely in the reservations made above: the greater or lesser degree of separateness of the subject and specificity of the ontogenic process. The bridge will be built within a somewhat idealized (and schematized) model of the primitive society, then extended along certain dimensions to cover pre-modern society and finally related in a differential mode to modern society.

Pre-modern orality

How does the mouth figure in a primitive society? What is the position of orality in it when regarded from the vantage point of the body, the self and the culture? Undoubtedly, orality figures in the primitive society not only as eating (the oral–ingestive dimension) but also as speech (the oral–aural dimension). Nevertheless, my argument is – as already noted above – that the interactive link which relates the subject to its environment, binding subjects to each other as a community, is primarily structured on the oral-ingestive dimension. The primitive society can hardly be reduced to a 'communion' or a common shared ritual meal, yet the rituals involving not only eating (meal) but also other activities concerning food, function as the integrative mechanism of the society. The primitive society is in a fundamental sense an 'eating-community'. This may be explicated by the topological scheme linking the three levels – body, self and culture – into one and the same network.

The body is characterized by a certain kind of *openness* – a theme which recurs in different variations within the anthropological field[14] – primarily focused on the eating mouth. Sharing and incorporating food in a ritual meal implies the incorporation of the partaker into the community simultaneously defining his/her particular 'place' within it. Here the oral bidirectionality is actualized in and as eating: eating into one's body/self and being eaten into the community. The bond is created primarily by *sharing* (communion) and not by *exchange* – if the latter is conceived of as a transaction between subjects recognizing each other's individual separateness and autonomy, be it a communicative relationship between 'speaking subjects' or an economic exchange between 'market subjects'. Sharing implies a two-way open body while exchange implies a body and self which controls that which is given/said *for* what.

At the level of self-formation the member of an eating-community may be characterized as a 'group-self'. This is a mode of self-formation the ethno-psychoanalyst Paul Parin describes in his study of the African Dogon community, noting that in the ontogenic scale the process of separation and individuation from the primal symbiosis does not proceed through those dramatic phases which are conceived of as 'natural' in the development of the modern individual self. This does not imply, according to Parin, that a member of the Dogon society never grows up, as it were, but that the culturally specific ontogenic process results in what Parin calls an 'oral type of self-autonomy' (Parin, 1978: 152).

In the Dogon culture, the process of individuation never reaches as far as it does in the case of the modern individual self which does not, however, prevent the Dogon person from acquiring the ability of autonomous conduct. The primal symbiosis is surely broken, but in a way which maintains a 'semi-symbiotic' relationship, now transformed into a community bond. This is the constellation which was characterized above as a membership of an 'eating-community' in which the reciprocal relationship is structured by the principle 'to eat and be eaten by'. Surely it does not make a primitive society into a big harmonious family but, nevertheless, it renders the society (as community) a much more emphatic character of insideness in relation to the subject when compared with the modern society as an 'outside' of an individualized self. In other words, the articulation of the inside/outside distinction lies primarily at the *collective* boundaries – as was illustrated by the case of the 'judgement of taste' above.

A tribal society is not lacking hierarchical structures, which are moulded according to the kinship system and whatever sub-categories it involves. Then again, the hierarchy itself is to be conceived of as a scheme of concentric circles, one inside the other, which is, according to Jonathan Friedman's (1983) formulation, the basic model of the (spatial) cosmology of primitive societies (dominated by a kinship system and personal relationships). This is a structure which, in topological terms, defines the next sphere outside the inner one as an inside of the outer one, and so forth, just like a set of Chinese boxes one inside the other (Figure 2.3c), as Stanley Walens characterizes the Kwakiutl cosmology (Walens, 1981: 54).

The 'eating-community' may now be illustrated by the following topological schemes. Figure 2.3a depicts the semi-symbiotic character of the group-self – incorporating the food which in turn incorporates the eater into the community (from the subject's point of view). It seems then that the figure is identical with the previous one (Figure 2.2b) presented in connection with the ontogenic scene. Even though there is a shift in its content – due to the undeniable difference between the mother–child union and a community bond – the relationship of these figures is not merely an analogical one: the self-formation of a member of an eating community really remains at a lower level of separation, even if it concerns only the dimension of social identity. The next scheme (Figure 2.3b) illustrates a shared ritual meal or a communion in which the bidirectionality of eating results in an 'inside-the-inside' topology which may then be conceived of as the core located in the inner circle of the concentric primitive cosmology (Figure 2.3c) – extending from culture to nature and the supernatural (Friedman, 1983) or from the house to village and finally to the physical universe (Walens, 1981: 54–5).

This is how the bridge between an open body, a group-self and a society as an 'inside' is built – all three levels are conceived of in terms of a shared topological scheme. At a cultural level, the model of an 'eating-community' points to the centrality of the ritual meal, and of the collective

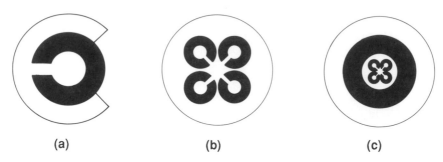

Figure 2.3 *The primitive 'eating-community'*

ritual in general, but the principle of sharing and the character of the
community as an inside goes beyond the paradigmatic model of communion and manifests itself more generally in the modes of transaction
preceding modern society and the individualized self, that is, 'trans-
missions' between 'dividuals',[15] as forms of sharing.

Sharing acquires the appearance of an exchange as soon as it is
transposed to the reciprocal relationships crossing the boundaries of the
inner concentric spheres, still defined as an inside of the community or,
illustrated by the Kwakiutl society (of the late nineteenth century, when it
was studied by Boas and Hunt): the inner spheres which in physical terms
reach from the 'box' via 'house' to 'village' and in social terms, from the
'individual' (= subject) via *numaym* to the 'tribe' (Walens, 1981: 54–5), are
all still conceived of as an inside, the community (culture) which sets its
boundaries towards the outside, to the 'others' (not-us), to nature and –
though more ambiguously – to the 'supernatural'.[16]

It is only when crossing the outer boundary that the transaction is
transformed into exchange. And, as the discourses on economic history
suggest, this is the very locus of the origins of economic exchange, the
'external markets' preceding the 'internal' ones (Polanyi, 1957), or in a
more relativized formulation, this is where the reciprocal or symbolic (gift)
exchange is transformed into an economic one (Mauss, 1967) both in the
form of barter and as money-mediated transactions. The latter of these –
gaining dominance in the coming of modern society – narrows the sense of
the term 'economic' to its contemporary sense, that is, referring to a
separate realm distinct from religious, political and social ones. On the
other hand, the former (barter) is conceived of as a more or less distinct
form located in between the reciprocal (gift) exchange and economic
market-exchange, that is, involving elements of mutual reciprocity
between the exchanging parties (devoid of the mediating 'third', money)
while being also an interested relationship to the object of desire in the
other's possession, thus rendering the relationship to the other (subject) an
instrumental role (see Humphrey and Hugh-Jones, 1992).

The reciprocal gift exchange as a temporalized and serialized form of
sharing gives primacy to the substantial connection between the parties of

the transaction, corresponding – in principle – to the 'internal' exchange or the uniting flow of substances in a shared meal. Here the boundaries between individual partakers are dissolved and consequently the line separating inside from outside is located around the ritual community (communion).

However, when moving towards the forms of 'external' exchange – along the discontinous scale from transactions between collective 'persons' to individualized market relations – the principle of 'internal' exchange becomes inverted in one crucial respect: now the exchange relationship presupposes the difference and separatedness of the parties involved and the transaction itself acts as an affirmation of the boundaries locating, reciprocally, the other party on the outside (of us/me). Surely external exchange still functions as various systems of distribution but it loses the characteristic of substantial sharing where boundaries separating the parties tend to be dissolved. Consequently it may be argued that the transactions between units do not become exchange proper until the parties define each other as something being outside (me or us), and consequently, the exchange between individual subjects is not actualized until the distinction of inside/outside is reduced to the scale of an individual self and body.

The more general coordinates formulated above prepare the ground – as I see it – for a generalization, in the historical dimension, from primitive to pre-modern society. It should, however, be recalled that this does not imply an interpretation which makes all 'other' and 'pre-modern' cultures into one and the same thing. As noted, the common denominator applies only to some 'dimensions which are, nevertheless, crucial from the vantage point of the present topic: the changing role of orality conceived of according to the topological scheme which links the body, self and culture.

The coordinates outlined above apply more generally to non-modern cultures even if they were not as thoroughly oral as the Kwakiutl society (of the late nineteenth century), which is characterized by Stanley Walens in a manner deserving of lengthy quotation:

> The Kwakiutl world is visually filled with mouths. It is a world where people, animals, spirits, sneezes, twitches, owls, dreams, ghosts, and even flatulence speak and sometimes forebode. It is a world where animals of countless variety all kill and destroy to satisfy their hunger, a world filled with gaping maws of killer whales, the fearsome teeth of wolves and bears, the tearing beaks of ravens and hawks. It is a world filled with omnipresent man-made images whose mouths betray their greed for food: of Thunderbirds who bring sudden death from the sky, of Cannibal Birds with beaks nine feet long that crack open human skulls and suck out their brains, of wild women with pendulous breasts and protruding lips, who watch for unwary travellers and misbehaving children and rip their bodies to pieces in the frenzy of devouring them. It is a world where babies calmly sucking at their mothers' breasts suddenly turn into monsters and eat them.
>
> An oral metaphorization of the universe is a cogent one since the mouth can be both a passive and an aggressive part of the body, and the processes of digestion and regurgitation mimic processes of creation and destruction; at the

same time, the powerful urges of insatiable hunger can be opposed to the controlled, learned, socialized nature of speech. (Walens, 1981: 12–13)

However, Walens also points out those characteristics of orality, dealt with above, which apply more widely also to cultures with less oral cosmologies. He refers to the 'rituality of eating and other activities concerning food' and to the importance of conceiving of meals as 'sacred occasions' which then help to realize that

> all large ceremonials that have as one of their parts the eating of a meal, the distribution of food, or the ritual enactment of any aspect of the gathering or eating of food are reinforced in their religiousness by virtue of their association with that food-act. (Walens, 1981: 35)

This is a description of an 'eating-community' in which 'oral/assimilative' metaphors are used to envision the identities of the members of the society and in which they act as the structuring principle of the 'primary mode of sociality' (Walens, 1981: 21–3). But, in more general terms, the same traits are also to be found in traditional society, in the *Gemeinschaft*'s of pre-modern Europe, where, as Karl-Heintz Osterloh puts it, 'the sphere of the fire place' functions as a continuation of the system of 'motherly-oral mode of need satisfaction' (Osterloh, 1976: 361).

The medieval union or guild are not the whole society but nevertheless they are more collective sharing communities than, say, the modern nuclear family. But beyond this, all the hierarchical power relations between 'masters and servants' are to be conceived of as relations of sharing – though in unequal parts – and forms of reciprocity defining an outer sphere of insideness not too far from the (spatial) primitive cosmological scheme (Figure 2.3c). Society is a more or less rigid hierarchy in which everybody has a certain 'place' conceived of both in concrete-spatial and in social-structural terms – and condensed into one 'name' (place/craft/person) – reminiscent of the Kwakiutl system (Walens, 1981: 63).

However, much of this is changed with the advent of modern society. To put it crudely, the spatial cosmology is overridden by the temporalized one which is oriented to the future (Falk, 1988a), the static social structure is replaced by dynamic ones and society gains increasingly the character of a 'second nature', which in the present context and in topological terms may be described rather as an 'outside' (than a second inside) of the subject becoming individual. So, it is no wonder that the 'eating-community' reappears in the nineteenth century as a utopia promoting the idea of sharing and reciprocity, manifesting its oral basis in its most articulate manner in the visions of an 'ideal community' (*Harmony*) outlined by Charles Fourier in the beginning of the century. According to Fourier, 'good food and good mealtime companionship' would play a central role 'in promoting intragroup harmony in the new order' (see Beecher, 1986: 171).

Returning again to the mouth, the next question to be posed is: what happens to the oral function of eating after the collapse of the eating-community and the loss of oral bidirectionality it involves; and, in the coming of the modern body and self, the shifting of the articulation of the inside/outside distinction to individual boundaries? Starting from cor-poreality, the change could be formulated in a preliminary way as a move from a (relatively) open body to a (relatively) closed one.

Closing the body?

As noted above in connection with the topic of taste, the erosion of rigid structures – from social hierarchies to cultural categorizations (the Order) – and the articulation of individual boundaries of body and self are to be conceived of as different aspects of the same process. Controlling the boundaries at an individual level implies a strengthened control over the flows in and out of the body. In other words, the body becomes more 'closed' in its relationship to the objects and subjects of the outside world. The medieval 'grotesque body' (Bakhtin, 1968) characterized by openness and flexible boundaries, allowing itself to be eaten into the carnivalistic 'communion' while eating the world into itself, gives way to the modern one in which 'all the orifices of the body are closed' (Bakhtin, 1968: 320), according to the idealized anatomical description of the Renaissance (cf. Kilgour, 1990: 141).

This is, of course, also an idealized description, but it nevertheless points to an essential change linked to the decline of the eating-community – also including its sporadic medieval form as a carnival: eating gains a much more individualized character implying a loss, or at least a marginalization, of its bidirectional character, in the pre-modern sense outlined above. Shared meals as such do not disappear: the family meal still prevails to some extent (usually at weekends) and people dine out (or in) with their friends. However, the role of the meal as a collective community-constituting ritual has been marginalized – even in the case of the nuclear family. On the other hand, the integrative function of a modern meal resides primarily in the other oral dimension, that of speech and communi-cation (in distinction to communion), aptly exemplified by a 'dining out' situation in which every individual partaker makes his or her individual choice of course in the menu.

Bakhtin's characterization of the closing body seems to fit rather well as a complement to Norbert Elias' model for the 'civilizing process' (Elias, 1978, 1982). In Elias' scheme the body becomes 'armoured' implying a control over the bodily openings and, more generally, a control over affective *ex*-pressions. In other words, the heightened 'self-control' concerns primarily the affective – sexual and aggressive – 'outlets' result-ing, as a kind of compensation, in an opening of an imaginary inwardness (*Innerlichkeit*) of emotional experience. The shift is depicted rather as a substitution than a sublimation, as a creation of a safety valve – if I may use the hydraulic metaphors on which Elias' thought seems to be based.[17]

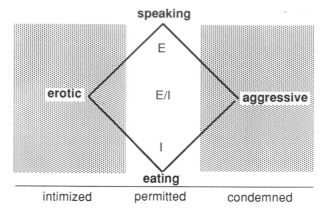

Figure 2.4 *Structuration of oral functions*

Thus, Elias formulates the 'civilizing process' mainly in negative terms, focusing on the modes of (bodily) conduct that are excluded from the public-social scene of manners. The imaginary inwardness – which actually can be regarded as a dimension of incorporation and consumption (reading novels, watching movies) – is thematized only in outline and the emerging new forms of social conduct to an even lesser extent.

Concerning the latter lack, one of Elias' disciplines, Cas Wouters, has pointed out that the interpretation of the growth in self-control should be complemented by a more detailed analysis of the emerging forms of expressive and communicative conduct which is not merely more 'civilized' but also more 'informal', so the civilizing process is actually accompanied by an 'informalizing process' (Wouters, 1977: 293–6). What could these informal modes of social conduct and self-expression be? Social interaction, social exchange or pure 'sociability' *à la* Georg Simmel? Perhaps. Anyway, they certainly presuppose a rather individually controlled body and self standing in an outside relationship to the other. But control taken to its extreme would result in a non-relation, so there must be a controlled influx and outflux constituting a relationship – even after the bidirectionality of the eating-community.

To make this clearer, let us return to the body – and the mouth – by means of a figure illustrating the re-structuration of the oral functions in the 'civilizing process' (Figure 2.4).

Elias focuses on the areas of exclusion from the vantage point of the public-social sphere. Affective *ex*-pressions – both erotic (kissing, etc.) and aggressive (biting, etc.) – are intimized or simply disapproved of, leaving the functions of speech and eating – neither of which Elias really deals with – in the 'permitted' area. The excluded affective oral functions are reduced to *ex*-pressions only from the self-control point of view, but viewed as interactive conduct they actually reside in an ambiguous position between excorporation and incorporation (E/I), that is, combining the *ex*-pressive and experiential dimensions of corporeality.

Then again, the 'permitted' oral functions are structured as a binary opposition in which speech is granted the status of pure (sublimated) excorporation (E), as expression and communication. So, maybe this is the locus of the 'informalizing process' Wouters refers to: 'eating-community' replaced by 'speech-sociability'. Consequently, eating – now lacking the 'original' bidirectionality – is re-defined as mere one-sided incorporation (I). So there is an eating and speaking body; eating in and speaking out? Surely, this is not what the reality looks like. Even the modern 'civilized' individual is moving somewhere along the sides of the oral square (Figure 2.4).[18]

The historical formation of an individual self – and thus also of an individual bodily 'being in the world' (Merleau-Ponty, 1981) – does undoubtedly strengthen the role of the human body as a *means of expression* in communicative social relationships. A move towards a more closed body which controls its bodily and affective *ex*-pressions and the flows from inside out and outside in may be also conceived of as a move from an *assimilative* body towards a *communicative* body (O'Neill, 1989), giving not only speech (as the sublimated form of excorporation) a more central position, but also assigning to the body-surface and whatever paraphernalia it is surrounded with more language-like communicative functions.

Now, what could the closing of the body imply for the incorporative dimension of *eating*? As noted above in connection with the topic of taste, the individual mouth is taken as a model of 'judgement' in the moral and aesthetic discourses (from the seventeenth century onwards), activating simultaneously a search for non-subjective standards of taste. Among other things, this may be interpreted as a symptom of the control function reduced to the individual level, specifically concerning the control over that which is *taken in* to the body and self – and is as such a crucial issue of self-definition.[19]

The controlling function of the mouth is, however, thematized in those same times in much more concrete and physiological terms, in the moral and medical discourses on 'dietetics'. The problem of the proper diet (questions concerning what to eat, how and when) was not dealt with as a separate topic but as an aspect of the whole normative system linking common 'goods' to individual – mental and physiological – 'goods'.

Even if the discourses focus primarily on the effects of specific diets on physical and mental well-being, they also, explicitly or implicitly, thematize the individual subject's relationship to food in a broader perspective, as a relationship to the outside world of objects and subjects. At least from Robert Burton's *The Anatomy of Melancholy* 1660 [1621] onwards these discourses are also concerned with the emotional, intellectual and social dimensions of outside relatedness, how to experience the world in visual terms, what to read and how, and with whom to associate and how – all this conceived of from a vantage point which articulates the distinction of the outside and inside on the individual level. So, what these discourses actually are dealing with is the individual subject's relationship to the outside world as a source of various stimulative flows – both material (food) and immaterial (the food of the mind or imagination) – which should be controlled individually according to the principle 'what should be taken in and what should be rejected', or 'what is for me and what is not for me'.

Then again, the problem of control is manifested in its most articulate manner precisely in the materiality of eating due to the predominance of the principles of 'humoral medicine' which emphasize the role of the body and its fluids in the formation of mentality and identifies these fluids with the substances outside the body (from climatic circumstances to the variety of foods). But the centrality of eating is understandable also from a more basic point of view: the individual powers of control are actualized most concretely in oral incorporation, in the realm of threefold 'judgement' called the mouth – which then, as a model (*paradigma*), is extended to less concrete modes of incorporation mediated by other senses.

Eating is turned into a problem not only as 'over-eating', or gluttony, as an unhealthy practice for the body or the mind but, in the last instance, for the whole society. The story is not only about the 'disciplining of the appetite' (Mennell, 1985) predominant in the pre-modern world of extremes: gluttony and fasting, surfeit and deficit, abundance and hunger. Eating is defined as a problem on a much more basic level, which in fact involves the very constitution of the appetite in a specific form, as an aspect of the constitution of individualized self and body. When the articulation of the inside/outside distinction moves to the individual boundaries and when eating is turned into a unidirectional incorporation into the body and self, eating becomes redefined as an act of 'self-fulfilment' in a literal sense. The closing of the body creates an empty inside – both in physical and mental terms – to be filled up with all the good things that it lacks.

This is where the 'oral character' in the specific modern sense emerges. It differs in an essential respect from the primitive or pre-modern one: it is not based on a continuation of – in psychoanalytical terms – the 'oral phase' transposed from the original symbiosis to a semi-symbiotic (or at least bidirectional[20]) community bond but exactly the opposite, the loss of the bond and its replacement with new kinds of social relationships which presuppose individuality and separateness. To simplify, the 'oral urge' of the modern individual self is not a manifestation of oral 'security' but on the contrary a symptom of its absence.

The latter formulation should not, however, lead us to too hasty pathologizing interpretations. It is true that the idea of an empty inside recurs in the anamnesis of the ambiguous 'modernity syndrome', as the inner void of a melancholic person (see Kleinspehn, 1987: 189) and, more recently, as the hollowness of the narcissistic personality, the 'empty self' (Kernberg, 1970: 219), but these interpretations should be conceived of rather as more extreme characterizations of the 'normal' existential conditions of the modern individual. The structural basis of the modern individual self involves a contradictory dynamics of separation and completion; to be a separate individual on the outside, or in social terms, in relation to the others, and to be whole – not as a part of a larger whole, a holy communion or a secular community but as an individual separate being with an inside to be filled up, completed. These two aspects are then structured in terms of a dynamic in which the pursuit of separation necessarily maintains a state of incompletion which then endlessly feeds the pursuit of completion (more about this topic in Chapter 5).

This is, of course, a rather schematic formulation of the basic dynamics of modern individual self-construction, which should be complemented by a number of reservations and qualifications. The modern individual is not an atomistic mouth moved around in an empty space by forces of aversion. Social relationships are not only necessary in themselves but are also embedded in the pursuit of completion even if they are no longer structured primarily according to the assimilative principle of the eating-community. This implies a shift to modes of social interaction in which individuals acknowledge – at least in principle – each other's autonomy as exchanging and/or communicating subjects.

However, in the present context the idealized individual self serves to outline the contours of the specific 'introjective' logic which is characteristic of eating in its individual and unidirectional manifestations. And, as we shall see below, the introjective logic figures as an essential aspect – as the 'other' logic – in modern consumption. This is the other side of modern orality, which, quite naturally, could be first characterized by outlining some basic tendencies in the modern 'eating-culture', referring not only to foodways in a narrow sense but also including other oral-ingestive conduct.

Modern orality (I) – the fates of the meal

The tendencies of modern eating-culture may be summarized as follows. First, the modern condition does not only imply a collapse of an eating-community as a structuring principle of social life but it also manifests a tendency towards a marginalization of the meal, even when conceived of as a less collective social event. Second, the decline of the meal is accompanied by the rise of different forms of non-ritual eating (snacks) and other modes of concrete oral-ingestive activity which concerns substances that are not considered to be food (sweets, titbits, soft and alcoholic drinks)[21] or which actually fall outside the category of nutrition (tobacco, chewing gum). A great part of the substances involved in non-ritual and mostly individualized oral-ingestive activities may be classified under the category of (oral) 'pleasurables' (corresponding to the German term *Genussmittel*). These oral-ingestive – but also inhalatory and masticatory – activities could be called 'oral side-involvements', to use Goffman's term (1967: 146) in a somewhat different sense, that is, focused specifically on orality.

There is nothing very new about these kinds of oral side-involvements in themselves. There is a lot of non-ritual eating in tribal societies, especially among the gatherer-hunters (MacClancy, 1992: 12–13, 49–50). Furthermore, all cultures have their own range of pleasurable 'stimulants' and actually most modern Western ones derive from the 'other' cultures, be it tea, coffee, tobacco or chewing gum. On the other hand, in the primitive society, not all oral-ingestive activities are bound into collective ritual settings. Nevertheless, what is new in the modern condition, is the way these activities are structured in relation to eating behaviour in general, to the decline of the ritual meal and to the rise of the food industry (see Levenstein, 1988). This is where we also have to make an historical and cultural specification, focusing on the turn of the nineteenth and twentieth centuries and, furthermore, focusing specifically on the new modern world, the United States, which may be granted the honour of being the augur of 'modern oralities' (see Chapter 6).

The United States at the turn of the century is the time and place where the mass production and consumption of soft drinks, cigarettes and chewing gum begins its breakthrough, where the food industry is oriented towards ready-made portions and where the snack-culture starts its invasion – all related to the social changes promoting the marginalization of the meal. These are the coordinates for the most articulated changes in the eating culture which may be summarized in Figure 2.5, illustrating a shift from the meal towards oral side-involvements.

Figure 2.5 is not to be interpreted as a description of a total transformation but of a tendency towards an individual and continuous oral mode of existence in terms of concrete oral-ingestive conduct. Then again, the tendency should be conceived of rather as a symptom of the oral character of the modern individual self in its relationship with the outside world as a source not only of stimulants but of *stimulation* in general, now referring to all sensory modes of reception, primarily, however, those which receive the 'stimulus' as representations.

Even the concrete act of oral incorporation, eating itself, does not escape the realm of representations, which then leads us to a rather odd-sounding conclusion: the oral character of the modern individual self cannot be traced back to the ingestive functions of the mouth but must be conceived of as an overall characteristic of the relationship to the outside world as the source of sensory representational stimuli. Thus, the expression 'eating with one's eyes' is not actually in a metaphoric but rather in a metonymic relation to actual eating (with one's mouth), which, as can be realized, corresponds to the psychoanalytical concept of 'primary identification' (above pp. 17–18). This is where the mouth must be redefined as a *model* referring to the introjective aspect of the modern self 'eating' the world as representations into itself by all sensory means, including the mouth.

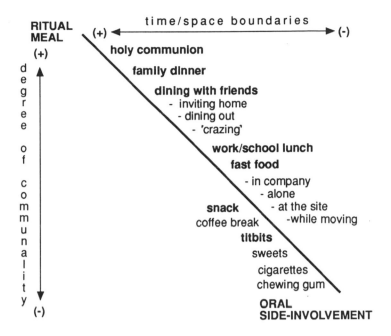

Figure 2.5 *Transformation of the eating-culture*

The mouth as model leads us inevitably to a redefinition of 'hunger' or 'appetite' too. The introjective hunger of the modern self has nothing to do with hunger in a physiological sense, not even when brought back to its original site, the mouth and the stomach. This does not, of course, mean that the physiological fact is denied. But what it does mean is that the oral side-involvements, the incorporation of oral stimulants, is actually located on the same continuum with the ocular and other modes of 'stimulus' reception, that is, the appetite for experience (*'Erfahrungshunger'*; Rutschky, 1980), for the 'spectacular' (Debord, 1977) or for 'events' (Nora, 1983) has as much to do with the physiological fact of hunger as, say, the 'thirst' for Coca-Cola has to do with the corresponding physiological fact.

This may also help us to understand the profound message of a Coke advertisement slogan from 1916: 'fun to be thirsty' (Falk, 1991; see Chapter 6). No doubt, a bottle of Coke fills up the stomach for a while, but what it primarily does as a *representation* is to fill up the individualized self, the insatiability of which is assured by the very dynamics of the self revolving endlessly in the circle of separation and completion. Perhaps Charles Baudelaire's characterization of the 'perfect *flâneur*' really applies more generally to the oral side of the modern consuming self: 'he is an "I" with an insatiable appetite for the "non-I" ' (cited in Bersani, 1990: 68–9).

Modern orality (II) – the art of conversation

The coming of the modern individual self is characterized by specific changes in the role of speech and the status of language as a means of communication and signification. Here I am not only referring to the fundamental cultural differences and historical changes in the functions of language – from 'primitive' word magic, in which spoken words are conceived of as indexically bound to referential entities or states of being, to language as an autonomized and neutralized sign system used without strong referential links and causal or 'performative' (Austin, 1975) presuppositions.[22]

Focusing on the constitution of the subject – as body and self – the scene of transformation might be formulated as follows. The control of affective *ex*-pressions (literally), including their oral and vocal forms, tends to civilize speech into the verbal use of language practised in 'pacified' social interaction (Elias, 1978). This is a transformation which is linked to the autonomization of language as a sign-system – breaking the magical ties between 'words and things' (Foucault, 1973) – in a certain way. The oral or, better, the verbal culture is essentially affected by the expanding literacy, in more specific terms, the skill of *reading*[23] – especially from the late eighteenth century onwards (Kittler, 1990). This constitutes a specific relationship between reading and speaking, concretely mediated by the practice of reading aloud.[24]

This is also where the purification of verbal orality from affective (vocal) *ex*-pressions is actualized. Alternatively, this is the context where the Kantian idea of the self-reflection in 'hearing-oneself-speak' (cited in Derrida, 1981b: 18)[25] is actually realized in a practical state. It is not realized in the ideal form of poetic speech, to which Kant refers and it is surely realized in interested and 'persuasive' modes of rhetoric, but nevertheless, it has a neutralizing effect on communicative (and dialogical) relations which could be characterized as follows: 'I hear myself speak to the other and vice versa.' In other words, the more detached the words become not only from things but also from the bodily states (*ex*-pressions) the more autonomous are the verbal 'messages' sent and received and the more is the body reduced into an oral-verbal *means of* expression (see Chapter 3).

The change in speech culture – related to the expansion and privatization of reading practice implying a certain reflectivity to speech as use of language – signifies the constitution of a social practice of speech, or in more autonomous form, a *speech sociability* corresponding on the macro level to the basic structural characteristics of modern 'market-society' as a realm of relatively free-moving subjects and objects (that is, commodities) – without, however, being reducible to the latter.

Speech sociability does not function as a structuring principle of modern society and it cannot be understood as a 'community'[26] in some stronger sense, even if it may be possible to point to certain social formations in which reciprocal speech as conversation' is actualized in forms approximating to the 'pure': from the 'academies' of Renaissance Italy and the seventeenth–eighteenth century French 'salons' and English 'coffee-houses' (Burke, 1993: 114–17) to the contemporary, less institutionalized settings for informal conversation.

Even though the market relations have – in structural terms – a significant role in the dynamics of modern society, it does not imply that speech sociability is a mere supplement of commodification. Informal conversation cannot be reduced into purely instrumental 'speech acts'. The modern condition, characterized by (relative) individual freedom opens up a whole heterogeneous realm of social interaction, room for speech sociability to manoeuvre which lies somewhere between reciprocal (gift) exchange and market-exchange.

On the one hand the 'dialogic connection' may be conceived of as a dyadic relationship in which the Maussian rules of gift exchange (to give, to receive and to give a counter-gift) are reformulated into the three 'obligations': to speak, to listen and to respond (Gurevitch, 1990). On the other hand, when applied to the modern settings of informal conversation, the dialogic connection is rather a relationship between individuals than dividuals, presupposing a reciprocal acknowledgement of the other as a separate autonomous person. This is a characteristic the modern 'speaking subject' shares with the 'economic subject' as a sovereign party of market transactions.

The mutual recognition of the other's sovereignity in both of the above cases is essentially a *formal* condition of social interaction which is not necessarily realized in equality in some more substantial sense of the term. The formal condition does not in itself exclude hierarchical structuring of the partakers of conversation insofar as it refers merely to the rules of 'dialogic connection' and leaves intact the 'external' (social) determinants defining the settings of conversation and consequently turning the speech into 'interested' intentional conduct.[27] However, when the formal condition is extended to include also the 'equal rights' of the speaking subjects to take part in the conversation, we end up with the scene of modern *informal* conversation where the rules aim at guarding the boundaries of the autotelic conversation rather than to determine the proper way of speaking to persons with a certain status.[28]

The description above is, of course, reminiscent of Georg Simmel's conception of 'sociability [*Geselligkeit*] as the autonomous form, or play-form, of sociation [*Vergesellschaftung*]' (Simmel, 1950: 43–57 [1912]), which is an abstraction of all content and materiality of social relationships (individual interests, etc.) and the social formations embodying them. Simmel abstracts, however, also from the specific substance of sociability, *speech* as a communicative reciprocal conduct, and ends up by referring to 'conversation' as a specific – though paradigmatic – realization of pure sociability.[29]

Food to words

Now let us now turn to the modern meal and to the specific mode in which the two dimensions of orality – eating and speaking – are structured within it.

A modern family meal – even if it too is becoming marginalized (Thurn, 1980: 129–42) – still carries some traits of the pre-modern eating-community: preparing, sharing and incorporating a common meal while rendering speech a secondary role (and reminding the children not to speak with food in their mouth). The situation is, however, quite different in the social gathering of 'dining out' where each makes his or her individual choice from the menu while contributing to the sociability and conviviality as a self-expressing, thought-exchanging (speaking) individual. The social event is of course still *shared* but the link between the partakers is now constituted primarily by the words expressed and exchanged and not the food silently incorporated.[30]

So the decline of the ritual significance of the meal manifests itself not only in the shift from food to words but also in the informalization of the reciprocal speech acts – into conversation in the modern sense of the term. The 'table conversation' (*Tischunterhaltung*) – analysed by Georg Simmel in his 'Sociology of the Meal' (Simmel, 1984: 210 [1910]) – may be given certain boundaries of 'suitability' concerning the themes of conversation, but it is not predetermined by strict rituals, rules which actually render speech a secondary and derivative role in relation to the rituals of sharing and incorporating – especially food.[31]

This is the difference between the pre-modern ritual meal and the modern one that Simmel's 'Sociology of the Meal' actually ignores, due to his scheme of form/content duality, where the latter is reduced to the (pure) materiality and physiology of eating. According to Simmel the act of eating is in itself an individual act that rather separates than binds together and is thus devoid of all social character. Consequently, the community-forming and socializing aspect of the meal emerges only as a form which compensates the 'natural' individuality of eating, as it were:

> This [the transformation of the meal into a sociological issue] gives birth to the rules regulating eating and drinking, rules that do not, however, concern food as substance (Materie) – which is here unessential – but the *form* of its consumption. (Simmel, 1984: 206–7)

So the development of the sociality of the meal – from the archaic ritual meals to the modern meal – takes place, according to Simmel, entirely in the realm of form(alities), from basic ritual rules of the primitive sacrificial meal to the 'aesthetic stylization' and the boundary-rules of the proper 'table conversation' of a modern meal, leaving the solitary eater in his pure materiality intact. What this means is that the 'pre-social' natural eater who has *not yet* entered the 'social contract' of the meal[32] is identified with the modern individual eater whose sociality is *not* longer based on the simultaneously material and representational sharing and incorporation of food. Consequently, Simmel's interpretation rules out the possibility of thematizing the fundamental change from the pre-modern bidirectional orality to the modern one in which eating becomes increasingly unidirectionalized and individualized while at the same time complemented by the 'sublimated' orality of speech.

Notwithstanding the ahistorical bias, Simmel's essay on the meal is, however, an adequate analysis of the character of the *modern* meal, rendering primacy to the sublimating (aestheticizing) forms and the sublimated mode of interaction as (dialogic) 'talk', the latter of which, according to Simmel, 'is the purest and most sublimated form of two-way-ness' (Simmel, 1950: 53).

The social bond – as interaction – really appears to be totally independent from the materiality of eating. This is a configuration which opens up an alternative (?) interpretation of the inverted meal scene in Luis Buñuel's film, *Le fantôme de la liberté* (1974).

The first impression of the scene is that it is a questioning of the relationship between social and intimate spheres by means of an inversion of the place of oral and anal functions. A middle-class gathering (a few couples) sitting in a 'dining' room on lavatories having a lively conversation while excreting. One man stands up, apologizes and withdraws to the 'toilet' to have his private/intimate meal, returning after a while to the table to continue the social event. The second thought opens up, however, the possibility of a further interpretation. The sociability of the 'meal' has been divorced from its substantial basis and sublimated to speech, so it does not actually matter anymore what the substance is about or which direction the flow takes – food in-take or ex-crement.

However, the above interpretation of the inverted meal scene disregards a crucial aspect to which Simmel also refers while characterizing the dialogic connection as the 'most *sublimated* form' of two-way-ness. In the Simmelian context the issue of sublimation is linked to the pure 'social form' exemplified by the speech-sociability which is 'the fulfilment of a relation that wants to be nothing but a relation – in which, that is, what usually is the mere form of interaction becomes its self-sufficient content' (Simmel, 1950 [1912]: 53). Nevertheless, the theme of sublimation has a wider context dealing with the hierarchy of the senses (from Plato to Kant and onwards) and especially with the *relationship between food and words*.

Actually this topic appears to be a kind of obsession throughout the Western Christian tradition where 'man does not live by bread alone, but by every word that proceeds from the mouth of God' (Matt. 4:4). However, the tradition is not only about the body vs. spirit (soul) dualism but also about the formulation of the relationship between food and words in terms of sublimation – at least from St Augustine onward, according to whom the 'separation of spiritual and bodily appetites involves [. . .] a sublimation of food into words' (Kilgour, 1990: 52).

When related to the long tradition of 'sublimation' of food to words the historical fate of the meal may be given 'a more sublime characterization: the sociability constituted in the autonomous realm of words returns to the 'original' in a reflective mode which (almost) literally turns food into words – as a verbalization of the pleasures of eating, giving words to distinctive tastes, evoking stories of past culinary experiences, etc. Thus we may delineate a path of orality from the ritual meal of the Kwakiutl where especially 'talking about food while eating is rigorously forbidden' (Walens, 1981: 13) to the culinary version of the modern meal which Claus-Dieter Rath (Rath, 1984: 321) has characterized in the following words:

> Every meal, every food is experienced by the individual persons as a 'taste event'. The fact that it may taste good (or not) evokes conversation on the food and leads to its verbalization. No more obligations of silent eating or partaking in 'general and non-intime' table conversation but the communication of one's own experience in a way which should show and express the individual desires. (Rath, 1984: 321)

The partakers of a modern meal are no longer 'dissolved' into a unity by means of the shared and incorporated food, but rather linked together through communicative (speech) acts in which the individual autonomy of those present is reciprocally respected. However, the great civilizing move from communion to communication characterizes not only meal rituals and foodways but the whole modern culture and the ways people relate to others, to themselves and – last but not least – to the objects of consumption. It is precisely in modern consumption that both the duality of eating and speaking and the dynamic circle of the individualized self 'sublimating' food into words manifest themselves in a most extensive and intensive way.

The gospel of self-realization

As long as the contradictory dynamic of the modern individual self is conceived of merely in terms of the maintenance and loss of self-control, the two oral dimensions of consumption – as eating and speaking – remain disconnected. What we would be left with is a dual characterization of the modern self as an insatiable (literally) self-fulfilling eater, on the one hand, and as a self-controlling ascetic resisting these temptations, on the other. However, the latter is more reminiscent of an autistic than a speaking person. So the point is to gain a conceptual grip of the process of transformation in which the mute self controlling its boundaries in purely negative terms is turned into a self-expressive being, that is, a self which articulates its boundaries by symbolic means of expression.

These two characterizations are commonly conceived of as historical phases in the formation of the individual self – as it is manifested at a discursive level dealing with the idea of 'individuality' – leading from a self-controlled 'character' to a self-expressive 'personality', as Warren Susman (1984) puts it.[33]

The shift from self-control to self-expression actually relocates the self from the boundaries to the inside which, in William James' formulation, was only something to be put and kept in order. In James' view 'the normal evolution of character chiefly consists in the straightening out and unifying the inner self' (cited in Kilgour, 1990: 47). The 'inner nature' was in fact already given a positive connotation in romantic thought – as a link to the true natural basis of the individual – but now it was transformed into something which should 'flow out' of the self as an expression and a realization of its unique individuality. The self-expressive outflux is defined both as the realization of the inner self and a communicative social act which opens up the individual self to the other. Charles Taylor describes the 'expressivistic' stance in the following words: 'Fulfilling my nature means espousing the inner élan, the voice or impulse. And this makes what was hidden manifest *for both myself and others*' (Taylor, 1989: 374; my italics).

In other words, the romantic idea redefined that which was formerly conceived of rather as 'inner noise' (to be controlled) as 'inner voice' which should be heard not only by oneself but also by others. But as long as the inner voice is conceived of as a manifestation of the inner nature, the romantic mode of being in the world is not opened up for a bidirectional relationship. It is, however, precisely the later derivative of the 'romantic self' defined by Colin Campbell (1987) as the model of the modern 'hedonist' and consumer which links the self-expressive dimension to the imaginary consumption of the outside world – as representations. This is where the consuming body is completed as an 'eater' who sublimated the food of the imagination into words, speech.

In an interesting way, the above-outlined romantic self turned into a consumer of representations – sublimating food into words – re-appears in a rather different context but still in a recognizable shape. The context is the therapeutic discussions in United States in the turn of the century, that is, right in the middle of the 'great transformation' of the modern oralities (dealt with above). Jackson Lears (1981, 1983) describes the re-orientation of the therapeutic principles as a shift from 'scarcity therapy' to 'abundance therapy' (Jackson Lears, 1981: 54; 1983: 12).

According to the former the over-stimulative character of the modern urban life was a major cause of both somatic and mental problems, summarized by one of the better known representatives of scarcity therapy, George Beard, under the category of 'neurasthenia', referring to nervous exhaustion. The cure was based on the idea of reduced stimulation. The patient should be kept in rest and peace and the environment should be as non-stimulative as possible. The principle was also applied to the diet, so the principle of scarcity was generalized to all forms of reception and 'intake'. Scarcity therapeutic thought was based on the 'old' principle of self-control: the stimulative flows of the modern (urban) world should be kept outside by means of self-control and if there was a lack of control, due to weak nerves, the only cure was to reduce the stimulus to the minimum and hope for a recovery.

The principles of the 'abundance therapy', gaining popularity during the first decades of the twentieth century, were formulated from the exact opposite stance. The problem lay in the attempt to keep the stimulative world outside and the cure was to 'open up' towards the world and make it the source of one's self-fulfilment and self-expression. The 'path to self-realization' was formulated anew. The pursuit of 'wholeness and security through careful management of personal resources' was replaced by the pursuit of 'emotional fulfilment and endless "growth" through intense experience' (Jackson Lears, 1983: 11). This was the therapeutic declaration of the 'ethic of self-fulfilment' (Jackson Lears,1981: 55) corresponding to what Campbell (1987) calls the 'Romantic ethic', the mental basis of consumerism.

Eating, reading and speaking

Eating, as a model and metaphor of consumption, is generally associated with the *passive* consumer. Consumption in the form of eating signifies receiving, the incorporation and assimilation of some ready object to make it part of the physical or mental self. And even if not everything can be 'swallowed whole', the act is not, as such, regarded as productive. This is, in classical economic terms, unproductive consumption proper as opposed to productive consumption, that is, material production in which the combined consumption of raw material and labour is materialized as the product of labour.

The portrait of the *active* consumer is drawn according to another model of consumption. The act of consumption, as purchase but especially as use, is seen as production – labour or expressive conduct. To the active consumer the world of goods provides tools for social competition (conspicuous consumption, status symbols, positional goods, etc.) setting him or her apart from others/inferiors (Veblen, Bourdieu) – but also for more passive imitating of those above (Tarde). These are the ingredients for building both a social and an individual identity.

According to this model, the objects of consumption act as a response to Dale Carnegie's famous problem, 'how to win friends and influence people'. On the other hand they also act in more general terms as symbols and signs the consumption of which (show and use) is interpreted as an active, expressive and thus also productive function of *communicating* or *speech*. As symbolic production consumption is not necessarily linked with the dynamics of social competition and distinction but can also be interpreted as an individualized practice – a self-strategy – in which a unique identity is expressed and at the same time constructed as something distinct from all others.

Concentrating specifically on the problems of *individual* consumption creates a situation in which the models for passive and active consumption begin to overlap. This was aptly expressed by the basic metaphor for consumption adopted by the French scholar Michel de Certeau, namely *reading*, which is passively receptive and ingestive (eating)[34] yet at the same time active, productive and interpretative processing of the significations of commodities. This implies that the symbolic dimensions of goods are not merely determined externally (e.g. according to the intentions of marketing), but are reinterpreted and transformed to become elements of the individual's life and identity (Certeau, 1984).

Certeau's model of consumption as symbolic production does not, however, necessarily imply a transformation of reading into speech, even if the former does lay the foundations of the latter. In other words, the act of consumption is conceived of as active elaboration even if lacking the communicative intention of expressive conduct. That offered (supply/ marketing) is not 'swallowed whole', and when swallowing is transferred from the realm of concrete orality to the symbolic realm of consumption in general, it becomes active and productive 'work' (Miller, 1987: 191; see also Appadurai, 1986: 31) that not only breaks the food down into a form that can be swallowed but transforms it and processes it into something else, something that is considered mine/ours.

It would be tempting to write off these three metaphors – eating, reading and speaking – simply as different approaches to modern consumption, or alternatively to conceive of them according to a social and cultural hierarchy in which the popular classes represent a more primitive and more passive *oral-introjective* logic of consumption and the elite correspondingly a more civilized, *distinctive* and *aesthetic-reflective* logic of consumption. In certain fields of consumption – especially that of cultural products – this interpretation seems quite convincing: the masses gorge themselves on 'circuses' (mass culture), while the elite savour the titbits of high culture in an expert and reflective manner or, to avoid the oral metaphor: read, interpret and assess the meanings and messages of (cultural) products, turning them into a form of rhetoric.

The set-up is, however, anything but unproblematic. To begin with, and adapting the interpretation of Certeau, the oral consumers of mass culture – and in fact of other objects of consumption, too – may well be, at the same time, reflective readers even though their reflection does not adhere to the legitimate code of 'good taste' and is not actualized in the corresponding speech (or rhetoric). The reflection – and the associated symbolic production – does not need to observe the legitimate aesthetic and intellectual code; it may just as well be a comparative assessment in the course of everyday life, such as while watching *Dallas*.

Secondly, if and when the elite is limited to that group in society that governs and dictates 'good taste', it ultimately gets reduced to a very thin layer of those in possession of 'cultural capital' (Bourdieu, 1984) excluding much of the economic capital elite. Furthermore, the elite is bound to its code in a manner which prevents it acting as a genuine avant-garde – the latter function being largely taken care of by professionals (cf. the fashion system). The progress of – (what is roughly called) – middle-class society further flattens the hierarchical structure, confusing the boundaries between highbrow and lowbrow.

Thirdly, even though consumption in the form of eating, reading and speech is undoubtedly classified in the various social categories under different types of graded importance, these forms are to be found in each of the social groups (along with the corresponding logics of consumption: introjective vs. distinctive). The characteristics of the passive and active, ingestive and productive, digestive and expressive consumer are complements of the modern individual self and present in every social category, and their manifestations are fragmented as the 'old' hierarchy (elite vs. popular classes) crumbles.

Thus tracking down the different logics of consumption involves the entire spectrum of modern consumption and cannot be tied in advance to given dualisms in the social hierarchy. We all eat, read (interpret) and speak, both in the literal and the metaphorical sense, and these logics of consumption are by no means literally tied to corresponding commodity categories – from food to (material) language.

Food can act as a text to be interpreted and eating can turn into rhetoric. Texts – especially in the form of (moving) pictures prevailing in the present – can be received in the culinary sense (Eco, 1979; Jauss, 1970: the 'different paths of reading'), as food for the eye and the imagination and as bodily experiences corresponding to culinary pleasure, just as much as creations stimulating interpretation and aesthetic-intellectual reflection – as food for the mind.

On the other hand these logics of consumption are also manifested in the field of ('non-food') material consumption in which the objects of consumption act both as metaphorical food 'filling up' the self and as words and statements in the material language used to distinguish from and identify with, to communicate and to speak, and ultimately to articulate the unique individuality. This is the topic which will be developed in more detail below (Chapter 5). But first the ground must be prepared in more bodily terms.

Notes

1. The other traditional, though less common categorization of the senses distinguishes sight, hearing *and* touch as 'objective' (Kant, 1820 [1798]) or 'projective' (cf. Balint, 1959: 63) senses, structuring the object-world outside, from smell and taste as 'subjective' or non-projective senses (cf. 'chemical' senses) which function inside the body and subject.

2. Perhaps only in the exceptional case of intravenous 'feeding' of an unconscious person we may speak about pure nutritional intake, or better, 'input', but this does not really weaken the general thesis of eating as a representation-related behaviour.

3. Even if there may exist some exceptional talented taste/smell-artists resembling Grenouille – the perfume-maker in Patrick Süsskind's novel *The Perfume* – who was able to compose new perfumes in his mind like music, the general rule applies, according to which

tastes and smells cannot be memorized or brought back to the mind as 'images' without tracing them back to the contextual (especially visual) characteristics (the smell of the *rose* – as distinct from the visual image of the plain colour 'rosa'). On the other hand, smells and tastes – in actual stimulation – have a significant power to evoke memories (with visual and auditory characteristics) from the distant past (cf. Sperber, 1975: 115–49). This does not mean that there would not be expressions designating smells and tastes. For example, the French connoisseur wine-vocabulary contains about 3000 words describing the taste of wine. But as Sperber notes (p. 115), the designation of tastes and smells is 'almost always' done 'in terms of their causes or their effects': the smell of a rose (cause) or a nauseating smell (effect).

4. In biological terms the openness of the body as organism may be illustrated by Stephen W. Hawking's minimalistic proof for the fact that life is impossible in a two-dimensional world: life, in a biological sense, presupposes a metabolic process and thus a channel linking the openings for 'input' and 'output'. So, the organism in the two-dimensional 'environment' would simply fall into two pieces.

5. One of the earliest thematizations of the various relations between individual and group selves was presented by Marcel Mauss in his essay on *The Gift* (Mauss, 1967) and especially in his essay on the notions of 'person' and 'self' originally published in 1938 (Mauss, 1989).

6. It was not until the eighteenth century that the problem of non-individual standards of taste was actualized, by the French classicists and the British moral and aesthetic thinkers. In fact it was precisely the 'natural' character of taste which provided the Archimedean point transcending the individual mouth, and the individual character of the judgement also considering moral and aesthetic issues as the concept of taste was expanded by analogy to these realms. The naturalness of taste implied that it was something not provided by culture and hence an inborn ability based , in the last instance, on natural (ethical and aesthetic) principles. This is where the slogan *de gustibus non disputandum* is redefined according to the principle: either you had the natural disposition of (good) taste or not, and thus there is nothing to argue about. Nevertheless, 'education' could serve as a means to bring out the hidden natural disposition, an idea that was in accordance with the German '*Bildung*' tradition (cf. Howes and Lalonde, 1991: 125–35; Ong, 1967: 4–5; Summers, 1990).

7. From an ontogenic perspective, this does not yet apply to the early oral phase in which the reception and perception of the outside world as objects is realized primarily in the mouth (Spitz, 1965). As is well known a child puts everything possible into the mouth in order to gain (experiential) 'knowledge' of an object and simultaneously makes an elementary classification concerning the edible versus inedible.

8. From the physiological point of view all sensory reception relating to the outside world ('exteroception' of the five senses) functions in an interactive mode. The reception is complemented by projection: for example, an object is felt on the body surface simultaneously defining the sensation as a characteristic of that object. Actually, hands have a specific role as active projective organs of the sense of touch.

9. The uncontrollable character of respiration is actualized in the sense of smell. To be *inside* an unpleasant smell is experienced as disgusting, even if one avoids breathing through the nose, simply because that which is experienced as negative cannot be kept outside the body. On the other hand the sense of smell functions also in a projective manner, in the case where the smell acts as a characteristic of an object (which one may choose to smell or not).

10. The eye is – in psychoanalytical terms – both an introjective and projective organ. Its excorporative function becomes most evident in ideas of sight lacking reciprocity, such as the evil eye (*mal occhio*) which is directed at the victim and beyond the victim's control, or the panoptical look, which sees but cannot be seen, or as the clinical gaze (Foucault, 1976) which objectifies the subject in terms of power and knowledge. Perhaps also the concept of 'ocular penetration', found in some critical feminist discourses on pornography (see Chapter 7), belongs to the same genre of looks in which something is streaming out of the eyes – a familiar motif in horror movies in which the demonic being shoots laser-like beams out of its eyes. Then again, there is also the feminine seductive look, a look aimed at eating the other, the deadly Medusa.

11. This is one of the few themes which may be turned from the ontogenic scheme to a

cultural one without too much analogical violence. It is hardly a coincidence that what Fenichel called 'primitive reactions' in the above quotation correspond very closely to the modes of so-called 'primitive' magical thought analysed by J.G. Frazer into two distinct types: 'imitative magic', corresponding to visual incorporation, and 'contagious magic' corresponding to the oral one (cf. Frazer, 1983: 14–58 [1922]).

12. This is not to be understood as a specification of the locus and moment in which the subject is born, or in which the representation comes into being. All that can be said is that there is a transition from a symbiosis to separateness which can also be said of the nature–culture transformation – both conceived of as a move from non-difference to difference. However, the subject can be thematized only as already constituted in the same manner as Derrida refers to culture as an 'always already'. It is meaningless to ponder the 'origins' of the difference because the difference is the very constitution itself. This is what Derrida's 'différance' actually refers to, both as an act and a fact, being the difference and an act of 'deferring'.

13. A similar tension figures in the *Da!-Fort!* (there-gone) game which Freud used to play with his grandson. The tension is created in the oscillation of disappearing and reappearing or losing and regaining of an object, in which the pleasure is less derived from the reappearance than from the experience of a continued existence of the object as a *representation* in the act of its factual disappearance and absence (= out of sight). That which stays present when the object disappears is not an eidetic after-image but a memory trace structured into a mental representation.

14. The primitive/non-Western/pre-modern open body is thematized for example by Walens (1981) concerning the Kwakiutl body, by Knauft (1989) dealing with the Melanesian body and by Marriott (1976) in his study on South-Asian Hindu 'dividuals'. On the other hand, the open body figures also as an historical 'other' in Western society, as the pre-modern 'grotesque body' outlined by Mikhail Bakhtin (1968) from Rabelais' texts.

15. Marriott's study of *Hindu Transactions* (1976: 111) points out that the South Asian person should be characterized as a 'dividual' as distinct from an individual – an 'indivisible bounded unit' – due to the mode of transaction in which the 'dividual person' both 'absorbs heterogeneous material influences' but also 'transmit from themselves particles of their own coded substances that reproduce in others something of the nature of the person in whom they have originated' (interpreted in Sanday, 1986: 37). These transactions also acquire other forms besides food exchange, but the principle of sharing (in the form of exchange) remains the same.

16. Sacrificial ritual may be conceived of as shared meals (with the deities and spirits) and/or as a relationship of reciprocal exchange in which the counter-gift is not necessarily only wished for but also demanded. In general, gift exchange is not reducible to disinterested conduct, and thus the distinction of reciprocal and (economic) equivalent exchange may become blurred (cf. Mauss, 1967). The logic is, however, basically different in these two modes of exchange: the former is focused on the relation to the other while in the latter it is focused on the object in the other's possession. Nevertheless, the variety of different modes of reciprocal exchange is considerable, ranging from an almost 'pure' gift to the proximity of equivalence exchange (cf. Gregory, 1982; Humphrey and Hugh-Jones, 1992; Parry, 1986).

17. Both Thomas Kleinspehn (1987) and Stephen Mennell (1985) have applied an Elias-inspired approach to the historical change of eating and food culture. Kleinspehn is focusing in a rather psychoanalytic mode on the genealogy of the insatiable eater while Mennell is primarily concerned with the disciplining and civilizing of the appetite.

18. Not even the speaking body – when defined broadly to include both verbal and non-verbal (gestural) expressive conduct – is reducible into a mere instrument of language use harnessing the 'sign-function' (Eco, 1976) for communicative purposes. Surely, the auto-nomization of language (as a sign system) is manifested in the possibility of lying - as Umberto Eco (1975, 1976) notes – but this does not imply a transformation of the speaking body into a neutral instrument of linguistic expression.

19. Judgements formulated into questions such as 'Is this for me?' or, 'Is this good for me?' then extended to the search for non-subjective standards for the 'good' (in moral and/or

aesthetic sense) and formulated into questions: 'What is virtue?', 'What is beautiful?' etc. – all referring back to the subject's stance ('Is this [for] me?'). The standards of taste as a problem is a search for an Order, which is just a manifestation of a collapse of rigid cultural categorizations functioning as a code which does not offer too much room for individual 'judgement'.

20. It should be noted that symbiosis is a reciprocal (bidirectional) relationship also in its biological sense, that is, symbiosis between two organisms, which does not, however imply any notion of equality or harmony. This is exemplified both in a mother–child union and in a master–servant relationship – both being forms of 'living together' which is the (Greek/Latin) etymological root of the term and referred in English use to communal and social life (from the seventeenth century onwards) before it was given a biological sense (in the nineteenth century).

21. An American food psychologist, Paul Fine found out in a study on food behaviour that people tended to record their own eating in terms of the normal daily meal sequence and disregard the numerous other 'food contacts', snacks and titbits, they had during the day (and sometimes also by night). These were simply not regarded as eating (see Hess and Hess, 1989: 6 8).

22. In distinction to the latter case, the former makes lying (almost) impossible: either there must be a presence of the thing spoken or, alternatively, the words will produce (into the presence) the referred thing or state of affairs. In other words, the break of the magical (or indexical) link between words and things creating an autonomous sign system and making lying possible is in itself a culturally conditioned historical process.

23. The term 'literacy' links the ability to read and write together, which is problematic from an historical point of view. The skill of reading expanded in fact faster and at an earlier stage than the skill of writing and thus reading 'should ideally be discussed separately from writing' as Peter Burke notes in his article on 'the uses of literacy in early modern Italy' (Burke, 1988: 23).

24. A history of reading should also thematize the 'slow but significant shift from public reading [aloud] to private reading' (Burke, 1988: 23), which, however falls outside the present topic.

25. The idea is repeated by Hegel ('Sich-Sprechen-Hören'; Wimmer, 1984: 122) and also by G.H. Mead, who regarded it as the basis for self-objectivization: due to the fact that we can hear our own voices, the self can be an object to itself. This is how the interactive (social) constellation for self-formation is constituted, a constellation where the (object) self is posited in a relation to the 'other' and where the response of the other acts as the productive loop of self-formation (Mead, 1934: 175–95).

26. Immanuel Kant points out the role of mouth as 'the organ of voice' in the constitution of a 'community'. According to Kant this is the way in which 'men, more easily and more completely, enter with others in a community of thought and sensations, especially if the sounds that each gives the other to hear are articulated and if, linked together by understanding according to laws, they constitute a language' (Kant, 1820 [1798]: §18).

27. Take an example from early sixteenth-century Italy where Castiglione formulated his ideas on conversation (1528). Castiglione stated that 'the idea of conversation implies a kind of equality and exchange in an equal basis' and then proceeded, without any inconsistency, to settings of conversation where the hiearchy was actualized – concerning especially 'the way in which a courtier should talk to his prince, or more exactly how he should not talk to his prince' (Burke, 1993: 100).

28. This implies the exclusion of interests – deriving from the 'external' social determinants – leaving, however, room for a hierarchical structure; only now the possible hierarchy grows from within, based on the differences in the skills of conversation (telling stories, jokes, etc.).

29. The abstraction process is actually doubled in the 'social exchange' theories, particularly as represented by Blau (1964) and Hohmans (1958, 1961). First there is an abstracting from the economic exchange of self-interested subjects (on the market), generalized into social behaviour as communication, and then an abstracting from its specific 'materiality', that is speech. This double abstraction is manifested, for example, in formulations in which

behaviour 'emits' something towards the other (Hohmans, 1958: 598–9). It is conceived of as some kind of natural radiation abstracted both from the material flow of economic exchange and from the significational flow of communication, but still modelled by the former.

30. This is, of course, a somewhat stereotypical depiction of the individualized modern meal. There is still a lot of sharing of food and even the same food – being still the predominant characteristic of meals for example in the modern Far East culture of Japan, analysed by Barthes in the early 1970s (Barthes, 1982 [1970]).

31. In his study on the relationship between ritual and speech Iwar Werlen analyses two examples – the 'Roman Catholic mass' and the 'beginnings and endings of everyday conversations' – in which the relationship between food and words or sharing and exchange are structured very differently: 'alltägliche Gespräche sind Tätigkeiten, deren Verbalität hoch und deren Rigidität niedrig ist; sie bieten sich daher einerseits an zur Überprüfung des vorgeschlagenen Konzepts von Ritual, das ja zuerst an rigiden und nichtverbalen handlungen entwickelt wurde, und anderseits zur Prüfung des Handlungscharakters der Sprache' (Werlen, 1984: 231–2). ('everyday conversations are activities characterized by a high degree of verbality and a low degree of rigidity; thus, on the one hand, everyday talk tests the proposed concept of ritual in which rigid and non-verbal modes of conduct are given primary position and, on the other hand, these conversations seem to support the idea of speech as action'.)

32. Marc Detienne and Jesper Svenbro (Detienne and Svenbro, 1989: 153) refer to Athenaeus' (the author of *Sophists at the Dinner Table*) understanding of 'the fact that the social contract is first of all a culinary operation'. In Athenaeus' case this involves the idea of an egalitarian meal but the basic principle of the social contract actually boils down to the distinction of edible versus inedible: those taking part in the meal acknowledge each other as eaters and thus as non-food, implying a 'contract' of not eating each other. This is the minimalistic version of 'social contract' formulated also by Rousseau (see Hénaff, 1992: 22) – and recently by Elias Canetti (1991) – which is, however, rather problematic according to knowledge concerning the variety of (endo)cannibalistic practices (see Chapter 4).

33. The shift has been given different names: as a change from 'utilitarian individuality' to 'expressive individuality' (Bellah et al., 1985), or as the coming of the 'psychological man' leaving behind the religious, political and economic one (Rieff, 1966), or some other sequence of 'personality types' (e.g. Riesman, 1955) constructed in a more or less mechanical fashion. Perhaps Charles Taylor's (1989) analysis of the genealogy of the modern individual self is the most detailed explication of the process.

34. This conception may be related to an historical discussion which took place two centuries ago. Voices raised in the cultural debate in Germany at the end of the eighteenth century were very worried about the new addiction for reading fiction (*Lesesucht*), which was conceived of as passive reception and as an introvert act comparable to seeking consolation in eating or in masturbation (see Bürger, 1980: 200). Similar arguments are nowadays being raised in assessing the harmful effects on children of watching television or playing video games. But, on the other hand, reading habits can be divided into active and passive, as was done by e.g. Jauss (1970) in making his distinction between aesthetic-reflective and passive 'culinary' reading – *Readers Digest*ing the words as food.

3
CORPOREALITY AND HISTORY

The tale of the human body and corporeality is not concerned with the phylogeny of the humanization of the ape. It is not the classification of generic traits into a consecutive evolutionary series; it is cultural history in the most general meaning of the concept. As such, any mere accumulation of generic features by the 'classifying reason' for defining the *differentia specifica* of man (as distinct from animals) provides only a fragmentary picture of the historicity of the human body. What makes the organic entity we call 'body' precisely the *human* body only becomes evident in the field of culture as constituted in the unity of the body's social status and functions and the cultural meanings of the body. The history of the human body is at the same time the social history, the cultural history and – combining both – the 'history of concepts' (*Begriffsgeschichte*) of the body. A body becomes a human body as part of an *Order* encompassing both social-practical structures (division of labour and power hierarchy) and cultural meaning structures.

The *historicity* of the human body is precisely the historicity of the Order. The social status and functions of the human body, the (cultural) meanings of the human body and ultimately the concept itself change and are transformed in accordance with the classifications, distinctions, hierarchies and oppositions contained within the Order. The fundamental concept-historical starting point for any examination of the historicity of the human body is thus the relationship between the body and something else: the body as opposed to or distinct from something else. The historicity of the body is the historicity of 'the body and/or/vs. x' arrangements, whose roots are to be found far in the dawn of human culture.

The second constitutional point in the history of the human body is that the *general concept* of the body emerged in very recent times – only a few centuries ago – as part of the evolution of so-called modern society. A general concept of the body is vital to the archaeology of the 'prehistorical' strata in the meaning of the human body (cf. Marx and labour), and the present chapter is likewise part of that reconstruction.

Body and ?

But where does the story of the human body begin? Should we start with the magical and animistic concepts of archaic societies, in which the body and the 'other' are two different things?

In its most general form, animistic thinking endowed all beings with a 'soul' or 'spirit' (*anima*), that is, conceived of these beings as 'living', be they animate or inanimate. The animistic concept is, however, specifically based on and centred around the mystery of the *life* and *death* of the human body. We could follow E.B. Tylor and say that the duality of body and 'soul' is determined in the relationship between the animate and the inanimate body. The soul is the outcome of the subtraction between them.

The concept of the world of the living (this world) and the world of the dead (the world beyond = of souls) is in turn the basis for the religious duality of *sacred* and *profane* (see Durkheim, 1954 [1912]).

In these fundamental dualities of life and death, sacred and profane the human body does find itself in the grips of the Order, but it nevertheless retains its basic ambivalence.

To begin with, although the duality of body and soul does in fact follow the duality sacred and profane, the body and the soul do not (yet) constitute two parallel entities but rather a cyclic succession of meta-morphoses: the soul/spirit is embodied in the living body – in its materiality and functions. The body's magic substance, especially blood, is not just 'one of the seats of the soul', it is in fact 'the soul itself' (Durkheim, 1954 [1912]: 259).[1] Secondly, 'sacred' is itself ambivalent in relation to the dualities of good and evil or pure and impure (see Caillois, 1959: 36 ff.) – a fact that is manifest in traditional attitudes to woman's menstrual blood.

The body and corporeality also retain their ambivalent nature in the early stages of the Christian tradition (see Bottomley, 1979). The origins of the straitjacket forced upon the body (both the practical and the concep-tual) must be sought elsewhere, in ancient Greek philosophy and especially the concepts of Plato. The duality of body and soul now loses its ambivalence and changes from a succession to a static parallelism marked by the duality *material* and *ideal*. Only then do body and soul become a hierarchical opposition, the body becoming 'the prison of the soul' (Plato).

Body, soul and reason

Making the body and corporeality part of a hierarchical opposition in relation to the Order (ideal and spiritual) does not as such mean that the body and corporeality become negative, but it does signify their definition as something inferior in relation to a superior. The relationship of the hierarchical opposition is far more sophisticated and complicated than simply contempt for the body or the negation of corporeality – a theme taken up in more detail by Michel Foucault in the final stage of his 'History of Sexuality' project (see Foucault, 1982b, 1987, 1988a, 1988b).

In this reorientation of the final stage Foucault examines the 'genealogy of the subject' from a perspective that no longer returns without trace to the concept of power relations which he formulated in the 1970s. 'Techniques of domination' are joined by 'techniques of self' (see Foucault, 1982b: 9–10), the roots of which can be traced from ancient Greece and Rome to early Christianity. In his 'genealogy of the subject' – which is at the same time the genealogy of both the moral subject and the subject of desire (*sujet de désir*) – he demonstrated how subjectivation is 'internalized' as a reflection concerning the subject's *own* body and (in particular) corporeality and 'the production of truth' concerning it. These techniques of self that can no longer be reduced to mere effects and continuations of techniques of domination subjugating *another's* body.

The production of truth concerning one's own body and corporeality (bodily pleasures) and the demand for their control did not imply denial of the body or simple internalization of prohibitions; it meant subjectivation and the building of the self. This principle was already crystallized in the reasoning of Plato and was later manifest among the Stoics and in the rules of Benedictine monastic asceticism.

On the other hand a gradual negativization of the body and corporeality took place in precisely the Christian tradition from Augustine and Cassian onwards and in connection with the principles of monastic asceticism. The ascetic principles of monastic life, the prime content of which was a striving towards chastity and the purity of the soul through freedom from the evils of the flesh and other wordly vices, increasingly marked out the body as the seat of human sin. The writings of Cassian, a predecessor of Benedict in the fourth and fifth centuries already contained a list of eight vices – a list that was later, in the moral code of the medieval Christians, reduced to seven deadly sins (see Foucault, 1988a). The first six of these eight sins constituted, according to Cassian, a causal chain: *gluttony* led to *lust* (and fornication), which in turn generated *greed* and *anger*, which were the cause of *sadness* and *sloth*. The list also included *vainglory* and *pride*.

Although corporeality and the pleasures of the flesh do occupy a leading position in the list of vices, the causal chain does extend beyond the body. Furthermore the two last sins mentioned appear to have no connection with the body and corporeality. Control of the body and the subjugation of corporeality were, in the principles of monastic asceticism, only part of the 'process of "subjectivation" ' (Foucault, 1988a: 239) in which chastity and holy union are more generally striven towards by the renunciation of the wordly sins.

> It is rather the opening up of an area [. . .] which is that of thought, operating erratically and spontaneously, with its images, memories and perceptions, with movements and impressions transmitted from the body to the mind and the mind to the body. (Foucault, 1988a: 239)

Foucault's ultimate turn (the emphasis on technologies of the self in the genealogy of the subject) could now easily be interpreted to the effect that the birth of the 'soul' of Western man, and at the same time the soul–body duality, is primarily an 'endogenic' process and not a product of power technology (directed at others). This interpretation, however, proves to be an exaggeration. Although the genealogy of the subject leads Foucault to make a distinction between the technologies of domination and those of the self, he himself emphazises their close relationship (in which the principle of confession plays a central part): 'One has to show the interaction between these two types of self' (Foucault, 1982b: 10).

In this sense Foucault's project was much further from completion than may appear at first sight. For the technology-of-self scheme of the genealogy of the subject as analysed by Foucault cannot be interpreted as an historical process in which the mechanisms of subjectivation change in accordance with some sort of principle of diffusion (cf. Norbert Elias) to become general in society. The question about 'the interaction between these two types of self' mentioned above can thus justifiably be formulated as: how is the relationship of these two technologies ('two types of self') structured at the dawn of the modern era as the 'soul' of modern man gets more and more societally generalized?

Although the genealogy of the moral subject does in fact extend to the time before the crystallization of a moral code, this crystallization of the moral code in medieval Christianity did imply a shift in emphasis to the control of *another's* body and the making of the soul the prison of another's body, for all are (in principle) 'others' in relation to the code. And further: in its societally (increasingly) generalized form the emergence of the duality of soul–body is bound up with precisely technologies aimed at another's *own* – and not, therefore, that *owned* by another – regardless of the prehistory of these technologies, be it in the monastery or some other closed institution.

Foucault analysed this birth of the soul of modern man in his work *Discipline and Punishment* (Foucault, 1979). The development of a power technology corresponding to modern disciplinary society – which paradigmatically is manifest in the history of new disciplinary practices and the prison as an institution – is (part of) 'the story of the birth of the soul of modern man' and thus the history of the crystallized duality of body and soul. The same process produces both the crystallized duality of body/soul and the general concept of the body.

But what is this body and its incorporeal double, the soul? The body is simply a body – or to be more precise, a living body with its own rhythms, flows and intensities; its pain and its pleasures. There is nothing more to be said about the body, for every additional epithet increases (paradoxically, it seems) the soul. On the other hand 'it would be wrong to say that the soul is an illusion or an ideological effect' (Foucault, 1979: 29). It really does exist, being produced perpetually:

> it is produced permanently around, on, within the body by the functioning of a power that is exercised on those punished – and, in more general way, on those one supervises, trains and corrects, over madmen, children at home and at school, the colonized, over those who are stuck at a machine and supervised for the rest of their lives. (Foucault, 1979: 29)

In this order and thus ultimately – as the network gains generality and density – it applies generally. All in all: 'soul is an effect and a tool of a political anatomy: soul, the prison of the body' (Foucault, 1979: 30). Thus Plato has been turned upside down.

The disciplining of the body does, of course, have its prehistory, in the subordination of both self and others. The slave's body is owned and it is constantly the object of potential (corporal) violence. But the presence of direct violence keeps the slave a mere body devoid of a soul, and we cannot then speak of the *human* body. On the other hand monastic asceticism meant not only the discipline of the body but also an overall striving towards chastity, purity and sacredness.

Not until the seventeenth and eighteenth centuries did disciplines become the 'general formulas of domination' (Foucault, 1979: 137) – a cornerstone of the emerging technology of power. The new forms of discipline did not merely involve the strict subordination of the body, not merely the schooling of bodily skills. It involved a close unity of the two: the body had simultaneously to be both useful (a tool) and obedient (controllable).

But in order to spread, this modern power technology, in which power begins to feature with growing prominence in a positive-productive form and less and less frequently as something openly repressive, demands something from society that could in general be described as 'freedom'. Although disciplinary *techniques* for the most part develop in a world marked by an absence of freedom (in institutions for persons isolated from the rest of the society), they spread and are diversified in a world of 'free subjects', in other words in a world in which 'individual or collective subjects [. . .] are faced with a field of possibilities in which several ways of behaving, several reactions and diverse comportments may be realized' (Foucault, 1982a: 221). Power, as a productive principle and relation, can only be directed at these free subjects. And thus the effect and medium of this power technology, the soul of modern man, also legitimized its role – the body's prison in a social state in which the other bars and chains fettering the body have more or less been thrown off.

The body is no longer actually owned; nor is the control and supervision of the body total in the way it used to be in pre-modern society or in special closed institutions. Nevertheless it is precisely these closed establishments that act as the laboratories for modern power technology and corporal disciplinary power. Thus the technology needed to produce the soul of the 'free worker' is already being developed in the institutions, especially the work houses (*Zuchthäuser*), where the framework of bars and walls has not yet been cut down to the size of the soul.

The body as a tool

It is, however, in the historical process which Foucault calls the history of the origins of the soul of modern man, that the body and corporeality gain a new social and cultural status. The body, in general, becomes the object of both intellectual and practical control. But an integral element of these two aspects is the instrumentalization of the body. The instrumentalization of the body is thematized in two forms that are inseparable at the discursive level.

First, we have, on the one hand, the instrumentalizing and instrumentalization of man's *own body*. In this respect the proclamation of the sovereignty of reason of the rising bourgeoisie – which embraced the principles of controlling corporeality (desires and needs) and were given their most pointed expression in the (English) Puritanism of the seventeenth and eighteenth centuries – constituted a proto-discourse. The norms of ascetic life of the bourgeoisie did have some connection with the forms of (Benedictine) monastic asceticism, but with the vital difference that the 'soul', defined as rational and calculating will, transformed the body into a medium for action based on rational will and especially action furthering personal interests.

Human passions or 'vices' became more and more firmly connected with the body and its natural tendencies (as desires). The opposite position was occupied by reason, whose task was to curb and instrumentalize the body into part of the dynamics of culture, or in this case, perhaps better, civilization. The subjugation and instrumentalization (exploitation) of external nature was thus paralleled by the instrumentalization of 'inner nature'.

The breakthrough of Western economic reason is not, however, an historical truism – a fact well appreciated even by Max Weber in debating the relationship between Protestant ethics and the spirit of capitalism. The rise of reason, and at the same time the crystallization of the duality of body and reason, meant a profound upheaval in the Christian moral code, finding its most illustrious expression in the Reformation.[2]

The history of the development of this upheaval can be constructed in the political and moral-philosophical tradition: for we are concerned here with the gradual re-formation of the moral code in which the 'dissolute' passion closely associated with corporeality, a craving for money and more generally the pursuit of personal interests, are replaced by *reason*, as the antithesis and guardian of the bodily passions.

For example, according to the concepts of St Augustine, which took on new life in the Middle Ages, the three main sins were the lust for money and ownership, the lust for power and sexual lust (of the flesh). The first (and to some extent also the second) of these deadly sins was for a long time still defined as a passion in moral-philosophical discourse (Bacon, Spinoza, Hobbes, etc.), even though private vices were in fact beginning to turn into positive forces conducive to the public good (of the commonwealth). The concept of the battle between passions with differing values (both beneficial and detrimental) on the 'battlefield of the soul' (after the medieval allegory) becomes crystallized step by step as the conflict of *interests* and *passions*, in which the former identifies with reason and the latter increasingly with corporeality, and in which it is the task of reason to govern the unreason of the body.[3] Reason now assumes an historically specific content as the leading principle in the brave new rational world.

The grounds on which the duality of reason and body is based differ radically from those behind the traditional Christian duality of body and soul. The latter, with a growing loss of ambivalence, looks increasingly towards the duality based on *sacred* and *profane*. Monastic asceticism aimed at chastity and purity of the soul by the disciplining of the body and the purging of worldly vices. But the reason–body duality of the bourgeois subject primarily centres around a different, clearly more worldly basic duality: that of *nature* and *culture* (or civilization).

Secondly, the instrumentalizing of the body is also notably thematized to apply to another's body, or to be more precise, another's *own* body. This is the same historical process in which the epithets for the ideal type of bourgeois subject are also crystallized. It concerns the inevitable complement to the bourgeois subject, the birth of the 'free' wage labourer. The history of the disciplining of the body does not refer to the wage labourer alone, but in the form of wage labour it was given its most general societal expression. The process is far more heterogeneous than the 'breakthrough of capitalism' and the increase in wage labour generated by 'mute economic forces' (Marx).

The technology of the disciplinarian mechanisms took root in the closed institutions, the worlds of those robbed of their freedom. Yet the discourse on the disciplining of the body, by no means a powerless reflection but part of effective practice, have numerous different undercurrents: the human scientific discourses (Foucault's *sciences humaines*) on institutions are connected with the moral codes of the ideal bourgeois subject, which are in turn impossible to distinguish from the discourses on the disciplining of the wage labourer.

There were in nineteenth-century England, for example, a number of discourses and practices that explicitly involved the instrumentalization and disciplining of others' own bodies, in other words those of the wage labourers: particularly in the enforcement of working time discipline (see e.g. Thompson, 1967), but also of 'rational recreations' (see for example Bailey, 1978; see also Falk, 1979a, 1983). But as the moral codes and (work) ethical principles, the origins of which could be interpreted as self-definition of the bourgeois subject, became individualized rational principles commonly applied within society, self-discipline and other 'self' norms now by no means referred to the idealized bourgeois subject but to every wage labourer (see Falk, 1979b) and even more widely to each individual subject in modern society.

The body becomes part of an increasingly dense network of order, classifications and measurements out of which grows a prison commensurable with the soul of the individualized subject. The body ultimately becomes the *medium of self*: the very use of the terms 'I' and 'my body' already makes this fundamental distinction.

Corporeal equality

The history of the instrumentalizing and individualizing of the body is also the history of the equalizing of bodies (see Gebauer, 1982: 314 ff.). Organically connected with this is the birth of the general concept of body.

The formation of a concept concerning the body 'in general' can be observed from the trend in human scientific discourse. In the 'oldest' archaeological stratum of human scientific discourse, anatomical-clinical medicine, the dead body really is the 'model for the body', as has been pointed out by Baudrillard (1982: 180), but examination of the pathological corpse at the same time provides the key to the mysteries of the living body (Foucault, 1976: 173–4). In anatomical-clinical medicine, the human body features simultaneously as both a generality (a body) and as an individual (medical) case. In this dual role the human being, and especially the human body, becomes an object and medium for positive knowledge (Foucault, 1976: 199–200). Man is objectified (the body in general) but is also subjectified and individualized (as a case).

On the other hand, the equalizing of bodies is a political process: it is a thread in the development of a (modern) society of equals. Gebauer (1982: 313) calls this concept based on the equality of bodies 'symbol theoretical' and further distinguishes it from the 'quasi-biological' concept of the human body that still prevailed in the sixteenth century.

According to the latter concept the body is the bearer of certain given biological properties, which biological properties to a great extent conformed with the social (estate) position of the bearer. The various estates in fact represented different races: the peasant was also physically 'peasant-like', as distinct from the nobleman and his body, just as a workhorse differs from a thoroughbred racing horse. But according to the 'symbol theoretical' concept that really gained ground in the nineteenth century (that is, alongside the anatomical-clinical concept of the body), the body is more of a 'symbolic manifestation' of certain properties (Gebauer, 1982: 313).

Bodies as such become equal, from nobles to the lowest rank of commoners. According to Gebauer the body concept, in keeping with the 'new reason', can be crystallized into three principles: (a) no man has the right to another's body (corporeal sovereignty, physical inviolability), (b) the bodies of prince and bourgeois do not differ (they are in principle alike) and (c) the body acquires its right according to the performances its owner achieves (Gebauer, 1982: 318). The body is the property of the free subject.

The body as a means of expression

The origin of the new (modern) concept of body is thus manifest in two parallel and interconnected ways: in the systematic form of human scientific discourse and, more generally, as a change in the social (political) status of the body. In the former the body becomes an object-subject – specific in its generality and general in its specificity – that submits to the 'clinical gaze' (Foucault, 1976) as a simultaneous object and means for the production of knowledge ('truth'). In the latter the body is individualized and instrumentalized both as a stand for reason and a working tool (bourgeois subject & wage labourer) and also – and this is gaining increasing emphasis in modern society – as the *means of expression* of the individual subject.

Whereas the clinical gaze interprets symptomatic bodily expressions, the equalized body comes in for cross-fire from interpreting gazes at societal level, the interpretation not being restricted merely to pathologies but also examining the soul or character hidden beneath the body's outer shell. The body now acquires a new duality: that of the *outer manifestation* (expression) and the *inner being*. The body is subsumed to the 'total culture of appearances' (see Baudrillard, 1990: 33) turning into a collection of signs to be interpreted. It becomes a façade (Goffman, 1959; Sennett, 1978), which at the same time both conceals and expresses the inner being. The body enters the realm of signs and becomes a mannequin (cf. Baudrillard, 1982: 180).

The body's new status both as a shell and as a means of expression is also evident in nineteenth-century human scientific discourses, in which attempts were made to interpret a person's inner nature from his outward *features*. This involved the application of the ethological perspective to the study of man (cf. Darwin's research into the expression of emotions by both humans and animals) and also, more generally, the typologizing and interpreting of outward physical features, physiognomy. One example is Bertillon's phrenology, in which criminal types were classified according to their skull measurements (cf. also Lombroso). First came pathological cases, and only later did scientists come up with psychological typologies proceeding from pathologies to the 'normal' (for example, Kretschmer's body-build and character types).

But the social breakthrough of the new instrumentalization of the body (its transformation into a shell and a means of expression) has its own historical prerequisites and roots that can be explicated by means of the interpretations of, first, how the body's shell comes into being and, second, how the 'language' of the body and the 'speakers' of this language come into existence.

One background interpretation is provided by Norbert Elias' concept of the 'civilizing process' (see Elias, 1978, 1982), in which man's affectivity (sexual and aggressive behaviour) is gradually, through the stages from court society to modern bourgeois society, restricted and transformed into an inner emotionalism. In fact Elias' interpretation, which displays the influence of both Freud and Weber, is concerned with the inhibition of bodily expressions and functions and their civilizing, but at the same time with the *armouring of the body*.

The tendency of affect expressions and bodily functions to become more intimate and private in fact signifies a radical change in man's public and social behaviour – a change that specifically emphasizes the importance of the body's visible outward armour. At sensory organization level this change may be described as a shift in emphasis in social intercourse from the close contact senses (smell, taste, touch) to the senses by distance (hearing, sight), especially the supremacy of the eye (see for example Kamper and Wulf, 1982: 13). This is the reverse of the bodily sovereignty of the free subject and a 'new sense of respectability' (Gebauer, 1982: 318 ff.): everyone has the right to physical inviolability but at the same time also the obligation to observe this principle in his or her (public) social intercourse regardless of the nature of another's bodily approach (aggressive/sexual).[4]

The civilizing of public-social interaction is admittedly one aspect of the disciplining of the body, but in this case the emphasis is on the part of the process applying to the body specifically as a means of *expression*. This is not, however, debated by Norbert Elias: what interests him is what remains inside the body's armour and not what functions the outer shell of the armour acquires in modern society. The problems surrounding the outer shell have, however, been debated by, for example, the classic authority Georg Simmel and, more recently, Richard Sennett and Jean Baudrillard.

Both Simmel and Sennett specify that the modern society of public-social intercourse emphasizing bodily sovereignty and the distant senses (especially the eye) is an urban way of life. In Simmel's interpretation (see Simmel, 1958, especially pp. 483–93) the emphasis on sight is connected with the individualized form of urban life and the spatial structure of the city. Sennett (1978) analyses the rise and fall of the 'public man' produced by the urban way of life in more detail. The public-social part of the city, especially its street life, forms a stage on which people perform to one another as façade bearers. *Outward* appearance, *exterior* and *outlook* act as means of expression.

The body and 'the body's body',[5] that is clothing, now act as expressions of social and personal identity, but at the same time also as creators of identity. The staging of clothed bodies and the silent language of gestures and behaviour become a fundamental form of the instrumentalization of the body. In the social public life of the city, each person appears as both an exhibitionist and a voyeur simultaneously: visual gastronomy becomes the primary sphere of silent speech.

The signs surrounding the body (from clothes to other requisites and behavioural habits) are no longer part of a static system in which the body with its signs and social status are one. In hierarchical estate society both the body and the signs surrounding it were bound directly to the status. But in a society of 'free' subjects and moving positions, where bodies are in principle equal, the body and its signs become something to acquire and to achieve. Whereas formerly (static) status preceded the sign (this in fact being an index of this status), the sign now takes precedence over status: by assuming certain signs a man achieves the status they signify (see Bauman, 1971: 279–91).

This expression of social status and identifying with it is still part of present-day reality (Bourdieu, 1984), but we are also dealing with a more sophisticated use of language: the signs surrounding the body (from the outer shell of the body to the surrounding requisites) also act specifically as ways of expressing and/or creating the individual identity or self of the subject. The signs surrounding the body are in fact part of the system of classifications, measurements and distinctions which, in Foucault's more general conception of the technology of power, is crystallized in the bodily prison of modern man, the soul. This becomes evident on examination of the constitution and the specific dynamics of the world of signs surrounding the body; neither bodily armour nor spatial analysis of the city are sufficient to explain this.

One interesting approach to this theme is developed by Jean Baudrillard, especially in his (earlier) interpretation of capitalist commodity production as 'sign production' and of consumption as consumption of signs (Baudrillard, 1981). It is precisely capitalist commodity production, as mass production, that creates the prerequisites for the birth of a (relatively) independent 'language of goods'. The world of goods constitutes a constantly growing and shifting system of signs which consumers use in their (silent) speech. This system of signs has a productive effect on its users, as does language in general. But in addition it also has its own dynamics as capitalistic commodity production.

We can, on the basis of these two criteria of effectivity, reduce the above-mentioned ambivalence of expressed vs. produced identity in favour of the latter: commodity production as the production of signs also creates the users or consumers of these signs. The outer shell of the body and the signs that surround it do not hide the 'inner being' – this inner being is the product of these signs and their sign production – which can now be conceived of as part of the *productive* power technology, as conceptualized by Foucault.

Silenced or silent body

The body is tied to a network of boundaries ranging from concrete practices to linguistic signs, from social hierarchies to classificatory codes. The subject and the 'soul' are the product of all this.

But is it even possible to speak of the human body without turning our definition into the construction of a soul? Can the human body and corporeality be approached as something positive without this approach becoming part of the Order defining and determining the body? And again: is it possible to reconstruct the concept of corporeality so that it at the same time implies the deconstruction of the Other (soul, reason, self)?

To a certain extent, the above formulations make our framing of the question less unconditional: the fates of the human body in the face of historically changing (discursive and non-discursive) orders help to bring out deconstructive elements, for the historicity of the orders confining and defining the body also speaks of the historicity of corporeality itself.

I shall now try to develop this idea by demonstrating that there is a close conceptual link between corporeality and 'transgression' (à la Georges Bataille). Corporeality is not 'nature', standing before or outside 'culture'. Corporeality is not an 'animal' that dwells in man, nor is it mere biology and physiology.

The body as Archimedean point

Be this as it may, we must in any case start with the problem: how to speak of the human body and corporeality? How to avoid calling corporeality 'nature', an absolute reference, a transcendental signified, Archimedean point that determines true humanity and at the same time provides scope for criticism of 'Civilization and its Discontents' (Freud)? And on the other hand: how to ensure that we do not lose sight of the indisputable fact that the concreteness of the human body simultaneously has a firm link with nature – as materiality? *Hic Rhodus, hic salta!* – or perhaps even better: *hocus pocus!*[6]

It is, of course, obvious that the human body cannot simply be postulated as an invariable essence. The whole problem can in fact be avoided by restricting ourselves to the examination and specification of the mechanism binding and defining the human body. This principle seems to have been followed quite consistently by Michel Foucault. According to Foucault the human body is primarily the 'raw material' for social and cultural processes and mechanisms, to which no positive (or absolute) qualities are attributed. In his later texts and statements Foucault consciously tried to avoid being branded as a corporeality mystic or a philosopher of desire.

Foucault's logic in avoiding the Archimedean point is not, however, infallible. This is apparent from, for example, the declaration towards the end of the first volume of *The History of Sexuality*, stating that the battle against confining and defining sexuality should draw not on 'sex-desire' but on '*bodies and pleasures*' (Foucault, 1981: 157).

Sexuality is both a tool and a product of knowledge/power technology: it is not 'genuine' corporeality but one (historical) form of binding and defining corporeality (the body and its pleasures). Adapting this to Foucault's earlier formulations, the sexual (sexualized) body is in fact part of modern man's soul – the prison of the body – and not a genuine corporeal existence repressed by the soul. Foucault's dilemma is, however, that constructing a counter-strategy to the 'deployment of sexuality' (Foucault, 1981: 77 ff.) seems in principle to be impossible. A counter-strategy would involve raising the body and its pleasures to the discursive level, but at the same time it would replace the rejected deployment of sexuality by a development of corporeality – which is just as much produced (and part of the soul) as the rejected sexuality (see Fraser, 1983).

But maybe it is, after all, possible to create a counter-discourse that is not just the reverse and thus a derivative of the predominant discourse and that is not just a futile extension of the endless (binding and defining) discourse texture. This does, however, call for a redefinition of the epistemological basis for the discourse/counter-discourse relationship, as Foucault did in fact try to do, with varying consistency, by replacing *theory* by *strategy*.[7]

The journey into the theme begins, however, rather conventionally with conceptual distinctions.

The corporeal being and corporeality

It would at first sight seem natural to begin with the human body as a being with certain universal properties – in other words properties that may be considered as physical generic features of man. This would yield an endless list of properties (from *homo erectus* to the naked ape) peculiar to the human being alone as distinct from 'other animals'.

This may in practice bring us up against certain characteristics fundamental to man's corporeal existence, but the conceptual tools for distinguishing them from the inessential features is nevertheless lacking. The final outcome would be a *description* of the functions and dimensions of the human body and not a *concept* of the dimensions of corporeality.

What if we were to start with a specific aspect of the corporeal being that, at the level of pre-conceptual understanding, is an integral part of something that could be called corporeality? Man is a *sensory being* – but so are all the animals that interact with their environment, and pointing to some special form of the organization of the senses (close vs. distant senses, etc.) by no means solves the problem.

Man is a being that experiences positive and negative sensations (pleasure and pain). We have now entered the field in which the question of the unique nature of man's corporeality begins to be actualized. True, a dog that has been beaten howls (from pain?) and a cat purrs when it is stroked (out of pleasure?), but can we speak of positive sensations if there is no sense which allows them to be registered and interpreted as such? The hedonistic concept of man emphasizing corporeality solves this problem by defining man as a being who acts so as to seek pleasure and avoid pain, but at the same time it transforms man from a sensory being to a *sensual being*. And, lo and behold: we have arrived at the mysteries of man's corporeality.

But the vulgar hedonistic concept is not enough. For if it is interpreted as behaviour on the stimulus–response scheme, the distinction between man and the worm that has learnt to avoid getting an electric shock or to find food in a T-pipe begins to be blurred. What is essential is to determine the special logic behind the sensuality and sensory experience of the human body and its striving towards positive bodily states. This unique nature may tentatively be represented by the conceptual difference between need and desire (Falk, 1983).

The mechanism behind the negative and positive (bodily) state of an animal (or more generally a living organism) operates on a scale ranging from unbalanced (state of need/hunger) to balanced (satisfaction of need/ hunger), whereas human striving towards the 'pleasures of the body' is primarily something more than the avoidance of the negative 'unbalanced' state; this striving is more in keeping with the *logic of desire*.

For man a particular bodily state (and now especially its positive dimension: pleasure) is more of a shift from normal state to hyper state. Pleasure is itself a shift to an exceptional state above what is normal and at the same time the characterization of the very state. In this sense the state of bodily pleasure peculiar to man cannot be analysed as a striving towards balance and the satisfaction of need in accordance with the logic of need. The state of satisfaction is foreign to desire: it is a constant striving.

It is already apparent by this stage that beginning with the human body as a being and distinguishing the characteristics of this being from animals and nature is inadequate and in fact leads to a dead end. Man's (bodily) sensuality, as characterized above with the aid of the concept of desire, cannot be reduced to any biological-physiological mechanics of pain and pleasure.[8]

The logic of desire as the operating principle for a living organism, however developed that being's sensory system may be, is simply irrational and impossible. It would ultimately lead to postulation of the self-destruction principle of the living organism. The logic of desire cannot be conceived of in the context of the individual organism any more than it can in the context of an ecological system.

The logic of desire presupposes a culture-as-constituted, a cultural existence of man, or simply humanity as the property not of the (species) being but of the societal existence.

The striving from normal to non-normal state, which may be called a *hyper* state rather than a *hypo* state, is a vital feature of the cultural dynamics which on a collective and on a social scale takes in more than the level with the closest relationship to man's bodily existence.

The duality contained in the cultural dynamics has been represented by various pairs of concepts: *profane* vs. *sacred* (Durkheim), *everyday life* vs. *fête* (Bataille and Caillois), *structure* vs. *anti-structure* (V. Turner) or *apollonic* vs. *dionysian* (Nietzsche). Each conceptualization stresses various aspects of the normal and the non-normal state in different ways, but one thing they all have in common is that corporeality is granted a special status as an element of the non-normal state.

The 'liminality' (van Gennep) in rituals or the more secular popular festivals includes dancing and singing, eroticism and orgy, intoxication and ecstasy and lack of restraint in general (feasting, drinking, debauchery) – in other words the manifestations of human corporeality in which sensuality and pleasure play a leading part. The articulating of corporeality is a major part of the dual cultural dynamics in which the profane or everyday order is momentarily laid aside and replaced by a sacred or festive order.[9]

Examining corporeality and its historic fate, the dual cultural dynamics can also be distinguished in the manifestations of corporeality that are not directly bound to social forms (rituals). This in turn calls for conceptual specification of the dual cultural dynamics: the emphasis must be shifted from duality (sacred/profane, etc.) to dynamics operating between the poles – the *transition* from the normal state to the non-normal.

The *principle of transgression* formulated by Georges Bataille (see esp. Bataille,1962) here takes on central significance, admittedly in a critical interpretation. Transgression, the crossing of borders, points to the dynamics in which the order of the secular and everyday world is shattered. Transgression is itself a transition to the other (non-normal) state, the sacred or festive world. But this time, from the point of view of corporeality, transgression also points to the breaking down and crossing of the borders confining and defining the body imposed by culture as an Order.

The dual cultural dynamics and principle of transgression permit us to abandon the futile debate of the generic features of the human corporate being and allows us to define corporeality as part of the 'inner' dynamics of culture.

But how can we justify the principle of transgression itself? Does the postulation of this principle as the Great Explanans not lead to the replacement of one anthropological constant by another? The danger is obvious, and Bataille's concepts in fact contain elements justifying such doubts. Bataille speaks of man's fundamental striving towards a 'continuity of being' – a state in which the 'discontinuity' of cultural existence is overthrown (Bataille, 1962). We could just as well postulate that the 'longing for natural state', away from the oppressive and discontinuous state of culture, is a fundamental generic feature of man. Transgression then becomes regression – a return to the (natural) state preceding human and cultural existence.

The concept does, of course, seem familiar. For example, Freud's concept of regression (also non-pathological) to the – oral and primary narcissistic – early stage of psychosexual development and the 'oceanic feeling' (*Ozeanisches Gefühl*) can be conceived of as a return to a symbiotic 'natural state' on an ontogenic level. The primary narcissistic natural state is the state before humanity, which is now defined as a psychic order produced by sane and correct psychosexual development.

The primarily narcissistic state is also a *bodily state* characterized decisively by the pleasure principle; in this state the body and its functions have not yet broken away from the 'nature' surrounding them as repre-

sented by the mother and the mother's breast. It is, of course, true that
Freud's concept of corporeality dominated by the dynamics of drive
(*Trieb*) is far more sophisticated than earlier concepts of 'the evil', 'beast'
or 'nature' within man, but even so the concept of regression rests on
precisely the binary opposition of *nature* and *culture*.

A similar nature/culture-oriented interpretation of regression also
appears in an anthropological version of Lévi-Strauss' interpretation of
contrasting feature in myth and ritual (see Lévi-Strauss, 1981: 668 ff.)

According to him a myth is an interpretation of the transition from chaos
to order, from the nature to culture. The logic of the ritual[10] is, however,
opposite to that of the myth.

> While myth resolutely turns away from the continuous to segment and break
> down the world by means of distinctions, contrasts and oppositions, ritual moves
> in the opposite direction: starting from the discrete units that are imposed upon
> it by this preliminary conceptualization of reality, it strives to get back to the
> continuous. (Lévi-Strauss, 1981: 679)

In other words ritual represents collective regression, a striving to get back
to nature, to a time and state before culture and Order. The corporeality
articulated in ritual can likewise be explained by this same regressive
principle. Regression itself becomes, both in Freud's psychoanalytical and
Lévi-Strauss' anthropological conception, a principle that can be explained
only as the parallel and simultaneous manifestation of culture and nature in
man and human society – a concept that turns out to be an unsolved
paradox. How can nature appear as a virgin *force* spared the 'corruption' of
culture, as an energetic principle, and yet be a materiality that is organized
and/or moulded by means of cultural meanings and practices? And, as
applied to corporeality: how can human existence also be being 'in a
natural state' at the same time, if and since this nature (or the animal in
man) cannot be reduced to or located in the characteristics of the human
body and its functions?

The dual cultural dynamics and principle of transgression cannot be
derived from the nature–culture duality and the associated energetic
principle. Transgression has to be defined as a principle that reduces
neither to a regressive longing for the natural state nor to a counter-effect
generated by the world of restrictions and order (cf. the functionalist
'safety valve'-interpretation). Transgression cannot be tied to the energetic
principle, nor to the corporeal being, as an absolute referent. The principle
of transgression can be presented only in weak form and in reverse: by
referring to the cultural and historical universality of practices manifesting
dual cultural dynamics and by proving the inability and reductionism of
rationalistic conceptions to explain these 'irrational' phenomena.

Only now can we make a precise conceptual distinction between the
corporeal being (and its properties) and *corporeality*. The body can be
perceived as a being freed from its cultural existence that has certain
properties, the sum of which does not, however, ever lead to the
comprehension and conceptualization of human corporeality (from sen-

sory being to sensual existence). Corporeality demands the existence of limits confining, restricting and defining the human body, just as transgression itself generally demands borders. Corporeality is a cultural and also an historical category. As the Orders, as a system of boundaries, change in history (and from culture to culture), so the crossing of boundaries and thus the forms of corporeality also change.

Although *eroticism* can indeed be conceived as a highly universal and suprahistorical field of human corporeality, the transgressions it embraces have their own historicity. But the origin of eroticism in any case lies in the limits of human culture and crossing these limits, as Georges Bataille has tried to show.

Bataille and the origin of eroticism

In his earlier concepts of eroticism (see Bataille, 1962) Bataille is still firmly entrenched in the sacred–profane duality of Durkheim and Mauss. Eroticism is defined as a broad category including not only (more narrowly defined) 'physical and emotional' eroticism but also the 'religious' (and mystical) world of experience (Bataille, 1962: 15, 23). All these forms of eroticism display man's fundamental striving towards a 'continuity of being', the ultimate form of which is death: 'Eroticism . . . is assenting to life up to the point of death' (Bataille, 1962: 11).

In his later concept of the origin of eroticism (see Bataille, 1981) Bataille restricts himself to sexuality and shifts the emphasis to the dynamics of transgression itself. Bataille links eroticism (which is peculiar to man) with 'death-consciousness' or the awareness of the limited nature of earthly life. 'Eroticism differs from the sexual drive of animals in that it is . . . a conscious striving towards a goal, in this case a striving towards sensual enjoyment' (Bataille, 1981: 45). Even the sexuality of prehistoric man was guided neither by any natural instinct nor any rational striving to continue the human line – the concept of the cause and effect of the sexual act and procreation is by no means inborn in man.

The enjoyment of sexual functions, erotic passion, is related to the fear of death. Both feature the border between life and death – the profane and the sacred – and crossing this border. In both 'one is occupied by an alien force and in both cases a strange event explodes over the established order of things' (Bataille, 1981: 35). According to Bataille eroticism always includes the proximity of death – the simplest absolute manifestation of transgression, though this is peculiar to human culture alone: crossing the border between life and death (the profane and the sacred). It is thus no mere coincidence that the climax of sexual enjoyment, the most intensive moment (orgasm) has been called *'la petite mort'*. The enjoyment experienced in the sexual act is not just a 'natural' or 'animal' bodily function, but lies in the momentary breaking of the bounds confining the body, a transition that is an imitation of death.

Bataille's interpretation of the origin of eroticism should by no means be conceived of as a suprahistorical scheme for explaining erotic enjoyment and sensuality in general. The history of sensuality is the historicity of transgression related to the body, in turn bound to the historicity of the borders confining and defining the body. There is thus no cause to wonder that the eroticism and sensuality of prehistoric man differed greatly from that of the medieval peasant and even more from the level of physical pleasures enjoyed by 'civilized' modern man. Revolving around these three fixed points, the history of corporeality cannot, however, be conceived of as a process of evolution devoid of all ambiguity – as the rise or fall of corporeality and sensuality. Paradoxically the historical fabric of corporeality is made up of threads from both lines of development, and distinguishing between these calls for a finer definition of the concept of corporeality.

The two dimensions of corporeality

We have already given a basic definition of corporeality: corporeality is a form of transgression and as such a cultural category. It has also been limited to apply to positive (sensory) experiences – sensuality and enjoyment.

The definition can simply be argued by saying that the idea of transgression is directed at, for example, the experience of pain, as in sadomasochistic eroticism (admittedly mainly at the level of fantasy), the sensory experience becomes reversed, i.e. positive. This reversal is partly emphasized by the fact that in intensive sensory experience the border between pleasure and pain becomes diffuse.

The conceptual distinction of greater importance as regards the historical fates of corporeality divides corporeality into two dimensions, which I shall call the *expressive aspect* and the *experience aspect*. These dimensions of corporeality may be described by numerous contrasting pairs of attributes: active/passive, externalizing/internalizing, etc., but classification does not lead to any more profound conceptual distinction. The distinction between the two dimensions of corporeality is, however, of major importance in solving the parallelism of the two directly opposed interpretations of the historical fates of the body. It may be claimed that only in the modern world have the conditions existed for rich sensuality, yet this same world also acts as a monster destroying man's corporeality and sensuality. How can these two interpretations be placed side by side?

Explicating the conceptual distinction associated with corporeality demands an excursus into the cultural historical and critical interpretations dealing with the fates of corporeality with the advent of the modern world.

Reference has already been made to Norbert Elias' theory of the civilizing process, according to which the control of affectivity and in general the growing intimacy of bodily functions leads to a shielding of the body. In accordance with the problematic nature–culture duality, the body's armour (affect control) disciplines the animal/nature in man but – by way of compensation and substitute – opens up a world of inner fantasies and emotions. In other words direct and functional *affect expression* – be it sex or violence – is replaced by an internally experienced *passive emotionalism* staged in the world of fantasy and drawing on fiction, from chivalry romances to adventure films as its raw material (Elias, 1982).

The duality of affect expression and passive emotionalism can be interpreted as a pair of concepts which come quite close to the duality of the expressive aspect and the experience aspect of corporeality. Shielding the body prevents the externalization of 'inner nature' and leads to compensatory daydreams. This does not mean a total disappearance of expressive corporeality – the intimized erotic practice indeed retains the expressive and the experience aspects as an organic whole – but the civilizing process signifies a marked narrowing of fields of expression, and growing privacy.[11] Collective carnal rituals (*carni*vals) for the most part become things of the past.

The same basic scheme, the inhibition of the externalization of 'inner nature', also recurs in a manner of Freudo-Marxist (and partly Foucault-influenced) cultural critique interpretations, in which the emphasis is not on the shielding of the body but on the instrumentalizing, disciplining and ultimately the subjugation of the body as a medium for the individual self (see for example Krovoza ,1976; Nitzschke, 1974; zur Lippe, 1978 and 1979). Krovoza speaks of the desexualization of (capitalist) production and Nitzschke of how 'the necessity to uphold the self which is constantly reinforced by work and individuation excludes experiences that are possible only when the self disintegrates' (Nitzschke, 1974: 8). In these concepts the expressive aspect of corporeality seems to give way almost totally to the *instrumental functions of the body*, which expands from work to dance and sport (see zur Lippe) and in general to the functions maintaining the individual self demanded by modern society. Sensuality is destroyed (Nitzschke), there is a shift in emphasis from the contact senses to the distant senses and, all in all, the senses become stupefied.

This latter aspect – the destruction of the experience dimension of corporeality – is particularly stressed by the critical interpretation based on the concept of use-value in which the emphasis is on the inhibition of the internalization of 'outer nature': commodity production destroys the 'true' and 'natural' world of use-values, turning it into an artificial, alienated, non-sensory and unsensual world of exchange-values (Pohrt, 1976). Ultimately we have an apocalyptic scene of the destruction of outer and inner nature as the fate of corporeality and man in general (Nitzschke, 1974: 139).

The above characterization of the culture and civilization critical conceptions is indeed quite crude, but it does reveal two things they have in common; first, the basis for their interpretation is either an implicit or an explicit postulation of the duality of nature and culture and, second, they are powerless in the face of the trends in the history of corporeality featuring an increase in sensuality.

The two dimensions of corporeality – the expressive and the experience aspects – and the relationship between them can now be made more precise by problematizing the above interpretations.

First, both corporeality dimensions are connected with transgression. The expression of corporeality does indeed take place as (externalizing) functions of man's bodily being, such as convulsive laughter or signs of sexual stimulation (erection, etc.), but this 'alien force' (Bataille) becomes sensuality and pleasure precisely because it transgresses boundaries; in the case of the modern individual it dissolves (momentarily) the boundaries of the self. The same applies to the other corporeality dimension, experience, which, according to the concept, is unmediated corporeality devoid of any cognitive self agencies.

The corporeality of sensory experience seems self-evident in the realm of the contact senses (taste, smell, touch), since they involve concrete physical contact, but this is not the case. In order to be transgressive and thus enjoyable, the contact sensory experience must also stand in relation to the world of boundaries. On the other hand the distant senses (hearing and especially sight) have just as naturally been interpreted as non-bodily, especially in concepts where a shift in emphasis from the contact to the distant senses (in modern life) is viewed as part of the destruction of sensuality. But this interpretation also proves to be problematic. It is true that the instrumentality of the distant senses becomes emphasized as the modern world of signs and symbols expands (speech, writing) but this does not eliminate the fact that the field of immediate experience has also expanded with the growing prevalence of the listener and especially the spectator.

The very civilizing process that shifts the sensory emphasis from the contact senses to the distant senses creates a growing band of 'spectator activities' (see for example Bailey, 1978; Cunningham, 1980; Malcolmson, 1973; Ozouf, 1975), from the theatre to spectator sport and the cinema, some of which do, admittedly, also contain elements of corporeal expression (the football match or the rock concert) but in which the lived (audiovisual) experience clearly plays the leading part. The football match and other spectator sporting events still clearly possess features of the traditional popular festival and even of the uprising (see Kutcher, 1983), and dancing and shouting are possible at rock concerts too, but at the theatre and in the cinema the expression of corporeality is limited to laughter (at the right moment). 'The rule of passive emotion' (Sennett, 1978: 212) applies in these institutions of experience transgression.

In fact the entire (modern) cultural history of laughter aptly displays a shift in emphasis from the expression of corporeality to 'inner' experience (see Thomas, 1977). In seventeenth- and eighteenth-century England laughter, especially loud laughter, increasingly became a mark of vulgarity – just like other forms of lack of physical restraint. The opposition to laughter and the pathologizing of laughter was not simply the outcome of the demand for disciplining the body but also of a socio-political attitude: laughter, as part of the carnival inversion and transgression of the common people, was the vulgar way of breaking down the barriers of the 'subject' in the older subordinate meaning of the word. Thus the repression of laughter also included the norms of forbidden and permissible laughter, which roughly speaking meant that the superior could laugh at the inferior, but not the other way round. The Great Laughter *à la* Rabelais (see Bakhtin, 1968) may no longer exist, but there are all the more little laughs (insofar as they are not stifled by the 'canned' laughter comedies on television).

It is, therefore, true to say that there has been a shift in emphasis in the dimensions of corporeality, from expression to experience, but this cannot simply be interpreted as the repression or destruction of corporeality and sensuality. From the point of view of transgression it is not a shift from the genuine to the non-genuine or from the real thing to a substitute. Nor is there any justification for such an interpretation of the change in sensory organization from the contact senses to the distant senses and especially the supremacy of the eye, for, as Gert Mattenklott (1982) has convincingly shown, the 'voracious eye' (*das gefrässige Auge*) has its own special logic of pleasure that cannot be reduced to a mere substitute for contact sensuality and bodily internalization, as is usually the case in interpretations of pornography (see below, Chapter 7).

Secondly, the problematization of the repression interpretations presented above is more fundamental in the case of the making absolute of the repressive effect of the boundaries confining the body and corporeality. For the growing disciplining and instrumentalizing of the body is in two respects only one side of the matter. On the one hand the instrumentalizing of the body, in the final analysis as an instrument of the self, simultaneously signifies an increase in individual freedom: sharp hierarchical boundaries break down and appoint the soul or the self of modern man as the body's guardian and instrumentalizer.

On the other hand, the increase in density of the limits, categorizations and norms related to corporeality produces a multiplicity and diversification of transgressions as a complementary opposition, though primarily in the experience dimension of corporeality. We may even claim that only in modern society has the individualized body, with all its restricting networks, been able to enjoy the full scale of sensory pleasures in all its richness, be they erotic, gastronomic, visual or combinations of all these. Modern man is not only sensitive to pain (see Jacobs, 1969; van den Berg, 1960): (s)he is also sensitive to pleasure.

The more articulated and multifarious the restrictions on corporeality, the more sophisticated the forms of transgression become. Lack of restraint emphasizing corporeal expression is replaced by a diversification of the scale of sensory pleasures. This in turn creates a new type of corporeal intensity that is no longer based on infinite quantity but on the multifariousness of qualitative distinctions.

This sophistication of sensory pleasures is evident in the nineteenth-century rise of gastronomy, in the course of which the gluttony tradition-ally representing oral pleasures was replaced by a qualitative scale of taste distinctions (as was put forward in Brillat-Savarin's *Physiology of Taste*, 1971 [1824]). But the food culture also has its own more tasteless history, as part of the discipline of the body. In this history, which can be traced back to the bourgeois puritanism of the eighteenth century (B.S. Turner, 1982) and the functionalization of the reproduction of the wage labourer (Aronson, 1982), food becomes an expedient fuel (healthy and economic) for the body-machine turned instrument (Falk and Gronow, 1985).

The history of corporeality is not merely the disciplining of the body and the destruction of sensuality any more than it is the great emancipation of the body's potential: it is the paradoxical combination of the two. The scale of corporeal expression becomes restricted along with the shielding and instrumentalizing of the body, yet the field of experience widens, diversi-fies and becomes more sensitive. There can be no special reason to yearn for the eroticism of the medieval peasant, the attraction of which soon turns out to be a mere romantic-naturalistic illusion. We may nevertheless experience a certain nostalgia when we compare the carnival revelry of past centuries with the culinary pleasures or cinematic experiences of the present day.

Notes

1. The entire cannibalistic logic is based on this concept (see e.g. Attali, 1981), the 'internalization' of the human body signifies the possession of magic forces or 'holiness', as in the Christian Communion ritual, in which the body and blood (= the soul) of Christ is taken in the symbolic form of the bread and wine.

2. Thus Max Weber could justifiably wonder how 'interested' conduct (in the form of both the rational pursuit of advantage and usury) received moral blessing, i.e. 'how this behaviour, which may even be morally tolerated, has become a "professional calling" in the sense used by Benjamin Franklin' (Weber, 1947: 60).

3. It should be noted that in late sixteenth-century European concepts 'interests' and acting according to them referred in broader terms to the reflective and calculating aspects of human strivings and were not narrowly confined to economic-materialistic actions and principles (Hirschman, 1977: 32).

4. In the field of anthropology of everyday life this theme has been conducted by Edward T. Hall. In his analysis of the 'distances' in human behaviour, their meanings and cultural differences, he presents a typology with the 'intimate distance', i.e. physical contact at one extreme and the 'public distance', the 'distant stage', which in American culture is at least 25 feet, at the other (see Hall, 1966: 107 ff.).

5. Erasmus of Rotterdam once stated that clothing is in a certain sense the body's body. It is one means of maintaining the bearing of the soul (quoted in Elias, 1978).

6. The roots of this magic expression have been traced back to Christian Communion rituals in which Christ's body appears in the symbolic form of bread (*hoc est corpus meum*/this is my body). 'Hocus pocus' is a folk culture and carnivalistic parody that emerged in the Middle Ages (see Grimes, 1982: 90).

7. It is in this context neither necessary nor possible to start explicating the 'alternative' epistemology. A brief account will suffice instead: the construing of a counter-discourse is the

questioning and deconstruction of the prevailing discourse, but the 'truth' produced by the counter-discourse cannot be canonized as a new Truth (a 'true' theory) in accordance with the epistemological principles by which the prevailing discourse justifies itself. The counter-discourse must justify itself in practice and as practice – in the organic unity of the discursive and the non-discursive. The counter-discourse is part of the functional strategy of the 'state of war'.

8. We can of course, try to refer man's sensuality back to certain special features of the human bodily being. For example, to the fact that man is the only mammal that has ears with flesh and nerves, and this 'non-functional' feature of the human body can now be conceived of as the enhancement of excessive sensory (touch sensitivity) and erogenous areas. This interpretation is, however, easily proved as being a pure teleological post-rationalization.

9. To be more precise: the articulation of corporeality occurs especially in the stages or types of ritual at which the reversal of profane/everyday order generates a liminal state devoid of order or at which the 'order' of the non-normal state is the everyday (normal) world turned upside down, as in carnival (superior and inferior change places, the forbidden becomes permissible, scarcity is replaced by abundance, etc.).

10. This refers to ritual elements and forms that are not mere dramatizations of a myth and thus do not directly reinforce order, but which overthrow order.

11. Elias also examines how the shielding of the body is manifest in the growing intimacy of bodily functions: defecation, farting, belching, and last of all perhaps spitting become forbidden bodily expressions in the public-social field. These expressions of the body nevertheless become expressions of corporeality only as transgressive practices (cf. defecation/urination in the realm of 'perverse' eroticism or the pleasure of sneezing in the golden age of snuff).

4

TOWARDS AN HISTORICAL ANTHROPOLOGY OF TASTE

My aim in the following is to reflect upon the different forms of cultural dynamics determining and moulding human taste (that is, gustatory) preferences as manifested both in the formation of specific food cultures and in the multiplicity or diversification of tastes from an overall historical perspective. The chapter may also be conceived of as an introduction to the study of modern 'tastescape', an elaboration of a conceptual scheme to be applied in the actual analysis of the nexus of modern taste preferences.

Taste preference is a multi-relational concept which cannot be reduced to a relationship between the objective properties of foodstuffs and the sensory-physiological reaction of the human ingestive and digestive organism. At the sensory level taste preferences are necessarily also related to and even determined by the symbolic principles which translate the material universe into *representations* of the edible vs. inedible, which are then further specified into different sub-categories according to taboos and ritual rules. And as these cultural categorizations seem to ignore to a considerable extent what I shall refer to as the objective facts of nutrition, as defined by contemporary scientific knowledge, they must be conceived of as the basic principle of human food behaviour affecting the constitution and development of food preferences and thus also taste preferences.

These principles of cultural dynamics are something other than a unilinear and cumulative evolution – the product of food-technological development or the dissemination of food discoveries from one culture to another, or a gradual learning process in which new edibles are discovered, accepted and finally regarded as pleasant-tasting substances.

These evolutionary processes presuppose certain basic preconditions which concern the relationship between the (cultural) *representation* and the (gustatory) *sensation* of foodstuffs and foods (Fischler, 1980), and specifically the ways in which the representation determine the sensation. This does not imply any strong 'one-to-one' relationship between *specific* representations and sensations[1] but rather a general set of rules according to which the representations determine the positive and negative value of sensations.

I am arguing for a multi-levelled set of principles which relates the food as 'good to think' – both in Lévi-Strauss' (1963) sense 'think with' (Lloyd, 1986: 8) and as a representational 'think of' – to food as 'good to eat' finally specified as 'good to taste'.

These relations and their different principles will be dealt with below in an attempt to formulate a preliminary answer to the following question: how can the 'sweetness of the forbidden fruit' be explained if it cannot be reduced (a) to a natural fact, or (b), without residue to the principle of positive representation? The former (natural fact) refers to the conception of innate taste preferences in circumstances of natural scarcity and thus valued in a specific culture. The latter refers to the idea of (intra)culturally valued food as a determinant of positive sensory responses to it.

Edible versus inedible

Starting from the trivial, in order to survive, man, like other more complex life forms must feed himself with natural organic substances called 'food'. Or, to be more precise, the term 'food' should be replaced by 'edible' because the most fundamental distinction made by man, the original *Homo culinarius*, divides the world into *edible* and *inedible*, into that which may be incorporated and that which may not. Accordingly, the Hua people (Papua, New Guinea) have a word for 'everything' (*do 'ado' na*) which literally translated means: 'that which can be eaten and that which cannot' (Meigs, 1988: 342).

Edible vs. inedible is a basic distinction closely related to analytically constructed and more abstract binary oppositions such as *us vs. them, same vs. other, inside vs. outside, good vs. bad* and *culture vs. nature*. Edible is something which may be accepted or 'taken in' to our community and, in the last instance, into our bodies. Everything else is inedible – not only as defined within the binary opposition (edible/inedible) but also as objects 'naturally' precluded from the cultural edible/inedible categorization due to material-physiological constraints: humans do not eat rocks, for example – even if they do eat 'earth' (Couffignal, 1970) – nor do they swallow fire (not even in circuses), that is, matter which cannot be assimilated into the body or which the body as an organism simply rejects.

The boundary between 'natural' inedibles and the cultural binary opposition of edible/inedible is, however, a fuzzy one. The latter does not obey the 'bodily wisdom' (Fischler, 1980) of metabolism and nutritional efficacy but rather follows a minimalistic principle of *dissolution*: incorporation must transform the object into substance and furthermore, the substance must have some effect on the body (assimilation) in the act of ingestion (sensory response) and/or in the process of digestion (from sating hunger to pharmacological effects). Consequently, the range of beings, objects and substances classified either as edibles or inedibles remains sufficiently broad to call for a dynamic system of categorization within a specific culture.

Looking at the edible/inedible classifications of a certain food culture reveals the fact that not nearly everything that is (objectively) edible and available is really eaten (for example, insects rich in protein). Then again, substances objectively defined as non-foods or even poisons are actually incorporated – from coca-leaves to tobacco.[2] Man differs here essentially from the rat which does not eat non-food or poisonous substances (rat poison *per se* is, after all, poisoned food). But, then again, rats do not give meanings to the stuffs they feed themselves with, so they do not incorporate 'good' substances in any symbolic or representational sense.

The dynamic character of the cultural edible/inedible categorization may be conceived of in terms of different levels. First, the categorizations are liable to historical change. Second, the intracultural food taboo systems relativize the distinction between edible and inedible according to time and place (ritual setting) and according to (changes in) social status. Third, the categorization not only concerns the *choice* of possible foodstuffs but also the means of *food elaboration*: from 'raw' to 'cooked' as the mythical representation of *nature–culture transformation* (Lévi-Strauss, 1987: 39), further expanding to other forms of 'culturalized' transformation such as controlled 'rotting' (souring, etc.), detoxifying, different techniques of food preservation (cf. Goody, 1982: 218–19; Thorne, 1986) and seasoning.

These transformation techniques constitute the developing corpus of the art of cookery which is, however, 'always already' (as Derrida would have it[3]) subsumed under cultural categorizations and ritual rules. This may be exemplified by the rules defining the *order* of cultural – or culturalized – transformations. The 'problem' dealt with by Aristotle concerned the Greek culinary code according to which it was forbidden to roast boiled meat whereas the reverse was permitted. The solution is to be found in the logic of symbolism which defines the former transformation as a regression from a civilized state into a primitive one unlike the 'progressive' direction of the latter (Detienne, 1977: 74–7).[4]

As one implementation of ritual rules, preparing food is a part of the taking possession of and incorporating of foodstuffs (making it 'our own') which culminates in the physical act of eating. The 'act of alimentary communion' (Durkheim, 1954 [1912]) is also an essential moment in the (re)constitution of the community, manifested in the Latin etymology of the word 'companion': *com* = together, *panis* = bread, or literally, 'one who takes bread with someone' (Barnhart, 1988). This may be understood as referring to those partaking of the meal (sharing the same food) or, more broadly, to the members of the same (food) culture, to those eating the same *kind* of food.

In its sacrificial form, ritual connects the preparation and incorporation of the meal with the exchange and communion with the 'supernatural' (spirits of the ancestors, gods). The rite of sacrifice may be conceived of both as an act of symbolic exchange which desacralizes the foodstuff (especially meat) into human (our) food, and as a communion – a shared meal with the deities – which sacralizes the partakers in the ritual (Valeri, 1985: 83). In both cases the substances become edible as legitimate food 'for us'.

As far as primitive societies are concerned though, it is impossible to distinguish practical techniques of detoxification (such as the preparation of the bitter manioc in South American cuisine) from the ritual procedures of purification, for example, those of the Indian caste system described by Mary Douglas (1988 [1966]). Here a member of the upper caste is not allowed to accept elaborated food from the representative of the lower caste because the human contact involved in cooking 'pollutes' the food. This does not, however, apply to 'raw' food which may be purified ritually by preparing (cooking) it within one's own caste and according to the proper rules. Here cooking signifies a 'ritual break' (Douglas, 1988: 127) which removes the impurity caused by the contact the food has had with the lower caste.

Real versus other foods?

It seems reasonable, however, to posit the existence of an early preconception, however vague, of the hunger-satisfying or nutritive character of a certain range of foodstuffs classified as edible. This implies a subdivision of the edibles into what could preliminarily be called 'real' foods and 'other' foods – both acceptable for incorporation according to the specific rules of the alimentary code. So, for example, the long tradition of tobacco use in the New World, whether ingested or inhaled (not to speak of other forms of incorporation, cf. Falk, 1988b; Wilbert, 1987), defines it beyond doubt as edible.

And yet there is still a difference, as among the Barasana Indians of the Vampés area of Colombia who make a distinction between 'ordinary' foods and 'anti-foods' such as coca, tobacco, yagé and beer. These two categories of edibles must not be consumed at the same time. Furthermore, the consumption of anti-food – regarded as the food of *He* people (first ancestors) and the souls of the dead – is far more severely taboo than the ordinary food. The consumption of anti-food is restricted to men and old women according to specific ritual rules (Hugh-Jones, 1988: 90–1).

The intuited and practically learned distinction between 'real' and 'other' foods – inscribed in the Barasana alimentary code as the binary opposition of food vs. anti-food – figures mainly in the phase preceding food preparation (cooking), that is, in the choice of foodstuffs. The 'other' foods have, however, one specific role in the system of cooking, that is, as substances giving and transforming the taste of the food (herbs, spices, etc.).

The 'other' foods as taste substances provide a basis for a second-order conception of cooking (= cultural transformation) as manifested for instance in the food (preparation) categories of Greek antiquity according to which the distinction between 'civilized' and 'primitive' is not only represented in the duality of boiled vs. roasted but also in the duality of salted vs. unsalted (Detienne, 1977: 78). So even the early forms of

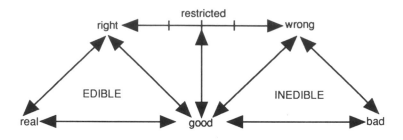

Figure 4.1 *The possible determinants of good (taste)*

cooking were more than a matter of transforming the foodstuffs into *right* or proper edibles and ingestible/digestible *real* foods. They were also means by which to make the food palatable, to make it taste *good*.

So, our first thematization deals with the complex of relations in the triangle of right, real and good food and in a later section we will move to the two complementary triangles concerning the relations between right (permitted), wrong (forbidden), good and bad (Figure 4.1).

The real thing

Let us start from the (socio)biological and cultural evolutionary conceptions which tend to postulate 'real' food as the basis for the constitution of food preferences, including not only the digestive and metabolic properties of foodstuffs but also the sensory dimension of taste.

The line of argument may be characterized roughly as follows. There is a natural basis for the human diet (both biological and ecological) which is guided by a genetically and/or culturally structured ability and tendency in food choice which optimizes physiological survival in nutritional terms within the given ecological context of the specific culture. In other words, the search for 'real' foods – including the later development of the techniques for food elaboration – determines food preferences in both sensory ('good') and cultural-classificatory ('right') terms.

Or, at least, this was the case in the innocent beginnings of human culture not as yet perverted by the unnatural principles of the culture which broke the harmonious chain of preferable nutrition (for the digestive system and metabolism) – good tasting and culturally valued. In this idyllic 'state of nature' (Rousseau on 'natural needs') the palatable and nutritional quality of food was one and the same thing (Boyden, 1987: 255–6). But then the bias-producing culture intervened: 'Certain variations in food preferences between human groups may result from *natural* selection of *cultural* variations. The evolution of human diets is almost certainly affected by genetically transmitted *biases* that make some foods taste good' (Boyd and Richerson, 1985: 177–8, my italics; cf. Lumsden and Wilson, 1981: 38–43).

The strong case – often referred to in this type of argumentation – is the universal preference for *sweet* (tasting) substances which actually crosses the boundaries between nature/culture and animal/human. As Paul Rozin puts it:

> Our species, and many other mammalian generalist or omnivore species, have an innate preference for sweet substances. [. . .] This taste bias presumably has its adaptive basis in the fact that sweet taste is characteristic of energy sources (sugars), particularly fruits, in the world of Nature. (Rozin, 1982: 228)

It appears quite reasonable to argue that the preference for sweetness could have a certain role in the generation of practical know-how concerning food choice and yet, to regard the preference as natural, that is, common to human and other species, is far from unproblematic. It appears unproblematic only if *innate* dispositions and preferences are simply equated with the *natural* – overriding the species boundaries. So, what does it mean to have an innate preference in the case of humans? Research concerning new-born babies has discovered a correlation between positive facial expression in neonatal infants and incorporating water sweetened to the same extent as mother's milk (for example Steiner, 1977).

This is pure biology manifesting the natural taste preference[5] for the natural nutrition of the suckling, but very soon (long before entering language, the realm of the 'Symbolic', in the Lacanian sense, and thus the possibility of representations) the preference is humanized and thus culturized into a primal 'sensing' which implies a crucial step out of pure biology and nature. The early experiences of symbiosis are structured into a kind of bodily memory or in psychoanalytic terms 'coenesthetic sensing' (Blanck and Blanck, 1986: 46–7; Spitz, 1965: 45). This builds a link between mother, breast, milk and the positive bodily state including the sensory dimension which we might call a taste preference – for sweetness [6] So there is a kind of pre-verbal 'unrepresentable representation' which could be illustrated with a line from a recent song by Leonard Cohen: 'I can't forget, but I don't remember what'.[7]

The cultural dynamics of taste preferences should, however, be related to the *cultural* representations (though not unrelated to the psychic ones). Consequently, the next step takes us (naturally?) to the question: in what ways could cultural food categorizations and the more specific taboo systems determine food and taste preferences? Now we are focusing on another of the triangle's axes, starting from the relationship between right and good (tasting) food.

Doing the right thing

Edmund Leach (1964) defines three categories of edible/inedible distinctions. In the first, 'edible substances [. . .] are recognized as food and consumed as part of the normal diet'. The second consists of 'edible substances that are recognized as possible food, but that are prohibited or else allowed to be eaten only under special (ritual) conditions' (consciously tabooed), and the third of 'edible substances that by culture and language are not recognized as food at all' (unconsciously tabooed; p. 31).

The relationship between the second and the third categories could be defined as a relation between relative and absolute taboos, the former functioning primarily in the intracultural context (sub-groups and their identities), and the latter in the intercultural setting – articulating the boundaries between the culturally generalized identity of 'us' in relation to 'not-us'.

There exist, however, strictly defined ritual means which make it possible to transgress (momentarily) even the stronger taboos which articulate the boundaries either towards nature (food of the beasts) or towards the divine (food of the gods; Vernant, 1989: 166–9), not to mention the complex principles of endo- and exo-cannibalism (Sanday, 1986). But the intercultural context of the edible/inedible distinction appears to be a rigid one which is at least partly due to the fact that it is the context for the constitution and reproduction of 'our' identity (Fischler, 1988).

Thus, we are back to the original distinction of edible vs. inedible, with just one specification: *for us*. Leach tends to ignore the role of this specification and so he ends up emphasizing the difference between the second and third categories of edibles (vs. inedibles), illustrated accordingly by 'the Jewish prohibition against pork' and 'the Englishman's objection to eating dog' (Leach, 1964: 32). In the former case, according to Leach, 'pork is food, but Jews must not eat it' while in the latter case 'dog is not food'. In both cases, however, pork or dog is not food *for us*.

The specification – for us – may be applied both to intracultural sub-groupings and intercultural distinctions which differentiate us (humans, civilized, etc.) from others (non-humans, barbarians, etc.). But, of course, one may 'know' that something which is inedible (and non-food) for us is eaten by others, but this does not change the fact that it still remains classified as inedible – for us. To take an example, the case of food taboos of Shokleng Indians (Brazil) studied by Greg Urban:

> in the Shokleng/non-Shokleng subsystem – or, translating more literally the native terms, the 'human being/other' – Shokleng is the marked category. The Shokleng consider inedible or 'repulsive' certain species, namely lizards and various snakes, that they know are eaten by non-Shokleng in the region, e.g., by Tupian speaking peoples and by local Brazilians. [. . .] Brazilian settlers consider the large lizards found in that region a special delicacy; to the Shokleng mind, this is a sure sign of barbarism. (Urban, 1981: 479)

Mary Douglas (1988) presents an elaborated analysis of the cultural categorization of what could be called the 'object-world': beings and things in the surrounding nature are classified according to certain criteria thus locating also the anomalous in-between cases found unclassifiable and defining them as taboo and inedible. The beings respecting the order are regarded as 'pure' and, within food categorization, edible. It could be said that these things or beings are symbolically and thus practically 'in control'. In contrast, those which transgress the boundaries and disregard the Order such as aquatic reptiles 'swarming' both in water (fish) and on solid ground (animal) – are anomalous, impure, polluting and inedible. As ambiguous beings they are symbolically and hence practically 'out of control'.

These cultural categorizations are to a certain degree arbitrary in the Saussurean sense, so far as the criteria for classification vary from culture to culture, defining in different ways the boundaries and consequently those respecting or disregarding them. The categorization may, however, be structured along another dimension in which the object-world is structured in relation to the subject, not as a taxonomy, but as a scale of distance reaching from the 'self'[8] to the far end of the 'unknown'. This is what Edmund Leach does using as a primary case the ordering of animal categories. According to Leach, 'language [. . .] does more than provide us with a classification of things; it actually models our environment; it places each individual at the center of a social space which is ordered in a logical and reassuring way' (Leach, 1964: 36).

The distance-scale is a form of cultural categorization following a specific principle – subject–object distance – and hence is non-arbitrary by nature. On the other hand, we may argue that the ordering by distance is already based primarily on the taxonomical criteria and not on 'objective' measurable distance, and so we are back to the (at least relative) arbitrariness of cultural classifications. This does not, however, explain away the difference between the two dimensions. The taxonomy structures the object-world into categories and those which are unclassifiable (that is, tabooed, impure, inedible) while the distance scale operates on the subject–object dimension defining both those 'too close' (to self) and those 'too far' as inedible, and, accordingly, those belonging to the middle categories as edible.

By way of illustration Leach offers the English animal categorization defining 'very close pets' as 'strongly inedible', middle categories of 'farm animals' and 'game' as edible (the latter according to more strict ritual rules), and 'remote wild animals, not subject to human control, inedible' (Leach, 1964: 44; cf. Sahlins, 1976: 170–9, on the American food system).

This illustration describes the 'civilized' condition characterized by a strong cannibalistic taboo, but the rules also apply to the 'primitive' condition which includes ritual means of transgression (otherwise endo-cannibalism would not be possible). There is a cultural variation on rules defining the 'too close' as inedible but the principle remains the same: eating the 'too close' equals eating oneself. The same principle is manifested in different forms, for instance concerning the status of the totem animal – 'eating the totem is a cannibalistic act' (Caillois, 1959: 82–3) – or in the case of more sensitive food taboos exemplified by Hua culture where 'to eat one's own food [that is, self produced/prepared] or the food of one's offspring would be to consume one's own' (Meigs, 1984: 107; cited in Sanday 1986, 68).[9]

Leach characterizes the inedible 'too far' end of the distance-scale on one hand as 'uncontrolled' and on the other as 'unknown' (Leach, 1964: 44, 60). Both characteristics apply also to the unclassifiable anomalies of the object-world taxonomy (cf. Douglas): not in symbolic and (thus) practical control or not (yet) classified.[10]

To eat or be eaten by

The distance-scale does offer an additional perspective on the inedible far end, implicitly present in Leach's model and partly explicated by Roger Abrahams (1984: 31–2). Starting from Mary Douglas' model Abrahams takes Leach's interpretation some steps further, referring to the

> complex system of creature categories based on principles of cleanliness and contamination, in which we are not only concerned with whether a 'thing' is edible, but also with whether it will consume us, or contend with us for our basic resources. (Abrahams, 1984: 31)

Focusing on the 'eat or be eaten by' parameter, the things or beings 'out of control' and 'unknown' may be conceived of as dangerous creatures or substances 'which may kill and/or eat us' (p. 31), such as wild animals and poisons.[11] Again, these 'wild things' may be brought under control and possession by (exceptional) ritual means, through the process of 'cooking' in the widest sense of the word (the nature–culture transformation). But they differ essentially from the edible middle categories 'under our control' which in the 'agricultural scheme', are represented by cultivated (controlled) 'domesticated animals and plants' (p. 32).

I would like, however, to further develop Abrahams' 'eat or be eaten by' theme to a point where the taxonomic and distance-scale categorizations find a common ground. First, as already noted, the things located at the inedible far end of the scale share the same characteristic with the boundary-transgressing anomalies of the taxonomical scheme – things out of control or things which potentially consume (pollute or eat) us. On the other hand, the two inedible ends of the distance-scale have one common property: they both confuse the primary subject–object distinction, that of *eater vs. food*.[12]

At the 'too close' end we are faced with the ambiguity of self as eater and food (eating one self; see Figure 4.2a). The eater/food ambiguity of the close end may be translated into a taxonomic anomaly, such as half-man/ half-animal (Valeri, 1985: 119). But if it is reduced to this (that is, according to the object-world categorization) we lose the common basic principle which also explains also the far inedible end of the distance-scale.[13] At the 'too far' end, then, the eater/food ambiguity is repeated, only this time in the form 'to eat or be eaten by' (Figure 4.2b).

As a rule, these uncontrolled things are inedible and this is a rule in function both in the taxonomic model and the distance-scale scheme: these wild things are unclassifiable and ambiguous whether we take them to be

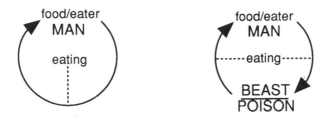

Figure 4.2 *The eater/food-ambiguity on the distance-scale: (a) too close; (b) too far*

transgressors of the object-world categories or violators of the subject–object distinction.

In the 'too far' end the roles of eater vs. food are not determined a priori, for example in hunting the 'man-eating animal' or in the exo-cannibalistic practice as part of warfare (Harris, 1986: 204). In both cases killing is the prerequisite for roles to be distributed and after that there is a need for additional (powerful) ritual means (rules of exception) to guarantee the stability of the roles eater vs. food. But as a rule, these uncontrolled things are inedible and this is a rule in function both in the taxonomic model and the distance-scale scheme: these wild things are unclassifiable and ambiguous either as transgressors of the object-world categories or as violators of the subject–object distinction.

In other words, on the meta-level – in the distinction between classifiable and unclassifiable – both logics of categorization end up with similar characterizations of the ambiguous, uncontrollable, dangerous – thus tabooed and defined as inedible. In the taxonomic categorization the emphasis is primarily on the lack of *symbolic* or conceptual control while the distance-scale, especially in the 'too far' end, shifts the emphasis towards the lack of *practical* control – or better: it explicates the parallel nature of the symbolic and practical aspect of the 'uncontrollable'. Eater/food ambiguity is both symbolic and practical in the case of 'man eating animal eating man'.

Valerio Valeri takes an anti-reductionistic stand in relation to the symbolic/practical question in his study on the Hawaiian sacrifice system noting that

> if it is foolish to ignore the idea that the value of an animal such as the turtle is due to factors that are first of all intellectual [. . .] it would be equally foolish to make the fear of sharks a phenomenon derived from some imagined anomaly. [. . .] the shark is divinized because people are afraid of it [. . .]; it is not feared because it has been divinized by its anomalous status. (Valeri, 1985: 24)

The point, however, is that the 'man-eating' shark is a categorical anomaly also due to its practically uncontrollable, and thus feared, role. As I have tried to show in the interpretation developed above there is no need to build a dualistic (anti-reductionistic) explanation based on a sharp distinction between 'imagined anomalies' and practically constituted 'real threats' (1985: 119).

Furthermore, in analysing 'species taboo to women' Valeri (1985: 115 ff.) constructs a categorization of the tabooed (marine) species which in fact supports the thesis of symbolic/practical unity. Mantas and rays are 'winged' fish and, on the other hand, marine mammals and turtles are animals 'that breathe on the surface of the sea'. Both are categorical anomalies: bird/fish and sea-animal/breathing animal. And further, the species of both categories are uncontrolled by man, and moreover, the former group 'constitute a real threat to man' (p. 119). The 'threatening' takes the uncontrollable into the extreme where the eater/food roles are switched (see the paradigmatic case of 'man-eating shark' classified into both above-mentioned categories).

So the key term here is *uncontrollable*, both symbolically and practically, imagined and real. And furthermore, as Valeri explains in reference to the Hawaiian attitude towards cetaceans and turtles, 'like everything that is uncontrollable, they have a negative connotation' (p. 119). They are dangerous, poisonous, polluting and ultimately disgusting. And, by the same token they are tabooed (especially negatively sacred), forbidden, avoided and disliked.

Now we may formulate the first constellation by which cultural representations are related to gustatory sensations. It would seem that we cannot find a direct link between 'right' and 'good' food. The connection is constituted in *negative* terms: from 'wrong' (that is, beings/things out of place and control) to 'bad' tasting (see Figure 4.1 p. 72). The influence of cultural categorizations extends over the system of strict taboos into the norms of avoidance. This may be illustrated by Valeri's (1985) example concerning whale meat which is explicitly tabooed for women (by formal proscription) but not for men, who, however, 'are averse to it because of its symbolic connotations'. Thus, Valeri concludes:

> the avoidance is explained in the same overall fashion as the taboo. If some animals arouse a certain distaste, it is because from a symbolic stand-point they have negative connotations. They are bad to eat because they lead one to think about bad things. (Valeri, 1985: 120)

Here the 'disgusting' is defined as the binary opposite to the 'good' (tasting) and it is conceived of as a derivative of their negative status these things or beings have in either of the models. In other words, negative cultural representations evoke 'negative connotations' (Valeri). This is how a mediation from representations to sensations is constituted. One such example are the Hua (Papua, New Guinea), whose young male initiates have to avoid certain foods 'resembling female reproductive anatomy'. These are foods, that are thought to be 'not only dangerous (because polluting) but also disgusting' (Meigs, 1988: 351). A similar idea is expressed by Sartre in his analysis of the disgusting character of the '*visqueux*' (stickiness, sliminess), into which one risks being dissolved (that is, eaten by; Sartre, 1966: 777): 'the disgust which it [sliminess] inspires can be explained only by the combination of this physical quality with *certain moral qualities*' (p. 771; my italics).

According to the wrong-bad connection the link between right and good (tasting) may be reformulated in terms of a negative definition: from right to not-bad. The search for a positive link between good as sensation and as representation requires, however, a closer look at the relative nature of the right–wrong dimension.

Beyond the statics of food taboos

If cultural food classifications and taboos were absolutely rigid – both between and within specific cultures[14] – there would not be many degrees of freedom for the multiplication and diversification of food and, accordingly, taste preferences.

But food classifications are not static and taboos tend to change, even in tribal societies, due to a constant reinterpretation of the mythological corpus reshaping the cosmological scheme (Sahlins, 1985). There is always room for '*bricolage*' (Lévi-Strauss, 1966) or interested and competitive conduct within the symbolic systems (Bourdieu, 1977).

This is also the situation Gilbert Lewis had to cope with when studying the Gnau of New Guinea (Lewis, 1988). He 'kept searching for a clearer system to the food taboos [. . .] but the people frustrated those attempts' (p. 159). He found out that 'the system of food taboos leaves room for variation in the details of observance, lapse, change or mistake intervening in transmission of the rules, and understanding of them and their timing' (Lewis, 1988: 161).

On the other hand, from an overall historical perspective, reconstructed from the standpoint of our globalizing modernity, taboo systems have been transformed into a much weaker system of distinction (Bourdieu, 1984), still based, however, on certain explicit or implicit rules concerning the good and the bad, the low and the high, what is to be avoided and what not – and what is edible and what is not. So, my aim in looking more closely at the dynamic aspects of food categorizations and taboo systems of the primitive condition is linked to an interest in outlining a kind of speculative history depicting what happens to food (taste) preferences in the course of the erosion of formerly rigid categorizations and unquestioned taboos. I will start with the intercultural setting and then move to the intracultural one.

Others' food and our food

Let us first pose a question which the 'diffusionist' explanation of the development of food preferences does not consider a problem at all: people just 'learn' from each other and that is about all there is to it. The question is: how can the others' food become our food?

The general precondition for the others' food to be conceived of as edible for 'us' is the relativization of their 'otherness' through a common denominator which puts us and them under the same umbrella – for example, as different kinds of human beings. This is the prerequisite for the others' food to become potential food for us – something to be adopted into our culinary culture or even valued as 'exotic delicacies'. But thus far we have already moved quite a way in history towards the (ac)culturated settings more familiar to us. So, whatever those historical-cultural factors may be which lower the threshold of specific cultural classification, the way is clear for a process of intercultural diffusion of food and taste preferences. But, of course, there is much more to it than that – historical factors determining the availability of foodstuffs, differences in the level of practical cooking (know-how), forms of cultural contact (migration, wars, colonialism, economic globalization), all these and more have a part to play in the process.

But still the problem exists: why would one culture adopt the other culture's foods? It is not 'right' food from the onset; it is transformed into 'right' food when included in our alimentary code. So, maybe it is first 'real' (effective) food and/or 'good' (tasting) food which is welcomed because of its superior qualities and thus redefined as 'right' food? This would imply first, a total rejection of the cultural food classifications, and second, a postulation of a universal principle of human food (taste) preferences – an interpretation already found to be problematic. Maybe, then, the others' food is conceived of as acceptable or even desirable just because it is *different* – but not too different – in order to become a part of our edibles?

The last proposition leads us to Paul Rozin's (1982) 'straw-model' explaining the evolution of food preferences. Rozin postulates a dual disposition of human food behaviour: the fear of new foods (as possible poisons), *neophobia*, and the desire for variety, *neophilia* (p. 230). Neophobia is a conservative principle manifested as preferences for familiar foods while neophilia is an innovative principle, a search for the new and unexperienced.

According to Rozin, the diversification of culinary and gustatory substances is guided by a multi-phase cultural learning process in which the use of substances originally and even innately found to be favourable – nourishing and/or tasting good (as in the case of sugar) – widens, developing technologies of production, etc. Using the same basic scheme, Rozin also explains the birth and spread of oral 'pleasurables' or stimulants proper, such as chili pepper, coffee and tobacco. To put the matter simply, man gets used to spices, bitter drinks and smoke that are originally repulsive and irritating (fiery) and finally begins to regard them with pleasure.

There are, however, some difficulties in applying Rozin's model to the intercultural setting outlined above. If the search for variety in food/taste experiences would define everything new as positive there would be no problem in explaining the adoption of others' foods. But this, arguably

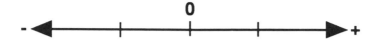

Figure 4.3 *Rozin's (1982) linear taste-value scale*

rather odd, assumption is not what Rozin has in mind. The food/stimulant preferences develop, according to Rozin, through exposure and social pressure, which lead to 'habitual use and liking' of these oral substances, even those with 'innately aversive taste' (coffee, tobacco).

There is no link between the experienced 'good' taste and some other abstract 'good' anchored outside bodily and sensory experience. The flexible taste preference may be moulded by other positive bodily responses (especially those based on pharmacological effects) but not by representational characteristics of the edibles. The 'liking' (taste preference) is simply learned – as an 'unlearning' of dislike and only a short step away from 'tolerable'.

The development of food/taste preferences described by Rozin appears as a troublesome journey along a linear taste scale (Figure 4.3) from the negative (distaste, aversion) just over the zero point (neutral, indifferent) to the positive side ('liking').

Although Rozin's evolutionary model is much more sophisticated than the (socio)biological interpretations, it still fails to explain the principle which pushes the taste preferences along the taste-value scale from the negative (aversion) to the positive (liking, addiction). In the case of intoxicants and stimulants he refers to the other, pharmacological, characteristics which are experienced as positive, thus overriding and, in the long run, unlearning the taste aversion. But this is far from sufficient explanation for the diversification and expansion of taste preferences in general.

For the food to become ours, that is, 'right' and 'good to think', it must act as a non-negative representation. And for the food to be regarded not only as 'good enough' but as 'good to taste', it must act as a *positive* representation.[15] In other words, it must *stand for* something valued, something or someone better and higher – on the positive scale, perhaps reaching finally to the divine, to the ultimate taste pleasure of the food of the gods ('ambrosia'; Vernant, 1989). This is the theme I will develop, albeit schematically, in the intracultural setting illustrated by anthropological material. Consequently we are now shifting the focus onto the second triangle which relates the right–wrong dimension to 'good' (see Figure 4.1, p. 72).

Food as a positive representation

In an intracultural context the distinction between edible vs. inedible functions in a certain manner, especially in the case of age-grade categories. The system of mobility in which the members of the community move from one age-category to the next, and accordingly, from one status to another (through rites of passage) is a dynamic aspect present even in the most 'static' (or 'cold', according to Lévi-Strauss' earlier formulation) societies. Here we are in the realm of food taboos in a narrow sense: a set of rules defining the boundaries between forbidden and permitted food-stuffs, forms of preparation and incorporation in terms of time (cosmic cycle, life cycle), place (situation), group (sex, age, status) and company (with whom).

Temporary food prohibitions and especially those structured along the age-grade categories, introduce a specific dynamic principle into the food categorization. A food which is now prohibited – regarded as dangerous or poisonous – for us/me will be permitted after the initiation or after passing through a sequence of achievements (Lewis, 1988: 147).

Here the food acquires a dual character: something to be avoided now but welcomed in the future. In a sense the food is bad and good (for us/me) simultaneously: bad now but representing the good to come. Above all, it is transformed into a representation of something *good*; something to be desired and therefore something which even tastes good. Now there is a link between representation and sensation which differs from the type of relation based on the fundamental cultural food categorizations into edible and inedible, that is, the connection between the 'right' and 'good' food which actually is determined through the negative sequence of taboo–avoidance–distaste.

The food's double role, as currently bad and forbidden but good and permissible in a future situation or position, creates a kind of enticement or anticipatory tension, making possible a positive representation. This tension is not just structured according to social boundaries. It is also manifested in temporal and situational distinctions: some foods are allowed within certain rituals but forbidden outside a specified time and place. This is the constellation constituting the duality of *everyday* food vs. *festive* food.

In primitive and pre-modern societies, consumption of festive foods is restricted to these ritual occasions which are structured primarily according to the yearly (cosmic) cycle, such as calendar rites. But the pendulum-like dynamics of everyday vs. festive foods function likewise in the modern condition, though in modified forms: according to the weekly cycle or sporadically, in reduced collective or even individualized forms and within specific institutions ('dining out'; cf. Finkelstein, 1989).

The duality of everyday vs. festive foods is traditionally connected to the seasonal variation in available foodstuffs (and even according to economic constraints). And yet, the difference is also culturally constructed: through taboos and norms marking off the special occasions. So the contrast – in quantitative terms – between everyday scarcity and festive abundance is also artificially produced, such being exemplified in the cyclic alternation of fasting and feasting (Heinisch, 1976; Wiegelmann, 1967).

But there is also a *qualitative* side to it: specific foods function as markers of festivity and thus act as positive representations. And this is the principle found in primitive society too, as illustrated by Lewis' Gnau study. Lewis records how he 'had asked Tuawei, a highly able married man, who was often perceptive in finding reasons for doing things, why coconuts should be forbidden. The answer he made was that they were forbidden because if we did not forbid them first, what could we give when we came to the time for decorating them? *Restriction is imposed so that afterwards there can come release*' (Lewis, 1988: 146; my italics).

What happens when the intracultural taboo system grows weaker, that is, when the prohibition loses its strength as an 'index' – in the Peircean sense[16] – of the (temporarily) inedible? The answer is that it loses the magical power to transform the forbidden food into deadly poison. This may be understood as a first step in the desacralization of the taboo system, which breaks the immediate (indexical) connection between the transgression of the food taboo and its consequence (pollution–poisoning–death). The transgression is still sanctioned – by divine or (later) secular powers – but it does not 'materialize' in the food itself. Consequently, the role food has as a representation of good is emphasized, constituting a link between 'restricted' and 'good' (see Figure 4.1).

As the food taboo system is replaced by more secularized hierarchies and systems of distinction a constellation is created in which even those belonging to a certain status (by birth: gender, lineage or estate) may think of themselves as eligible for the food of the other social groups within any specific cultural context. The food is *present* enough to be imagined as my/ our food but *absent* enough to become a representation. But the question remains – of what?

In a hierarchical context – from lower to higher – it becomes a potential representation of the (higher) good. This makes the representation of good (food) possible but not necessary: the boundaries between 'us' and 'them' may still operate according to the principle of mutual exclusion, as different or opposed cultures (see note 14).

The traditional mobility along age-grades is still far away from the modern form of individualized social status-seeking which actually functions in reverse: taking possession of certain foods and goods, and 'all the manners' (Mennell, 1985) involved in their use, grants the person a certain status (Bauman, 1971). Nevertheless, the representation of an attainable good is already there. And that at any rate is more present than mythical visions of the food of the gods.

Thus, in the pre-modern condition – still characterized by rigid hierarchies – representations of the good based on social categories do not yet function as an effective principle of social conduct. They become effective in the modern condition of dynamic social hierarchies, making social mobility possible and replacing sanctioned boundaries by social norms. This is the 'law of imitation' (Tarde) wherein the lower always seeks to emulate the mores of the elite, who constantly adopt new ways of distinguishing themselves from the rest (Bourdieu). Thus it becomes possible to 'learn' to like the taste of a food representing the prestigious and valued – or 'good taste' in the reflective sense taken to its extreme in the Kantian pure aesthetics (Kant, 1987 [1790]).

These foods are not available for me/us 'here and now' not only for objective and 'natural' reasons of scarcity but also because they are prohibited, and will be permitted in an anticipated and attainable status, time and place. They are *possible* objects for possession and incorporation, and as objects which are strived for, they are defined as *good* objects.

This positive representation implies a hierarchical situation in which the food (object) represents the higher, the valued and something attainable. But this is not enough. As long as the reason for prohibition is conceived of as materially present in the food's substance or essence (maintaining the double meaning: as the inner nature and as the existential form of the 'matter') there is no likelihood of an *effective* representation of 'good' being formed. The food is simply polluting, poisonous and even deadly for me/us, here and now. It is not until the *indexical* (material and causal) link between the food and the negative consequence of taboo transgression is broken that the positive representation becomes effective. Only now is it possible to desire the food just because it stands for the 'good' – the higher, prestigious, etc. And only now may we formulate a chain of determination in which the food is part of, and thus represents, the 'sweet life' and those living it, and furthermore, makes the taste of the food, now as an index of the representation, 'sweet' (in semi-metaphorical sense; interestingly, in the Finnish language the words for 'sweet' and 'taste' [*makea, maku*] are etymologically connected – see note 17).

Keeping in mind that 'the rules are no game' it is always possible to point out cases (Harris, 1986) which show that those in privileged and dominant positions tend to monopolize all the 'sweet things of life' – in a literal, semi-metaphorical and metaphorical sense.[17] And while this is an adequate interpretation of one essential aspect of the dynamics of the 'game', as an explanation of the development of taste preferences it would take us back to a postulation of 'natural' taste preferences.

As the indexical link is broken in this way, the incorporation of certain foods ceases to be a question of 'life and death' but the question of individual and social *identity* becomes the more crucial. While the *magical* conception of being transformed according to the characteristics of the food incorporated still survives, it is now accompanied by an *imitative* conception based on the representational status of the food.

In the former case the slogan 'You are what you eat' (Feuerbach: *Der Mensch ist was er isst*) refers to the causal-magical transformation: if you eat a fast-running animal you will run faster, or, if a Hua male initiate eats the *dguripa* mushroom – resembling a young woman's breasts – his growth into manhood is at stake (Meigs, 1988: 351). In the latter case the same slogan must be specified within the representational scheme: when eating the *food of* (that is, representing) the valued model, your identity is transformed into his or her kind. Now the incorporation of a certain food produces that identity both through imitation and through the material nature of the same shared food (the magic relic), the index of which is the taste sensation. The similarity of the experience, or taste sensation is, however, necessarily an imaginary construction based on the 'mimetic desire' (Girard, 1977, 1987) expressed towards the model but relocated in the substitute, or what the food 'stands for'.

This imitative constellation may also be interpreted as an imaginary (and abstracted) common meal, a ritual communion creating a bond and identity between those sharing the same food and (imagined) experience. Incorporating the same food is experienced as an act in which the eater is incorporated into the 'model'-community, status group, etc. even if it is merely an imaginary alimentary communion.

The constitution of food as a representation of 'good' offers a partial answer to the 'forbidden fruit' dilemma. As for the prohibition of food according to status or situation (time/place) there is always the temptation to give up the abstinence and transgress the rules – or, psychoanalytically speaking, to sacrifice the 'reality principle' for the immediately rewarding 'pleasure principle'. There does seem, however, to be something more fundamentally fascinating about 'forbidden fruit', something that makes it especially 'sweet' (that is, good) *just because* it is forbidden.

The sweetness of forbidden fruit

The interpretation developed thus far seeks to explain the conditions for the constitution of positive representations of food through the relativizing dynamics of the food taboo system (restricted). The forbidden fruit dilemma takes us back to the link between wrong/forbidden and good (see Figure 4.1).

The question we are now interested in is this: is it possible to trace a connection between the 'good' (tasting) and the 'wrong/forbidden'? Or, to put it another way: is there an ambivalence of positive vs. negative in the wrong/forbidden pole which might explain the grounds for making this connection?

As noted above, the common denominator of the tabooed intermediate cases, that is, those not fitting with the object-categorization (Douglas), confusing the eater/food distinction (Leach) or situated anomalously half-way in the nature–culture transformation (Lévi-Strauss), is that they are regarded as *uncontrollable*, both symbolically and practically. These ambiguous beings (objects and substances) are dangerous and to be feared precisely because they tend to invert the eater/food relation; incorporating them does not result in gaining possession over them. In fact, the very reverse is the case.

But why would this uncontrollable something have a positive dimension? Is it because an uncontrollable thing represents exceptional powers? Then again, in order to become positive, they have to be subjected to control, by some exceptional ritual means, and thus they cease to be uncontrolled.

What I am now arguing is that the ambivalence is located in the uncontrollable itself – as fear *and* desire to be eaten by or dissolved into the other (being, object, substance), subsumed to the first-order ambivalence of 'to eat or be eaten by'.

This is the situation psychoanalysis defines as the 'oral' stage where the 'oral introjection' is simultaneously the executive of the 'primary identification', as Otto Fenichel (1982) puts it. He continues:

> The ideas of eating an object or being eaten by an object remain the ways in which any reunion with objects is thought of unconsciously. The magical communion of 'becoming the same substance', either by eating the same food or by mixing the respective bloods, and the magical belief that a person becomes similar to the object he has eaten are based on this fact. (Fenichel, 1982: 63)

But, as Fenichel notes, 'the idea of being eaten is not only a source of fear but under *certain circumstances* may also be a source of oral pleasure. There is not only a longing to incorporate objects but also a longing to be incorporated by a larger object' (p. 64; my italics). In other words, there is not only 'a lust for swallowing up the other' (Kristeva, 1982: 118–19) and a 'fear [to] be swallowed up by' the other (Sanday, 1986: 69–70) but also the lust or pleasure of being swallowed up by the other. The question now is: what could these 'certain circumstances' of oral pleasure be?

As for the 'to eat or be eaten' situation being a matter of survival (to be or not to be), the ambivalence is projected in terms of the negative: oral fear and/or disgust. This is the case when confronted with a man-eating animal or deadly poison. This applies also to the food which irrevocably endangers the basis of identity: eating female-polluted or 'woman-food' destroys manhood, etc. The oral fear is the fear of losing one's self/identity, in the last instance, the fear of death.

As soon as the situation 'to eat or be eaten' is transferred to the realm of non-fatal and repeatable experience the positive pole of the ambivalence becomes explicit. There is a transgressive logic of pleasure (see Chapter 3) which operates both in opposition to and in demarcation of the feared and disgusting.

The transfer into the realm of non-fatal and recursive experience may be conceived of as another mode of taboo relativization, and yet transgression presupposes the existence of boundaries, of prohibition and order. Or, in the words of Georges Bataille: 'the transgression does not deny the taboo but transcends it and completes it' (Bataille, 1962: 63; Caillois, 1959). The 'pleasure principle' of transgression is not constituted in the existential state beyond the boundaries – the state of death or psychosis – but in the very act of transgression. Thus transgression also functions as an affirmation and reproduction of the Order.

This implies a meta-order making the recursive transgression – break into disorder and undifferentiation – possible. On the collective scale the meta-order is manifested in the ritual boundaries which define the limits to the 'liminality' (van Gennep, 1960; cf. Leach, 1961; V. Turner, 1969) marking off distinctively the time and space of transgression.

On the subject level the meta-order, realized both as collective (external) and/or individualized (internal) control, transforms the fatal act into a repeatable bodily and sensual experience of pleasure. Here the boundary to be transgressed is specified into that which separates the subject from the other – from mother (Kristeva, 1982) and ma(t)ter.

This is the locus of transgression which in the last instance is concretized in relation to the bodily boundaries separating the inside from the outside – boundaries which are crossed in the sensual practice of erotic and oral pleasures. Here both the ambivalences of 'to eat or be eaten by' – one of the key themes in erotic love poetry[18] – and the fear/desire to be eaten are actualized. Due to the meta-order the latter ambivalence is, however, constituted primarily on the positive dimension of pleasure, but, nevertheless, in demarcation of the threatening, polluting and disgusting.

The positive characterizations of 'oceanic feeling' (Freud) or the (regressive) 'striving for a complete harmony between the subject and his environment' [which 'may be approximated (a) in our sexual life, in particular in its most intense phase – during orgasm, and (b) in all forms of ecstasy' (Balint, 1959: 64)] refer to the same phenomena as the negative characterizations of the disgusting risk of 'being dissolved in sliminess' (Sartre, 1966: 777) or being drawn into the horrifying 'state of undifferentiation, the state of abjection' (Harpham, 1987: 191; Kristeva, 1982: 68).

Focusing on the bodily boundaries – and transgressions in relation to them the theme of anomalies and ambiguity may be elaborated more specifically with categories of materiality and sensory qualities thereof. This is what Mary Douglas does when she examines the 'disorder' not only within the system of classification but also 'within the set of forms' (Meigs, 1988: 349). Here, the 'ideas of form and formlessness' (Douglas, 1988: 98) may be conceived of as referring to material properties.

Referring to Sartre's essay on 'stickiness' Douglas points out the anomalous character of this form of materiality being 'a state half-way between solid and liquid' (Douglas, 1988: 38). An object/substance of this kind ('treacle', the example given by Douglas) produces an 'ambiguous sense-impression' in addition to the fact that it is 'anomalous in the classification of liquids and solids' (p. 37). But the ambiguous sense-impression of the sticky/slimy, usually considered with fear or disgust, is not reducible to an effect of the classificatory anomaly, and this becomes explicit also in the further characterization Douglas offers.

The sticky and slimy is something which threatens bodily integrity: stickiness is clinging, like a overly 'possessive dog or mistress' (p. 38). It creates on the level of sense-impression an ambiguous confrontation with the uncontrollable which may be specified as the 'eat or be eaten by' situation: am I taking that object/substance into possession or is it breaking my bodily boundaries and dissolving me into itself? The object/substance ambivalence is now restructured according to the formula.

object/substance → *object/subject* → *food/eater*

The common denominator – the uncontrollable – nevertheless remains the same.

But, then again, this kind of ambiguous sense-impression also has its place on the positive side of sensual pleasures, especially in the realm of erotics but also in the more narrowly defined field of oral pleasures. In the latter case we must now analyse the 'ambiguous sense-impression' and the transgressive principle of pleasure connected to it, focusing especially on the sense of taste.

The 'sweetness' of the forbidden fruit may now be understood in the following way: according to the different levels of classificatory anomalies it is a confrontation with the 'uncontrolled' the incorporation of which challenges the eater's role thus endangering his or her bodily boundaries. Being transformed into a non-fatal repeatable experience, itself conditioned by the meta-order, the pleasure derives from the transgressive 'dissolution' into the taste sensation.

In a sense, the 'forbidden' food – indexically the taste sensation – takes control of the eater. The eater is *overwhelmed* by (the taste of) food – allowing himself to be consumed by the experience.

This sounds more like a characterization of a gourmand indulging in culinary pleasures, and in fact it is this very context which institutionalizes the meta-order for transgressive oral pleasures. But the same principles apply more generally to the 'neophilic' tendencies (see Rozin) in the development of taste preferences manifested in the intercultural diffusion of foodstuffs and foodways.

As noted above, Paul Rozin does not explain the principles on which neophilia is based; it is simply postulated. On the other hand, the intracultural setting producing the positive representation of food is not without its problems when applied to the *inter*cultural setting. The 'forbidden fruit' scheme suits also, however, the case of intercultural diffusion: as the basis for neophilia directed to the 'unknown' and thus potentially uncontrollable, though on the other hand counteracted by the neophobic clinging onto the known and acknowledged 'right' food.

The rise of the culinary art, condemned as 'unnatural' by many pregastronomic (Bonnet, 1979) and dietary (Falk and Gronow, 1985) discourses of the eighteenth century,[19] and its segregation into a specific field of oral pleasures turned the neophilic dimension into a systematic search for new and unexperienced pleasurable tastes. Development within elite cuisine[20] also built bridges for the intercultural transfer of foods and recipes – literally from court to court (Braudel, 1973; Mennell, 1985).

Cookery is transformed into an innovative practice systematically breaking the old rules and replacing them with new ones. The innovative cook is accompanied by the neophilic epicure (later, in the 'gastronomic' nineteenth century civilized into a *gourmand*, see Falk and Gronow, 1985) reaching for new and unknown oral pleasures: uncontrollable foods, combinations and compositions with tastes which take possession of the eater.

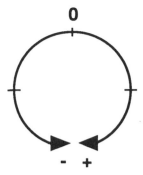

Figure 4.4 *The curved taste-value scale.*

Pre-gastronomic culinary culture (that is, before the nineteenth century) operated mainly with excesses in quantity – both regarding the amounts of food eaten and spices used to produce strong taste sensations. Anyway, both these forms of excess can be interpreted as transgressive practices threatening the bodily boundaries – the former almost literally and the latter in the sensory register where the strong tastes enter into a demarcation of pleasure and pain.

Nineteenth-century gastronomy shifts the emphasis from quantity to quality condemning excessive eating as gluttony and replacing strong tastes by refined and sensitive taste distinctions (Brillat-Savarin, 1971 [1824]). Nevertheless, the neophilic search for new taste sensations, new combinations and mixtures, remains as the dynamic principle of innovation – the transgressive practice located in the demarcation of pleasure and disgust. This is the theme Ulrich Raulff touches upon when referring to the culinary sub-category of cheese, the 'rotten' food – especially at the ripe end of the scale   which is regarded either with utmost pleasure or disgust (Raulff, 1982: 245–6).

We may now depict an alternative 'taste-value scale' to the one describing Rozin's 'unlearning aversion – learning liking' model presented above. The *linear* scale must be replaced by a *curved* one (Figure 4.4) bringing the positive and negative far ends of the scale into mutual proximity. If the linear scale describes the constitution of 'good' tasting according to the neophobic principle, then the curved scale depicts the constitution of the 'delicious' following the neophilic or transgressive principle of oral pleasure.

In the curved universe of neophilia, the journey from pleasurable taste to the disgusting never passes the zero point of the neutral or 'tasteless'. The highest degrees of oral pleasure are located in the dangerous zone nearest the disgusting (Raulff, 1982: 252). This also explains why 'our' delicacies may be inedible and disgusting to those of 'others' (and vice versa) but never indifferently near the zero point.

A true gourmand, as Grimod de La Reynière declares in his *Almanach des Gourmands* (1803/1810), 'has no false delicacy; his first duty is to sample everything and to have an aversion to nothing' (MacDonogh, 1987: 187). This is a characterization of the innovative and neophilic side of the modern *homo culinarius*. But there is the other side too, the critical alter ego who not only controls his or her appetite (cf. Brillat-Savarin, 1971) but is suspicious of everything entering the mouth. This is the neophobic side emphasized in François Revel's characterization of a 'gastronome' – being 'curious but also suspicious, a researcher and a coward longing for new experiences but also fearing them' (Revel, 1982: 113).

It is this duality which, in 'matters of taste', is quite literally realized in the ambiguous zone of the mouth, located on the boundary between the outside and inside of the body (cf. Derrida, 1986: xxxviii). Physical tasting is really 'a yes-or-no sense, take-it-or-don't sense' as Walter Ong (1967: 5) puts it. The mouth acts both as an organ of *sensory* and sensual experience and of *censorship*: either you swallow it up or spit it out.

Notes

1. Actually it is impossible to translate 'gustemes' – Lévi-Strauss' term for the 'units of taste' – into corresponding representations (cf. Tyler, 1987: 124; Sperber, 1975: 115 ff.) which was the aim of Lévi-Strauss' earlier (1958) formulation regarding the food system as a structure of gustemes corresponding to Roman Jakobson's conception of linguistic phonemes (Lévi-Strauss, 1967 [1958]). Later (1965) he modified the model replacing the taste units with semantic elements – which Jack Goody (1982: 20) calls 'technemes' – referring to modes of food elaboration corresponding to basic cultural representations, as exemplified in Lévi-Strauss' (1965) well known 'culinary triangle' (raw–cooked–rotten).

2. In the 1920s the German toxicologist Louis Lewin wrote an extensive study on man's craving for all kinds of 'poisons', from more familiar intoxicants and stimulants of various cultures to incredible addictions such as 'arsenic eating' (Lewin, 1927). Lewin's book dealing with the positive uses of poisons is about as thick as his earlier study on the negative uses, the *World History of Poisoning*, in which these substances are used against 'others' (Lewin, 1920).

3. The 'always already' is one aspect of Derrida's '*différance*' – 'the non-representable principle of representation' (Harvey, 1986: 203) – which Jonathan Culler has illustrated as the non-traceable 'original' scene of both language and food choice:

> For a caveman successfully to originate language by making a special grunt to signify something like 'food' is possible only if we assume that the grunt is already distinguished or distinguishable from other grunts and that the world has already been divided into the categories of food and non-food. Signification always depends on difference: contrasts, for example, between food and not-food which allow 'food' to be signified. (Culler, 1979: 164)

4. This reminds me of a personal experience I had in Cambridge some years ago. A South Korean anthropologist offered me a liquid made of dog meat – first boiled (into a bouillon) and then fermented into a light alcoholic drink. As I later analysed my adverse reaction to this substance I realized it didn't rise primarily from the semi-cannibalism of dog eating (cf. Leach, 1964; Sahlins, 1976: 170) but from the 'confusion' of transformations and foodstuff categories: meat first boiled and then fermented did not fit my classifications of foodstuffs and modes of transformation.

5. Actually, this is also problematic. How can we judge the 'taste preference' of a newborn infant when the gustatory response is undistiguishable from the reaction of the organism as a whole? How can we talk about taste preferences when there exists no differentiation of tastes? And also: how do we decode the facial expression into a 'hedonic' response to the taste

if it cannot yet be differentiated from the positive reaction to nutritional satisfaction? I will, however, ignore these problems as secondary to the present line of argument.

6. The 'mystery of sweetness' (Falk, 1987) was dealt with by Edmund Burke long before psychoanalysis with a remarkable insight: '*Milk* is the first support of our childhood. The component parts of this are water, oil, and a sort of a very sweet salt, called sugar of milk. All these when blended have a great *smoothness* on the taste, and a relaxing quality to the skin. The next thing children covet is *fruit* . . .' (Burke, 1792: 253 [1757]).

7. © 1988 Leonard Cohen Stranger Music Inc.

8. The 'self' may be specified – depending on the context – either as individual self (me) or collective, 'group-self' (we) as is done, e.g. by the ethno-psychoanalyst Paul Parin in his study of the Dogon (Mali) (Parin, 1978; cf. Marcel Mauss' concept of 'Person' in his essay *The Gift*, 1967).

9. Then again, there are the ritual 'rules of exception', making possible – and even necessary – the eating of the totem animal 'in ritual communion to renew the mystic principle' etc. (cf. Caillois, 1959: 82). As Anthony Wilden points out in the title of his book (1987), *The Rules are No Game*.

10. The 'unknown' must be understood in relational terms, i.e. constituting a meaningful relation to the object (real or imaginary). In absolute terms the 'unknown' would be non-existent and thus outside any categorization.

11. Freud's (1977: 156) definition 'poison is nourishment that makes one ill' should be radicalized into the form: poison is food that consumes the eater.

12. Roger Caillois characterizes this fundamental subject–object relation as follows: '. . . just as in marriage, a specifically polar relationship is required between the food and the eater for their mutual advantage' (Caillois, 1959: 82).

13. The cannibalistic eater/food ambiguity is also conceivable within the culture–nature scheme as exemplified in the Greek thought of the Orphic era. From the stand point of Greek 'culture' cannibalism represents 'savage customs' (Herodotus) and 'bestial tendencies' of the barbarians (Aristotle), those belonging with wild 'nature' (Detienne, 1977: 58). The strong taboo against cannibalism removes those eating the flesh of his kind (– eating one's self) to the far (wild) end of the distance-scale, in other words, 'eating human flesh means entering an inhuman world' (p. 59) or to be transformed into beast, as manifested in the Lycaean ritual: 'wolf is the man who tastes human flesh' (Detienne and Svenbro, 1989: 157).

14. This is a problematic distinction which should be specified case by case. Namely, the food cultures have remained remarkably local even in the formation of larger societal units. Flandrin and Hyman (1986: 6–7), for example, find in fourteenth–fifteenth-century France mutually exclusive local (peasant) cuisines which also stood against the more unitary culinary code of the elite: escargots, the delicacy of the higher estates were considered inedible by the lower ones. Actually, in Europe the elite (courts) had a central role in the creation of cuisine transgressing the local boundaries, especially from the thirteenth century onwards (see Braudel, 1973: 125; Revel, 1982).

15. Actually Rozin's model contains a hint as to the role of positive representation concerning the development of 'liking' in the 'coffee & tobacco' case: the 'exposure' is realized 'under strong social pressure from peers, and *motivation by desire to "be adult"* ' (Rozin, 1982: 248; my italics). 'Being adult' functions here as a positive representation pushing the (taste?) sensation along the scale from the negative to the positive.

16. 'Index' refers to signs wherein there is a spatio-temporal or physical connection between sign vehicle and entity signified – like in the relation of smoke to fire.

17. Combining the literal and metaphorical or the semi-metaphorical (sweet = good tasting) or the metaphoric to the metaphoric (good 1 – good 2) the line of the song goes: 'sweets for my sweet and sugar for my honey'. Or as L.A.G. Strong declares in his book in defence of sugar: 'we cannot think without the idea of sweetness, any more than our bodily chemistry can work without the fact of it' (Strong, 1954: 14).

18. This is the idea underlying the conception of sexual intercourse common in 'primitive' cultures, as exemplified by Andrew Strathern's description of the 'sexual ideologies' of the Melpa and Gimi (New Guinea): 'in sexual intercourse, the sexes "eat" each other . . . females

consume male semen, but do so in order to achieve reproduction through a combination of semen and their own blood . . . ' (Strathern, 1982: 129). The symbiotic relationship blurring the distinction between eater and food is not only a typical theme of love poetry but also something expressed in myths of cosmological scale, exemplified by a verse from Taittiriya Upanishad (cited in Hyde, 1983):

O wonderful ! O wonderful! O wonderful!
I am food! I am food! I am food!
I eat food! I eat food! I eat food!
[. . .]
Whoever gives me away has helped me the most!
I, who am food, eat the eater of food!
I have overcome this world!
He who knows this shines like the sun.
Such are the laws of the mystery!

19. The same line of argument is also found among the (socio)biologists who locate the bias or perversion into the development of culinary art which sets 'endless traps of sight, taste and smell to break down the restraints of appetite' (Brock, 1963: 48).

20. The culinary art of the elite already flourished in China in the fifth century, in the Arabic world in the eleventh to twelfth centuries and in Europe from fifteenth and sixteenth centuries onward (Braudel, 1973: 125).

5

CONSUMING DESIRE

There is, of course, no reason to deny that consumption – even in its modern forms – involves the satisfaction of needs and rational use of tools. But to construct the concept of consumption on these anthropological universals does not lead us to a deeper understanding of the specificity of *modern* consumption which is, primarily, something over and above 'eating' (using up) and 'building' (using tools). The universalistic postulations naturalize the dynamics of consumption into an abstract principle which is not so very far from the definitions of matter/energy-transformation offered by physics.

After all, consumption in the universalistic sense is simply a synthesis of entropic and negentropic processes; matter dissolving into energy and maintaining or producing more complex and ordered forms of matter, or an endless chain of transformations – of destruction and construction – which is based on the same universal principle even if the historical and cultural forms change. This is in accordance with the bivalence inherent in the etymological roots of 'consumption' deriving from the Latin '*consumere*' (*cum sumere*), that is, to use up entirely, which involves destruction of matter, and '*consummare*' (*cum summa*) or to sum up, to carry to completion (Barnhart, 1988; Williams, 1982: 5). The duality is manifested in the distinction of the English words 'consumption' and 'consummation', a distinction which fails, however, to resolve the fundamental bivalence but gives it only one specific expression.

The perspective on destructive vs. constructive aspects of consumption has a central role in the (programmatic) ecological discourses concerning 'waste' – both as irrational and excessive dissipation of natural resources and as the problematic refuse causing pollution and other environmental dangers. It is not without good reason that, in a sense, the contemporary ecological discourse revives the 'old' meaning of 'consumption' prior to the material and economic uses of the term, referring to 'a wasting of the body by disease' (Barnhart, 1988) – the body being now writ large as the superorganism or ecological system of the earth and the 'disease' being re-defined as the material culture of modern Western civilization.

Nevertheless, in order to go beyond moralistic argumentation and programmatic policy formulation the riddle of modern consumption must be dealt with as a phenomenon in its own right. We have to advance the question concerning the constitution and genesis both of 'consumer society' and of 'consumer behaviour'. And this is what the contemporary

historical, anthropological and sociological discourses on consumption are
mainly about. The following is a comment – or maybe a 'supplement', in a
sense to be explicated further below – to these discussions.

The riddle of the modern consumer and the whole consumer society
inevitably confronts us with questions concerning (a) the *constitution of
desire* exceeding the 'necessary', (b) the *limitlessness* of the desire and
(c) the endless longing for the *new*. These are the questions upon which the
contemporary interpretations of modern consumerism are focused. On the
other hand these interpretations attempt to go beyond the two conventional models, the first of which is based on production determinism and
the second on the dynamic principle of social competition (imitation,
emulation and distinction).

The search for an alternative mode of thematization of modern consumption is aptly exemplified in the recent studies by Colin Campbell
(1987) and Grant McCracken (1988). Both take distance from the Janus-
faced consumer stereotype depicting the consumer either as a rational
being maximizing not only need satisfaction and economic utility but also
social 'goods' (prestige, status) or as an irrational hedonist driven by an
endless craving for immediate pleasure. Both attempt to locate a rational
kernel behind the 'irrational' desire for novelty which would explain this
peculiar trait of modern consumption as a sensible mode of behaviour.

But as I shall try to show further below, both interpretations involve an
inexplicable residue. In Campbell's case the problem of how desire is
realized as actual consumption and in McCracken's case the principle
which constitutes the goods as objects of desire. And in both cases there is
a tendency to slide back towards the Janus-faced consumer which both
rejected in the first place. The dualism seems to derive from a more basic
dilemma – that concerning the constitution of object-relations in the realm
of consumption – which I try to explicate and reconceptualize in the
following starting from a broader contextualization and thus also from the
basic question: 'what is consumption?'

Consumption before 'consumption'

Starting from the basic etymological bivalence of 'consumption' would
dissolve the concept into an endless list of natural and cultural life-
processes lacking any definite boundaries. In other words, there is no
prehistory of consumption without a post hoc conceptualization which
posits the term in a binary relationship to the 'other'. But what could this
'other' be – other than the concept of 'production' in relation to which
'consumption' is defined in the economic discourse from the eighteenth
century onwards?

The 'the history of concepts' (*Begriffsgeschichte*) of 'consumption' can
be traced to the old meaning (prevailing till the end of the fourteenth
century [Barnhart, 1988]) reducing the etymological bivalence to the

negative and destructive ('consuming disease'). But if we generalize the concept, thus specified, into the natural and cultural life-processes of subsistence – in the last instance referring to oral consumption or 'eating' – we would again face the basic bivalence. Eating implies the consumption (dissolving, using up) of the food but it is also simultaneously a process of production – or better, construction:[1] (re)producing or constructing life on all levels from the physical to the social. Thus we end up with the concept of reproduction which in material terms is nothing short of the variety of life-processes or different modes of metabolism within the body, between man and nature and man to man.

We may, of course, give the name 'consumption' not only to actual eating but more broadly to the activities involving the satisfaction of (basic) human needs including all the social and cultural forms of their realization (ritual, meal), and accordingly define 'production' as all that effort expended for the subsistence, but still the distinction would remain empty. Imagining a subsistence economy reproducing itself on the physical survival level there would be no way to categorize the activities of the community into production vs. consumption. But such a society is largely an imaginary construction[2] as mythical as the Lost Paradise or Golden Age of abundance – or even more mythical because in most cases the 'Stone Age economics' (Sahlins, 1972) of the archaic and primitive societies have functioned far beyond the subsistence level even if the surplus could also be 'wasted' in simple idleness.

Perhaps the archaic 'consumption' can be located in the different forms of doing away with the produced surplus? Yes and no. On the one hand, even if it were possible to postulate a subsistence level defined into a range of necessities meeting certain physical or other needs and correspondingly categorize the excessive part – in whatever form – as unnecessary and luxurious we would still be left with the problem of how to relate these forms of consumption to corresponding forms of production in a social or cultural system which subsumes all conduct into different forms of symbolic and especially ritual action regardless of their 'productive' or 'consumptive' character. Ritual sacrifice and material production ('work') cannot be distinguished any more than the material practices of preparing, sharing and incorporating food can be distinguished from their ritual and mythical meaning.

So, we are back to the heterogeneity of life-processes – now in terms of culturally meaningful practices. If we project, anachronistically, our (Western) 'productivist' scheme upon the archaic 'economies' we will end up with evaluative categorization of productive vs. consumptive activities. But it is still our scheme and not the 'other's'.

Bataille's 'dépense'

On the other hand we may formulate a positive answer to the question posed above which forces us to replace the (pre)conception of consumption with that of 'waste' or 'expenditure' specified into particular forms of cultural practices such as sacrifice, feasting or festive rituals and other ritual ways of expenditure which Georges Bataille calls *dépense* (Bataille, 1975 [1933, 1949]). The excessive part[3] to be wasted or simply destroyed – as in the potlatch ritual of the Kwakiutl originally studied by Franz Boas and later (re)interpreted by Marcel Mauss (1967 [1925]) offering inspiration to Bataille's thought – presupposes the existence of a surplus, but this surplus cannot be defined according to the productivistic model which implies a postulated distinction between the necessary and the superfluous. The '*dépense*' follows a principle other than that of economic scarcity.

Following Bataille's conceptions, the 'unproductive' modes of expenditure are manifestations of a transgressive cultural principle which cannot be rationalized into an economic scheme, in the narrow sense. Doing away with the excessive (cursed) part can be *generally* characterized merely as the other side of the dual dynamics of human culture (see Chapter 3) counteracting the Order, regressing back from Cosmos to Chaos and opening 'liminal' (van Gennep) spaces for transgressive forms of conduct.[4]

And yet, the non-rational expenditure may be extended to include modes which are not unambiguously destructive though 'unproductive' in the narrow economic sense. This is done by Bataille in his 'general economy' (Bataille, 1975 [1933, 1949][5]) turning the economistic idea of original scarcity upside down.

Actually Bataille's 'general economy' is a cosmological model which transcends the boundaries of human culture – to nature and finally to the universal laws of matter and energy. The principle of excess, waste or expenditure (*dépense*) is the universal law which manifests itself in nature both as wasteful solar radiation (only a fraction of which hits the earth and is transformed into construction/production) and as the wasting of semen in relation to the procreational function. The same applies – according to Bataille – to the cultural dynamics: contrary to the economistic scarcity thesis human culture, in its different forms, evolves on the basis of the 'wasteful' general economy. Using Derrida's expression, the excess or luxus is 'always already'.

Bataille's cosmic generalization undoubtedly accords his interpretation some mystic features but it does, nevertheless, represent a profound critique of the 'productivist' economy, and the corresponding economic thought, attempting to show their historical specificity as a mode – not of production (Marx) but – of *dépense* or expenditure. In Bataille's view an economic system which is based on the principle of 'production of commodities by means of commodities' (Sraffa, 1960) is a mode of 'consumption', or a specific cultural formation with particular forms of doing away with the 'cursed part' – even if the obvious telos of the system seems to be to *produce* excess without limits.

Bataille's model for the general economy and the notion of *dépense* leads rather paradoxically, however, to a concept of 'consumption' which is too universal and yet too narrow. Its universality derives from the postulation of the energetic principle of 'over-consumption' governing both the natural and the cultural. On the other hand – and specific to the realm of human culture – this implies a narrowing of the concept of consumption to the destructive dimension. There is no conceptual distinction between the constructive and destructive modes of wasteful expenditure: 'idleness, building pyramids and (inebriate) drinking' (Bataille, 1975: 153) are all forms of *dépense* exemplifying the basic destructive or entropic dimension which goes not only beyond any notion of need or utility but also beyond any notion of meaning.

While dissociating himself from the economistic idea of *productive* activity Bataille ends up subsuming the *constructive* (or negentropic) aspect of *dépense* under the basic destructive (or entropic) principle – corresponding to the second law of thermodynamics. Constructing 'useless' monuments is merely a phase in the overdetermining process of destructive waste which is paradigmatically manifested in festivals or potlatch rituals as well as in the 'consumption' of warfare sacrificing human lives and the destruction of material constructions whether useless or useful.[6] But, after all, looking at the world from an entropic viewpoint: what else is the entirety of human culture than a 'useless' monument tumbling down some not so sunny day?

Yet, Bataille is very much aware of the fact that in the history of human cultures the principle of *dépense* is responsible for the whole *constructive* dimension manifested in more or less material forms ranging from magic to works of art and sciences – now called 'culture' in the specific sense, that is, as a separate realm distinct from the functional fields of economy and politics. Manifested both constructively (the cumulation of arts and sciences) and destructively (as unique rituals or performances, e.g. fireworks), 'cultural production'[7] is much older than the economic distinction between production and consumption.

The genealogy of luxury

Notwithstanding the above, the essential point to be gleaned from Bataille's cosmic system is the opening of an 'other' perspective on *luxury* – not as a produced remainder or surplus measured according to a postulated norm of 'the necessary' but as the transgressive desire of man and human culture to go beyond the Order – to break the prevailing boundaries both in regressive and progressive forms.

Thus we have to transcend the naturalized distinction between the necessary and the unnecessary or excessive. Furthermore, in refocusing on the concept of luxury, the emphasis falls on how, by whom, and for whom the boundary is defined. This question takes us (back) to the Garden of Eden which is the primal scene of luxury in John Sekora's interesting study on the history of 'luxury' (Sekora, 1977). According to Sekora 'the story of Adam and Eve' (Genesis 2–3) 'is a natural starting point for a survey, for it contains the simplest definition of luxury: *anything unneeded*' (Sekora, 1977: 23).

The archetypal luxury of Adam and Eve involves five elements the first of which 'is the legislator, Yahweh, who defines the limits of necessity and thereby the threshold of luxury' (p. 24). Yahweh sets the Law (Order) but in order to be a law demanding obedience, and not an unconditional natural necessity, there must be the possibility of transgression. This is where the second element comes in, 'the object of testing and temptation. In Genesis, the fruit of the forbidden tree is by definition inessential to sustenance and comfort [. . .] it is present to fulfil not human happiness, but the conditions of the Law' (p. 24).

The third and fourth elements – the tempter and 'imperfect human nature as subject to the Law and victim of the tempter' (p. 24) – resulting in the Fall completes the formula of luxury as 'thought arousing desire impelling action', a definition which is to be found, according to Sekora, both in the writings of early Jewish commentators and the English political orators of the eighteenth century. In other words, luxury is defined as *transgressive desire* translatable in the Bataillean scheme into *desire for transgression*.

Finally, there is the fifth element, the punishment (expulsion), 'a movement from enjoyment of all good things to enjoyment of few or none' (p. 24). A movement from the state of innocence and complete satisfaction to the state of knowledge and neediness.

Taking Sekora's depiction of the 'original state' some steps further, reveals something deeply paradoxical in the Edenic situation: no *lack* in terms of *needs* but a fundamental lack in terms of *desire*. The Garden of Eden supplies everything that is needed but, on the other hand, it involves an additional element, the forbidden tree and fruit, creating or articulating the lack, that of human imperfection in relation to the all-perfect God. This is lack in terms of desire, a desire for limitless unity and completedness. The Law, being the boundary which ought not to be trespassed, calls for man's subjection to God. But it also defines (in the words of the tempter, the serpent) the forbidden fruit as a supplement, making man God-like. It defines the *object* of desire. So, there is simultaneously a desire for transgression (breaking the Law) and a transgressive desire (to acquire the perfecting supplement).

But which comes first: the unnecessary and forbidden addition or the lack, and furthermore, the lack or the desire? Adam and Eve were lacking nothing. In other words, they had everything they *needed*. So the desire for the unneeded, the excessive and luxurious, was already there. But on the other hand, the prohibition and the forbidden tree were also already there, thus breaking the harmony and constituting the lack.

Thus there is no solution to the problem. The additional (forbidden) element both creates and articulates the lack, the latter being an expression of desire as much as the desire is an expression of lack. All we are left with is *transgression* presupposing the Law (boundary) presupposing the possibility of transgression. The forbidden fruit will always be eaten and the Pandora's box opened – and that is what human culture in the last instance is all about.

The point is, however, that there is always someone who establishes the Law and Order defining the boundary between forbidden and permitted and that which someone does, or does not, need. The definition of luxury begins with a prohibition and this gives rise – in Sekora's words – to 'the social and political meaning of luxury: *anything to which one has no right or title*' (Sekora, 1977: 25) to be found already in the Deuteronomic writings. Luxury is first of all defined negatively, as a violation of Law and Order. On the other hand it is expressly the Order constituting the boundary which creates luxury, as motivation (desire), conduct ('luxuriate') and the 'supplement' desired. Translated into the Derridean scheme: 'différance produces what it forbids, making possible the very thing that it makes impossible' (Derrida, 1976: 143).

Luxury is a threat to Order in which the latter refers not only to God's will but further to cosmologic principle, to social order and finally to the unity of the individual human being. These three principles are found in the classic Greek and Roman thought – from Hesiod to Aristotle and from Cicero to Seneca – and they are predominant in the Western tradition till the eighteenth century (Sekora, 1977: 29–39, 66–7). The principles are the same in 'the just and healthy state' proposed by Socrates and those ideals depicted in Augustine's *City of God* or Hobbes' *Christian Commonwealth*: 'man's needs are few, and incipient luxury is incipient anarchy' (Sekora, 1977: 30).

The classical economic discourse

From the eighteenth century onwards the discourse on luxury is paralleled by and intertwined in the economic – especially 'productivist' (the physiocrats and especially the British classical political economy) – discourses on production *and consumption*. Now luxury, in the sense of supplementarity or excess, is rationalized and neutralized as (private) consumption into a more or less functional part of the economic system aimed at the production of surplus, both in material (*produit net* of the physiocrats) and in economic value terms (Adam Smith's *wealth*).

The moral problem of luxury is related to the new distinction between productive vs. unproductive consumption (and labour) in a manner which, step by step, erased the boundary between necessaries and luxuries.

Mandeville (1970 [1714]) still labelled luxurious conduct as 'private vices' producing, however, 'public benefits' and thus redefined luxury as something positive. But for Adam Smith this was not enough. If 'luxury, sensuality, and ostentation are public benefits' then there is no reason to call them vices. They are virtuous passions – or passions in virtuous use – as far as they add to the common good, to the wealth and progress of the nation (*Moral Sentiments*; cited in Robinson, 1970: 22).

But the argumentation was complicated due to the productive vs. unproductive distinction. On the one hand, seen from the vantage point of the 'economic man' producing value, that is the capitalist, the situation looks different: frugality is a virtue and prodigality a vice simply because that part which is reserved 'for immediate consumption' is consequently 'withdrawn from his capital' (Smith, 1970: 432 [1776]). This is, however, an argument against the luxurious private consumption (or *self-consumption*) of the entrepreneur, not against the production and consumption of luxury in itself. On the contrary, producing luxury for the market and for others' consumption increases the wealth: 'the consumption is the same, but the consumers are different' (Smith, 1970: 438).[8]

On the other hand, the distinction between the necessary and the unnecessary (luxurious) is thematized in connection with the labour and wages problem. The fair price for the commodity called 'labour' (which Marx later redefined into labour *power*) was the concern of classical political economy and the answer was formulated most clearly by its last significant representative, David Ricardo, as follows:

> the natural price of labour is that price which is *necessary* to enable the labourers, one with another, to subsist and perpetuate their race, without either increase or diminution. (Ricardo, 1971: 115 [1821]; my italics)

Here the definition of the necessary derives from the capitalist's focus on the labour *costs* which should be minimized (among other costs of production) according to the rationality of surplus-value. Thus the *ideal* limit of the necessary is reduced to the minimal (= optimal) level of the reproduction of wage labourers. But while the definition is dependent on the historical and moral factors determining norms for 'human life' and its requirements, the definitions of the necessary determine the limit to be more or less above the physical minimum – a notion which is nothing more than an abstraction in itself.

Within the discourse of classical political economy the relativization of the limit derives from the 'macroeconomic' perspective (the wealth of *nations*). This is a standpoint found in Smith's answer to the 'common complaint that luxury extends itself even to the lowest rank of the people'. According to Smith,

> it is but equity, [. . .] that they who feed, clothe, and lodge the whole body of the people, should have such share of the produce of their own labour as to be themselves *tolerably* well fed, clothed, and lodged. (Smith, 1970: 181 [1776]; my italics)

But more generally, in the moral, philosophical and social discourses of the eighteenth and nineteenth centuries, it is linked to the themes of human needs, the good life and good society thus combining the 'old' luxury discourses with the 'new' conceptions of natural human needs. (I shall return to this theme in the next chapter).

In classical economic discourse the boundary between necessity and luxury is both thematized and relativized (according to the productivist perspective) in two ways. The first focuses on the entrepreneur's luxurious self-consumption which is condemned, not because it breaks the divine Law or cosmic Order but because it violates the productivist principle of capital. This may, however, be conceived as a continuation of the old luxury discourse for the reason that it starts from the thematization of *luxury* as a transgression of Law. And in fact it is linked to the closely interconnected (Banta, 1983) moral and medical discourses on the vicious or unhealthy nature of excessive conduct: idleness, indulging in oral or other pleasures and lack of self-restraint were among the major causes of both Burton's 'Melancholy' (1660) and Cheyne's 'English Malady' (1991 [1733]), the melancholic disease of the 'professional man' which George Cheyne wanted to conquer with his 'dieteticks' (Porter, 1991; B.S. Turner, 1982, 1984).[9]

The second focuses on the wage labourer, from the entrepreneur's point of view. Now the thematization follows an inverse direction: it begins with the necessary or ideally with the lowest limit of (re)production (costs) of the commodity 'labour power' and defines negatively all that beyond the limit as excess, that is luxus. This mode of thematization is essentially discontinuous in relation to the old luxury discourse but it has, however, a link to the moral, philosophical and social discourses on human needs, primarily critical of the productivist and progressivist ideas on 'civilization'.

Both discourses – on human needs and on workers' necessity – attempt to define what is *really* needed but they differ in one essential respect. The discourse on human needs seeks universal and natural norms while the economic labour-costs discourse restricts itself (by definition) to the wage labourers. Both share, however, the interest in 'genuine needs'; the former in moral and philosophical terms and the latter in practical economic terms. Thus it is not surprising that early Marx (of the *1844 Manuscripts*) was rather critical towards needs as 'a limiting concept' (Springborg, 1981: 94). It was not only due to his productivist view (involving certain elements critical of civilization) but due to his interpretation which traced the idea of 'genuine needs' back to its crudest economic manifestation as workers' survival or reproduction minimum. For the 'political economist', Marx notes, 'every *luxury* of the worker seems to be reprehensible, and everything that goes beyond the most abstract need – be it in the realm of passive enjoyment, or a manifestation of activity – seems to him a luxury' (Marx, 1976: 308).

Even though Marx's early view on classical political economy was unjustly reductionist – disregarding the macroeconomic perspective – he succeeds in highlighting the fact that there is always a 'legislator' defining the boundary between necessity and luxury and, furthermore, that the Laws have been generally applied to a social target (group) more specific than humanity – at least since Paradise Lost.

In medieval Europe, church and civil governments acted together in combating luxury: developing sumptuary legislation and prosecuting 'victimless crimes' such as 'profuse spending, drunkenness, swearing and gambling' (Sekora, 1977: 61). But they also

> evolved the doctrine of 'consumption by estates' under which standards of conduct and comfort were fixed according to social ranks; liberty and magnificence were reserved for the highest rank but prohibited to all others, and so on down the great chain of social being. (Sekora, 1977: 61)

The hierarchical structuration of luxury prevails also in the productionist era though in modified forms. Even if both entrepreneur luxury and wage labourer luxury – according to their specific standards – were condemned, luxury configuring as produced commodities to be consumed by *others* was in accordance with the laws of productivity and even added to the common, especially material, good (Ferguson, Smith, Ricardo).

But who were the *others*? According to the Lauderdale–Malthus thesis (Lauderdale, 1804; Malthus, 1820) the 'unproductive' consumers, represented mainly by the landed gentry, are seen as a functional and beneficial part of the economy. They counteracted the 'too rapid rate of accumulation' (Dobb, 1973: 94) while taking care of the effective demand. In other words, the unequal distribution was still legitimated according to the doctrine of 'consumption by estates' but now, in contrast to the medieval situation, without any upper limit imposed on the luxury of the 'highest rank'.

In contrast to the Lauderdale–Malthus thesis, Ricardo's view appears to be radically egalitarian due to his economically neutralized concept of the *market*: from the macroeconomic point of view there was no reason to establish a hierarchy of demand according to a priori postulated norms. So, if the unproductive consumers happened to be parsimonious, the market would take care of distribution and the 'wants of consumers' would simply be 'transferred with power to consume to another set of consumers'. And furthermore, 'the power to consume [. . .] is not annihilated but is transferred to the labourer' (cited in Dobb, 1973: 94).

The economic concept of unproductive or private consumption, then, is cut off from its negative luxurious past and it begins to merge in the rising level of needs and wants considered tolerable (Smith) and reasonable. Nevertheless, the generalized, anonymous and individualized consumer was still waiting to be born in the economic discourse. It is not until the neo-classical economics of the late nineteenth century and especially the 'marginalist revolution' of the 1870s that the economically idealized and generalized modern consumer was theoretically defined. I shall return to this theme after an excursus concerning the discourse on natural vs. artificial needs exemplified by Jean-Jacques Rousseau.

Natural and artificial needs

The thematization of human needs is, as noted above, both a continuation of the old luxury discourse and a parallel to the economic theorizing about the necessary in labour reproduction. The discourse on human needs is, however, constituted in a way which underlines its distinctive character in relation to both of these other discourses. The problem is posed in a new manner.

First, it seeks to postulate a natural basis for human needs which would give the criteria to define the 'unneeded', luxurious and artificial. In this respect it differs from the old luxury discourse which does not thematize that which is needed but focuses on luxury as a desire or conduct transgressing Law and Order – whether divine or profane. On the other hand, here the discourse on human needs finds parallels with some applied fields linked to the economic necessity theme, that is, to discourses and corresponding (social) policies aiming at the 'rationalization' of workers' lives both in terms of nutritional (Aronson, 1982; Falk, 1979a) and recreational behaviour ('rational recreations'; cf. Bailey, 1978). The former is, however, of moral-philosophical character and the latter practical.

Second, the discourse on human needs does not stop at moralizing luxury but goes on to *explain* its origins and development – and now concerning all three senses of luxury: as desire (motivation), as conduct and as the 'thing' (object) desired. As a discourse critical of civilization – paradigmatically though not unambiguously represented by Rousseau – it shares the entropic and eschatological view of the old luxury discourse and stands in opposition to the progressivist and especially the productivist ideas about growing material wealth regarded as a journey towards society's completion. But beyond that, it attempts to explain the rise of luxury and artificial needs as an outcome of civilization's development and not merely as a sign of the basic human imperfection and/or as an effect of the original 'supplement', the unneeded and forbidden tree in the Garden of Eden leading man to Fall.

Third, it operates with a concept of man simultaneously *universalized* and *individualized*, manifesting the ideas of equality and freedom attached to the emerging modern man both in political and economic terms: as a citizen and as a commodity owner (seller and buyer) in the market. This implies a clear distinction both in relation to the old luxury discourse and the contemporary economic necessity discourse. In the discourse on human needs – and most significantly in its romantic version represented by Rousseau – man is above all an individual being and only as such universalized and naturalized into a species-being. Thus all questions concerning good and bad in general (for society, etc.) are measured in terms of the 'naturally' virtuous man true to his/her 'inner nature' as an individual (self) then projected back to the mythical 'state of nature' where the *inner* nature is equated with a harmonic unity with the *outer* nature (vs. culture).

In other words, man does not gain his generalized character as subject to God and he does not carry some common characteristics as a representative of a particular social category (estate, class); man is generalized as an *individual* whose virtuousness and perfection forms the basis for the common good – and not the other way round as it is formulated in the utilitarian scheme. Thus, based on the realization of his innate goodness and natural needs, the individual's perfection offers a measure for the evaluation and critique of the civilization producing the unnecessary and 'dangerous supplement' (Rousseau) evoking unnatural and artificial needs (desires), or to put it the other way round, the 'selfish' desiring (*amour-propre*) giving impetus to the endless production of surplus.

Nevertheless, Rousseau's view on civilization is basically ambivalent. Following on from the strange 'double bind' of Rousseau's 'nature' (inner/outer) natural needs are defined on the one hand in the state of nature *preceding* culture (Rousseau's civilization) but on the other these natural needs presuppose civilization as a *prerequisite* for their realization. Civilization both promotes and expresses human striving to self-improvement (perfectibility), towards rationality and thus towards the possibility of realizing the 'natural' existence. Now the natural is defined as man's inner nature which, however, is modelled according to the (outer) natural state of unity and completion.

Rousseau's 'state of nature' preceding culture and civilization is characterized by the balance of needs and abilities (for their satisfaction) characterizing man as a natural and physiological being who is 'self-sufficient' – as Rousseau puts it in *Emile* – 'so long as only physical needs are recognised' (cited in Springborg, 1981: 46). The rise of civilization with its division of labour and the production of surplus creates endlessly artificial needs and an incessant state of *desire* which as *lack* necessarily causes pain, dissatisfaction and unhappiness (Springborg, 1981: 38).

Rousseau's Paradise Lost differs, however, in one essential respect from the Garden of Eden described above. The one thing missing in Rousseau's state of nature is the unnecessary supplement of the Garden of Eden, the forbidden tree and its equally forbidden fruit. The original state was simply perfect: needs and abilities were in balance and there was nothing to break the harmony, no desire or temptation, nothing unneeded and forbidden to be desired. Thus Rousseau had to look elsewhere for the causes of the Fall and while doing this he was forced to apply different – mutually complementary but also contradictory – strategies of explanation which later, as we shall discover, reappear as distinct sociological interpretations of the constitution and dynamics of modern consumption.

On the one hand, the roots of evil lie in the birth of human civilization manifested in the division of labour and the development of private property, producing both material surplus and selfishness. Here the original harmony of natural needs is broken by the production of the 'supplement' giving rise to artificial needs.

On the other hand, Rousseau formulates a relative criterion for the distinction of true/natural and false/artificial needs which is no longer based on the surplus produced by civilization but on man's 'inner' dispositions and motives. In similar vein to many other Enlightenment thinkers who pondered the psychic basis of man's conduct (cf. Springborg, 1981: 35–7.) Rousseau makes a distinction between positive and negative 'self-love'. With the former (*amour-de-soi*) he meant 'self-regard' of one's inner and thus natural needs while the latter (*amour-propre*) refers to 'selfish' desire evoked by the comparison with others and in the competition to be better than others. The former is oriented towards *need*-satisfaction, into a state of equilibrium modelled according to the lost state of nature now sublimated through reason into sociability and virtue. The latter represents *desire* created by selfish comparison with others; a desire which knows no satisfaction or state of equilibrium. Here we have a distinction between two different logics – the logic of *need* and that of *desire*.

To sum up then, first, the unneeded and unnatural supplement (where luxus is excess) comes into existence as a produced surplus, corresponding roughly to the later consumption theoretical interpretations according to which the commodity production produces the consumer and the whole 'consumer society' (cf. Marxian models). Secondly, man is turned into a desiring creature transgressing the boundaries of natural needs. This transformation is explained by the exogenic factor of social comparison but, on the other hand, it presupposes the endogenic factor of man's (perverted?) second nature manifested in the desire for comparison and competition.

In other words, the desire is both a *consequence* and a *cause* of social comparison. The former case (desire as consequence) comes close to the sociological interpretations of modern consumption as represented both by Thorstein Veblen (1970 [1899]) and more recently – and in a more subtle manner – by Pierre Bourdieu (1984), that is, explanations which are based on the social dynamics of emulation and/or distinction. The latter case (desire as cause) is reminiscent of the principle of *imitation* postulated by Gabriel Tarde (1962 [1890]) as a basic human disposition: to imitate the other('s person) and hence the other's conduct, desires, etc. especially in the realm of consumption. It is also reminiscent of René Girard's universalistic idea of 'mimetic desire' (Girard, 1977, 1987) in which the object of desire is constituted as the object desired by the other, the 'rival' (Girard, 1977: 145). Tarde was explicitly concerned with the dynamics of consumption but even Girard's model has recently been applied to 'solve' the problems that neo-classical economics have had in explaining consumer behaviour (Orléan, 1988; see below pp. 131–2).

Rousseau was not concerned with modern consumption. He was certainly moralizing against luxury, according to the received wisdom of the old luxury discourse, but this was only a part of his attack against the degenerative and entropic traits of civilization and against the different forms the 'dangerous supplements' (*Confessions*) manifested in the dynamics of civilization: writing in relation to speech or masturbation in relation to heterosexual love (the themes deconstructed by Derrida [1976]), and finally generalized, natural needs in relation to artificial ones (that is, desires).

The economics of consumption

Even though Rousseau outlined in effect the basic arguments of the later sociological interpretations of modern consumption he still lacked the theoretical object and the concept of consumption. These were to be thematized in the late nineteenth century in the dawn of 'consumer society' (cf. Fraser, 1981; Hayes, 1941), both sociologically (especially Tarde and Veblen; cf. Williams, 1982) and economically; in neo-classical economics and especially in the 'marginalist theory' (Jevons, 1970 [1871]; Menger, 1871; Walras, 1954 [1874]) which completed the neutralization and generalization of the concept of consumption.

The neutralized and generalized concept of consumption presupposed an interpretation explicitly annulling the distinction between needs and desires. Classical political economy was already operating with a neutralized concept of consumption in relation to production but it also still operated with 'luxuries' in relation to 'necessaries'. In neo-classical economics the metaphysical model distinguishing needs from desires is replaced with another one making them interchangeable (or better; reducing needs to desires) on the basis of hedonistic-utilitarian principles and the concept of *utility*. In the marginalist economy, 'utility' was transformed from a universalistic principle into a category referring to individualistic desire (Birken, 1988: 29). Later, the metaphysics was simply rejected as useless speculation about what might lie behind the factual *wants* or preferences as manifested in the market.

The modern consumer is (re)defined as an economic factor and thus as a problem of economic theory: he/she accompanied with his/her kind represent the aggregate function called 'demand' to be subjected to theoretical and practical control. The marginalist theories defined consumption as the key problem of economics, or as Jevons put it, 'the theory of economics must begin with a correct theory of consumption' (Jevons, 1970: 103 [1871]).

An essential feature in the portrait of the consumer sketched by the marginalists was that the consumer (universalized into civilized man and *homo oeconomicus*) realized his/her own desires and wants, the generation of which were in principle limitless. The marginalistic consumer is still a hedonist guided by a pleasure and pain principle but now civilized or, better, rationalized into a utilitarian aiming at other (especially mediated) 'goods' and avoiding accordingly the 'bads'. He maximizes his individual 'utility' which Jeremy Bentham still defined in universalistic terms:

> By utility is meant that property in any object, whereby it tends to produce benefit, advantage, pleasure, good, or happiness (all this, in the present case, comes to the same thing), or (what comes again to the same thing) to prevent the happening of mischief, pain, evil, or unhappiness to the party whose interest is considered. (Bentham, 1789; cited in Jevons, 1970: 102)

The principle of utility does not thematize the difference between natural vs. artificial needs nor the endogenic vs. exogenic origins (Rousseau) of the generation of needs or desires. When the hedonistic orientation towards immediate (bodily) pleasure is broadened into a utilitarian 'good' towards which the individual (consumer) is striving according to his/her abilities, the model expands into an all-embracing explanation of human conduct. From this vantage point production itself is turned into a derivative of consumption; it is understood 'as the deferral of consumption' (Birken, 1988: 29).[10]

The whole economic system is redefined in the marginalistic theory. The three 'factors of production' – capital, labour and land (nature) – are complemented by the energetic principle of *desire* which takes a primary position in relation to the three other factors, as the prime stimulus to the economy (cf. Goux, 1990: 199–201). If the basis for and 'cause' of economic values lies in the intensity of desiring, it follows that the production of these values does not concern primarily the satisfaction of needs nor even the gratification of desires – it implies a production of the desire itself. Otherwise there would not be any production of 'value'.

The consumer society outlined in marginalist economics is at once a society of abundance and of scarcity. It must produce both plenty and paucity, both repletion and appetite, satisfaction and desire. This is the contradictory constellation which constitutes the 'metaphoric thirst'. Or in Goux's words:

> Superfluity is required for the thirst to become metaphorical and to seek satisfaction in *signs* and *imagination*, which make it potentially infinite. [. . .] But in order for the metaphoric thirst to be intensified, there must be a lack, evanescence, disappearance. (Goux, 1990: 200–1; my italics)

The market economy of consumption cannot be based on a non-elastic demand of needs satisfaction. It presupposes above all a 'vanity fair', a market for the unnecessary and superfluous characterized ideally by an 'infinite elasticity of demand', as the economists would have it: 'demand is all the more elastic when it concerns a "need", appetite, or thirst that is not essential to survival – a *substitutable* object' (Goux, 1990: 201). The metaphorized thirst transforms both the objects of consumption and the objects of desire into a chain of *substitutes*, substituting one thing for another and thus offering alternative objects for the fundamentally 'objectless' desire to be fixed upon. The substitutive character of goods – good (object)s – manifests their excessiveness or, according to Rousseau's view, their 'supplementarity' and the 'artificial' character of the needs they are supposed to satisfy.

Due to their substitutive character the objects cannot any more be defined as 'use-values', in the sense of classical political economy (Marx included). Here we are not so much concerned with a material relationship between the subject and the object of consumption – in which the 'utility' lies in the materiality of the object satisfying the needs of the subject (cf. Bentham, 1789), as with a subjective relationship following the pleasure and pain principle in which the the object is defined in pure and abstract terms as an object of desire disregarding the source of that desire. Thus the marginalist 'subjective value theory' sets off with a rejection of the 'metaphysics of use value' (Falk, 1982; cf. Baudrillard, 1975, 1981) and focuses on the individual fixing his or her desires on a range of objects. This has already been expressed in the modification which the pre-marginalist representative for subjective value theory, Nassau Senior, made to the universalistic concept of utility: 'Utility denotes no intrinsic quality in the things which we call useful, it merely expresses their relations to the pains and pleasures of mankind' (Senior, 1836; cited in Dobb, 1973: 107).

The consumer society is constituted precisely on the consumption of the exceeding part liberated from its original (?) curse (Bataille's *la part maudite*) and prohibition (Forbidden Tree) and finally generalized to the whole world of goods. In other words, we are consuming supplements in the irreducible double sense the term has in French language (*supplément*) – as *addition* and *substitute* (cf. to *supplant*) – and which Derrida deconstructs out of Rousseau's conception on writing:

> Supplement adds itself, it is a surplus, a plentitude enriching another plentitude, the *fullest measure* of presence. [. . .] But the supplement supplements. It adds only to replace. It intervenes or insinuates itself *in-the-place-of*; if it fills, it is as if one fills a void. [. . .] As substitute, it is not simply added to the positivity of presence, it produces no relief, its place is assigned in the structure by the mark of an emptiness. (Derrida, 1976: 144–5).

But the dual sense of the supplement as both addition and substitute is also linked to another ambiguity which may be characterized with the concepts of 'complement' and 'subtraction' being in itself or causing 'deficit'. If the state preceding the supplement is conceived of as a state of deficiency – contrary to Rousseau's idea of original perfection – then the supplement may be understood not only as a substitute but as a complement, an *inside* addition taking the vacant place left by the lacking object. But if the preceding (or original) state is conceived of as completeness (Rousseau) the supplement is defined as an *external* – excessive and superfluous – addition disrupting the original harmony. Thus it is re-defined as an actual diminution and 'subtraction' or transformed into a substitute for the real and original, producing and/or articulating the lack. The substitute, taking the place of the original (authentic) as a mere 'stand in' (the-place-of), never fills the place of that substituted and hence it becomes a sign of the lack (loss), 'the mark of an emptiness' (Derrida, 1976: 145).

Illustrated as a procedural scheme starting from the produced addition, Rousseau's 'supplementary logic' looks something like this (Figure 5.1).[11] The addition interpreted as excess breaks the harmonic state of perfection thus causing a state of imperfection or deficit or, alternatively, the addition is revealed to be a substitute which does not correspond to the lost original and is thus redefined as a subtraction causing deficit. The loop from deficit to surfeit sets off the accelerating dynamics of the supplement-generator.

Only if the substitute, standing in and for, is granted the status of an *equivalent* (corresponding or even being identical to the original/lost one *as*

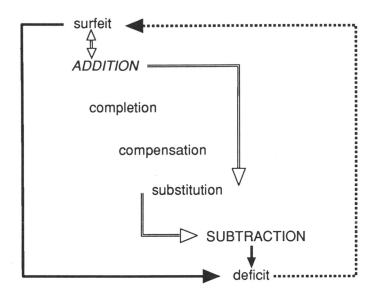

Figure 5.1 *Rousseau's first supplementary scheme*

an object of desire and filling completely its place) it regains the status of a *complement*. This implies, however, that the empty place complemented (filled in) is generalized and abstracted into an objectless lack or, in positive terms, into an objectless desire focusing on alternative objects which stand *in* and *for* each other.

The concept of an objectless desire does away with the whole supplement dilemma transforming the distinction of original vs. substitute (natural vs. artificial, etc.) itself into an unnecessary 'supplement' – but at the cost of confronting a further problem: the postulation of desire as a universal *energetic principle*.

According to the energetic principle of desire the procedural scheme of the supplement-generator is, in its simplest form, merely the productive relation from the never-ending desire for addition. But it may also be formulated in two more detailed forms: as a positive striving towards an abstract ideal of completion, or negatively, as a ceaseless (metaphoric) thirst demanding satisfaction.

This is the *perpetuum mobile* behind the rise and progress of the civilization and this is precisely the line adopted in the civilization-affirmative interpretations concerning both economic man and moral/aesthetic man especially articulated in the traditions of British utilitarian and moral-philosophical thought. Let us start with economic man and consequently return to the problem of the supplement to the topic of consumption.

The economic man

The marginalist discourse, which takes the psychological interpretation of utilitarian principles to their extreme, naturalizes desire into an anthropological constant according to the hedonistic and utilitarian principles. Man's desire is an energetic principle manifesting itself in the pursuit of pleasure (and avoidance of pain) further expanded to include other – indirect and instrumental – individual 'goods' (cf. Bentham, 1789).[12]

This is the basic outline of *homo oeconomicus*, both as consumer and as producer. As a consumer he is acting in accordance with the 'law of variety' (in human requirements) formulated by Senior (1836) and later characterized by Jevons as follows:

> The necessaries of life are so few and simple that a man is soon satisfied in regard to these, and desires to extend his range of enjoyment. His first object is to vary his food; but there soon arises the desire of variety and elegance in dress; and to this succeeds the desire to build, to ornament and to furnish – tastes which, where they exist, are absolutely insatiable, and seem to increase with every improvement in civilization. (Jevons, 1970: 103 [1871])[13]

As producer he abstains from the pleasures of immediate realization and orients himself towards some postponed and anticipated utility. Senior calls this 'third productive principle' *abstinence*, a characteristic of the entrepreneur which embodies the 'factor of production' called capital. 'Abstinence stands', according to Senior, 'in the same relation to profit as labour does to wages' (Senior, 1836; cited in Dobb, 1973: 104).

The abstinence of Senior's ideal entrepreneur is not, however, pure asceticism. The ascetic aims not only to fight the temptation (the realization of desires) but to extinguish the desire itself (cf. Foucault, 1988a; Harpham, 1987). Economic man as a producer, on the other hand, postpones the immediate pleasure in order to reach the higher – or better: quantitatively greater – utility and thus he maintains the state of desiring, the state of non-realization.

Here the civilizing refinement of desires and pleasures is realized as a process of *rationalization*: an ability to resist immediate pleasures and to orient towards mediated or instrumental utilities in a calculated manner. Thus the self-interested pleasure and pain principle is complemented and controlled by the calculation of costs and benefits.

The moral and aesthetic man

If economic man incarnates the refinement of pleasures and desires as rationalization and evolution of self-control, his virtuous brother, the moral and/or aesthetic man, depicted by the British moralists in the fifteenth and sixteenth centuries, represents another line of human development which is more aptly characterized as *cultivation* and a process of self-improvement. The process is primarily conceived of as an endogenic one – even if, more or less, susceptible to educational intervention – resembling the concept of *sublimation* Freud was to formulate some centuries later. Both discourses involve an energetic principle of desire which is not only subjected to (self)control on the basis of ascetic or rational principles (cf. abstinence) but actually transformed into higher moral, aesthetic or psychic faculties of the human mind. According to the British moralists the lower (physical) pleasures are not denied or post-poned but cultivated to the higher and even greater pleasures of 'sympathy' and the 'moral sense', as David Hartley (1749; Monro, 1972: 123–40) put it. Basically a similar idea – though lacking moral tones – is also found in the psychoanalytical interpretation of the development of the human individual.

The sense of morality and beauty – interconnected in the concept of 'taste' ([Lord] Shaftesbury, 1699) – derives from the same faculty of the human mind which is, on the one hand, a natural characteristic but, on the other hand, a potentiality to be actualized through cultivation. Neverthe-less, on the basis of the energetic principle of desire there is a continuum from the lower pleasures to the higher ones and thus the pleasure seeking is merely reoriented to other objects offering other kinds of pleasure.

This is the basic idea in Edmund Burke's (1792 [1757]) sensualistic aesthetics (Grimminger, 1986) which draws a line from the bodily (and maternal) origins of hedonistic pleasure to the 'sympathy of love', and further to the 'experience of beauty' (Schaper, 1987). Accordingly, Burke still emphasized the essential link between 'taste' as a sensation and as a reflective (aesthetic) judgement – a link which was subsequently broken in Kant's 'pure' reflective aesthetics (Kant, 1987 [1790]).

Purified pleasure

Kant distinguishes three types of delight: delight in the 'agreeable' which is based on inclination, delight in the 'good' based on respect, and delight in the 'beautiful' based on favour (*Gunst*). The first two delights are 'interested', that is, the relationship to the object involves a desire either because the object renders immediate 'gratification' (the 'agreeable' sensual pleasures) or because the object is defined as 'good' due to an external (for example, moral) purpose. In contrast to these two the third delight is 'disinterested' representing the primary realm of the judgement of taste which is merely 'contemplative'. Accordingly, this judgement is 'indifferent to the existence of the object' and it considers 'the character of the object only by holding it up to our feeling of pleasure and displeasure' (Guyer, 1979: 170–87; Kant, 1987 [1790]: 51).

Regarding the object-relation, Kant's conception of aesthetic pleasure goes beyond both of the two models for desire and pleasure refinement. The subjectivized principle of utility (from Senior to the marginalists) transforms the object into an abstraction which exists only insofar as it is related to the 'pains and pleasures of mankind' (Senior), understood as the

pains and pleasures of the *individual* man (marginalists). Nevertheless, the
desire is oriented hedonistically towards immediate pleasure in spite of the
rationalistic principle which directs the conduct to intermediate and
instrumental 'utilities'. The same energetic principle of desire is at work
also in the pursuit of higher (moral and/or aesthetic) pleasures, formulated
by the British moralists, only now with the difference that the pleasures
themselves are cultivated into higher forms corresponding to the sublimated object choices; gaining pleasure from compassionate feelings and
experiences of beauty.[14]

In contrast to the rationalization and cultivation interpretations, Kant's
conception of aesthetic pleasure implies a process of *purification* which
denies its 'lower' origins and excludes the desire (as a manifestation of
interest) from the object-relation, introducing a type of pleasure which
ultimately transforms the relation into a non-relation. A beautiful object
'merely pleases' (Guyer, 1979: 170) without constituting any relationship
to the object, and all the more so because it is 'indifferent to the existence
of the object'. The delight in the beautiful is not conceived of as a higher
stage of pleasure but as a negation of all pleasure defined in terms of
desire. Cultivation turned into purification and denial produces a paradoxical definition of delight as that which negates pleasure and likewise forms a
paradoxical relation to the object, simultaneously denying any relationship
to it. Or as Derrida puts it:

> The purely subjective affect is provoked by what is called beautiful, that which is
> said to be beautiful: *outside*, in the object and independently of its existence.
> [. . .] *The entirely-other cathects me with pure pleasure by depriving me both of
> concept and enjoyment.* (Derrida, 1987: 47)

Kant depicts a transcendental subject of pleasure characterized by a
paradoxical unity of an ascetic ideal (the extinction of desire) and an
imaginary substitute-pleasure. The experience of the beautiful transcends
the realm of consumption – and thus the dilemma of the supplement – by
introducing a principle of non-consumptive consumption devoid of all
desire. The supplement (as desire and that desired) belongs to the lower
and interested delights of the agreeable, offering immediate gratification
and including the other 'goods' (utilities) subsumed to an external purpose
– be it moral or amoral and instrumental in the self-interested utilitarian
sense of accumulating the future pleasure realization (abstinence).

But as we shall discover, even the detached and distanced 'indifference'
towards objects – and towards the world in general – occupy an important
role in modern consumption, though not primarily in the ideally 'cool'
mode corresponding to Kant's reflective aesthetic attitude but rather in the
auto-affective and masturbatory forms of imaginary 'self-consumption'
(Campbell, 1987: 77; see below pp. 139–40) – a theme which surfaced
already in Robert Burton's *The Anatomy of Melancholy* (1621) as one of
the major ills of 'idleness',[15] and which has been the key topic also in the
later characterizations of the 'disease of civilization' (B.S. Turner, 1982) –
from George Cheyne's *English Malady* (1733) and William Stukeley's

Spleen (1722) to George M. Beard's *Neurasthenia* (1869, 1881) and Freud's first formulations of 'neurosis' (1895).

Desire historicized

The universalized energetic principle of desire – both as crude hedonism and in its refined forms (rationalization, cultivation and sublimation up to the limits of purification and denial) – shares common ground with those explanations of the rise and constitution of modern consumerism which locate the 'primal cause' within man and not in the external apparatus producing the supplement, that is, the economic system of (surplus) production. Here I not only refer to the marginalist (neo-classical) conceptions but also to a range of sociological and historical interpretations – from Thorstein Veblen (1970 [1899]) and Gabriel Tarde (1962 [1890]) to Pierre Bourdieu (1984) and from Werner Sombart (1922 [1912]) and John Nef (1958) to the contemporary, historically more subtle approaches (for example, McKendrick et al., 1982 and Mukerji, 1983). In general terms, this is the approach also represented by Colin Campbell (1987) and Grant McCracken (1988) to which I shall return later on.

The *universality* of the energetic principle of desire very soon leads, however, into difficulties when explaining the *historical* character of modern consumerism (or the consumer society), and consequently to a need to complement the explanation with exogenous factors: desire is a universal potentiality which is actualized and realized according to evolving abilities which again are dependent on the production of (new) means of satisfaction. The actualization of 'higher' needs or desires is not only paralleled but made possible by the progress in (surplus) production. And thus we are back to the dual explanation: from desire to object and from object to desire (cf. above; the tautological definition of desire and utility).

In this respect the historical and sociological interpretations follow another line of argument. In order to explain the constitution of modern consumption the historical and sociological constitution of the desire or 'metaphoric thirst' itself must be explained – without relegating it to a mere effect of the (surplus) production. This is the explanatory strategy already developed by Rousseau and used as the 'second' explanation based on biased human nature (*amour-propre*) which gives impetus to the creation of the additional, excessive and supplementary.

The historical and sociological models dealing explicitly with modern consumption locate the problem in a more specific historical context compared with Rousseau's macro level of 'civilization'. Now the roots of modern consumerism are related to those of modern society in general and the origins are located in Western history somewhere between the sixteenth and nineteenth centuries, depending on whether the origins are identified with the first symptoms or with the massive breakthrough of consumer society.

In the following my aim is to demonstrate how the dilemma of the supplement figures in the historically and sociologically specified explanations of modern consumption – starting from some 'classical' schemes and then moving to the contemporary interpretations. I will start from Norbert Elias' conception of 'the civilizing process' (1978, 1982 [1939]) which may be regarded as an historicized and sociologized variation of the refinement schemes outlined above.

The hydraulics of deficit and compensation

Elias' basic idea may be characterized as follows. Contrary to the endogenic refinement schemes, Elias emphasizes the exogenic (social) nature of the 'civilizing process'. He still operates with an energetic principle but reduces it to man's affective disposition which manifests itself both in sexual and aggressive forms.

Due to external restrictions and control – the monopolization of the use of physical force by the state which results in the pacification of social intercourse – the immediate affective conduct is turned into 'inner' emotionality. Or, to put it in simple terms, the whole story of modern man boils down to the transformation process in which external control is internalized into 'self-control' – combining the Weberian concept of 'rationalization' with the Freudian concept of 'super-ego'[16] – defining and maintaining the boundaries to immediate bodily expression of drives and passions. Consequently, as a kind of compensation, an inner world of imagination and experience (*Innerlichkeit*) opens up in which the affective impulses are realized imaginarily in the form of emotions.

The civilizing process transforms the drives and passions into a harmless imaginary consumption the raw material for which is supplied by the fictional production:

> Life becomes in a sense less dangerous, but also less emotional or pleasurable, at least as far as the direct release of pleasure is concerned. And for what is *lacking* in everyday life a *substitute* is created in dreams, in books and pictures. So, on their way to becoming courtiers, the nobility read novels of chivalry; the bourgeois contemplate violence and erotic passions in films. (Elias, 1982: 242; my italics)

When related to the broader theme of modern consumption the above characterization seems to cover only a part of it. It concerns primarily the consumption of cultural products and especially the expanding realm of mass culture (which, however, falls outside the historical scope of Elias' study). But so far as the whole world of consumer goods is turned into *representations* – the material carriers of meanings and images – the difference between fiction as commodities and commodities as fiction is becoming more and more blurred.[17]

Thus the world of goods supplying fuel to imaginary self-consumption is defined as a realm of substitutes which discharge the affective 'pressure'

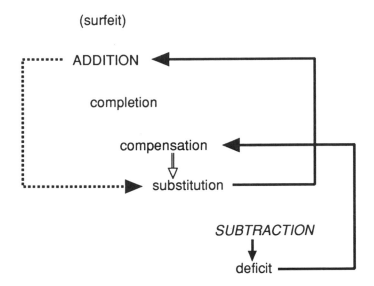

Figure 5.2 *The hydraulics of the 'civilizing process'*

(the term Elias repeatedly uses) without the harmful and uncivilized consequences of their actual realization – or in psychoanalytical terms, excluding the 'acting out' of inner impulses. But of course with regard to modern consumption as a whole this is still only a partial explanation which requires supplementing with other factors which I will return to in the next chapter.

In Elias' 'theory of civilizing processes' (Elias, 1982: 229–333) the energetic principle of desire is transformed into a hydraulics of 'drive-control and drive-transformation' (Elias, 1982: 307) which is primarily understood as a channelling of the (drive) pressure into socially accepted and surrogate modes of imaginary consumption. But now the energetic principle – conceived as hydraulic pressure – is historicized into an outcome of certain historical and social structures regulating the immediate *ex-pression* ('pressing out', in a literal or hydraulic sense) of drives and passions.[18] Thus the inferential chain of the supplementary starts not with an addition but rather with a subtraction, with the blocking out of the 'natural' outlets and the creation of substitute and compensatory 'safety valves' instead. Outlined into a procedural scheme the supplement-generator of modern consumption would look something like Figure 5.2. The blockade of affect expression as subtraction causing deficit is compensated for by substitute channels of self-consumption stimulating the addition of these substitute means.

According to Elias' hydraulic model the control of affect is not necessarily conceived of as a repressive system. On the contrary, it is the prerequisite for the constitution of modern sociability. But if the 'animal-istic' drive pressure is replaced by a normative conception of 'true human nature', the realization of which is hindered by these restraints, we are back to the civilization-critical interpretations which in the nineteenth century were targeted both against the repressive character of bourgeois society (from Saint-Simon and Fourier to Marx and his followers) and against 'mass society' promoting the 'democratization' of mediocrity – in the nineteenth century from Tocqueville to Nietzsche and the 'crowd psychologists' such as Gustave Le Bon and in the twentieth century, more exactly in the 1930s, exemplified for example by Ortega y Gasset and F.R. Leavis (see Brantlinger, 1983: 113–221; Swingewood, 1977: 1–23). In the twentieth century attention was also directed more specifically towards mass culture, mass consumption and the mass media as the main ingredi-ents for the deformation of true human nature preventing its actualization.

For example, in the Marxist tradition the critique of mass culture or 'culture industry' (especially the Frankfurt school: Horkheimer, Adorno, Marcuse and Lowenthal) locates the source of the deficit in the sphere of production. Alienated wage labour suppresses humanity and produces a deficit, a state of deprivation in terms of real needs or self-realization, thus demanding compensation (cf. Brantlinger, 1983: 222–48; Jay, 1973: 173–218). To simplify, the pursuit of compensation takes place in life outside work – in various (escapist) leisure-time activities, in the privacy of family life, hobbies, mass culture, consumption, etc. (cf. Cohen and Taylor, 1976).

According to the hydraulic model the pendulum-like dynamics of deficit and compensation may be regarded as an unproblematic rhythm of life corresponding to the duality of activity (work) and rest (recreation). But postulating 'real needs' turns most forms of compensation into substitutes which fail to meet these needs thus leaving them frustrated. Men are turned into the passive audience of mass culture or consumers longing endlessly for ever brand new goods.

Thus, once again we are entering the world of endless substitute chains: actual life is replaced by imaginary worlds of daydreaming nourished by the 'culture industry' (Horkheimer and Adorno, 1972 [1944]) or 'con-sciousness industry' (Enzensberger, 1974) and – as the realm of substitu-tion is expanded – the vacuum is filled up also with consumer goods offering empty promises of fulfilment. Real needs are dulled by unneeded things, circuses and other time-passing entertainment.

Here the source of the deficit is still located outside the apparatus supplying material for substitute compensation (addition). However, if it is placed within the same mechanism and unified into one principle we are close to an interpretation which could be called a *manipulation model* – referring primarily to the critiques of mass culture, mass consumption and advertising presented after the Second World War. It is structurally analogous to Rousseau's scheme of 'addition causing deficit' but is now specified historically in terms of modern mass consumption redefining the consumer as an innocent victim manipulated by the vicious apparatus of surplus production.

Manipulation nullifies the long and troublesome process of refinement and sublimation diminishing the consumer into a childlike being who seeks for immediate gratification. Typically this line of thought appears in conceptions concerning the manipulative power of advertising, exemplified by Vance Packard's classic book *The Hidden Persuaders* (1957). According to Packard, marketing and advertising represent 'regress rather than progress for man in his long struggle to become a rational and self-guiding being' (Packard, 1979: 13 [1957]).

The purest form of manipulation model is primarily found in moralizing discourses. In the more analytic discourses the origin of deficit is traced to other factors besides the apparatus producing addition. Thus, for example, Lasch's (1980, 1985) psychoanalytically inspired interpretation of the rise of the *Culture of Narcissism* (1980), and the 'narcissistic orientation to experience' (1985: 185) it nourishes, refer not only to the productive effects of the mass consumption–culture–media complex but also to the altered conditions for primary socialization (see also Kovel, 1981). Or listed in a condensed form:

> the emergence of the egalitarian family, so-called; the child's increasing exposure to other socializing agencies besides the family; and the general effect of modern mass culture in breaking down distinctions between illusions and reality. (Lasch, 1985: 185)

Nevertheless, the addition-apparatus is in essence responsible for the creation of the passive, regressive and 'oral' modern man – as a consumer.

This is basically a portrait of the 'masses' characterized by the novelist Wilkie Collins in mid-nineteenth century (Swingewood, 1977: 104) as 'the unknown public' and who are offered the role of passive spectators (audience) and consumers in the discourses on *mass* culture and *mass* consumption from Collins' times to our own. The portrait is conventionally modelled by the lower classes of the society, from workers to the expanding middle classes, with the moralistic aim of educating the regressive and irrational consumer who merely 'eats' into himself with his mouth, eyes, mind and, through purchase, takes in(to) possession any thing 'agreeable'.

But the regressive and 'oral' consumer has an alter ego depicted already in the sociological discourses of the late nineteenth century. These discourses render 'social comparison' (Rousseau) a constitutive role in the generation of desire – now specified as the disposition and conduct of the modern consumer. Desire is conceived of as socially constructed and as a phenomenon gaining general significance in the mobile modern condition, making both positions and possessions more attainable than ever before – starting from the higher levels of the hierarchy and expanding gradually to the lower ones.

The social construction of desire

As noted above, Rousseau's second formulation of the vicious circle of supplement has its starting point in the false self-love of man (*amour-propre*), or the disposition to compare with and outdo the other. This is the basic formula for the social construction of desire presented in the late nineteenth century in two well-known formulations. One is Thorstein Veblen's *Theory of the Leisure Class* (1970 [1899]) and the other (lesser known) is presented by Gabriel Tarde, especially in his study on the *Laws of Imitation* (1962 [1890]). The former emphasizes the competitive and the latter the imitative aspect of social comparison but, all the same, the basic idea of the social origins and constitution of 'metaphoric thirst' (desire) – acting as the primary impetus of the supplementary dynamics – remains the same. In the following I shall concentrate on Tarde's 'laws of imitation' as a means of illustrating the basic line of argument which is largely applicable to Veblen's scheme too.

Tarde does not postulate desire as an anthropological constant – contrary to his contemporary and opponent Emile Durkheim (see Durkheim, 1951 [1897]). Desire is constituted in the dynamics of social relations governed by 'laws of imitation'. These laws are, according to Tarde, the sole foundation for social harmony and progress, but two of them in particular – the first and second 'extra-logical' laws of imitation (Tarde, 1962: 189–243 [1890]) – are closely related to the topic of consumption.

According to the first extra-logical law imitation proceeds 'from within to without', or, 'from the inner to the outer of man' (Tarde, 1962: 199). Only in appearance have people begun by imitating the outer signs of those superior. But in fact imitation begins with the internalization of inner characteristics, those of spiritual and mental nature. In other words, 'imitation of ideas precedes the imitation of their expression' and 'imitation of ends precedes the imitation of means'. The new things desired are primarily 'new ends' creating 'needs for a novel kind of consumption' (Tarde, 1962: 207) and are only secondarily new means or expressions for the old ones.

The second extra-logical law of imitation determines that imitation proceeds from the inferior to the superior (Tarde, 1962: 213–14) implying a hierarchical structure of imitation in which the lower looks upon the higher. This 'relation of model to copy, of master to subject' (p. 214) is the basic constellation of historical universality. Or, as Tarde notes, 'in all periods, the ruling classes have been or have begun by being the model classes' (Tarde, 1962: 198–9). But modern society – as Tarde understood it in the late nineteenth century – gives a greater degree of freedom to imitation in the opposite direction (from superior to inferior) even if the basic order remains predominant: 'it is also the inferior who, in a certain measure, much less, to be sure, is copied, or is likely to be copied, by the superior' (Tarde, 1962: 215).

Both directions of imitation are, however, in accordance with the basic principle of imitation present in all forms of human intercourse which Tarde reduces to a dyadic situation: 'when two men are together for a long time, whatever may be their difference in station, they end by imitating each other reciprocally, although, of the two, the one imitates much more, the other much less' (Tarde, 1962: 215). Thus Tarde replaces the energetic principle of desire with that of imitation. Imitation is regarded as the contagious aspect of social interaction reaching from the lower level of stimulus and response (contagious yawn or laughter) to the higher level of ideas and manners.

Tarde's concept of imitation gains the status of a transcendental principle and in this respect it is reminiscent of the concept of 'mimetic desire' presented by René Girard, even if the scope of thematization differs significantly (Girard, 1977; 143–68; 1987: 283–98). Furthermore, Girard's mimetic desire is postulated as a universal principle of human conduct and cultural evolution, and even beyond this applicable in an ethological context too.

Both Tarde's *imitation* and Girard's *mimetic desire* are basically object-less and, accordingly, both of them emphasize the pre- or non-representational character of imitation/mimesis. In other words, a desire expressed towards an object is not constituted due to its representational role – as 'standing for', being symbol of, or representing something valued and desired. An object is desired only derivatively on the basis of an imitative relation to the other subject. proceeding 'from within to without', to 'expressions' (Tarde), or by adopting mimetically the other's desire and resulting in a rivalry concerning the other's object of desire (Girard).[19] Tarde's scheme starts from the imitative relationship between subjects (copy to model) then extending to external signs (including objects) as positive representations while Girard's scheme starts from the 'rivalry over objects' (Girard, 1987: 19) in which the other's desire for the object constitutes, on the basis of reciprocity, the object of desire in general.

Tarde does not see any problem in the move from universal imitative disposition to the realm of representations. Imitation proceeds 'from within to without' – from the spiritual characteristics of the model to the outer signs (conduct and objects) – somehow naturally. A likewise natural fact, according to Tarde, is that the inferior is more likely to imitate the superior than the other way around. But Girard's theory is in this respect much more ambitious: it is a theory of the 'origins' of both *desire* and *representation* or, taken together, of the origins of *culture*. Mimetic desire is a transcendental (energetic) principle already present in the wild and war-like state of nature (Hobbes). Nevertheless, the same principle prevails in the pacified state of culture (Order) created and reproduced through the ritual 'sacrificial substitution' (Girard, 1977: 250–73) which channels the open violence of the mimetic desire towards the victim representing all the members of the community.[20]

Although Girard emphasizes the continuum from ethology (animal behaviour) to ethnology (or human conduct), both dominated by the principle of mimetism,[21] the pacified state of culture actually constitutes mimetic *desire* as a state of non-realization. After all, if open violence in the struggle over the other's object of desire is controlled more or less effectively by ritual means (later crystallized into Law prohibiting imitation; Girard, 1987: 10–19), then desire is transformed into a state of being, that is, constituted as desire (non-possession) in the proper sense. On the other hand, the (other's) object of desire is transformed into a *representation* standing for the other who has or is imagined to have access to it. This is where the other's object of desire becomes indistinguishable from the other's object of *possession*.

So even if the metaphysical foundation of imitation or mimetic desire anchors the concept in the realm of non-representation – as 'primary mimetism' (Girard, 1987: 294) – it becomes representational as soon as it is interpreted as an element in social dynamics. The desire for an object is not constituted in a dyadic subject–object relation but in a triangular drama in which the third corner is occupied by the other subject (the 'rival'). Thus, whether the basic motive is to be like the other (Tarde) or to take the place of the other (Girard) the objects desired and/or possessed by the other gain a representational character – standing for and signifying the (desire of the) other. When oriented to an object the mimetic desire is necessarily directed to a 'substitute' or sign standing in-the-place-of the other and hence not being the other.

As long as the conflictual acquisitive mimesis is controlled by ritual means (the 'surrogate victim')[22] and by laws prohibiting imitation (cf. Girard, 1987: 10–19) the representational character of desired objects (from women, food and weapons to the expanding range of other 'valuables') are not transformed into elements in a dynamics of imitation. For the representational character of desired objects to become an element in this dynamic system presupposes a certain degree of *free movement* of both objects and subjects and, accordingly, a certain degree of *separation* between the world of objects and the world of subjects. The concept of the *market* expresses these conditions in ideal typical form, but then the term should be given a broader sense than the narrowly economic one. And here we are already alluding to the basic preconditions of consumption, in the modern sense.

If the world were reduced to Tarde's two men imitating each other, lacking both external objects and other subjects, the imitation would never proceed 'from within' to outer expressions, beyond the simple mimetic and gestural body-language. Likewise, there would be no difference between the superior and the inferior, only reciprocal aping converging to similarity. The world is, however, built up of subjects and objects and the various relationships between them which make the two extra-logical laws of imitation possible. But only in principle: as long as there are strict boundaries (structured in terms of the 'social order') for imitation by means of outer signs and expressions, the disposition to imitate remains latent.[23] Only when these boundaries grow weaker making their transgression possible and, finally, turning the sanctions for transgression into rewards, is both the Tardean imitation and the Girardian mimetic desire actualizable as a social dynamic principle.

Surely these preconditions do not apply to modern Western society only. Nevertheless, this is the scene for their full-blown manifestation. 'Conspicuous consumption' may be traced back to its archaic forms of prestige ostentation among and between the chiefs and kings – as described in Marcel Mauss' classic essay on *The Gift* (1967 [1925])[24] – and emulative dynamics are already found within the courts and among the nobility of pre-modern Europe (cf. Elias, 1982; McKendrick et al., 1982; Mukerji, 1983). But the broader basis for imitation oriented to objects as representations is constituted as soon as the lower ranks can aspire to higher status by these representational means. This is the pattern Norbert Elias specifies to the rising bourgeoisie aping 'the nobility and its manners' (Elias, 1982. 304) and which Pierre Bourdieu in a more subtle manner updates to apply to the imitative practices (especially) of the middle classes.

The possibility of upward social mobility is, however, not enough. Imitation by means of object representations (not in the psychoanalytic sense in this context) is made possible by a (separated) world of *object-imitations*. This is precisely what mass production is basically about: producing a mass of the same and, in its purest form, to produce copies without an original.

Although the actual breakthrough of mass production and the mass market of consumer goods does not take place until the nineteenth century (see W.H. Fraser, 1981; Williams, 1982), the historical roots can be traced back to the printing 'production' of the eighteenth century – as is done by Chandra Mukerji: 'Printing, as heir to the stamping techniques used to print coins in the Middle Ages, was the first mass production technology, the first technology that would allow the mass production of exactly identical objects' (Mukerji, 1983: 16).

The growth and diversification of the mass production (of object imitations) opens up the world of consumer goods and makes possible the imitative consumption of materialized representations. By consuming – possessing and using – the *similar* the consumer identifies himself with the status, lifestyle or social identity the object stands for. Now the imitation – still structured hierarchically from lower to higher – is offered materialized external 'expressions' (Tarde) which go beyond the mimic, gestural and verbal aspects of conduct, that is, of 'manners' (Elias). The mass-produced object imitations form a reserve of words (or perhaps better: enunciations) in a material language which is not as inexhaustible as the immaterial verbal language and the use of which is conditioned by economic resources, but which, however, makes the representational imitation possible. In other words, it becomes possible to be 'like' the other, to identify oneself with the other and even gain the same status the other occupies without actually taking the place of the other.

On the other hand, the creation of a realm of representational imitation does not lead to an idyllic scene starting from upward social mobility and perhaps ending in the 'democratized' entropy where everybody is imitating one another both by non-representational and representational means. Even Tarde, who regarded this as the main tendency of modern society, also pointed to a kind of counter tendency or reaction, 'the need for individual divergence, for *dissimilation*' (Tarde, 1962: 203).

But when the perspective is shifted from the individual to the social it opens up another kind of view: the *imitation* 'of the superior by the inferior' is complemented by the other side of comparison, the pursuit of *distinction* by the superior in relation to the inferior. However, the pursuit of distinction may be present also in the relationships between those of the same status, as the pursuit to outdo the other. This is also exemplified in Mukerji's interpretation of the origins of mass production and consumption: 'the first form of mass culture, [the] popular pictorial prints' actually 'marked a deep cultural shift, the differentiation of elite from mass culture', and, generalized into consumption at large, a differentiation of elite and mass markets (Mukerji, 1983: 17).

This differentiation of mass production to masses and elite production to elites was still built upon a distinction between an original and genuine, on the one hand, and a copy or fake, on the other, insofar as it involved an imitative constellation. But the differentiation also reflected more fundamental differences in 'tastes' thus rendering the 'masses' one of its own without reducing it merely to a poor imitation.

Then again, the social dynamics of imitation and distinction is not dependent on the original or genuine vs. copy or imitation distinction. The ever more completely mass produced world of goods still functions according to these principles. This is due to the fact that the object world of consumption itself functions as a generator of ever new differences, specifically in the form of fashion but also as technical progress and systematic product differentiation and diversification; the two dimensions of change which are hardly distinguishable from the dynamics of fashion. Thus mass production – a term which itself should be conceived of in a differentiated manner: reaching from the 'nearly' handmade and unique to the true massive scale – accumulates, reproduces and recreates the reserve of material language.

There is still a difference – in a relative sense – between the original (genuine) and its copy and also between the 'original' copy and its copy and so forth. They do not disappear in the 'Age of Mechanical Reproduction' (Benjamin, 1969b [1936]). The situation is not changed even when the actual models copied and turned into mass products (the elite style) are replaced with – what I would call – innovative *prototypes* (especially design objects). It just manifests a shift from 'old' static hierarchies to 'new' dynamic ones resisting the tendency towards social homogenization. Furthermore, mass production creates its own 'rarities', as collector's items such as the 'errors' desired by the philatelists. As Michael Thompson

(1979) has pointed out, the biography of things is not reducible to buying and using (up): the things turned into 'rubbish' may be resurrected as collector's 'valuables' (see also Stewart, 1984).

Then again, even if there is an interesting link between the collector and the consumer, in the latter case the primary system of differences is, however, constituted within the world of goods as a dynamic system producing means of distinction in the form of *novelties* – including the re-invention of 'old' models, but nevertheless implying a distinction between the new and the old, the better and the poorer, or that which is 'in' and 'out' of fashion. This is, of course, a simplified depiction not only of the fashion mechanism but of the whole (economic) apparatus producing *addition*. It also seduces us towards an explanation reducing to the inner dynamics of the apparatus producing addiction by producing addition (the manipulation model). But this is precisely the reductionism the 'social construction of desire' approaches explicitly reject. The addition apparatus (production and marketing) surely has an inner dynamics of its own but the supply is – according to the social construction model – rather a response to the demand governed by 'the laws of imitation' and the principle of distinction.

Structured as a hierarchy, the social dynamics of imitation and distinction launches a process where the lower adopts the models and manners of the higher while the higher keeps a distance towards the lower by strategies of distinction. This is how Norbert Elias characterizes the dynamic relationship between the (old) nobility and the (new) bourgeoisie, and further, between the upper class and the middle class (Elias, 1982: 304–9). Here Elias is especially focusing on the diffusion of self-controlled and self-restrained manners but also referring to what could be called the *material culture of goods as representations*.

According to Elias the trickle-down process is not, however, especially successful. The imitation 'vulgarizes' the models and transforms them into 'kitsch' (Elias, 1982: 312).[25] The maintenance of the distance between the imitator and the imitated is not created, however, merely because of the lack of 'good taste' in the former but also due to the strategies of distinction of the latter, motivated by a 'social fear' for the lower ranks challenging their superior position (Elias, 1982: 304). Thus the process escalates, corresponding aptly to the expansive character of the supplement-generator.

Pierre Bourdieu in his *Distinction* (1984) emphasizes strongly the negative basis of the social construction of lifestyles and, accordingly, consumption patterns. Surely, the lower (especially the middle classes) imitate the higher but – according to Bourdieu – the whole dynamics of consumption is primarily based on the strategies of distinction of those representing 'good' or 'legitimate' taste. Thus *taste* – in its reflective sense – is for Bourdieu a purely negative category, or as he puts it:

> Tastes (i.e. manifested preferences) are the practical affirmation of an inevitable difference. It is no accident that, when they have to be justified, they are asserted

purely negatively, by the refusal of other tastes. In matters of taste, more than anywhere else, all determination is negation. (Bourdieu, 1984: 56)

According to Bourdieu, the purest aesthetic judgement as formulated by Kant is a negative principle of distinction taken to its extreme. Or, as he puts it,

[the] 'empirical' interest enters into the composition of the most disinterested pleasures of pure taste, because the principle of the pleasure derived from these refined games for refined players lies, in the last analysis, in the denied experience of a social relationship of membership and exclusion. (Bourdieu, 1984: 499)

The social dynamics of (negative) distinction formulated by Bourdieu represents, in a sense, a marginal case of the explanatory model here labelled 'social construction of desire'. The dynamics is now based on – what could be called – 'distinctive desire' which can be conceived as the complement to and counterpart of the 'mimetic desire' (Girard) in the relationship of rivalry, that is, maintaining the distance and difference towards those (classes) reaching for the same or similar position and identity by imitation. The strategies of *exclusion* presuppose, however, the strategies of *inclusion*, and vice versa, both in the weaker Tardean scheme where imitation aims at being similar to the other – especially when evaluated as higher – and in the extreme Girardian rivalry where the inclusion into the place-of-the-other presupposes the exclusion of that other from his position (corresponding to the mythical case of Oedipus).

Especially the latter (Girardian) interpretation seems to point towards something not very far from pure social Darwinism (*à la* Herbert Spencer). But, as noted above, when focused on the realm of consumption – consisting of an expanding reserve of object imitations differentiated into a likewise expanding number of sub-categories – even the Girardian 'duel' (it's either me or you) is transformed into a more civilized, or at least less obviously violent 'consumer behaviour' drawing on the representational role of 'positional goods' (Hirsch, 1975).

So far as the interpretations based on the social dynamics of imitation and distinction – both combined in the concept of 'social comparison' (Rousseau) – are presented as explanations for the generation of desire and thus the creation of material surfeit of consumption, we end up with a procedural scheme of the following kind (Figure 5.3).

Comparison affirms a state of (social) deficiency activating the pursuit of the model (imitation), or the pursuit of keeping distance from the lower or outdoing the rival (distinction). This gives impetus to the production of addition (surplus) with a loop back to comparison, and so the round begins again. Regardless of whether the starting point is located in imitation (inclusion and identification) or distinction (exclusion and separation) the procedural scheme remains the same.

Then again, the social construction model still poses severe problems, if it is presented as an explanation of the supplementary logic of modern

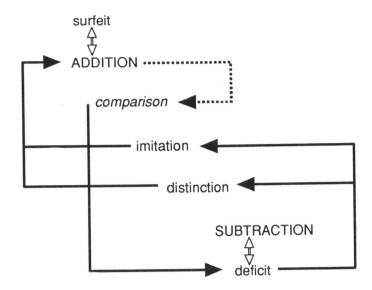

Figure 5.3 *The social construction of desire*

consumption. First, let us consider the conception which gives a primary role to the dynamics of *distinction* (esp. Bourdieu) Taken to its logical conclusion the principle of distinction moves towards practices which are beyond the supplementary logic of consumption. The system of differences upon which the 'taste' distinctions are based grow and change, primarily as a process of *intensification*, into ever more subtle distinctions rather than as a process of extensification which would merely serve to expand the material language of goods. The refinement of distinction strategies presupposes change and variation but it does not necessarily demand an endless production of novelty.

The distinction game does not require material excess, first because the existing stock of material signs offers unlimited possibilities for ever smaller differences in detail, combinations, etc.; and secondly, because the drama of fine distinctions is mainly acted (out) in the form of manners and style involving the *use* of both material and immaterial goods but not reducible to plain consumption. This is as far from the mere purchase, possession and display of 'status symbols' as the operations within the realm of 'cultural capital' (Bourdieu) are from the unidimensional socio-economic scales. In other words, the point of the distinction game, formulated by Bourdieu, lies in the elaboration of rhetoric and not in the expansion of the vocabulary.

Secondly, let us consider the conception which fixes *imitation* to a starting point. The postulation of a transcendental principle of imitation is in itself a dubious move (to say the least) and so too is the inexplicated leap into the more or less hierarchical structure specifying the roles of imitators versus the imitated. The mere existence of the other (Tarde) or the other's desire (Girard) does not suffice as a basis for an imitative disposition. There is no way to by-pass the question of *what* those who are imitated *represent* for those who imitate. The general and almost tautological answer is, of course, that those who are imitated represent something worth imitating for the imitators: the imitated are or have something the imitators are not or do not have (yet), they are or have something more than the imitators.[26] And, as it was, the realm of *object imitations* representing those who are representing something valued makes the imitator's task easier – at least in principle. It is possible to be *like* the other (at least in some respects) without being transformed into the other, either by means of cannibalistic magic (eating up the other) or by actually taking the place of the other (Girard). But then you have to know how to do it, if you can afford it, if you are included and accepted as one of them, and so forth.

Representing whom – representing what?

It seems clear that Girard is aware of the changed role of mimetic desire in the 'modern world' (Girard, 1987: 284–98). He points to the decline of ritual means of excluding mimetic rivalry, a situation which creates a chronic 'mimetic crisis'. This is the 'liberation of mimetic desire' which generalizes rivalry to the whole social dynamics 'from eroticism to professional or intellectual ambition'. The 'dynamism of desire' is re-defined into a specific characteristic of 'modern life' (Girard, 1987: 287–91). It is still based on the universalistic (energetic) principle but now it is actually realized as an effective force in social relationships. And even if Girard does not explicitly thematize consumption, he nevertheless refers to some features of the modern dynamism of desire which are undoubtedly closely related to the topic.

One of the central characteristics of the liberated mimetic desire is its escalation into a continuous and repetitive process of realization. Desire as a state of being is not maintained by (ritual) control or prohibitions preventing its actual realization but by an endless chain of realizations. The recursive realization – transforming non-possessed objects of desire into possessions and hence into non-desirables[27] – does not, however, lead to the extinction or reduction of desire (which is granted the role of a constant energetic principle) but rather reproduces it by refocusing the desire to the next, new and unexperienced, object.

The value of the object 'grows in proportion to the resistance met with in acquiring it' consequently increasing the value of the 'model' to whom it is linked and who signifies it as an object of desire (Girard, 1987: 295). And yet this is complemented with a counteracting process of devaluation in which the Girardian individual 'is always ready to condemn the objects he has once possessed and the desires he has already experienced – the idols of yesteryear – at the very moment when a new idol or a new object comes over the horizon' (Girard, 1987: 298). And so the dynamism of desire escalates into an endless process moving both subjects and objects, and when specified to consumption, moving subjects towards new objects and these towards new subjects, that is, accelerating the supplement-generator of consumption to ever higher speeds. This corresponds by and large to the simple model of the energetics of desire, except in one respect: the desire is conceived of as *socially constituted*

As noted above, for all this to function smoothly and (relatively) non-violently presupposes the existence of *object imitations*. And thus the focus is necessarily directed to the world of goods – to the markets of object imitations and to the mechanisms which, on the one hand, promote the dynamic system of differences (overdetermined by the mechanism of fashion) and on the other hand, ceaselessly transform the goods into representations (modern advertising; see Chapter 6).[28]

However, fashion and advertising are not, according to the Girardian scheme and the 'social construction' model in general, the mechanisms setting off the supplement-generator. They just respond and back up the dynamism of desire based on the universal principle of mimetic rivalry. In other words, these mechanisms exemplify the liberated movement of *objects* which is preconditioned, however, by the liberated mobility of *subjects* implying a pulling 'down of all barriers to "freedom" of desire' (Girard, 1987: 291).

But then we are faced with a further problem: how should we conceive the notion of 'realization' as a repetitive practice of the modern consumer acquiring goods as representations?

Insofar as the consumer moves in the market purchasing goods, realization is a simple act of economic exchange: buying and selling. But, of course, consumption is primarily something else and more, especially when consumption, from purchase to use (whatever it includes), is looked upon from a symbolic point of view, that is, regarding goods as representatives or representations.

If the acquisition of 'positional goods' (Hirsch) effectively grants the position these goods stand for (cf. Bauman, 1971)[29] then consumption functions as a means of gaining a certain social status and/or constructing a corresponding social identity. This may even end up in actual membership of a certain group which defines itself by excluding others (lacking those material signs, not to mention the more subtle units of imitation and distinction; manners, style, etc.). Here the possession of goods as representations functions pragmatically or (in the case of intentional conduct) *instrumentally*, as a means of realizing a specific social status or identity (in simple terms conceived of as an upward social mobility along the unilinear socio-economic scale).

Then again, consumption of goods as representations functions also as an *imaginary* practice which, in most cases, does not lead to the realization of a certain social identity. Or, related to the situation described earlier, it is always possible to identify oneself with a model by means of goods (as representations) without the affirmation of a 'realized' status based on social recognition. Now the realization takes place within the boundaries of the imaginary – or within the 'order of the simulacrum' (Girard, 1987: 17)[30] – being nevertheless still a mode of realization.

But realization in what sense? Is consumption, then, preoccupied only with 'dream worlds' (cf. Williams, 1982), turning the acquired goods into mere (transient) experiences of 'wish-fulfilment' in day dreams, in the Freudian sense? Yes and no. For this implies a shift towards consumption as *experience*, moving away from the instrumental use of goods as representations, and still further from the instrumental use of goods as material use-values. But when specified at the level of *individual self construction*, the imaginary 'realization' turns out to be effective and productive after all. Labelling such a (imaginary) mode or aspect of consumption as mere illusory compensation for the absent 'real' is not a valid argument against its efficacy in the 'self-building' of the modern individual. Referring to Lacan, even if the 'ego's function' is regarded as 'purely imaginary', as 'an agency organized to misread the truth which comes to the subject from the unconscious' (Benvenuto and Kennedy, 1986: 60) it still functions in a social network of real effects. And the same also applies to the agency named 'self' consisting of all (conscious and unconscious) functions which constitute a differential relationship to the Other – be it (m)other or ma(t)ter; subjects as objects (for 'love and/or hate' etc.) or objects as (stand-ins for) subjects.

Focusing on the theme of individual self-construction should not be understood simply as a change in viewpoint, from a social to a psychological one. The thematization of self-construction should, of course, be legitimated with a theoretically based interpretation of the cultural, social and historical factors which point (a) to the increasing emphasis on individuality (as an existential condition and mode) and (b) to the increasing significance of consumption as the stage of identity formation in the development of modern society. There is, of course, a substantial literature dealing with these themes and actually some of the discursive traditions which outline the genealogy of the 'modern individual' were already touched on above (economic man and the moral/aesthetic man; pp. 110–12). However, I will here proceed with the idea a few steps further, though in a somewhat speculative manner, before returning to the theme of the modern individual and its specific relation to the realm of consumption in a more detailed fashion.

In the following I will take up some further aspects concerning the relation of the pragmatic or instrumental and imaginary dimensions of consumption by going back to the imitative situation in which the consumer strives for a certain social status or identity by consuming goods representing the model.

In an effective case, the instrumental consumption of goods as representations may result in actual membership of a certain group and so the imitative project is completed and consumption is turned into a repro-ductive maintenance of the identity or position gained. This is, of course, a simplified hypothetical formulation which does not take into account the distinctive and exclusive strategies of the model aimed at keeping the imitator at a distance (Bourdieu). But there is still something else this formulation disregards. Goods as representations are not uncovered wholly in answers to the question 'representing *whom* . . .?' The question must be complemented with '. . . representing *what*?', an additional question which must be repeated until the answer turns to silence.

Obviously, the representational character of goods is not reduced to their role as indexes of a 'model' class, group or individual: the meanings attached to goods draw from the vast pool of shared cultural (and subcultural) representations[31] and thus the second question (representing what) is not only a complement to the first one (representing whom) but also its parallel. Goods act both as material representatives of valued models and as materializations of cultural values and ideals. In either case, they act as *positive* representations, as 'good objects' to be striven for. The point is, however, that even if the mystery of representation is approached by posing the question 'representing whom' we still end up with question-ing the 'what'.

To take a hypothetical example: what happens to a man buying a Porsche?[32] First of all, he affirms his social status and identity as one who can afford a Porsche and he may even become a member of a Porsche society (if there is one) but at least he gains a minimum identity which may be formulated into a tautology: he belongs to those who own a Porsche – whatever it means to the others with or without a Porsche.

But the questioning continues. Porsche represents those others possess-ing one, but, then again, what do they represent? Yes, they represent a highly valued lifestyle (offering prestige, etc.) which again is conceived as a realization of the image of the good life or happiness – *standing for* it and pointing, in the final count, beyond the horizon of representation towards a plain and unrepresentable 'good'. Thus, even consumption as instrumental use of material signs (representations) turns out to be, in the last instance, *imaginary* consumption aiming at – what? Yes, aiming at the 'good', or aiming at that which is *lacking*, the latter being in fact only an alternative formulation of the *good*.

The pursuit of happiness

It may well be argued that there is nothing new in the 'pursuit of happiness', or at least, nothing new in the dreams and ideals of a good world and good life. There is no human culture without mythical visions of a state devoid of any lack, of the Paradise Lost or the Kingdom of Heaven to come. These utopias located in indefinite Otherness (*u-topos*), the

models of the Good World, are primarily negations of the existing reality –
either as simple inversions of scarce life, the carnivalistic 'Land of
Cockaygne' characterized by abundance and endless pleasure, or as
elaborated depictions of Perfect Order in which well-being, virtue and
justice are finally realized.

Then again, the shift from mythical projections to utopian projects takes
us more specifically to the Western tradition, to the roots of modern
society and to the idea of progress locating the good state of being (and
beings) to the attainable temporal world (cf. Falk, 1988a). But what is
really new in the pursuit of happiness of modern (consumer) society is that
the utopian project is reduced in scale to the *individual*, into a modern
mode of self-building aiming at completion within the boundaries of one's
own self and one's own life, and that this is done primarily by means of
goods as the building bricks (McCracken, 1988: 111). This is a utopian
project of *self-fulfilment*, in the externalizing sense of the word as 'self-
realization' but also, more literally, as 'taking in' and 'filling up' the self
with something that could be called 'good objects' (to use Melanie Klein's
[1932] psychoanalytical terminology).

The individualized utopian project of self-building survives despite the
collapse of the Great Projects of Enlightenment – the Great Narratives
(Lyotard, 1984) of the modern world. And, in a way, it may be also
regarded as a, perhaps ironic, realization of the ideals of individual
freedom (of choice), self-improvement by means of good [object]s and
self-expression by means of goods as representations. Thus, the tradition
of philosophical, moral and economic ideas which build on the individual
search for happiness and count on the public virtues born out of it – that is,
the desire both *liberated, disciplined* (economic man) and *cultivated* (the
moral and aesthetic man) – becomes reality in the form of a 'consumer
society'. It may not be perfect harmony but at least it is less violent than the
original (?) 'mimetic rivalry' depicted by Girard.[33]

So, we are faced with the dilemma of a desire oriented towards
something beyond the mere mimetic relationship, towards something
which is 'always already' (Derrida) a representation, but which, nevertheless, cannot be represented. What could it be?

As it appears, even Girard fails to escape the paradox of the unrepresentable representation which is already found in the (hypothetical)
'primal scene' of mimetic desire. Although Girard postulates mimesis as
the basic principle which constitutes desire he is still forced to give some
explanation for the constitution of the mimetic relation, for example in the
following way:

> Once his basic needs are satisfied (indeed, sometimes even before), man is
> subject to intense desires, though he may not know precisely for what. The
> reason is that he desires being, something he himself *lacks* and which some other
> person *seems to possess*. (Girard, 1977: 146; my italics)

The mimetic desire returns to the order of representation after all, even if
the representation itself, towards which the desire is oriented, remains

undefined, at least almost: the other has, or is imagined to have, something the imitator lacks. Something more, better, higher, etc. Or simply, something 'good' which the imitator does not possess and hence desires.

This is of course an all too negative basis for any definition of the representation 'behind' the mimetic desire, which is now, however, something more than the object of the other's desire and, furthermore, which in fact is transformed in the above presented formulation into an object in the other's *possession*. But in another context Girard offers a second formulation which characterizes the representational basis of desire in positive terms:

> The model, being closely identified with the object he jealously keeps for himself, possesses – so it would seem – a self-sufficiency and omniscience that the subject can only dream of acquiring. The object is now more desired than ever. Since the model obstinately bars access to it, the possession of this object must make all the difference between the *self-sufficiency of the model* and the *imitator's lack of sufficiency*, the model's fullness of being and the imitator's nothingness. (Girard, 1987: 296; my italics)

Now we have the basic ingredients for a formula defining the representational character of the objects desired: they are elements the possession of which – 'so it would seem' – makes the other (model) complete or 'full' thus articulating the imperfection or 'nothingness' of the imitator. Thus, from the desiring subject's point of view we end up with the following equation: *the object of desire = a (part) object representing perfection = representing 'good' = representing something lacking.*[34]

But, as noted above, the unrepresentable representation – as perfection or plain 'good' – is only the ultimate ideal goal beyond the horizon of representation. In the chain of representations heading towards it (representing whom – representing what?), it gains a number of names, and the same applies also to the case of specified context such as the realm of consumption.

This is aptly exemplified in André Orléan's interesting article on 'Money and Mimetic Speculation' (1988: 101–12) in which he uses Girard's conceptual scheme attempting to overcome the problems that neo-classical theory has in explaining the market dynamics of consumption.[35] According to Orléan

> the Girardian individual and the subject in the marketplace are characterized by the same *radical incompleteness*: a desire whose law they do not know, one which does not resolve itself into a more or less lengthy list of objects. Like the Girardian individual, the subject in the marketplace never views his desire head-on; he always reads it obliquely in the gaze of others. This suffering from his lack of closure is something which the producer-exchanger experiences in the unforeseen conjunctures that are forever upsetting his production and consumption plans. (Orléan, 1988: 102)

This tension within the 'economic agent' leads to the emergence of 'a specific desire, the desire for *wealth*', as Orléan puts it. He proceeds with the following characterization of the concept:

> Wealth is that principle that Girard calls desire's ultimate goal, the possession of which would finally allow the subject to accede to self-sufficiency. It is what all things are measured against; it is the very substance of social evaluation. (Orléan, 1988: 102)

On the one hand, resting on the Girardian methodological individualism Orléan ends up defining the desire for wealth as 'a specific desire' deriving from the object-related desires read 'in the gaze of others'. But, on the other hand, he inevitably slides, just like Girard, into formulations which point to the primary role of the 'individual desires for fullness' (Orléan, 1988: 103). This is where the relation is inverted: the desire for wealth – as a desire to possess everything worth possessing, that is, everything 'good' – is redefined as a *general* desire which consequently is transformed into an indefinite number of *specific* desires fixed to specific objects according to the principle of mimetism.

One thing remains, however, unchanged even after this inversion: the (general) desire oriented towards the ultimate goal or 'objective' – perfection, good or wealth (in the above sense) – is still a desire lacking an object. If 'wealth' is defined in terms of objects – as a hoard of gold, silver or other 'quasi money'[36] – it is just turned into another representation of the unrepresentable; a fortune representing (the) fortune, one might say. Or, as Marx puts it in his analysis of the contradictions of wealth and its general form as money (with special reference to pre-capitalist hoarding of wealth in contrast to capitalist circulation):

> As the *general form of wealth*, the whole world of real riches stands opposite it. It is their pure abstraction – hence, fixated as such, a mere conceit. Where wealth as such seems to appear in an entirely material, tangible form, its existence is only in my head, it is a pure fantasy. Midas. (Marx, 1973: 233)

Gold (etc.) represents all the 'good things of life' it gives access and possession to. Money – whether bound to the referent (gold standard) or liberated to a 'floating signifier' – is merely a doubled representation of everything 'that money can buy'. And even if that 'everything' exists only in the order of the imaginary (as the *other's* perfection), the expansion of the world of goods makes the idea much more real-like: there is practically no end to the 'good objects' desired and acquired. This turns the 'pursuit of happiness' (*everything* desired) into an effective reality of consumption – or, better: it characterizes one of the basic traits of modern consumption, regarded in the perspective of 'self-building', which I have called the *introjective logic of consumption* (Falk, 1990).[37]

The good things of life are not reduced merely to the (good) objects of consumption. Nevertheless, the expanding consumer markets undoubtedly multiply the opportunities to define the objects of one's life (= one's self, temporalized) in terms of goods. And this may be noted without any moralizing tones and, furthermore, there is no need to apply pathologizing labels such as 'neurotic personality' (Horney, 1937) or 'narcissism' (cf. Kovel, 1981; Lasch, 1980, 1985), not in the present context, anyway.[38]

But this is only half of the story. The introjective logic of consumption is complemented and conditioned by the *distinctive logic of consumption* which I shall attempt to explicate below.

The exclusive and inclusive self

If mimetism – both in its instrumental and imaginary modes – turned out to be an individualized imaginary pursuit of completedness (the unrepresentable representation), then what could be said about the negative strategy of distinction, when transposed to the scale of individual self-construction?

As long as the principle of distinction is linked unambiguously to the social categories (class, group), self-formation is thematized merely in its social dimension – from the affirmation of social status to the construction of social identity. Taking distance – by symbolic means – from one class/ group is necessarily complemented by an affirmation of one's own class/ group identity. Or, the exclusion of 'them' implies an inclusion as one of 'us'.

In a mono-hierarchical system (cf. Bourdieu, 1984) the excluded is always defined as the 'lower', but even in a more heterogeneous social constellation – which is not governed by one hierarchy or which may even be regarded as non-hierarchical – the identities are defined in collective terms: us versus them. This is the simplest formulation of social identity which no doubt prevails also in the modern condition, but which also becomes problematic due to the dynamic character of social categorizations and due to the segmentation and fragmentation of 'life spheres'.

On the one hand, in the mimetic situation the model group acts as the reference group resulting eventually in the paradox of self-exclusion from one's 'own' group, that is, a denial of one's own social identity (in the simple sense presented above) which redefines it into something devalued and left behind. On the other hand, the fragmentation of life spheres – reaching from the basic distinctions of work vs. leisure and public vs. private to the emergent 'second-order' heterologies[39] – multiplies the reference points (that is, actual groups and autonomized representational models) of social identification resulting in 'partial' social identities which necessarily overlap in one and the same individual subject.

But the partial social identities not only overlap but may also relate in a contradictory way to each other thus problematizing the whole concept of 'social identity', as group membership or identification. This is where the sociological interpretations which tend to reduce self-formation to the social, turn either to dualistic conceptions concerning formal individuality (separateness, continuity), that is, to the social aspect of being part of some group (Simmel), or to dramaturgical metaphors reducing the partial social identities into 'roles'. Modern man is turned into a 'market-oriented' (Fromm, 1955), 'other-directed' (Riesman, 1955) or 'plural' (van den Berg, 1974) personality responding to the expectations of others and keeping his/her 'private' self behind the façade or losing it altogether (cf. Brittan, 1977: 115).

The same tendency towards dualism and absolutization of the 'social self' is manifested in the interactionist tradition – from G.H. Mead (1934; 'I' versus 'me') to Erving Goffman (1970; 'personal identity' versus 'social identity'; cf. Erikson, 1959). The whole dynamics of self-construction is conceptualized in a setting of generalized and/or abstracted social inter-action complemented, however, by the other pole of the duality. There is still a need for an instance which overrides the fragmented social identity, a need for that somebody playing the different 'roles'. This task is given to the 'personal identity' which synthetizes the contradictory elements and thus has a certain (reflective) *distance* to all of them. Consequently, the individual self – not reducible to any of the 'social selves' – is defined, in the last instance, as mere distance from the particular selves, or as an anonymous inner space created in the repeated acts of distancing. Concep-tually the personal identity (individual self) is emptied into a (teleological) principle of *self-maintenance*, which is nothing other than the construction *site* of the individual self. What happens at the site is another issue.

I am not suggesting here that we should move to the psychoanalytical scheme of ontogenesis accompanied by the argument that this is what really happens at the site: a child 'grows' into a self-maintaining being thus filling the empty place. This would merely repeat the reductionist dualism in an inverted form: individuation takes place in a separate world (family) after which the full grown individual enters into the network of social relationships (society).[40]

What I am arguing for is an approach emphasizing the *continuous* character of individual self-construction, from the ontogenic scene to 'social interaction' (as a complex of relations between subjects and objects). The argument may be formulated into two interconnected theses:

First, there is no such thing as a fully developed individual self coming out of the 'ontogenic tube'. This is because the modern conditions of social existence demand a continuous reconstruction of one's self. A child may grow up to be a 'healthy' human being, as luck has it, that is, capable of 'work and love' (Freud's simple formula for 'health'), but this does not free him/her from the burden of continuous self-building. He or she may give up the quest for individual self by becoming a part of a strong (traditional) community, such as a religious movement, but this kind of regression into a group-self (Riesman, 1955: 'traditional personality type') is a marginalized alternative in the modern condition of loose and/or sporadic social 'associations'.[41]

Secondly, the general principles underlying the formation of both 'personal' and 'social' identities are fundamentally the same, which means that the 'social' is already present in the 'personal' and vice versa.

The latter thesis may be formulated in topological terms as follows. Starting from the binary opposition of *inside/outside* – the binary oppo-sition lurking in all the others, as Derrida has noted (see Chapter 2) – we may characterize the common denominator of both 'social' and 'personal' identity as follows: both are constituted in a differential relationship to that which is conceived to be outside and thus not inside. The social or collective counterpart to Freud's distinction of *me* versus *not-me* (identified with the distinction of inside versus outside) is of course *us* versus *them* (cf. Marcel Mauss' concept of the 'person' as a collective; Mauss, 1989 [1938]). So, identity, be it social or individual, is always defined in terms of its opposite, non-identity.

In addition, the two distinctions are hierarchically structured locating the personal identity within the social one. And this applies not only to the modern condition – with its fragmented social spheres – but also to the stronger community forms from tribal societies to the pre-modern estate society. Only in exceptional cases – and sporadically – are the selves of the subjects dissolved into a (semi) symbiotic group-self – as was the case in the 'Jones-Town' tragedy in which the whole community committed suicide.

So, even the most primitive society leaves open a certain degree of individual freedom and thus makes possible 'self-interested' conduct (Bourdieu, 1977; Sahlins, 1983). This implies that the 'group-self', as characterized by Paul Parin (1978) in his study of the 'oral character' of the African Dogon culture, is still a mode of self-construction and not its denial. The members of the community must be able to act as separate beings even if their conduct is largely determined by their given *place* in the community (kinship, age group, sex, etc.).

Nevertheless, the (primitive) group-self situation does not actualize the inside/outside opposition primarily at the individual level but rather in collective terms ranging from group identity to the whole community. In other words, the group-self has not gone through the process of separation (and individuation) to that degree which from the modern individual self point of view appears as 'natural'. This implies that the factual outside of a subject is conceived of as a 'next' inside – configured as a spatial cosmology of concentric circles (Friedman, 1983) tending to identify the inside/outside opposition with that of culture (us = human) versus nature (not-us = non-human).

From an historical vantage point this is a constellation which prevails, at the expense of losing its rigidity, in all social formations whose members occupy a *prescribed* place in the social or community order. And, to make a crude simplification for reasons of economy, this is the constellation which is broken by the rise of modern society, implying a shift from the group-self towards individual self-construction. In topological terms, the opposition of inside/outside is increasingly focused on the individual self-boundaries (and bodily surface) as manifested in the discourses on self-control, self-discipline and self-cultivation especially from the sixteenth century onwards.[42] What these intellectual roots reveal (cf. Taylor, 1989) is a mode of self-construction in which the process of separation goes far beyond that of the group-self, and which then becomes generalized in the rise of modern society.

But what about the 'inclusive self', the introjective aspect of individual self-construction? How is the *inside* of the individual self thematized? Still applying the topological scheme, a fundamental change may be detected in the role of introjection – taking into one's body and/or self – in the case of individual self-construction, compared with the group-self situation. In the latter case and with the focus on the basic mode of introjection, that is, *eating*, the act of incorporation can be characterized as a *bidirectional* process. In a ritual meal, in which the community is both actualized and reproduced, the *sharing* and (bodily) *incorporation* of food also implies the incorporation of the partaker or member into the community (Kilgour, 1990; Stjernfelt, 1987). That is, while eating the shared food the subject is eaten into the community (communion). This may in fact be conceived of as an aspect of the diffuse and relative inside/outside distinction of the group-self.

In the case of individual self the introjective principle tends to turn into a *unidirectional* one – eating into the body and self without being eaten into the community. Expanding the scope to the outside as a world of objects in general (beyond the actually edible ones) the unidirectional introjection may be conceived of as an act of 'self-fulfilment', in a *literal* sense but not reduced only to the body but related to the (entity of) self. Or, to characterize the shift of emphasis in another way: the aspect of 'I belong to x' (x = community) is marginalized in the act of introjection rendering a primary position to the aspect 'x belongs to me' (x = 'goods', in whatever senses one may imagine). Accordingly, this may be conceived of as an articulation of the inside/outside opposition on the boundaries of the individual body and self (conceived of as the other side of the decline of 'group-self' communities). In other words, what is 'taken in' and what is rejected turns into an individual issue (see Chapters 2 and 4).

The consuming self

When related to the 'other side' of self-construction – separation and distinction – and incorporating the social dimension of 'belonging to' and 'sharing with'[43] (cf. above: the theme of social identity), the outside is surely something more heterogeneous than a world of desired objects (to be taken into one's body or self). It is a network of object and subject relations which relativizes the dichotomy of outside/inside. Hence, I am not arguing for an atomistic model in which autonomous units – both subjects and objects – cruise around charged either with positive or negative ions.

Nevertheless, when the outside is specifically related to the realm of consumption, *qua* the historical *novum* – which is simultaneously a world of object imitations, making mimetism by means of objects possible, and a dynamic system of differences, harnessing the world of goods to the purposes of distinction – we still end up with the constellation of subject versus objects (of consumption) emphasizing the inside/outside opposition on the level of individual self-boundaries. Only now the world of goods is not reduced to 'good objects' but manifests itself rather as a 'material' language articulating or making visible to the subject those objects which are 'not for me' precisely because they represent specified other(s) towards which they want to maintain a distance – and distinction.

This turns the imitative principle upside down: the object is desired not because it belongs to or represents the (valued) other but, on the contrary, because it does not belong to, or represent the (non-valued) other. In other terms, the realm of the objects of consumption exists now not only as desired but also as non-desired objects; thus we are complementing the portrait of the modern consumer with a more 'civilized' characteristic, that is, with the ability of making 'object choices' applying both positive and negative evaluation. A choice always implies an exclusion of the alternative but now it is not only an inevitable outcome but an act of reflection preceding the decision.[44]

But, as noted above, when the distinctive logic (of consumption) is taken to the individual extreme – or alternatively formulated, when it is thematized as an aspect of individual self-construction which cannot be reduced to social identity – it becomes disconnected from the hierarchical orders (Bourdieu, 1984) of 'us versus them' or those one wants to identify with and those one wants to distance oneself from (effectively and/or imaginarily). This is of course an idealization but as such it may be justified as a characterization of a tendency towards an increased emphasis on individuality.

Thus we may construct a parallelism of the social dynamics of consumption and its counterpart in individual self-construction – a parallelism which, furthermore, points to a shift of emphasis from social identity to the individual one (Figure 5.4).

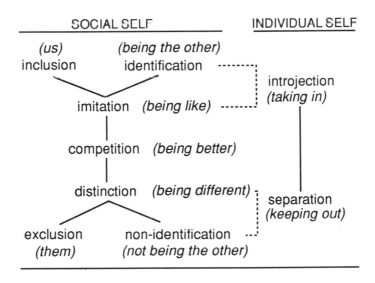

Figure 5.4 *The relation of social self to the individual self*

Viewed from either perspective – the social and the individual, both located on the same continuum – the realm of modern consumption functions as the primary mechanism supplying material for both ends of the scale. In social terms, it serves both *imitation* (realized as inclusion or as imaginary identification) and *distinction* (with corresponding alternative realizations). In terms of individual self-construction these two poles may be equated with the two aspects of self: *introjection* (or that which is 'taken in' to one's body or self) and *separation*, or the maintenance and articulation of (body/self) boundaries.

The principle of distinction or separation appears to be an unproblematic one. It figures both as an element in social differentiation – without which society would collapse into an entropic mass – and as a prerequisite of individual existence: there simply has to be a difference and hence an individual distinctiveness. Then again, the principle of imitation or introjection still remains a mystery, as noted earlier when tracing the chain of representations beyond the horizon (see the section 'representing whom – representing what?'). We still lack an explanation for the introjective logic of consumption and its relation to the distinctive one. This brings us back to the problem of *desire* – as a characteristic of consumer behaviour and as an impetus for the supplement-generator of the 'consumer society'.

In the following I shall approach the mystery of desire via a description of two recent interpretations, by Colin Campbell (1987) and Grant McCracken (1988), focusing strictly on their depictions of the modern consumer as a subject of desire.[45]

The evolution of the modern hedonist

Campbell outlines in his book *The Romantic Ethic and the Spirit of Modern Consumerism* (1987) a 'civilizing process' in which the traditional hedonist, who indulged in sensual pleasures is transmuted into the modern hedonist entertaining himself with the imaginary and the emotional. The evolutionary process is completed when the 'soul' of the modern hedonist inhabits the more profane body of the modern consumer, standing as he does amidst the landscape of commodities.

The traditional hedonist oriented to the realization of sensual pleasures, is transformed into a consumer of imaginary pleasures. The shift of emphasis 'from sensations to emotions' manifests an opening of an 'internal psychic world' (Campbell, 1987: 70–1) in which the pleasures are realized imaginatively. Here is the 'romantic self' (Campbell, 1983) within which the evolution continues as 'deliberate cultivation of emotions' (Campbell, 1987: 71). Hence the modern hedonist gains features reminiscent of Kant's 'pure aesthetic': the inner experiences of pleasure are refined, if not into 'disinterested' pleasures then at least into emotions lacking any compulsion towards realization or even presupposing the exclusion of a realization (interest), focused on an external object.

Moreover, Campbell's modern hedonist *realizes* his or her pleasures – but at an imaginative level. This is still consumption, however, even if it has been transferred into the imaginary realm. It is 'self-consumption' (Campbell, 1987: 77) but as such nevertheless realizing. This is a characterization which brings Campbell's modern hedonist very close to the reader of fiction (or the cinema spectator) depicted by Norbert Elias (1982). But now – in contrast to Elias' interpretation – the 'self-consumption' taking place in the 'inner psychic world' is not understood as substitutive and compensatory. Campbell's 'self-consumption' is an outcome of a refinement of pleasures rather than a substitute release of repressed desires. It is sublimation rather than substitution caused by external or internal(ized) denial. Self-consumption manifests simultaneously both auto-erotic pleasure and sublimated pleasure of the moral-aesthetic subject replacing the sensual experience with emotions and, furthermore, the lower emotions with the higher ones – such as the pleasure gained in empathy, in the imaginary identification with the other's suffering (*Mitleid*, translatable as 'co-suffering').

Yet we are still left with the problem: how are we to explain the transformation of the imaginary self-consuming hedonist into a consumer oriented to *external* objects? The modern hedonist may easily be conceived of as a reader of novels or a movie watcher or even as a 'window-shopper' but why would he regress back to realizing material consumption just when he has reached the higher level of imaginary self-consumption?

Campbell attempts to solve the dilemma by sketching another face for the modern hedonist. The 'principle of pleasure-seeking' is linked to 'the normal process of imaginative anticipation of, or speculation about, the future' (Campbell, 1987: 83) transforming the desiring or longing into 'a state of enjoyable discomfort'. Now 'wanting rather than having is the main focus of pleasure-seeking' (p. 86). Desire is redefined in terms of pleasure. The object and the realization are distanced into the future (or otherness) thus creating a state of enjoyable discomfort.

In other words, the modern hedonist is not only self-consuming imaginary goods (as representations) but also self-consuming non-consumption – longing, desiring while intentionally postponing the realization or abstaining from it altogether. Like an ascetic, the modern hedonist abstains from realizing any carnal pleasures (cf. Foucault, 1988a; Harpham, 1987) but then – unlike an ascetic – he transforms the 'suffering' caused by temptation into enjoyment. Thus the modern hedonist is a half-way ascetic not striving after the extinction of desires but after maintaining the continuous state of desiring. On the other hand, he still allows himself the auto-affective joys of imaginary self-consumption.

The problem can now be formulated as follows: the alter ego of the modern hedonist, outlined above, is even less fit as a realizing consumer than the first one simply because his/her pleasure derives from the postponement of realization. But the even more severe problem is this. How is the imaginary self-consumption and/or the non-consumption of pleasurable longing turned into actual, realizing consumption?

The modern hedonist projects the 'idealized pleasure which he has already experienced in day-dreams' onto ever newer products as the old and familiar ones have lost their ability to embody them and to redeem the promise of fulfilment. Here Campbell is forced to bring back the modern hedonist to the 'evolutionary stage' of his pleasure-realizing forefathers because otherwise the whole expansive dynamics of consumption would never have been thrown into motion. According to Campbell 'the basic motivation' of contemporary consumers 'is the desire to experience *in reality* the pleasurable dramas which they have already enjoyed in imagination, and each "new" product is seen as offering a possibility of realizing this ambition' (Campbell, 1987: 89–90; my italics).

This is what kicks the supplement-generator – or, what Campbell characterizes as 'the cycle of desire–acquisition–use–disillusionment–renewed desire' (p. 90) – into an expanding spiral movement.

Transformed into a consumer, the modern hedonist loses his/her ability both to gain pleasure from imaginary self-consumption and to maintain the state of longing through abstaining from realization. The 'gap between the perfected pleasures of the dream and the imperfect joys of reality' is reduced in the last instance to the duality of *dream and reality* giving 'rise to a continuing longing' (p. 95). The dream of perfect pleasure or absolute 'good' is attached to an object which, when taken into possession is transformed into reality – into a non-dream – and hence the dreams are attached or projected to the next, still unexperienced object.

This is how the difference between dream and reality is affirmed, but then again, how should we interpret the difference? To follow the logic of desire takes us nowhere, or more precisely it leads to mutually exclusive categories: what is in possession cannot be desired and what is desired cannot be possessed. Only that which is outside, elsewhere or absent, something lost (mourning, nostalgia) or something not (yet) attained (hope, anticipation, expectation) can be desired or longed for. The object of desire and longing, the 'good' may be given an endless list of names – for example as goods on the market – but the chain of substitutes never leads back to an 'original good' which would explain the mystery of continuous longing.

Consequently, Campbell is forced to back up his model for the consumer as a modern hedonist with arguments which rather poorly accommodate to the logic, and in fact turn against it. At the end of the chapter depicting the 'modern autonomous imaginative hedonism' (pp. 94–5) he refers to the unlimited 'wants' in relation to the 'limited resources' of the consumer. He also points to another 'fact' besides the continual indulgence of wants, namely, 'the fact that [wants] are also continually created, with the consequence that "frustration" is a permanent state' (p. 95) – a deficiency which now seems to have lost its enjoyable nature.

The replacement of the term desire by *wants* may be regarded as symptomatic of this dilemma and in fact the formulations come very close to those of the tradition of economical thought from Nassau Senior to W. Stanley Jevons. Man is just endlessly 'wanting' for reasons of pleasure, comfort or convenience and that is all. Nevertheless, Campbell does make an additional point: the wants are predicated upon the difference of dream and reality presupposing an ability to imagine the (day) dream worlds beyond the 'real' one. This is nothing modern in itself, as noted. But what is new is a utopian project reduced to an individual level. And this takes us to the second illustration, to Grant McCracken's (1988: 104–17) less ambitious yet interesting interpretation based on the analogy between cultural utopias and individual ideals, figuring specifically in the realm of consumption.

Materialized ideals

According to McCracken, cultures project the ideal 'good' into mythic or utopian Otherness – to another time and/or another place (Paradise Lost or that to come). At the individual level of modern consumption the goods have a similar position – as fixed points and material carriers for 'displaced meaning' (McCracken, 1988: 105). They represent the good(s) to be striven for in which the 'good' not only refers to hedonistic pleasures or its refined forms (cf. Campbell) but to a whole range of values and ideals both defined by the cultural code and actualized as individual likings.

McCracken refers to specific ' "high involvement" goods such as a car, a watch, an article of clothing, a perfume, a special foodstuff' which individuals buy 'in order to take possession of a small concrete part of the style of life to which they aspire' (McCracken, 1988: 111). These good (part) objects are 'bridges' which lead towards the 'ideal'. Thus consumption oriented to realization – purchase and use – does not necessarily lead to 'literal disillusionment' (Campbell, 1987: 90) or 'disappointment' (Hirschman, 1982: 10; Scitovsky, 1976) because each object represents only one part of the ideal whole which is approached step by step. The pursuit of ideals makes life into a goal-oriented project. It structures the existence into a movement focused on future and aiming at an end state simply called 'good'.

McCracken illustrates the importance of the life-project with a true story of a lottery winner who lost control over her life because all 'ideal' part objects became immediately obtainable – by means of money. This resulted in a collapse of the future perspective.

McCracken finds, however, 'a way out of this dilemma': a *nouveau riche* suddenly suffering from (relatively) unlimited resources may always become a *collector*: 'the virtue of pursuing collectables rather than merely consumer goods is precisely that they have their own special scarcity'. So as a collector it is always possible to maintain the future-oriented life project and, for example, dream of 'that magic day in which one owns every Renoir outside of public collection' (McCracken, 1988: 113).

At this stage there is a shift in McCracken's interpretation, almost imperceptible but nonetheless crucial. Before the appearance of the collector, the 'ideals' were conceived of in terms of *content* – mainly as culturally constituted values and goals: as aspired lifestyles or more generally as aspirations of 'the good life' embodied in certain symbols. In the case of the collector the content of the ideal is, however, emptied. It is transformed into a *formal* ideal which can be characterized only in one way – as perfection. The pieces of the jigsaw – the ideal part objects – are structured into a whole but it is not formed into an identifiable and nameable image. The jigsaw is upside down on the table, as it were. The ideal or magic limit pursued by the collector is simply and formally a *perfect* collection.[46]

Thus we may ask: in what sense is it possible to talk about the 'displaced meanings' of the part objects pursued by the consumer/collector? As it appears, the only 'meaning' of these parts, in the last instance is that they are parts of an ideal whole striven for. Symptomatically, McCracken ends up characterizing the collector's situation in the following words: 'the individual can now *pretend* that there is a distant location for his or her *personal* ideals and that these ideals will be realized when the bridge to them is obtained' (McCracken, 1988: 113; my italics). The collector's ideal, a perfect collection, may perhaps be interpreted as a substantialization of 'the abstract notion of a perfectly happy life' (p. 114) but only if it boils down into the following equation:

happiness = perfection = perfect collection = collector's life = collector's perfected self

It is not easy to decide which of these equivalence relations are metonymic and which are metaphoric but what can be argued is that the perfection of the collection is not merely a metaphor for the 'fulfilment' of life and the perfection of consumer's or collector's self but essentially also the material form of its realization.

Thus we are faced with a situation corresponding to that which was uncovered in the 'mimetic desire' pointing in the last instance towards an unnameable completeness beyond the horizon of representation. But if the object of desire turns out to be an unrepresentable representation or an ideal emptied and formalized into mere perfection – as in the present case – then it follows that the ceaselessly renewed desire cannot be explained with reference to the 'goods' represented by the objects of desire. The 'goodness' of the object is revealed as a derivative of the lacking object, or more precisely of a *lack*. Something is desired precisely because it is lacking – from the collection and the self. The object is constituted simultaneously as lacking and desired or 'good'. And hence the question about the endless desiring must be turned into a question of chronic *deficiency*.

Consuming supplements

But what do we gain by inverting endless desire into a constant state of deficiency or lack? To be sure it does not take us to any final solution but, nevertheless, it opens up the possibility thematizing that unrepresentable perfection or simply 'good' towards which the 'goods' as individualized utopias are also pointing.

It is not too hard to realize that the Garden of Eden (even if it already included a 'supplement') or Rousseau's natural state are names for the same state of being which in the psychoanalytical discourse appears on the ontogenic scale as the (mother–child) symbiosis preceding the steps towards separation and individuation. Then again, whether regarded in a cultural (and mythical) perspective – as a constitution of culture separated from nature – or from the perspective of individual development (towards a more or less autonomous self), that which was lost never existed as an *outside*, and furthermore, never existed as an *object* to be related to, either as a culture or a subject.

This is precisely where the parallelism of culture and subject is more than an analogy: to say that culture can be conceived of only as already constituted (Derrida) is based on the same principle as the notion that the object is constituted through its *absence* (Lacan). This is also how the distinction between inside and outside or the elementary subject–object relationship, and thus the subject, is constituted – all at the same point.

So, that which was lost was certainly not an object because it was turned into an object through the loss. Thus the objects of desire – as a chain of substitutes or representations leading beyond the horizon – never refer to an original object which could 'fill up' the empty place, the lack. It simply points to the undifferentiated and nameless state of being preceding separation – and thus the object.[47]

Relating back to the theme of *objectless* desire which tempts to the postulation of desire as an energetic principle, we may now present an alternative formulation. Desire is constituted by a loss, but not by a loss of an original object simply because the object (of desire) is constituted in the act of separation itself.

Consequently, the 'original' object of desire is already a substitute because the ultimate reference point of desire is situated in the state preceding the separation – of subject and object. Thus we have reached the paradoxical constellation in which the desire is objectless as far as it lacks the original object, but at the same time, desire is constituted in relation to an object which is already a substitute. What this implies is, that *lack* and *desire* are ultimately one and the same thing. And this is also why the 'goods' as objects of desire gain the irreducible ambiguous character of the 'supplement', being 'neither a plus nor a minus, neither an outside nor the complement of an inside, neither accident nor essence, etc. – a neither/ nor, that is *simultaneously* either *or* ' (Derrida, 1981c: 43).

This outlines the general principle of 'consumer society' as a supplement-generator, as an apparatus creating *simultaneously* both addition and subtraction, both surfeit and deficit, both superfluity and lack, as Goux put it.

What this implies is that there is no point in the pursuit of defining the supplement-generator of consumption as one which (re)produces *either* lack *or* desire. But this does not mean that the conceptual distinction loses its relevance. On the contrary, when applied to the dynamics of individual self-construction it is revealed to be a crucial distinction – supplementing the universal scheme of desire/lack with historical coordinates.

At this point it would be tempting to jump straight into interpretations which pathologize modern consumption by reference to 'the culture of narcissism' (Lasch, 1980) and the 'empty self' (Kovel, 1981: 125) of the modern man which must be constantly filled up with all kinds of things – experiences as goods and goods as experiences. There is no reason to deny the existence of 'consumer pathology' (Schlereth, 1982) which takes the introjective logic of consumption to the extreme of 'addiction', but to expand the pathology to modern consumption in general turns the analysis into little more than moralizing.

The logics of modern consumption – both introjective and distinctive – are rooted much deeper in the existential conditions of individual self-construction involving an historically specific mode of the reproduction of lack – and desire. More precisely, it is constituted by the reciprocal effects of the two moments of self-construction: the pursuit of separateness and distinction on the one hand, and the pursuit of introjective self-fulfilment on the other.

On the whole, the modern individual cannot reach for completion by giving up his individual self (autonomy) and becoming a part of a more or less symbiotic group-self. The modern individual is bound to the freedom of maintaining his self boundaries, his separatedness, thus creating a state of lack acting as an impetus for the further pursuit of completion – a project which is, as a rule, implemented within the boundaries of the individual self. In an essential sense the modern individual has to stand *alone* – to be *all* and *one* (in line with the etymological root of the word).

This is the dynamic conflict of modern individual self-construction which corresponds to the social dynamics of imitation and distinction, and is finally linked to the dynamics of the supplement-generator of consumption (see Figure 5.5).

The pursuit of completion is the core around which the whole system revolves precisely because it is writ to the level of the individual self. Self-building is simultaneously an act of separation or an articulation of self boundaries in relation to the outside, being thus both an 'addition' (complement) and a 'subtraction' with an effect of lack.

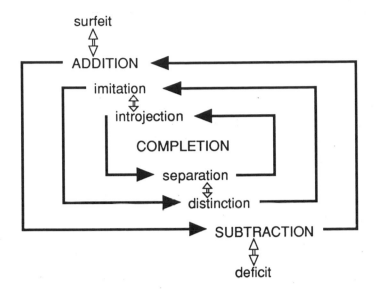

Figure 5.5 *The supplement-generator of consumption*

Modern man acquires the right and freedom to be alone, but the existential condition of separateness is simultaneously a state of lack, activating the individualized utopias of perfection. And the remarkable thing is that both moments of modern self-building are supplied by the supplement-generator of modern consumption.

Notes

1. This is just to remind of the problematic 'productivist' point of view and its unproblematic use of the concept of production.

2. Maybe the 'Mountain People' (the Ik, Uganda/Africa) studied by Colin Turnbull (1984) come close to the survival model but even if the 'society is too poor for morality' it still practices rituals of sacrifice 'consuming' the surplus.

3. For Bataille it is the 'cursed part' (*la part maudite*) which is destroyed in different forms of transgressive practices (Bataille, 1975 [1949]).

4. The dual dynamics of culture may be expressed in the binary relationships of profane vs. sacred – as Roger Caillois (1959 [1939, 1950]) does reading Durkheim and Mauss through Bataille – or everyday life vs. festival (*fête*), the latter of which Caillois characterizes as 'a paroxysm of life' (Caillois, 1959: 98).

5. The original subtitle of Bataille's 'La part maudite' (1949) reads 'Essai d'Economie Générale I. La Consumation'. Bataille uses mostly, however, the term *'consommation'* which refers in contemporary French both to (private) 'unproductive' consumption and more abstractly to the other etymological root corresponding to English 'consummation'. The term *'consumation'* – nowadays rarely used – refers more generally to 'use of matter' corresponding to the German *'Konsumtion'* or *'Verbrauch'* in distinction to *'Konsum'* referring to private and/or unproductive consumption.

6. Roger Caillois – the other 'sociologist of the sacred' besides Bataille in the Parisian Collège de Sociologie (1937–39) – presented an interpretation according to which, in modern societies, war has replaced festival as the dominant form of 'dépense' (Caillois, 1959: 163 [1950]). The 'consumption' in the recent six weeks Gulf War – and only in material terms – is surely the world record of potlatch so far. Merely the 'using up' of war-consumption goods of the US army – a fraction of all material costs – amounted to about $15,000,000,000 per week.

7. The economic system of commodity production surely transforms a large part of 'cultural construction' into commodities to be produced, sold and bought (esp. the so-called 'mass culture'), but this does not justify the 'productionist' idea of 'cultural production' formulated by some British culturalists in the late 1970s as follows:

> the notion of culture which we would advance hinges on the concept of production. We see cultural products and practices in terms of the relations between their material conditions of existence and their work as representations which produce meaning. In other words, our concern is both with modes of production and with modes of signification.(Barrett et al., 1979: 10)

8. Consequently, in searching for a basis for the dual perspective in anthropological universals Smith is led into somewhat contradictory statements: on the one hand prodigality is a 'natural tendency of both to individual and public' (Smith, 1970: 432 [1776]) and on the other, frugality is 'generally a predominating principle in human nature' (Smith, 1970: 441).

9. George Cheyne's analysis of the 'diseases of civilization' (B.S. Turner, 1982: 262) caused by different modes of consumptive excess and abundance (and not of scarcity) is located in the same discursive tradition that Robert Burton represented in the previous century with his monumental work on the *Anatomy of Melancholy* (1660). Burton emphasized the role of idleness as the cause of both social and mental disorder, noting that 'there is no greater cause of melancholy than idleness, *no better cure than business*' (cited in Lepenies, 1972: 22). 'Business' refers in the English language of Burton's time generally to the state of being busy (orig. bisines) and by Burton especially to physical 'exercise' and 'work' but not to intellectual labour or 'overmuch study' which was considered as one of the causes of melancholy with idleness, solitariness, passions, etc. It is also noteworthy that Burton introduced in his *Anatomy* the term '*luxuriate*' into the English language (Barnhart, 1988).

10. The 'abstinence' (Senior) which production requires is interpreted as an orientation to future consumption. According to Alfred Marshall 'it was "human nature" generally to prefer immediate to delayed consumption. In this scheme, the capacity to undertake production develops in proportion to the capacity to envision future consumption and, thus, delay immediate consumption in order to achieve a greater consumption in the future' (Birken, 1988: 25–6).

11. The explication of the symbolics in the figure(s): (1) the italic term acts as the 'starting point' in the dynamic model; (2) the double line denotes a conceptual identity, inference or link; (3) the solid line denotes a functional-causal link; (4) the dotted line denotes a functional-causal 'feed-back' or loop setting off the 'engine'. The disconnected terms are kept in the figure for illustrative reasons: to make the comparison with the figures to follow easier.

12. But the ambivalence concerning the location of the 'primal cause' still remains: is it the desire within or the object without? In the marginalist model the 'supplementary logic' (Derrida) is formulated in terms of a tautological circle: the objects of consumption have a utility because they are desired and, by the same token, the objects are desired because they have utility. In other words, the relationship is constituted both from inside out and outside in, or from the subject to the object and from the object to the subject. The source of desire resides within the subject and precedes its (external) target but, on the other hand, the desire is created by the addition (surplus).

13. If we replace the 'desires' with the 'needs' and formulate the hierarchical progression in more abstract psychological terms we end up with a conception resembling A.H. Maslow's 'needs-hierarchy' reaching from the lower boundary of basic physical needs to the higher needs (or 'meta-motives') of 'self-actualization' (Maslow, 1973).

14. Actually the difference in this respect between the rationalization model and the

cultivation model appears to be less significant as soon as we move away from the simple formula of self-interested utilitarian conduct according to which the postponement of immediate pleasures is a means to gain those same pleasures 'with interest' in the future. In other words, all the intermediate and instrumental utilities (advantage, prestige, etc.) attained may also produce a certain kind of pleasure which differs from basic hedonistic pleasure but also from higher moral pleasures due to its egoistic nature. But there is more to this: if the state of desiring is redefined into pleasure – as is done in Colin Campbell's (1987) portrait of the 'modern hedonist' – then the abstinence and postponement in themselves becomes a source of pleasure. I will come back to this theme later.

15. According to Burton 'idleness' as the opposite of 'exercise' is the cause of all kinds of ills and maladies and the major cause of the 'sickness of the soul' named Melancholy. The characterization is followed by an illustration from Homer's *Iliad* where Achilles is 'eating of his own heart in his idleness, because he might not fight . . .' (Burton, 1660 [1621]: 85).

16. According to Elias 'rationalization is only one side of a transformation affecting the *whole* personality, the level of drives and affects no less than the level of consciousness and reflection' (Elias, 1982: 326). On the other hand Elias reduces the Freudian perspective to the role of the 'super-ego' which is then linked to the Weberian model. Elias' formulation 'Protestant super-ego formation' (Elias, 1982: 300) is a condensed expression of this linkage.

17. This process of diffusion is strongly stimulated by modern advertising (from the early twentieth century onwards) the major function of which is to transform goods into representations (see Chapter 6).

18. As Elias notes, 'the degree of anxiety, like the whole pleasure economy, is different in every society, in every class and historical phase . . .' (Elias, 1982: 326).

19. Girard characterizes the mimetic constellation as follows:

The rival desires the same object as the subject, and to assert the primacy of the rival can lead only to one conclusion. Rivalry does not arise because of the fortuitous convergence of two desires on a single object; rather, *the subject desires the object because the rival desires it*. In desiring an object the rival alerts the subject to the desirability of the object. The rival, then, serves as a model for the subject, not only in regard to such secondary matters as style and opinions but also, and more essentially, in regard to desires (Girard, 1977: 145)

20. According to Girard, this is the 'first substitution' followed by the second, the 'strictly ritualistic substitution' in which the victim is replaced and represented by the 'surrogate victim' (Girard, 1977: 269).

21. In other words, 'acquisitive mimesis' does not disappear even if open violence is (largely) excluded. Thus Girard emphasizes the prevalence of social conflictuality unlike Tarde 'who sees in imitation the sole foundation of social harmony and "progress" ' (Girard, 1987: 8). This is also why Girard prefers the term 'mimesis' to 'imitation' as the former 'makes the conflictual aspect of mimesis conceivable' (Girard, 1987: 18).

22. Girard formulates the idea as follows: 'As a catalyst for the sacrificial crisis [mimetic desire] would eventually destroy the entire community if the surrogate victim were not at hand to halt the process and the ritualized mimesis were not at hand to keep the conflictual mimesis from beginning afresh' (Girard, 1977: 148).

23. To take an example, it was prohibited (by law) in the fifteenth and sixteenth centuries for Japanese merchants to dress according to the code of nobility, in precious silks etc., even if they could have afforded it. This led, according to Brain (1979: 62) to a compensatory body decoration of elaborated tattoos hidden beneath the 'restricted code' of merchant clothing.

24. This is actually the basis Veblen built on for his concept of 'conspicuous consumption' which he accordingly regarded as a universal social form realized in a specific mode in modern society (cf. Campbell, 1990).

25. Elias uses the term '*Verkitschung*' to describe this process (Elias, 1969: 426). The English translation 'vulgarity' (Elias, 1982: 312) loses this dynamic sense of model deformation.

26. Here the argumentation with different levels of 'need satisfaction' lurks just behind the corner, but even if it is not without relevance in many specified contexts (on the global level) it

is quite out of place when applied to the modern consumption of affluent societies. In a sense, modern consumption repeats the Edenic situation: the lack must be conceived in terms of desire and not in terms of needs.

27. This does not necessarily imply a devaluation or the loss of meaning of an object. Man's relation to the world of things is much more heterogeneous than the consumer's relation to the world of goods. Goods may be transformed into meaningful and valued things which give material form to memories (souvenirs), important relationships with people (gifts) etc. In other words, the possessions are transformed into belongings (see Carrier, 1990; Kopytoff, 1986). Nevertheless, whatever meanings and values the possessed objects materialize, they cannot be objects of desire, which (by definition) presupposes both non-possession and the possibility of (at least imagined) possession. And these are precisely the fundamental characteristics of the consumer's relation to goods.

28. Advertising does not create representations out of nowhere. It draws from the pool of cultural representations elaborating them and attaching them to specific objects according to a kind of 'bricolage'. So the 'manipulative' practice of marketing is not primarily directed towards the consumer but rather to the cultural representations (see Chapter 6).

29. Zygmunt Bauman makes a 'semiotic' distinction between 'sociocultural systems, in which rights to signs are derivative from social position' and those 'in which social position is derivative from possession of signs' (Bauman, 1971: 287). Even if Bauman's formulation is based on a somewhat simplified dichotomy of the pre-modern static social structure (status inherited) versus the modern dynamic one (status acquired), the basic point in the distinction is, however, relevant while thematizing the conditions and boundaries for a material sign-system to function as a language.

30. Girard uses this formulation while referring to the 'modern use of the term' *imitation* which 'is restricted to modalities of imitation in which there is no risk of provoking conflict and which are representational only, on the order of simulacrum' (Girard, 1987: 17). In contrast Girard's use of the term 'mimesis' emphasizes the conflictual and (socially) effective.

31. The Girardian model has also inspired explanations concerning the origins of cultural, that is, shared, representations expanded into a theory of the origins of language in general. Girard's disciple, Eric Gans (1981), explains the origins of representation as a 'sublimation' of mimetic desire. According to Gans, the sacrificial, sacralized and sacred object – both desired and feared – is transformed by ritual means into a shared representation or into a 'sublimated' form of possession 'in which the sign or "word" is a model of the object' (Gans, 1981: 51). But even if the symbolic and sublimated possession is removed from the 'world of action' and 'real possessions' there is still a pursuit to realize the desire: '. . . possessions within this imaginary model gives rise to a desire for possessions in the real world, and to the paradox entailed by such (imaginary) fulfilment' (Gans, 1981: 58). Then again, as long as the sacred object remains unique – even if that object is endlessly reproducible as a representation (a 'word') to be possessed by anyone – their acquisition would be plain sacrilege. But as soon as they are duplicated they become at least in principle obtainable. Actually, this condition is fulfilled long before profane mass production: the 'market' for faked relics may be conceived of as a transitional phase between the unique sacred object and profane mass production – corresponding to the immaterial goods of the papal pardons. (I am grateful to John Calton for drawing my attention to these pre-modern 'mass-products'.) But, of course, we should not forget the long history of (coining) money, which, in Marx's words, is the 'community' or 'common being' (*Gemeinwesen*) to end the 'ancient' ones (Marx, 1973: 223) or, translated into Durkheimian language, the secular 'sacred' to end the sacred.

32. I will pass, in the present context, all the 'what?' questions concerning the culturally constituted meanings of the car, of a sportscar, of a German sportscar, especially a Porsche, especially the 'classic' Porsche model named 'Carrera', etc. I will proceed starting from the 'representing whom?' question.

33. Zygmunt Bauman (1990) has recently presented an interesting interpretation of the collapse of communism based on the system's paradoxical role as a 'dictatorship of needs' promising to satisfy the needs of people but ending up repressing them. The Western course of development 'in its capitalist version turned consciously, explicitly and joyously to the

production of new needs' (Bauman, 1990: 187) and generalized the markets for individualized utopian projects redefining 'human happiness' as 'the expansion of one's consuming capacity and the cultivation of new, more capacious and ever more refined needs' (Bauman, 1990: 188). This resulted in the 'privatization' of both hopes and failures as fates of one's own life-project. The situation in communist society is dramatically different. As the state was responsible for the overall satisfaction of needs and failed to respond to the 'liberation of desire' (to use Girard's expression), the dissatisfaction was structured into a collective political protest against the state and not interpreted as an individual fate – expressed in 'guilt and shame' – of the individual life-project, as is the case in the 'postmodern' West. Then again, what launched the Eastern liberation of desire? Is there a deeper 'inner source' explaining the aspirations towards to more 'refined needs' or is it the Girardian 'mimetic desire' related to the Western Other (= consumer), that is, his/her object of desire.

34. Applied to a situation of actual (physical) need deprivation the equation sounds rather grotesque. If the model has bread to the 'fullness' of his stomach while the imitator is left with 'nothingness' the notion of the object of desire (bread) as a representation of the fullness of the stomach is of course reduced into a poor joke. Then again, we are not concerned here with an idealized scarcity economy functioning on the lower level of survival but with the 'additional' world of goods acting primarily as representations.

35. Orléan's solution is a kind of game-theoretical application of Girard's scheme conceptualizing the uncertainty of the consumer market. The explication of Orléan's model is not, however, necessary in relation to the present argumentation.

36. In economic terms 'quasi money' can be defined as any object that has a high enough degree of liquidity (Goux, 1990: 206–7).

37. The term 'introjection' is adopted from psychoanalytical discourse and in the present context it is used in the sense Sandor Ferenczi (1926 [1909]) originally gave to it, that is, referring the primary phase and mode of ego-formation characterized by a pursuit of completedness or unity with means of 'eating' the good world into the ego/self while 'projecting' everything bad to the outside. Or, formulated in Melanie Klein's (1932) terms: taking in the 'good objects' and rejecting the bad ones. Related to the imitation theme (developed above) it is of some interest to note that from the psychoanalytical point of view, (oral) introjection and imitation are closely related, as forms of 'primary identification' (Fenichel, 1982: 37 [1946]), characteristic of early phases of ego-formation (ontogenesis) but also at a cultural level referring the two principles of magic (thought) which J.G. Frazer named 'the law of contact or contagion' and 'the law of similarity' (Frazer, 1983: 14 [1922]). Even if one should be careful not to transfer by analogy the psychoanalytical interpretation from the psychic to the cultural, I venture to argue that this is one of the cases in which the transfer is justified. It concerns the basis of subject vs. object constitution, a theme dealt with in more detail in Chapter 2.

38. This is not to say that the interpretations focusing on 'pathological' traits in modern man would be totally without interest. On the contrary, focusing on characteristics defined as 'pathological' may give sharper contours to some phenomena which also underlie the prevailing 'normality'. But, of course, then the standards according to which something is labelled 'pathological' should be carefully explicated. So when David Riesman (1955) gives to the 'other-directed personality type' a negative characterization, just as Erich Fromm (1955) does to the 'market-oriented personality' or Philip Rieff (1966) to the 'psychological man', it is done from the normative 'sane society' point of view. Alternatively, the measure may be based on a psychoanalytically postulated idea of 'ortogenesis' which again may be revealed as a pure ideal type without a counterpart in the real world. It is also worthwhile noting that in the psychoanalytical discourse there is also a name for an overly 'normal' personality, the 'normophatic' (McDougall, 1986).

39. It is not enough to refer to a shift 'from production to consumption as a source of identity' – as Richard Harvey Brown (1987: 44) formulates it in a rather mechanical and moralistic manner. The restructuration is linked primarily with the erosion of the 'dividing line [. . .] between work and leisure', the two areas of activity which now 'flow together', as Michel de Certeau (1984: 29) puts it. This does not imply, however, a collapse into a 'mass

society' run by the 'captains of consciousness' (Ewen, 1976) or likewise, even if the media apparatus undoubtedly strengthens the 'hyperreal simulation' (à la Baudrillard, defining people at least formally into a 'silent majority' or into a big 'audience'). But what it implies is a change of social affiliations and thus a changed basis for the construction of social identities, which ranges from specific audiences to likewise specific 'communalities' and associations which may carry some characteristics of both Daniel Boorstin's (1973) 'consumption communities' and Robert N. Bellah et al.'s (1985) 'lifestyle enclaves' without reducing to the idea of strong community formation based on exclusion found in these two interpretations.

40. This could be characterized as a 'tube model' in which the society is present, on the one hand, *before* primary socialization (the social and historical factors determining the family structure, etc.) and, on the other hand, *after* the tube, when the more or less properly equipped individual faces the society outdoors. For example, Lasch's theses on the 'culture of narcissism' are largely built on such tube-thinking.

41. The stronger community bonds (cf. Tönnies' *Gemeinschaft*) still survive in the reduced form of the nuclear family which is, however, only a unit of the social whole (*Gesellschaft*) the structuration of which follows other, less solid principles.

42. This is surely not the beginning of 'self-technologies' the roots of which Foucault in his last works (1987; 1988b) traces back to the Greek Antiquity. But while the 'free man' in Greece was still building his individual self in accordance (or inside) the cosmological harmony (microcosmos–macrocosmos) and the Benedictine ascetic inside the divine order, the modern individual self, in an articulated manner as 'economic man', faces the world as an *outside* realm of intervention.

43. There is no reason to deny the social and even communal aspects of modern consumption – even if 'communities' in a stronger sense seem to be established rather on consumption-critical principles at the present. But as far I can see the forms of sharing the same or common are hardly comparable with the archaic ritual forms of sharing. Contrary to this, Mary Douglas and Baron Isherwood (1980) find a common denominator for the 'tribal society' and the modern one precisely in the rituals. According to them, in both cases 'ritual serves to contain a drift of meanings' and in both cases the 'rituals are conventions that set up visible public definitions' (Douglas and Isherwood, 1980: 65). The essential difference is, however, that in modern society the actual consumption is primarily realized in the form of private acquisition while the 'sharing' concerns merely the code according to which the attached meanings of the goods are interpreted. Thus what is shared resembles rather a language which can be used both for inclusion and exclusion, and this is certainly something other than shared values or ideals, not to speak of more substantial forms of community.

44. This is where the civilized consumer resembles the 'rational' one. Both make choices, but the former is related to goods as representations while the latter is dealing with the (metaphysical) 'use-values' measured in a calculation of exchange-values (or prices). I am certainly not denying the existence of rational choices, but as the argument goes, these do not reside in the core of modern consumption.

45. My description of Campbell's fascinating study is bound to be rather unjust as I am concentrating merely on the dilemma of desire and disregarding the whole subtle and innovative thematization of the intellectual roots of modern consumption.

46. This is surely a partial characterization of the collector, who is often a less systematic and less obsessed dilettante (in the positive sense of the word) who rather gains enjoyment from the continuous activity of collecting than of the idea of reaching perfection. This is in accordance with Campbell's thesis on the pleasurable nature of desiring itself – or as the Japanese proverb (cited by R.L. Stevenson) states: 'It is better to travel hopefully than to arrive'.

47. Kristeva (1982) has characterized this nameless state of unseparation as an 'abject' (= non-object) which, however, involves a reduction into the negative: that which threatens the boundaries of the body and self. Yet, the unrepresentable state preceding separation should be conceived of as essentially ambivalent and figuring also as the basis for the desirable dimension of 'to be eaten by' (see Chapter 4).

6

SELLING GOOD(S): ON THE GENEALOGY OF MODERN ADVERTISING

If consumption consisted simply in the satisfaction of basic needs or in the rational application of tools and implements, advertising would have no other function but to inform people where they can obtain the tools they require for need-satisfaction, how they should use these tools, on what sort of terms they are available and what sort of effects they have. In other words, advertisement would be plain consumer information, in the most fundamental meaning of the term. However, as a function of modern 'consumer society', consumption is much more than that; and the same goes for the advertisement, which today is much more than the announcement or public notice of the early nineteenth century in which potential 'customers' were informed about the existence and availability of specific goods.

Put differently: the advertisement, in its modern and proper meaning (Leiss et al., 1986), originated with the massive breakthrough around the turn of the century of consumer society and its huge markets for consumer goods in the major European centres and particularly in the US (W.H. Fraser, 1981; Hayes, 1941). The step from *announcement* to *advertisement* came with the recognition that it formed an integral part of sales and marketing; or, to paraphrase the famous statement of Clausewitz's, when it was recognized as a continuation of sales by other means. An early formulation of the idea was presented in 1904 by American advertising guru John E. Kennedy, whose simple but ingenious thesis was: 'advertising is salesmanship in print' (Pope, 1983: 238). At first glance the statement may seem trivial, even tautological, but this was in fact the first definition of selling as an *active strategy* whose principal tools were public words and images.

The growth of mass markets for consumer goods where the potential (local) customer was redefined as a 'consumer', at once as an anonymous mass and as an individualized target of communication, was not of course the only condition for the emergence of a modern advertising strategy. As well as a particular mode of production (Marx), modern advertising required a particular 'mode of information' (Poster, 1990) that made possible the transformation of concrete products into representations, into complex meanings carried by words and images.

The expansion of mass consumption and the development of mass communication on a corresponding scale, were not only inspired and made possible by the same process of technological development; they were in fact interwoven components of one and the same process. This connection between mass markets and mass communication is crystallized in modern advertising. In the mass production of consumer goods, the target, on the one hand, is an anonymous 'mass'; on the other hand, that mass is recognized as consisting of individual buyers. The same duality is repeated in the sender/recipient logic of the mode of information: the message is sent out equally to the whole body of recipients, but it is received individually by each one of them.

This paradoxical duality helps to explain the image of a Janus-faced consumer that unfolds not only in marketing philosophies but also in theories of modern consumption since the late nineteenth century: the mass of consumers was represented as more or less irrational 'adult children' – as it was put in the *Printer's Ink* magazine in 1897 (Jackson Lears, 1984: 376) – and on the other hand as consisting of individuals who were capable of making sensible decisions and choices (even though the conduct would not be considered as strictly rational in economic terms).

What really lies behind this dual consumer role is a confrontation of two antithetical perspectives: on the one hand the producer's concern is to realize the material mass of similarity (mass product) on what is regarded as a homogeneous consumer market. This is supposed to happen with the help of a marketing the aim of which it is to make sure that the correspondence between the two masses is established. On the other hand, the producer and the apparatus marketing must recognize the individual consumer's inalienable freedom of choice; the consumer will always retain the power to decide whether or not he or she wants to buy, if not in the capacity of a sovereign king then at least on grounds that are not (fully) controlled by marketing. In other words, the realization of mass products takes place in a sequence of choices by individual consumers; it is the sum of individual acts (of will), no matter what the underlying motives for these choices – from 'purely' rational cost-benefit calculations to the social dynamics of imitation and distinction, not to mention the more irrational motives.

Need, desire, will

An advertising and marketing point of view opens up, however, a more specific perspective on the Janus-faced consumer. Here, we need to refer to the (somewhat problematic) distinction between *needs* and *desires* (see Chapter 5).[1] If the consumer were a rational need-satisfying creature, the only function left for 'advertising' would be to inform. In fact, the whole business would never have developed into advertising in its modern sense but remained a form of consumer information, simply providing hard facts about product qualities and prices (which one does in fact sometimes see in modern advertising as well). Whether or not such consumer information were available, this ideal creature would make each and every choice autonomously and endogenously, carefully weighing all relevant needs; it would go to any length to obtain the missing information, and ultimately the missing means of need-satisfaction.

On the other hand, even though no such ideal creature exists, needs and deliberation do play a definite role in the portrait of the modern consumer. Thus one should also doubt the inverted image where the irrational consumer is driven solely by desires and makes choices on the basis of internal and external impulses – and is again beyond the control of marketing.

In fact the distinction between needs and desires has only marginal relevance from a marketing and advertising point of view. At the point where a willingness or readiness to sell is transformed into an active intention to sell, every product that is for sale becomes necessary ('you need this'), desirable ('this is what you desire'), missing ('you still lack this'); in a word, it becomes something that is *good* ('for you'). As far as the intention of selling is concerned it is of course a basic condition that the product is realized in the transaction of exchange, which from the buyer's (consumer's) point of view is defined as a choice, as a realization of a definite *will* to buy a certain product.

Marketing 'wants' the potential buyer to want this particular object of consumption for which they are a representative and which they transform in a representation. Because of its strategic significance, will becomes a key concept that supersedes both needs and desires. This reformulation is also found in the neo-classical economics of the late nineteenth century: the discourse on needs and desires is replaced by theorizing of the consumer's 'wants' and 'preferences' (cf. above Chapter. 5, p. 106).

The irony of the setting lies in the fact that this viewpoint of the shopkeeper's ('will you take this one . . .',[2] 'would you prefer this one to that . . .') transcends, innocently, as it were, the awkward distinction between needs and desires. The shopkeeper's point of view does not expose the paradox inherent in this distinction (see note 1), but simply by-passes it as irrelevant. As far as the business transaction is concerned, the most important thing is what the buyer wants, regardless of how the underlying motives are described.

The situation appears in a somewhat different light when it is approached from the marketing theorist's or the advertising psychologist's point of view. In an attempt to establish what sort of representation most effectively attracts the will and attention of the consumer to the product that is marketed, the advertising expert will need to go beyond the surface and probe into the possible motives that lead to the act of will to buy. At the same time, the advertising expert is confronted, time and time again, with the problem of the multitude of these motives. The solution to that problem lies (seemingly) in the Janus-faced consumer, in its different variants. One of the most interesting versions was presented back in 1926 in the American journal *Advertising and Selling*, which said that 'consumers made purchases on emotional impulse and then justified them with "reason-why" rationalizations' (Marchand, 1986: 153). Later a different approach was adopted to the problem of the Janus-faced consumer: the analysis was now based on a classification of different types of consumer goods – a theme that nowadays occurs mainly in the discussions on the dimensions of 'high and low involvement' in consumer behaviour (for example Rajaniemi, 1992) – and on different types and groups of consumers ('market segmentation'; see Pope, 1983: 291 ff.).

The good things in life

But no matter what approach they adopted to arranging and classifying motives, marketing theorists and advertising psychologists still remained captive to the seller's point of view. That is, no matter what words or images beyond the simple statement of availability were attached to the product, they had to promote a positive expression of want, a positive decision to buy. There are various different ways to argue in favour of a product; you may say it is 'useful', 'comfortable', 'healthy', that it brings 'social prestige' or simply that it 'makes you feel good'. The crucial thing is that an image is created of a 'good object' – to use the psychoanalytical concept introduced by Melanie Klein (1932) – that *you* do not yet have.

Some of these arguments may of course appear as more 'rational' than others, but even so their function remains the same. Even the rational argument serves to provide a representation of the (good) thing you are lacking, and in this capacity it often boils down to straightforward rationalization (in the psychological sense of the term). An example is provided by a fairly recent American advert where the argumentation for a 'completely new type' of deodorant bottle says it saves time, thanks to the new wider ball; you need just one stroke instead of two (Wills, 1989). Gary Wills demonstrates in his analysis that this 'advantage' - 'rolls on fast/dries fast!', as the slogan goes – is in fact an imaginary product quality: it is a new name for an ultimately anonymous (lacking) good the 'rationality' of which lies in your saving a few minutes of time per year; a few minutes you could just as well allocate to rolling on a few extra touches of deodorant, just to be on the safe side.

Arguments attached to the product and/or its consumption may even exploit the register of negative images, but the overall effect must be positive, otherwise people are not going to come in and buy the product. The idea that both the positive and negative register could be used was formulated by Roy Johnson, father of the 'impressionistic principle' of advertising, in 1911 as follows: 'we suggest the comfort or profit which results from the use of the product, or the dissatisfaction, embarrassment, or loss which follows from its absence' (*Printers Ink* 75 [25 May 1911] pp. 10–11; cited in Jackson Lears, 1984: 382). In other words, even where indirect or inverted means are applied, these must help to transform the product and its context into a representation of 'good'.[3] The negative register is used for depicting the state of deficiency that follows with the absence of the product and/or its use.

First, on the one hand, a negative image may be linked up with an identifiable moment in the present time, in which case it will appeal to the buyer's actual experience of deficit (the classical 'before–after' scheme); alternatively, it may interpret the consumer's current situation as 'relative deprivation' in comparison with the better situation that will (should) follow with the purchase and/or use of the product. This type of advert played an important role not only in the advertising of patent medicines towards the end of the nineteenth century (more on this later), but also in the socially stigmatizing, 'anxiety format' adverts of the 1920s and 1930s (see Leiss et al., 1986: 52–3; Marchand, 1986: 18–21). The latter appealed to the glances of reproof from neighbours and significant others and in general depicted the evil, the deficit that the absence and non-use of the product would cause to social relations, career prospects, etc.

This type of advertisement was used in the marketing of mouthwash, for instance, a product which promised to resolve once and for all the problem of bad breath and at once the distress, discrimination and loneliness that followed. It promised a completely different world of happiness, a world that was to be later outlined by Dale Carnegie in his famous guidebook for those who wanted to win friends and money and influence people. It is symptomatic that the marketing of this particular product named not only the product itself (Listerine) but also the deficit it promised to do away with. Discovered in an old medical dictionary, 'halitosis' was defined as a condition that could be cured by Listerine, opening the doors to a happy (social) life: 'For Halitosis use Listerine!' (Marchand, 1986: 19).[4]

In modern advertising one is hard put to find such uses of the negative register, although it may sometimes occur in the form of self-irony, with parodic repetition of 'outdated' advertising jargon and 'old' styles and patterns appealing to a sense of anxiety and guilt. Modern advertising operates almost exclusively with the positive register, depicting the happy and content soap user for whom there is always room even in a cramped lift rather than the distressed non-user who is left out.[5] The negative ('before') is excluded from the positive representation ('after') and has only an indirect, alluding presence, as in a margarine advert we had in Finland some years ago: 'what did we use *before* there was Flora . . . ?'

Secondly, on the other hand, a negative image may be projected into a conceivable future as a threat or as an otherwise undesirable state of affairs – loss of health, loss of face – that the product promises to keep at bay. Whereas negative images referring to the present time have more or less disappeared from advertising, images of threats projected into the future continue to occupy a quite firm position in present-day advertising jargon. This is most particularly true of adverts for beauty and health products, which do not portray horror scenes but rather hint at the prospect. Here, too, the negative is excluded from the frame of representation.

The strategy is applied most notably to selling today's 'patent medicines', that is the various vitamin products, the consumption of which has been increasing significantly in the Western world during the last two decades (Klaukka, 1989). Unlike their precursors in the nineteenth century, these products do not need to make promises that they have curative effects because their 'use-value' is located in a possible future – and in the threat contained therein – rather than in the present time and its verifiable effects. In this sense these products make for an ideal marketing item: no-one can say they don't work because there is no argument that the effects are visible here and now. The promises of future health and longevity cannot be falsified unless one lives one's life all over again in a 'control group'. This has to do with more than just the placebo character of a product (cf. Richards, 1990: 193): the utility of this product is equally verified by the presence and absence of any effects; after all things could have been worse if . . . .

Modern advertising: dimensions of change

Whether the advertisement uses the positive or the negative register of representation, the outcome must establish a positive link between the identified product and the 'good' that characterizes it. The building of this link implies a metamorphosis in which the product transforms into a representation – and it is this that modern advertising is basically about. The basic pattern has remained unchanged through the century-long history of modern advertising, but the modes and methods of creating representations of 'good' have changed. These changes can be roughly outlined in three stages of development:

1   the shift from product-centred argumentation and representation to a thematization of the product–user relationship and further to the depiction of scenes of consumption which emphasize the *experiential* aspect of consumption;
2   the shift from the emphatically rational mode of argumentation supported by essentially falsifiable 'evidence' of product utility towards representations of the satisfaction that comes with using the product – again emphasizing the experiential aspect of consumption; and
3   the shift in communication from verbal and literary means to audio-visual means, based on the development of communications technology that is closely related to the two former dimensions. Pictures were introduced to printed advertising in the 1880s, photographs in the 1890s and the next century offered the new powerful media of cinema, radio and TV.

These trends in development would seem to be heading towards a form of representation which has increasing independence vis-à-vis its point of reference, that is, the product, and which increasingly operates with expressions of the positive register. In other words, the language and argumentation of advertising is moving towards a pure 'good', towards a true positive experience. Of course, this argument needs to be backed up with a closer definition of what is meant by representation of 'good', and this is in fact one of the chief concerns of the discussion that follows. Suffice it to note at this point that the shifts identified above characterize not only the history of modern advertising, but more generally the completion of the modern world of consumption, particularly in its emphasis on the *experiential nature of consumption* – a theme to which we will revert later.

The argumentation above should not be read as a totalizing interpretation that we are heading towards a fully homogenized language of advertising. In the heterogeneous world of modern advertising, in the 'postmodern' simultaneity of diachrony and difference, advertising still applies rational, use-value arguments as well as a product-centred mode of representation, etc., but the predominant trend now is towards rhetorics and depiction which no longer involve falsifiable promises. Rather, advertising is now creating an endless stream of representations in which products are transformed into positive experiences. The link between different kinds of 'goods' (as the positive) and goods (as products) is established chiefly through connotations and associations. Sometimes the message is so veiled that practically-minded marketing critics say the actual product (name) may in some cases be overshadowed by the advertisement, which lives an independent existence as an experiential product (cf. for example Kroeber-Riel, 1984, 1993).

The transformation of goods, that is, physical objects and substances into *positive* representations, into an endless succession of good objects, is not only an integral part of the history of modern marketing and advertising; it is also a phenomenon which tells us something very important about the whole world of consumption and how it has taken shape. In saying this I do not want to express my support for the manipulation model (see for example Ewen, 1976; Packard, 1979) where demand is simply the product of an effective marketing machinery. As many recent historical and theoretical analyses of modern consumer society have shown (Campbell, 1987; McCracken, 1988; McKendrick et al., 1982), there is no proper justification for this sort of reductionism. Here I am also referring to the interpretation developed above (Chapter 5, pp. 129–45) showing how the fundamentally objectless desire for the 'good' is re-organized into individualized and singularized object relations and attached to the goods of the modern world of consumption. This story is about how this world of goods becomes visible to the consumer and how this visibility constitutes a direct consumer–product relationship.

Not by bread alone

There is no law of nature which automatically leads from the growth of mass markets for consumer goods to the birth of modern advertising. As we saw earlier, the large-scale transformation of products into messages, into words and images or into representations, requires a specific 'mode of information' (Poster). Although that mode of information does correspond to a certain stage in the development of mass production and mass markets for consumer goods, it cannot be reduced to a product of that stage. In the seventeenth and eighteenth centuries, mass markets did not yet exist, even in England. The range of consumer goods was still fairly narrow and heavily segmented according to the 'natural' social hierarchy of the estates (Brewer and Porter, 1993).

Most everyday consumption items used by 'common' people were essential necessities that had no names. Bread was bread; in the best cases it was good bread from the local baker's, but no arguments of a surplus 'good' were attached that would have made it 'something more' than just bread. This principle of 'something more' was formulated literally by an American advertising man in the 1930s: 'bread is not just bread' (Jackson Lears, 1984: 370).

This does not mean to say that bread (now in its literal meaning) was just a fuel to keep the human engine going, that it carried no other meanings and representations. In fact our 'daily bread' carried very strong mythical, religious and ritual meanings at this time, but these meanings did not single out a certain loaf of bread among other loaves, nor did they allow for an individual relationship between subject x and a specific object (of desire) y. In these circumstances the differences between 'our'[6] loaves of bread (y and z) were reduced either to the existence of different types of bread that otherwise were fully comparable or to the people who baked the bread having different names; there quite simply was no room for an individual-ized representation of (surplus) 'good' for a specific bread-product. It is a different matter altogether that different types of bread, a whole bread hierarchy has served as a system of social distinctions, as Piero Camporesi has shown in his description of seventeenth-century Italy where peasants used to eat bean bread and the townfolk wheat bread (Camporesi, 1989: 120–30).

However, beyond the basic necessities of everyday life, the common folk did have access to some other consumer goods as well. Some of these were in fact serially produced (by contemporary standards) and carried mean-ings which spilled over into the decorative: prints (Mukerji, 1983), pottery, buttons, etc. (McKendrick et al., 1982; Wernick, 1991). And although the internal differences within these product categories could still be reduced to their 'origins', to the producers, this system of differences also provided some sort of basis for a commodity language that was used to formulate distinctive statements. This was particularly so among the better-off whose vocabulary of consumption (the range of product categories and their internal differentiation) was wider than the average.

The first printed announcement-advertisements were published as early as the eighteenth century. In British newspapers and magazines, *customers* were informed about the availability of certain products at the same time as the majority of consumer goods were selling perfectly well without any marketing (beyond the direct interaction between shopkeeper and customer) and without any names. On the other hand, in those days there was no attempt even in announcements to create a distinguishable identity (name) for a product, and any positive characterizations of the product were also quite rare. In the words of John Styles (1993: 541), these announcement-advertisements 'simply listed the goods available and sometimes asserted their quality, cheapness, variety, novelty or metropolitan origin', without any effort to single out a specific brand name or the name of the manufacturer. Only the wholesaler and/or the retailer were mentioned by name. According to Styles, this was not particularly surprising in that the development of eighteenth-century consumer goods markets was manifested primarily in the continuing increase in the number of shops – and it was this that had the greatest impact on the individual consumer of manufactures (Styles, 1993: 441–2).

This stage of development in effect implied a redefinition of market;[7] markets were transformed from temporal events that followed an annual cycle into spatial sites where continuous commodity–money relations follow a daily and weekly cycle (see for example Polanyi, 1957).

Eighteenth-century 'marketing' did not yet address consumers but customers, that is retailers as well as the customers of retailers. This helps to explain why the name of both the producer and the product was not really significant. Marketing consisted chiefly in the practical conduct of personal relations (of commerce), which could hardly be described as 'public' in the modern sense of the word. In other words the world of goods was still lacking a realm of representations that would have covered the markets, not only because the mode of information made possible by this realm was only just beginning to take shape, but also because it simply was not necessary in the situation of local consumption and virtually non-existent competition.

So the time was not yet ripe for modern advertising; the necessary conditions were not yet there. Modern advertising requires a concept of 'consumer' which is at once general and specific, just as democracy requires a concept of equal and individual state citizens. This implies not only an expansion of consumer goods markets beyond the local level and the expansion of consumption downwards to lower strata of the population, but also the development of the 'mode of information' so that the message can be addressed to the potential consumer *en masse* but at the same time as an individual, using the print press and later electronic media. It is at this juncture, after the mid-nineteenth century, that we witness the emergence of the sphere of words and images, sound and light, in which products are transformed into representations.

This provides the basis for a mass communication system in which the producer = an identified product = a *trademark* = a potential *brand* sends out a message to an individualized consumer. It is this tendency to *single out* the individual that can be regarded as the distinctive characteristic of

modern advertising – a characteristic that has become increasingly promi-
nent during the twentieth century. The individualizing mode of communication creates an imaginary relationship between the assumed consumer
and the identified product that is personalized by means of positive
characteristics, a relationship which appears to every consumer to be as
unique as a romantic love affair. As a representation, the product takes on
an identity (name), a recognizable outer appearance (packaging) and a
voice, which will tell you in a seducing, sometimes in a declarative or even
threatening voice: 'this is/I am for you = you need me'. Perhaps the most
impressive (inverted) version of the statement is the recruitment poster
from the early days of modern advertising in which Uncle Sam looks you
straight in the eye and points his demanding finger and says: 'Uncle Sam
Needs You!'

Individualization did not imply a wholesale rejection of all earlier forms
of marketing: the nursing of client relations, travelling salesmen, merchants of patent medicines (those spectacular swindlers we have seen in so
many Westerns). Nor will modern marketing shy away from organizing or
sponsoring major spectacles. But the main trend in the modern advert is
very definitely towards *individualization* in communication, whose nature
remains essentially unchanged even when adverts begin to grow into
experiential products in their own right, with a tendency to overshadow the
product or brandname marketed.[8]

Naming the nameless

Modern advertising identifies and singles out products as representations
which are intended to appeal to the consumer at once as an individual and
as a mass. Or, as Leo Lowenthal puts it: the individualizing 'for you'
actually adresses 'all of you' (Marchand, 1986: 108). On the other hand,
each argument and quality that is attached to the product identifies it
precisely as a positive thing or (in psychoanalytic terms) as a 'good object'
which in one way or another promises to fill in the 'empty space' that
consumers feel is there, *even though they do not know how to name it.*

What could the identification of this unnameable deficit mean? If hunger
were plain hunger and bread just plain bread, then the whole problem of
anonymity wouldn't even exist. The naturalist theory of needs has a name
both for the deficit (hunger) and for whatever it is that fills the stomach
(bread). However, as we saw earlier, a fundamental thesis of modern
advertising is that 'bread is not only bread', which necessarily means that
the same applies to the other side of the equation; 'hunger is not only
hunger'. In other words, both are (also) something else and more; but
what? This leads us inevitably to the problem of namelessness, which has
two addresses – but which as we shall soon discover are just different
entrances to the same house.

First, on the one hand there is the problem of the nameless *product*, which is resolved by naming and individualizing the product and by setting it apart (in positive terms) from other products by means of marketing (packaging, adverts, etc.). A paradigmatic case of product identification is the pioneering work that was done by the American Quaker Oats Company (renamed as The American Cereal Company in the early twentieth century) towards the end of the nineteenth century (Marquette, 1967). In 1880, an oat producer by the name of Schumacher started packing his produce – which so far had been known simply as 'oat' – into sacks that had the producer's name printed on them (Marquette, 1967: 16). This was the first step in creating a brandname, which was soon to be followed by a technological innovation (steam mill) that made possible the processing of oats into a specific, identifiable form (rolled oats) and finally by the packaging and naming of this product: Quaker Oats.

Hence the transformation of plain oats into a potential *brand*; a potential that in this case was well exploited. The relationship of people to oats was of course nothing new, but the individualized (albeit imaginary) relationship of the (mass) consumer to Quaker Oats very definitely was. It was in this particular packaged, identified form – as a representation – that the product became more than just 'plain oats'.[9] The making of the product did of course require some real effort in terms of product development (from grain into flakes), which changes the sensory qualities of the raw material. However, the crucial thing here is that all the characteristics that emphasize the distinctive identity of the product are packaged together in the form of a representation. And if the physical characteristics no longer suffice to support the unique identity of the product, the other elements of the representation, the surplus 'goods' will have to take their place.

No product can expect to have the market all to itself for very long. Quaker Oats was soon followed by Kellogg's Company, Postum Cereal Company and many others who went after the consumer with cornflakes and rice krispies, which by now have become the staple food of breakfasts the world over.[10] Therefore a positive character must be continuously created and re-created for a named product.

Secondly, on the other hand, as a message to the potential consumer, the building of a positive product identity implies a representation of that product as a *complement*. It is in this function that the advertisement has to name something that is fundamentally nameless, the negative form of which is the consumer's *deficit* (which is eliminated by the complement) and the positive form of which is the *wholeness* that buying the product and/or using it promises to bring. 'It' is fundamentally nameless, not representable, and that is why *it* is always given new names, over and over again.

But regardless of whether the naming of 'it' focuses on the negative (deficit) or on the positive (wholeness), the role of the product as a *complement* is always and necessarily positive. As a representation appealing to the potential consumer, it promises something good, either in terms of eliminating the evil or in terms of offering surplus good; in this latter case the state preceding the surplus good is necessarily redefined as a deficit. In other words the duality of deficit (negative) and wholeness (positive) is present in the representation either explicitly or implicitly, on the reverse side of either deficit or wholeness. In any event the role of the product as a complement remains positive, as Ray Johnson (see p. 154 above) clearly understood.

So in the end the two addresses of identification or naming in modern advertising – the singularization of the product and its representation as a complement to an identified deficit and/or as a surplus which produces the wholeness identified – lead to exactly the same place. Transformed into a representation, the product must stand clearly apart from other similar products, in which case it will also be individualized to the potential consumer as a party to a bilateral (albeit imaginary) relationship. All the attributes of 'good' attached to the product in its representation fulfil both of these functions. In fact the full range of 'goods' – which has since been repeated in various combinations by modern advertising – was already in use in the marketing of selected pioneer products (that is cereals) in the late nineteenth century:

> Every device of the Advertiser's art was used by *American Cereal Company* between 1890 and 1896. Techniques later men claim to have innovated were tested by Crowell as early as 1893. In his ads he appealed to love, pride, cosmetic satisfactions, sex, marriage, good health, cleanliness, safety, labor-saving, and status-seeking. His boldness, at the height of prudish Victorianism, reached its peak in 1899 in an advertisement in *Birds* magazine and several other periodicals of the day. The illustration was a voluptuous, bare-breasted girl, her torso draped in Roman style, sitting on a *Quaker Oats* box. (Marquette, 1967: 51)

If for reasons of distinction or competition advertising has to resort to the positive register ('our' product is better than 'theirs', or 'better value for money'), the situation is somewhat more complex as far as the building of a product–consumer relationship is concerned. This is because the naming may concern both the deficit that the product 'promises' to make disappear and the 'good' that is secured by ownership and use of the product. It is on this dimension of duality that we can follow the development of the modern advert towards the positive. This process is made visible by the history of patent medicines, which in effect lies at the very root of modern advertising. Indeed, the thematic shift from the novelty products of the foodstuffs industry to patent medicines is not all that dramatic; most of the former were introduced to the general public precisely as 'health' products (see for example Levenstein, 1988; Porter, 1989; Young, 1967), such as one particular successor of patent medicines called Coca-Cola.[11]

Patent medicines

Patent medicines have played a central role in the history of modern advertising. These cure-alls were first 'advertised' in announcement or public notices, in the mid-seventeenth century in England (Wright, 1991), but the product group was still going strong when modern advertising made its breakthrough around the turn of the nineteenth and twentieth century (Holbrook, 1959; Schudson, 1986; Young, 1961).

Given the special nature of the product – a 'medicine' (+) that cured many different 'illnesses' (−) – patent medicines had no choice but to try and build up a positive image for themselves. It was a magical substance which affected change, so it had to inform people not only about its availability but also about its effects and efficiency. The announcement that was published in the London *Perfect Diurnall* in 1652, for instance, contained not only information on where the medicine could be obtained ('at the Physitians house in Flying Horse Court in Fleet Street'), but also an assurance on its effectiveness:

> a water for 3sh the ounce that will purifie the face to an exact clearness and fresh colour, keep it from wrinkles, take off freckles, morphew, sunburn, etc.
> An oil for 4sh an ounce that will change red hair brown or black.
> A powder and a plaister for 20sh that in 6 weeks time will cure the Kings Evil perfectly . . . (cited in Wright, 1991: 8)

The very same distinctive characteristics make the advertising of patent medicines, especially upon entering the nineteenth century, a paradigmatic case of the *naming of deficit*. In these adverts not only known diseases were named but also vaguer psychosomatic syndromes which effectively boiled down to anxiety and not feeling well. Patent medicines entered this vague domain of deficit as a saviour by naming known ailments but also by inventing new ones so that potential users could easily identify their very own deficiency and neediness.

The wider (and vaguer) the range of deficits that patent medicines came to identify, the more closely their promises of complementation began to resemble religious conversion. The favoured self-representation of patent medicines was indeed one of saviour: they could get rid of all evil and replace it with good. The affinities between religious conversion and advertising for patent medicines extend all the way to the individualizing mutuality of the (object) relationship that is aimed at – insofar as the salvation of the religious convert is based on an individualized 'god-relationship'. However, the crucial difference here is that the salvation of the convert requires subordination to a larger whole (= holy), that is, a partial rejection of the (individual) self, whereas the happiness of the consumer (wholeness) presupposes the maintenance of the individual self in which the good (object) is internalized. In the former case wholeness requires self-denial, subordination as 'lamb of the Lord', but in the latter case the attachment to oneself of an object that exists 'just for you'.[12] Nonetheless, 'it' still remains nameless and the same in both cases: salvation, healing, freedom and happiness.

However, this correspondence with religious conversion in the identification of deficits is found not only in adverts for patent medicines in the nineteenth century; it is still evident in modern marketing during the early decades of the twentieth century. For example, in a psychology textbook published in the early 1920s and intended for the training of salespeople, the model of religious conversion is applied with the aim of getting the potential buyer to recognize his own deficit, which will be complemented by the product sold:

> For an excellent example of tactics to pursue at this stage the seller may profitably study the methods used by a professional evangelist in 'selling' religion. He begins by showing the prospective convert (buyer) *how great a lack there is in his life*. (Kitson, 1921: 180; my italics)

But the message of salvation only makes sense if there exists a threat of damnation, and it was in this domain that nineteenth-century advertising for patent medicines operated, all the way till the turn of the century. Advertisers did not even have to go to too much trouble to identify illnesses; physicians and 'alienists' (now known as psychiatrists) had plenty of names in stock, especially of vague syndromes that seemed to cover virtually every form of 'not feeling well' known to modern man. For example, one of the mid-nineteenth-century patent medicines, Helmbold's Buchu, promised in its announcement-advertisement (1860) that it will cure at least the following ailments:

> General Debility, Mental and Physical Depression, Imbecility, Determination of Blood to the Head, Confused Ideas, Hysteria, Absence of Muscular Efficiency, Loss of Appetite, Dyspepsia, Emaciation, Low Spirits, Disorganization or Paralysis of the Organs of Generation, Palpitation of the Heart, And, in fact, all the concomitants of a Nervous and Debilitated state of the system. (cited in Young, 1961: 117)

The lists of ailments were longer for some patent medicines than for others, but as a rule (with only few exceptions) the list contained at least one ambiguous psychosomatic syndrome which meant that the series of ailments remained open ended – towards all possible variations of the theme 'not feeling well'. The Helmbold's Buchu advertisement, cited above, does this in explicit terms ('all the concomitants of the Nervous . . .') but the same applies also to the patent medicine advertisements which referred to a civilization-illness diagnosed and named by the American neurologist George M. Beard as 'neurasthenia' (nervous exhaustion) in the late 1860s. The open-ended nature of the specified illness called neurasthenia is immediately revealed as soon as one takes a look at the list of symptoms presented by the inventor:

> Insomnia, flushing, drowsiness, bad dreams, cerebral irritation, dilated pupils, pain, pressure and heaviness in the head, changes in the expression of the eye, neurasthenic asthenopia, noises in the ears, atonic voices, mental irritability, tenderness of the teeth and gums, nervous dyspepsia, desire for stimulants and narcotics, abnormal dryness of the skin, joints and mucous membranes, sweating hands and feet with redness, fear of lightning, or fear of responsibility, of open places or closed places, fear of society, fear of being alone, fear of fears, fear of contamination, fear of everything, deficient mental control, lack of decision in trifling matters, hopelessness, deficient thirst and capacity of assimilating fluids, abnormalities of secretions, salivation, tenderness of the spine, and of the whole body, sensitiveness to changes in the weather, coccygodynia, pains in the back,

heaviness in the loins and limbs, shooting pains simulating those of ataxia, cold hands and feet, pain in the feet, localized peripheral numbness and hyper-aesthesia, tremulous and variable pulse and palpitation of the heart, special idiosyncrasies in regard to food, medicines, and external irritants, local spasms of muscles, difficulty of swallowing, convulsive movements, especially on going to sleep, cramps, a feeling of profound exhaustion unaccompanied by positive pain coming and going, ticklishness, vague pains and flying neuralgias, general or local itching, general or local chills and flashes of heat, cold feet and hand, attacks of temporary paralysis, pain in the perineum, involuntary emissions, partial or complete impotence, irritability of the prostatic urethra, certain functional diseases of women, excessive gaping and yawning, rapid decay and irregularities of the teeth, oxaletes, urates, phosphates and spermatozoa in the urine, vertigo and dizziness, explosions in the brain at the back of the neck, dribbling and incontinence of urine, frequent urination, choreic movements of different parts of the body, exhaustion after defecation and urination, dryness of the hair, falling away of the hair and beard, slow reaction of the skin etc. (Beard, 1881: 7–8)

And this, Beard assures us, is by no means an exhaustive list. If an ailment is discovered that as yet has no name, it can easily be fitted under this civilization-illness or 'modernity syndrome'[13] which in this particular case is called neurasthenia. The same applies more generally to lists of ailments that can be cured by patent medicines; just about any ill(ness) was acceptable. While adverts for patent medicines in the late nineteenth century utilized the entire register of the mythical to produce powerful images of the ill and the evil – with dragons (Swaim's Panacea), skeletons (W.M. Radams Microbekiller, 1887), and alike – and dramatized the scene as a struggle between good and evil (Pilules Pink, 1899; see Illustrations 6.1–6.3), the endless lists of all sorts of ailments actually served to expand the evil into a category of general ill-being or not-feeling-well that accommodated just about every expression of deficit.

In other words, the generalized ill (deficit) became the inverse image of generalized 'good' (wholeness); and that was what the patent medicine promised to achieve in its capacity as an agent for good. So by the late nineteenth century adverts for patent medicines were already operating in the good (feeling) world,[14] albeit indirectly through its inverse image ('deliver us from evil . . .'). Even though the 'before–after' format of advertising, as a typical intermediate form was still commonly used, the argumentation for and depiction of the products had by now come fairly close to using a purely positive register of representations. But obviously a more in-depth explanation is required of this shift towards plain good in which the nameless 'it' appears as variations of wholeness with different names. To resolve the mystery we have to continue our journey for a while through the wonderful world of patent medicines.

The metamorphosis of patent medicines

One reason for the move to using the positive register in representations of patent medicines was that the producer wanted to expand his markets to

Illustration 6.1   Illustration 6.2

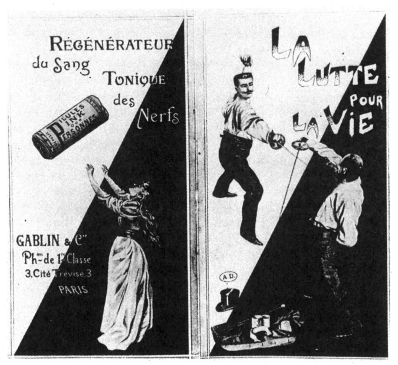

Illustration 6.3

include not only people who were (or felt) ill but also those who were (did) not. By the end of the nineteenth century all patent medicines had redefined themselves not only as a cure for the sick and frail, but also as a preventive elixir for the healthy. A patent medicine called Pure Malt Nectar, for instance, was advertised under this slogan in the United States: 'invigorating tonic, alike for invalids and those in health' (Petersen, 1969: 321). At the same time, advertisements started to identify and visualize the 'good' that followed for those who decided to use the product, defined either as a succession of specific 'goods' or in more ambiguous terms, as in this slogan for a very popular patent medicine: 'HADACOL – for the better tomorrow!' (Brigham and Kenyon, 1976). This advert no longer includes the negative condition which remains behind; from the identification of a deficit, it has moved on to naming the desired (good) state of being that can be attained by the goods (that is the products) specified.

The redefinition and expansion of the identity of patent medicines was instrumental in pulling down the barriers between different categories of oral consumption: the line between preventive medicines and foodstuffs was blurred. Preventive medicines promised to keep the evil (illness, ageing and ultimately death) away and turn the 'normal' life into a better one by providing extra energy, happiness, beauty, etc.[15] The same arguments were used also in the marketing of cornflakes, rice krispies, etc., in the name of 'good health'.[16] This trend was very much reinforced by innovations in organic chemistry and nutrition science, which shifted the focus of attention somewhat away from invisible enemies, the bad 'microbes', to the good invisible helpers, that is vitamins and other 'protective foods' (Levenstein, 1988: 147–8).

Another factor with dramatic effects on the identity and advertising of patent medicines is a less modern aspect of how they were promoted, that is their direct *promises* of 'good' that, in principle, were falsifiable. It was these 'empty promises' that inspired rather heated debate in the early twentieth century, first in the United States and later elsewhere, on the ethical principles of advertising. Soon after it was established in 1911, the Associated Advertising Clubs of America launched a 'Truth-in-Advertising' campaign in order to drive through legislation to stop untruthful and misleading advertisement (Jackson Lears, 1984: 366). This proved an important impetus for consumer protection legislation both in the United States and in other Western countries.

All this promoted the 'rhetorical turn' of advertising for patent medicines (the single biggest product category advertised at that time), that is its reorientation to assurances of 'good' and particularly to such forms of representation that precluded any risk of breaking promises. It is easy to retrace this process of transformation by looking at how the slogans for an early wonder drug called Coca-Cola have changed with time: in the 1890s it was marketed as a remedy for headache and as a brain tonic (1893: 'The ideal brain tonic'); in the early twentieth century (1906) the product was associated both with good health and with happiness ('A toast to health and happiness'); and ten years later the deficit (thirst) had become plain fun (1916: 'Fun to be thirsty'). This process is not just a case of Orwellian Newspeak where the negative is redefined as positive, but of a fundamentally new formula in which the 'good' offered by the product (wholeness) is associated with a positive *experience*, which covers both thirst and its satisfaction. As it is put in the longer slogan from the same year: 'It's fun to be thirsty when you can get a Coca-Cola'.[17] The same pattern could hardly be applied to a medicine ('It's fun to be sick . . .').

The more recent slogan from 1982 for the same product: 'Coke is it!', is perhaps the most simple and straightforward expression of the positive form of 'it', of the secularized state of wholeness which acquires ever new names: Americanism, youth and beauty, sunny beaches, partying people, anything *good* that can be imagined in this world.

The transformation of Coca-Cola from a patent medicine into a stimulant and soft drink is an obvious step towards plain good, but does it really tell us anything important about the development of modern advertising in a more general sense? In the case of Coca-Cola the shift to the positive register of representation is closely linked up with the change in the identity of the product. Many other patent medicines of the late nineteenth century went through a very similar metamorphosis. Some of them became food (Kellogg's Cornflakes), others were redefined as spices and seasonings,[18] such as (Heinz) ketchup (which was preceded by Dr. Miles Compound Extract of Tomato: 'a sovereign remedy for mankind's ills'; Young, 1961) and peppermint (Essence of Peppermint; Jones, 1981); and one became a scented skin cleansing agent for external use: Eau de Cologne, brandnamed as 4711, was also originally a patent medicine for internal use (Bongard, 1964).

A major factor behind the transformation of patent medicines was the new legislation that entered into force in the early twentieth century (in the United States The Pure Food and Drug Act of 1906), which prohibited the free sale of hard drugs in the form of medicines and forced many patent medicines to leave out the substances that added to their magical potency.[19]

Towards pure experiences of good

So while patent medicines and their successors had clear reasons to move towards the positive register of representation, there was also under way a more sweeping process of change in advertising. That is, the language of *modern* advertising was now beginning to take shape, a process which clearly highlights the connections between the dimensions of change mentioned earlier (see pp. 156–7). As naming and representation begin to move away from the actual product and its qualities and towards the act and context of consuming the product, the fundamentally nameless 'it' becomes thematized in the domain of satisfaction and wholeness. This means that the building of the connection between the product and 'goods' turns round: the positive elements no longer refer (primarily) to the qualities of the product (for example to the efficacy of the patent medicine, which may turn out to be an embarrassing fraud), but the product is associated with representations of wholeness. The first part is wiped out of the 'before–after' scheme (see Illustration 6.4), but so is the obligation to meet 'use-value promises' (Haug, 1980) because the depicted 'good' has gained independence from the product and its qualities.[20].

Insofar as this process of change boils down to a change of identity from medicines to foodstuffs and stimulants (a change paradigmatically represented by the case of Coca-Cola), there is no need to explain the shift to the positive register of representation: pleasing experiences are obviously marketed by means of pleasing images. However, the trend towards the experiential good cannot be fully reduced to the identity of the product because positive representations cut across different product groups. This is clearly seen if we compare the destinies of Coca-Cola and another mythical product, i.e. Aspirin as product types and on the other hand as advertised representations. Both originated towards the end of the nineteenth century; the former as a classical patent medicine that in the early decades of the twentieth century is transformed into a soft drink, and the latter as a modern painkiller that in spite of its cure-all character is intended for specific uses (unlike traditional patent medicines).[21]

In the late nineteenth century the identities of the two products were still more or less indistinguishable; Coca-Cola was emphatically represented as a brain tonic and a medicine that would cure headaches. Even their announcement-advertisements were very similar (see Illustrations 6.5a and 6.5b). But then their ways parted. In the new division of labour, Coca-Cola's role was to produce surplus 'good' (pleasure), while the job of Aspirin was to exorcize the evil, the ill being the (head)ache. This division of labour is repeated in the representations of their adverts: Coca-Cola depicted the world of pleasure and Aspirin the pain to be eliminated (see Illustrations 6.6a and 6.6b). Coke has persisted with its positive line up until the present day, whereas Aspirin (not the product but the representation) has recently undergone a transformation. An advert from 1989 describes the world of pleasure and joy that Aspirin can help to maintain: 'It's great to feel great again' (see Illustration 6.7). We have come full circle, but this time at the level of representation: the image suits equally to both products.

What is it that makes possible this interchangeability? True, we have seen a shift from product orientation (qualities and effects) to the contextual representation of consumption, but on the other hand this shift itself requires the redefinition of consumption as an *experience*. In its capacity as producer of a consumption experience, the product must be located within a scene of consumption acts that allows for positive identification and imagining oneself in different situations. This is why the painkiller must adopt a different strategy and begin to represent a world in

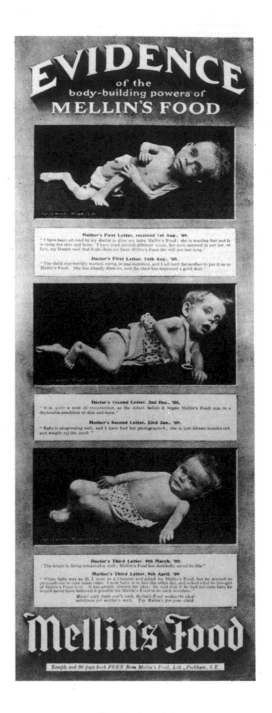

Illustration 6.4

Illustration 6.5a   Aspirin advertisement from 1899 (Germany)

Illustration 6.5b Coca-Cola advertisement from 1892 (USA)

Illustration 6.6a   Aspirin advertisement from the 1930s (Italy)

Illustration 6.6b   Coca-Cola advertisement c. 1912 (USA)

ASPIRIN® PLUS C

Hızlı ve güçlü etki, mükemmel tolerans

ASPIRIN® PLUS C

Illustration 6.7

which pain does not exist (any more). Consumers do not need to be reminded about the experience of headache; they know enough about headaches as it is and they don't really want to imagine themselves in that situation. On the other hand, there is no way in which the *absence* of headache can be represented, for that is just an empty place. Therefore the representation must be based on the elements of good (full) life, on the fun and pleasure that the medicine makes possible and with which consumers want to identify themselves.

This points at an important principle of representation where the depiction of the good world has assumed full independence as a process of building an experiential target for identification and to which the product is attached retrospectively, as it were. As already noted, the product (name) is attached to good rather than the other way round, as was the case during the early stages of modern advertising (in terms of explicit promises and rhetoric assurances of surplus good). In order to explicate this difference, we need to make one further excursion into the early history of the modern advert; and again we start out with patent medicines.

The rhetoric assurance or guarantee was already present in the mid-seventeenth-century announcement we examined earlier (see p. 163) for a patent medicine which says: 'all these medicines have often been proven'. Two centuries later, the very same products were marketed by 'testi-monials' (Apple, 1986: 14) that followed the pattern of religious revival, undersigned by a host of satisfied users, people who had been healed. In

Illustration 6.8

this genre of written advertising, promises and rhetorical assurances flowed into each other.

On the other hand, the rhetorical guarantee also appeared in a more independent form, in a manner that did not refer directly to the qualities of the product, that is, in the case of patent medicines, to their curative effects. In these products the rhetorical guarantee actually resides in their name: the word *patent* referred originally to the authorization given to the product by (H.M.) the King.[22] In this way the named product acquired not only a guarantee of originality but also a surplus 'good' – prestige – which as such had no substantive connection to the actual product. The same principle of 'surplus value' was followed in various purveyor slogans ('Purveyor to H.M. the King/Queen') and more generally in references to public figures who used the product, which served as rhetorical and/or iconic guarantees. A case in point is the Hadacol advert from 1950 which copied the style of the late nineteenth century and had none less than Abraham Lincoln as the guarantee (see Illustration 6.8).

Rhetoric and iconic guarantors were used for selling not only patent

THE "JUBILEE" SCENT BOTTLE.

May be purchased throughout the Empire.

Wholesale only of

S. MORDAN & CO., LONDON.

Illustration 6.9

medicines, but also velvet or perfumes; in England, for instance, the prestige of Queen Victoria was harnessed for this purpose (see Illustration 6.9). Thomas Richards (1990) has analysed – in line with the interpretations of Henri Lefebvre (1971), Guy Debord (1977) and Jean Baudrillard (1983) – what he calls Victorian 'jubilee advertising'. In these adverts Richards discovers the 'decline of referentials' (originally formulated by Lefebvre), where the picture of the Queen and the text describing the product no longer have any reference to each other. As Richards puts it:

> In Jubilee advertising, Victoria did not speak; as a consumer, she was spoken for. Jubilee ads muted the speech of the consumer and substituted in its stead the voice of the advertiser. In this way Victoria's image was a model of irreferentiality: it burst the confines of traditional iconography and made it possible for any language to be attached to any image. (Richards, 1990: 107–8).

Richards is definitely in the right in the sense that a symbol of prestige that is reduced to an icon does not provide even a rhetorical guarantee, nor does the icon represent Queen Victoria as a 'model consumer' of the product (although there were some jubilee adverts which did try to hint in this direction). In this sense jubilee advertising does indeed represent a step towards irreferentiality. On the other hand, the surplus 'good' which is represented in these Victorian adverts (but which does not as such refer to the actual product) still appears as a guarantee which, in the form of a simple juxtaposition, still refers to the actual product. The relationship is not, therefore, completely arbitrary, even though the link in terms of content (between Queen Victoria and a certain perfume, for instance) is missing.

The crucial step towards irreferentiality does not occur until the representation of 'good' focuses on the act of consumption and (later) on the scenes of consumption that make possible an experiential identification with the users and the use of the products and in general with the good world that is represented. And again, the representation is now built the other way round: the 'good' is not attached to the product but the product is attached to the 'good' – either personalized into model consumers or constructed into scenes, situations and events.

This difference in the constitution of representations can be illustrated by comparing our Victorian advertisement with the adverts for Lux soap in the 1960s, in which a Hollywood filmstar says she is one of those 'nine out of ten moviestars who use Lux'. Although this advert may seem a bit outmoded today (mainly because it is based on identification with the person rather than on the modern trend towards situational identification), its function differs essentially from the adverts that referred to Queen Victoria in the late nineteenth century.

Queen Victoria lends her prestige ('guarantee') to the product but she does not provide a model for identification, even with the hint that she uses the product herself. No potential consumer could even *imagine* being like Queen Victoria (even if they wanted to) or gaining admission into her court. The situation is different with the advert for Lux, where the filmstar perfectly fits the role of a model consumer, representing all that good from beauty to the 'sweet life' of filmstars with which ordinary consumers can, at an imaginary level, identify themselves – even though they would be perfectly well aware that they will not turn into a filmstar by using the product.

In psychoanalytic terms, this advert for Lux which stresses identification with a person serves as an object for ideal-ego projection – primarily in the Lacanian sense (Lacan 1968; on the application to advertising, see Williamson, 1978: 60–70; cf. Chasseguet-Smirgel, 1985) – where the object of identification represents 'everything I ever wanted to be'. This is just one short step away from imagining oneself into the good world (scene, situation) 'in which I would like to be/where I could imagine being'. This is why the shift in representations from model consumers to scenes of the good world (such as from the Lux advert here to the Aspirin advert discussed above; see Illustration 6.7) is essentially a less significant one than the shift from jubilee adverts to the Lux advert, where product representations have gained independence as a separate sphere of imagined involvement.[23] The first symptoms of this turn appeared long before the Lux advert, during the early decades of the twentieth century (and most particularly in the United States). The turn cannot be reduced to a mere change of advertising jargon; we are looking at a more profound cultural change where the experience of consumption and the consumption of experiences appear as mutual prerequisites for each other.

A perceptive analysis of this broader cultural change has been offered by the American historian T.J. Jackson Lears (1981, 1983, 1984) by relating (perhaps somewhat surprisingly) two rival concepts of 'therapy' (in the broad sense of care of both body and mind) from the turn of the century to the massive breakthrough of 'consumer society' (see above Chapter 2). The receding concept of caring, 'scarcity therapy', stressed the importance of asceticism, withdrawal and rest and the avoidance of stress and overstimulation (characteristic of 'modern times'), while the emerging 'abundance therapy' favoured the opening up to new stimuli in the modern individualized project of self-realization and self-expression.

In relation to the receding therapy concept, this implied giving moral permission to accept the goods (now in both senses: see note 3) of the expanding mass consumption and mass culture. The new 'therapeutic ethos' rejected the principles of ascetic self-control promoting instead the ideals of psychic growth and perpetual education of the personality capable of enjoying the gifts (goods) of the civilization. This was the 'new basis of civilization' as the economist Simon Nelson Patten put it in the title of his book from 1907 – implying 'a new morality' which 'does not consist in saving but in expanding consumption' (Patten, 1968: 143; cited in Jackson Lears, 1981: 54). Against this background it is hardly surprising that by the turn of the century, as Jackson Lears has shown, the latter therapeutic principle had won a firm position also in advertising psychology.

In this broader context of cultural change, modern advertising as a whole had a key role not only in the marketing of certain products but more generally in creating more permissive attitudes towards consumption. Advertising has an 'historical mission' which was later formulated by advertising psychologist Ernest Dichter as follows:

> In the promotion and advertising of many items, nothing is more important than to encourage this tendency to greater inner freedom and *to give moral permission* to enjoy life through the use of an item, whether it is good food, a speed boat, a radio set, or a sports jacket. (Dichter, 1960: 189; my italics)

Modern advertising is born with one foot in the world of goods and the other in mass culture. The precondition for the birth of modern advertising, as we have seen earlier, was the expansion of consumer goods markets as well as the formation of a specific mode of information, in which entertainment, and more generally, the 'spectacular' was to assume an important role. At the beginning of the century figures for the consumption of mass culture and the world of goods skyrocketed: films, magazines, department stores, and the advertising that links all these together. Mass culture transformed experiences into marketable products and advertising turned marketable products into representations, images and, with time, into experiences again. In other words, the consumption of experiences and the experience of consumption (in its elementary form) have been interlinked from the very outset, as it were (see Eckert, 1978: 1–21; Jackson Lears, 1984: 351; Mayne, 1988: 69).

In the world of representations, the issue of 'truth' is replaced by 'credibility' (Jackson Lears, 1984: 361) and 'believability' (Boorstin, 1962: 226), which are tested against the *verisimilitude* of the experience rather than in terms of its veridicality. This concept of the experiential 'real' can hardly be expressed more succinctly than in the American pop song I happened to hear some time ago, in which the intoxicating state of being in love is described by the words: 'I feel so real!'

The question of the 'truthfulness' of advertising is accordingly pushed into the background. An illuminating case is the justification for an acquittal in a hearing against misleading advertising in the United States in 1963: 'A representation does not become "false and deceptive" merely because it will be unreasonably understood by an insignificant and unrepresentative segment of the class of persons to whom representation is addressed' (cited in Pope, 1983: 279). So you need to know how to read adverts, just as you need to know how to read the fiction (of) film. But an advert is not just entertainment, except perhaps to the Parisian intellectuals who gather once a year to watch advertisements through the night in a cinema theatre. The advert is still a representation of a product even if it no longer is product-centred but focuses on the experience of consumption. The advert attaches a meaning to the represented product, which is then not merely adopted but also transformed by the other party to the bilateral relationship, that is by the potential consumer. But in spite of the freedom that the consumer enjoys in the 'productive' act of (re)interpretation (Certeau, 1984) – which marketing tries to anticipate the best it can[24] – the building of representations has a special logic of its own. In entering the experiential world of consumption, the advert begins to operate with the positive images of wholeness.

It is hardly a coincidence that the representation of the good world begins with stimulants and other oral goods, which are the most basic areas of experiential (sensory) pleasure. But the representation of the world of wholeness does not remain within the boundaries of certain product types. If Coca-Cola invented the 'pleasure of thirst' in 1916 ('Fun to be Thirsty'), just three years later the American markets saw the appearance of a car advert that stressed the 'pleasure of driving'. In 1919 the Jordan Motor Car Company launched an erotic-experiential car advert:

> In a motor car youth will have its fling. The road skims beneath you, winds before you, and unless a man is bloodless he cannot but surrender himself to that fine intoxication that comes of such motion in the open air. It begins in a sort of breathless sensation and ends with that pleasing drowsiness – a silence in which

two people need exchange no words to understand. (cited in Jackson Lears, 1984: 394–5)

In today's advertising shaving is no longer just efficient and easy; it opens the way to the world of (erotic) sociability (Gilette) and finally redefines shaving as a pleasurable experience in itself (a recent Philishave advert). And if you have happened to see the erotically-tinged fantasy-like television advert for Whirlpool household appliances, which begins with a symptomatic 'Imagine!', it must be clear that even these fundamentally 'sensible' goods have entered the realm of experiential representation. Ernest Dichter's thesis gets down to the essence of this logic of representation, rather by intutition than due to theoretical insight: 'Strictly speaking, a new car, a colour TV-set, cigarettes, beer, or French wine are not necessities. *But they all represent aspects of a full life*' (Dichter, 1960: 14; my italics).

Epilogue

The overall shift towards good experiences, characteristic of modern advertising specifically during the last decades, does not, however, imply that the representations produced operate solely within the positive register. The scale of positive experience goes far beyond unambiguous images of pleasure and happiness (beautiful bodies, smiling faces, sunny skies, etc.). Contemporary adverts – posters and especially TV-spots – are filled with dramatic and spectacular elements, touching mini-stories of life which may bring tears to one's eyes and, of course, spiced with humour of different kinds. In other words, today's advertising exploits/uses the same themes as other contemporary experiential goods such as fiction film and music videos. The advert is located at the same continuum, more precisely, in the 'compressed' end of the line not so far from film trailers and music videos (the duration of a TV-spot is about 30 seconds compared to the 3 to 4-minute music videos and slightly shorter film trailers).

The common ground of these categories becomes the more obvious as the advert's autonomy as an experiential product strengthens. Nevertheless, even though the advert is turned into entertainment and perhaps even art, it still has to refer to the product it wants to sell and, consequently, the advert should leave a positive impression on the potential consumer – an impression which is associated with the product. So, even if the mini-story contains representations of negative feelings – sadness, aggression, fear, etc. – it still must have a 'happy ending', a positive effect which (as hoped) associates with the marketed product. It may well be that an 'average' consumer of experiential goods (fiction novels and films) prefers happy ends to tragic ones but in the case of adverts the necessity of a positive end effect is already defined by the basic function: advertised goods must be positively charged in order to act as objects of desire for the potential consumer.

The point is, however, that the positive charge may be produced by many other means besides a straightforward display of happy faces etc. The advert may evoke a whole range of feelings provided the overall effect – the after-image or after-taste – remains in the positive side. A compressed 30-second version of a happy end story is one way to do it but the aim may be reached also by various combinations of metaphoric, comic, dramatic, aesthetic and spectacular elements. So, returning for a while to the advertisement for painkillers, if the recent Aspirin advert presented above (Illustration 6.7) is a paradigmatic case for the shift towards the positive register displaying a world without pain (representing merely the happy end), it should not be too difficult to come up with counter-examples which disregard this simple formula of the positive. The negative – the pain to be cured – may still be represented but this is done, as a rule, in a way in which the negative is given a secondary role in relation to the positive value of the style of representation.

This principle of stylistic elaboration could be illustrated by two recent Finnish TV-ads for painkillers: the first one (Nurofen) shows two fighting yaks charging each other, their horns and heads crashing together with an impressive bang!, and the other (Orudis) is a scene of miners working with their drills in a coal mine accompanied by dramatic opera music. In both examples the negative element of pain is actually reduced into a sign (bang!, drills) contextualized in a metaphorical scene giving priority to the positive experiential aspects of the aesthetic (both cases), the comic (former case) and the spectacular (latter case). The negative (pain) enters the representation only as a sign subordinated to positive experiential (aesthetic etc.) values and not as a figure inviting to identificatory experience – thus affirming the dominance of the positive register. This is a strategy which allows even the return of the 'old' stigmatizing adverts, exemplified by a recent (Finnish) TV-spot for Pepsodent mouthwash: a boy and a girl dancing and having fun while the girl wears a huge clothes peg on her nose signifying her partner's 'lack' (= bad breath). Perhaps the advert contains a self-ironic (?) comment on the old stigmatizing style, nevertheless the message is still there, a reminder of the negative thing the product promises to send away. But, here again the negative is subordinated to the positive value of the humorous (the *huge* clothes peg) thus excluding the negative identification and the 'bad feeling' (of lack) it was supposed to evoke in the 'old' times.

But what about Benetton's new line of advertising launched some years ago (1991–2)? How should we interpret the documentary genre of photograph-posters and prints which is indistinguishable from the 'catastrophe aesthetics' so characteristic of contemporary network news? A ship packed full of Albanian refugees (Illustration 6.10a), some of them falling over the rail, an exploded car burning, a killed man lying in a pool of blood and an AIDS victim and his family by the bed just three minutes after the death (Illustration 6.10b).

Surely these images do not respect the representation code of advertising as characterized above. These Benetton adverts transgress not only the

Illustration 6.10a

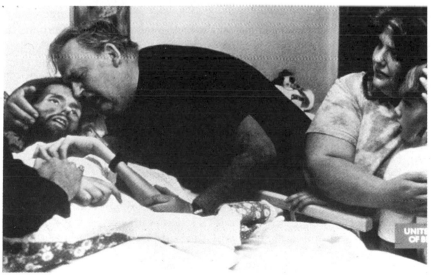

Illustration 6.10b

boundaries of more traditional advertising depicting the 'good things of life' but they also break the rule of the contemporary ad-language by disregarding the principle of the positive end effect. These adverts evoke anxiety rather than some version of 'feeling good'. Nevertheless, the effect is undoubtedly strong, evoking not only strong emotional reactions in the big audience but also among the authorities guarding the code of public representation, that is, defining what may be shown to people, where and how.

Mr Benetton himself stated in an interview (*The Independent* 1992) that it would be a pure waste of money to 'speak about the products' (clothes) in the adverts and that he wanted to create adverts (with his art director Oliviero Toscani) that would 'touch people', and make them *feel* the reality of today's world. Perhaps in order to heighten the awareness of the people and to make them realize their responsibility in building a better tomorrow? Fighting against inequality and human suffering – clothed in the 'united colors of Benetton'?

This is, of course, a noble intention. Nevertheless, it cannot override the fact that the documentary posters should still function as adverts selling the goods of Benetton and appealing to the individualized consumer. Thus we have to take a closer look at the 'special effect' of these adverts. First of all, these adverts function very efficiently in promoting the brand and distinguishing it from the others clinging to the conventional modes of advert representation. And, as many marketing theorists have claimed, this may be the most important function because the negative images associated with the product will fade away with time and all that will be left will be a recognized name occupying a firm place in the consumer cosmology.

On the other hand, these Benetton ads certainly succeed in making people *feel* – something and thus themselves. The experience effect is strong even if it does not fit very well in the 'feeling good' scheme. So, could it be possible that the 'society of the spectacle' (Debord, 1977) should also be conceived of as a 'society of experience' (*Erlebnisgesellschaft*; Schulze, 1992) where emotional and bodily experiences in general are charged positively in relation to the state of 'not feeling anything'. Even the anxiety experienced in front of a photograph of an AIDS victim in the 'act' of death makes one feel oneself – alive – as long as it remains in the regime of 'co-suffering' (Ger. *Mitleiden*) and does not mirror one's own fate. From this point of view, the Benetton adverts are not primarily about 'social concerns' but exemplify a strategy in which the spectacular effect is taken to the limits of representation towards the illusion of 'real presence' ('Look, this is really happening!') which is not too far from the pornographic effect dealt with in the following chapter.

Notes

1. Jacques Derrida has referred in one particular context to the law of 'need *or* desire', observing in passing that he has 'never believed in the radicality of this occasionally useful

distinction' (interview with Derrida, 1991: 115). I, for my part, would be prepared to argue that if the distinction is not transcended, then it will be reduced to an interpretation not dissimilar to the distinction between 'natural' vs. 'artificial' needs which does not avoid the paradoxical fate of the 'supplement' (see Chapter 5) – even if a positive, primary and productive role were assigned to 'desire' in a critique of the concept of 'need'. On the other hand, the transcending of this distinction is actually equivalent to making visible the paradoxical nature of the 'supplementary logic' of desire and need. In this respect the deconstructive strategy may be conceived of as the antithesis of 'resolving' (= making invisible) the paradox.

2. It is no coincidence that the shopkeeper's implicit or explicit question to the potential customer bears a close resemblance to the question that the minister asks in the marriage ceremony ('do you [x] take this [y] . . .'), albeit without the obligations attached ('to have and to hold, to love and to cherish till death us do part'). In both cases people are being asked to make a fundamentally voluntary choice and to express what they *want* rather than to make a binding promise or contract. From this point of view Colin Campbell's (1987) reference to the link between modern consumption and romantic love seems quite appropriate.

There is of course a contractual element involved in the exchange of money and commodities, as well as in situations where marriages are terminated. However, the modern marriage that is based on romantic love and free will is quite far removed from the pre-modern marriage arrangement that could only be cancelled in the event of a serious defect (such as impotence or infertility) in the other party or 'product' (Duerr, 1988: 324 ff.) – consumer protection of sorts for the pre-modern newlyweds.

3. The terminological identity of good(s) as positive and good(s) as product(s), being in itself significant (goods as materializations of the 'good objects'), is differentiated in the following by putting the former in single quotation marks – whenever there is a possibility of confusion.

4. It is interesting to note that the discovery and naming of the ill is linked to a transformation of the product identity 'from wound dressing into an antidote for "halitosis" ' (Jackson Lears, 1983: 24). Thus the (new) product identity – branded Listerine – may be conceived of rather as a derivative of the naming of a deficit (halitosis) which, due to its vague nature, opens up much wider markets than the former identity of the product of the same name. A similar logic may be detected in the metamorphosis of patent medicines, to be dealt with further below.

5. It is not surprising that the use of the negative register today is commonest in informational advertising, which is chiefly concerned to lower consumption levels of 'hazardous' products (alcohol, cigarettes) and to encourage the use of products that can help to avoid obvious risks (AIDS and condoms). However, even here the trend is now away from intimidation and towards tempting tactics, or at least a combination of these.

6. The bread of 'others', the bread outside a particular 'bread culture' (com-*panions*), is defined either as non-bread or at least as not-proper-bread.

7. Arranged more or less sporadically during the annual cycle, markets had a dual nature, and indeed as late as the thirteenth century the terms 'market' and 'fair' still meant the same thing. In these days markets were still ritual events the liminality of which was manifested by the festive denseness of both economic exchange and social interaction. In this context it was impossible to distinguish the potential 'buyer' from the viewer of spectacles, nor the 'seller' from the performer. It was not until the nineteenth century that 'market' and 'fair' began to take on distinctly separate meanings, the former referring chiefly to business and the latter to pleasure. With the appearance in the mid-nineteenth century of the term 'fairground', the latter meaning was also anchored more firmly to a specific place. In a sense, the present situation is bringing these two meanings closer together again, now as a kind of second-degree spatiality and as a linear temporality, characterized in a way by Guy Debord's 'society of the spectacle' (1977) and Jean Baudrillard's 'hyperreality' (1983).

8. The increased potential of self-irony and self-reflectiveness in modern advertising is clearly seen in a recent Finnish TV-spot for a chocolate bar called CHAP. The comical theme of the advert is the marginalization of the product name (although at the same time it also

pokes fun at the 'action movie' type of advert favoured by its rival TUPLA). The 'frame story' of the CHAP spot has two elderly gentlemen, looking very much like a combination of chemist and cook, watching a blueprint film produced by an advertising agency which is supposed to heighten public awareness of the fantastic product these men have created. They are totally baffled by the action-packed scenes; slowly recovering, one of the gentlemen says something like: 'What happened? Did they even mention the chocolate bar!?' The self-irony is underlined by the text in the closing picture: 'CHAP – as yet we have no advert for it'.

9. W.F. Haug (1980), the 'commodity aesthetics' theorist would say that this represented a transition from real use-values to empty promises of use-value. However, the problem cannot be brushed aside as easily as that, as I have tried to demonstrate elsewhere (Falk, 1982). It is also interesting to note that in her recent critique of the world of goods, Susan Willis (1993) uses precisely the case of Quaker Oats as an example of how marketing (naming and packaging) distorts people's 'natural' relationship to oats.

10. In a way the American Cereal Company anticipated the things to come when in 1902 they attached a slogan to their huge outdoor advertisements for Quaker Oats: 'The World's Breakfast'. However, cornflakes and rice krispies have had even greater successes in conquering the world.

11. The erasing of the line between medicine and other oral substances was not merely an outcome of a deliberate strategy of the producers and marketers but based on the dominant discursive formation deriving from 'the Enlightenment's dream of perfecting health and prolonging life' (Porter, 1989: 39) and promoted by the rise of nutritional science in the nineteenth century. Today it is supplemented with the more 'narcissistic' theme of eternal youth, beauty and fitness.

12. From the point of view of orality this distinction corresponds to the difference between the (pre-modern) bidirectionality – to eat and to be eaten into the community (holy communion) – and the (modern) uni-directionality of eating, filling one's stomach and self (see above Chapter 2).

13. I am exploring in more detail the long tradition of vague civilization-diseases from the seventeenth-century definitions of melancholy to the late nineteenth-century neurasthenia and beyond, including its contemporary variations such as the ME (*myalgic encephalomyelitis*) or the 'chronic fatigue syndrome', in a forthcoming study on 'The Modernity Syndrome'.

14. Many of the patent medicines did in fact live up to their promises of 'good feeling', at least in the short term: they contained intoxicating substances. A typical patent medicine of the nineteenth century (Laudanum, Hoffman's drops, etc.) contained alcohol as well as some hard drug (opium, cocaine).

15. This effectively implied a redefinition of 'normalcy' as a deficit, which was no longer understood in terms of specific ailments but which had already been reduced to a general sense of 'not feeling well'. Or as Jackson Lears notes, 'As early as 1873 an advertisement for Tarrant's Seltzer in *Harper's Weekly* noted that "thousands of people who are not actually sick complain that they are – never well . . ." ' (Jackson Lears, 1983: 25).

16. In the marketing of certain types of cereals a more 'pharmaceutical' identity was favoured. An example is provided by the adverts for Postum Cereal Company's flakes, in which the product was represented as a medicine for a self-invented (named) illness called 'coffee neuralgia' (Carson, 1959: 161).

17. It could also be argued that in this slogan as well as in later representations of the product along these lines, Coca-Cola is actually inventing the *fun* and *pleasure* of thirst and in this way doing a great service to the sunny world of soft drinks in general. In the same way as other pioneering products of mass consumption (cf. Ford and cars or Kelloggs and breakfast), Coca-Cola is here identifying and opening up a whole new domain of consumption not only to themselves but to the competition as well.

18. According to Richards (1990: 193) about half of the patent medicines on the English market in 1909 called themselves 'food or drink'.

19. Only one old-style patent medicine managed to continue its career after these legislative changes: Hadacol survived well into the early 1950s. One important reason for the continued success of Hadacol (apart from the forceful marketing) was the modernization of

the product: in its new form the product included vitamin B, although it was still mixed with 12 percent alcohol and also contained other magical substances such as ginseng (Brigham and Kenyon, 1976). Today's wonder-drugs – varying combinations of vitamins and trace elements – which are sold both by chemists and by shops specializing in 'alternative' medicine (cf. Starobinski, 1993), are not proposed to have the same sort of omnipotent effects as their predecessors, but even so the magical element is still there.

20. This change in the connection between the products and 'goods' should not be understood too categorically. Goods are, after all, still sold by reference to their positive qualities (better, best, inexpensive, etc.), but these assurances have turned into mere *rhetorics*. The ordinary consumers who have lost their innocence are aware of this: 'well that's what adverts are like' (much in the same way as the 'promises' that politicians make before elections).

21. The nature of Aspirin as a universal remedy has to do with what it is used for curing, which is not a specified disease or condition but a symptom – (head)ache – that may be brought about by several different reasons. As an experience the condition is not in fact all that different from the vaguer 'not feeling well' that was named, in various different ways, by nineteenth-century patent medicines. In this connection I am not referring to the recent discovery that Aspirin can also be used for such purposes as thinning blood, which in a sense strengthens the role of the product as an all-purpose drug.

22. In fact the 'King's patent' is the origin not only of the 'good' (prestige) attached to one product, but also of the *brandname* in that it provided the product with a certain protection in relation to potential competition and imitation, and at the same time with a name. Thus, for instance, a long-lived patent medicine from the eighteenth century which survived until the late nineteenth century, could only be sold as a patented product: 'By the King's Patent / Essence of Peppermint' (Jones, 1981). In this sense the individualization of the product was closely bound up with the building of a positive identity for the product.

23. Then again, the shift from the negative to the positive register is equally dramatic. This may be illustrated by comparing the above-mentioned Lux advert to an older one using the same 'nine out of ten' argument. In 1913 the White Cross Electric Vibrator was advertised in The American Magazine in the following words: 'nine out of ten people are only half alive. How about yourself? Vibration is life. It will chase away the years like magic [. . .] you will realize thoroughly the joy of living. Your self-respect, even, will be increased hundredfold . . .' (cited in Jackson Lears, 1983: 26).

24. The (problem of the) active role of the audience was recognized already by Roy Johnson, the inventor of the 'impressionistic principle' of advertising (1911). According to Johnson,

> The meaning of a word isn't determined by the dictionary, but by the thoughts and feelings and sentiments of the man who reads it. In other words, it requires constant study to make sure that the reader will get out of our ads precisely what we put in. He will read between the lines in spite of us. Let's try to see that he reads the right things there. (*Printers Ink* 75 [25 May 1911] p. 8; cited in Jackson Lears, 1984: 382).

PORNOGRAPHY AND THE
REPRESENTATION OF PRESENCE

What makes pornography into an exciting topic of study is its role as the excluded other. Depending on the type of discourse it is characterized as evil, immoral, pathological or ugly. On one hand, from an 'orthodox' psychoanalytical perspective the sexual stimulation by visual (or generally: representational) means is turned into a perversion if it does not lead into an actual realization of the sexual act. Thus pornography is not *real enough* or, as Alan Gowans puts it, 'the basis of all pornography is substitute imagery; insofar as painted or photographed or carved bodies serve the purposes of the real thing *in absentia*' (Gowans, 1980: 141). On the other hand, the aesthetic discourses condemn pornography precisely because it is *too real*, abolishing the reflective distance. But the same arguments are found also in moral-juridical discourses, for example in the report of the Attorney General's Commission on Pornography (1986) in which Chairman Hudson notes that, 'what emerges is that much of what this material involves is not so much portrayal of sex, or discussion of sex, but simply *sex itself*' (Report p. 266; cited in Stewart, 1988: 177; my italics). So, in terms of (sexual) conduct pornography is not real enough while in terms of representation it is too real. The ambiguous role of pornography as an in-between of realizing action and imaginary consumption of representations inspired me to open up a broader perspective on pornography, especially relating it to two historical topics, which may be characterized as follows.

First, as regards the aesthetic argumentation, pornography reveals an alternative approach to the historicity of aesthetic and moral conceptions, in somewhat the same way as Michel Foucault's early approach to the archaeology of Western rationality via its repressed Other – madness – which is negativized into insanity and non-rationality (Foucault, 1965). Pornography is the paradigmatic case of the *anti-aesthetic*, the obscene part of what Karl Rosenkranz in the mid-nineteenth century called 'the aesthetics of the ugly' (*Aesthetik des Hässlichen*; Rosenkranz, 1853).

Second, there seems to be an interesting parallelism between *photography* and *pornography* in the context of the aesthetic-philosophical discourses of the nineteenth century. The tendency to exclude photography from (visual) art as a medium and mode of (re)presentation goes hand in hand with arguments excluding the pornographic from (classical) aesthetics. This curious parallelism can, according to my tentative hypothesis, be interpreted on the basis of one common feature: both fight against the principle of representation, in ways that I will try to explain.

This parallelism becomes a unity in the form of photographic pornography, arguably the basic form of modern pornography, later expanding to include the photo-based moving images such as film and video. The semiotic aspects of the article are developed mainly in the context of modern pornography thus defined. This is where the tension between presence and absence or *present*ation versus *re*presentation is actualized in its most articulate manner. However, when historically contextualized the problem of the *boundaries* of representation forces us to trace the discursive roots prior to the invention of photography; or, in more specific terms, we must return to the historical scene where the discourses on obscenity, on one hand, and the discourses on (iconic and literary) representations, on the other, were not yet linked together.

The focus in the genealogical section to follow will be precisely on the modes in which the two themes – obscenity and the role of representations – become interconnected in both moral and aesthetic discourses – from the ecclesiastic debates in the sixteenth century to the modernist 'anti-aesthetic' turn in the nineteenth century (and after). The genealogical part is then followed by a more detailed analysis of the modern hard core pornography which – according to the definition I will propose – is based on the specific character of the 'photographic message' (Barthes). Here the problem of representation is approached in a more semiotic manner aiming at an explication of the historically and culturally specific principles that define the boundaries of representation.

Obscenity: from conduct to representations

The historical contextualization of pornography could, of course, also take us back to prehistoric times, to the cave paintings of the Palaeolithic era depicting explicit sexual acts and organ themes. Then again, the cave-man 'pornography' would just be a manifestation of the culturally primal scene in which the ritual, magical, erotic and 'aesthetic' are merged into an undifferentiated whole. It would be a story of the origins of almost everything cultural, also about the 'origins of art', as Georges Bataille formulated it, inspired by the Lascaux caves uncovered in the 1940s (Bataille, 1981).

Alternatively, one could start from the etymology and the conceptual history of pornography – from the Greek '*pornographos*' or the 'writing about prostitutes' – but then we would just experience a huge leap from antiquity into somewhere between the mid-eighteenth and mid-nineteenth centuries, to the times the term (re)appeared referring to something quite different than it does today. An English medical dictionary from 1857 still defined pornography as 'a description of prostitutes or of prostitution, as a matter of public hygiene' and it is not until the *Oxford English Dictionary*

from 1909 that the term is given, besides the medical sense, an alternative
definition as the 'description of the life, manners, etc., of prostitutes and
their patrons: hence, the expression or suggestion of obscene or unchaste
subjects in literature or art' (Kendrick, 1987: 1–2).

So, the actual key terms are *obscenity* or *unchastity*, not, however, in the
general sense, referring to morally and/or juridically condemnable modes
of conduct, especially of a sexual nature, but as a theme concerning
representations. Consequently, the discursive roots of pornography, in the
modern sense, are structured into two distinctive, yet intertwined, topics,
the first of which concerns the prevention and control of obscene
behaviour, and the second the nature and effects of representations.

There is nothing very new in either of these topics by themselves. The
public conduct of people has always been regulated by rules in one way or
another and the theme of the nature and effects of the representations is
already taken up in Greek philosophy, especially in Plato's *Republic*
(Socrates), concerning, for example, the falseness of myths and the ills of
theatrical representations that disregarded reality (Kendrick, 1987: 36–42).
However, what may be conceived of as an historical *novum* in the Western
tradition, is the specific mode in which these two topics are linked. And
this is something which can be traced back to a number of changes and
processes of separation, the first symptoms of which are found in sixteenth-
century ecclesiastical discourses dealing with the good and evil effects of
images (Ginzburg, 1990: 77–95).

Thus, a bridge was built linking the theme of obscene and unchaste
behaviour to the question of the corrupting effects of representations.
While the Catholics defended the role of the holy icons against the
Protestant iconoclasm referring to their power to evoke virtuous thoughts,
they logically ended up expanding the discourse on the negative side too –
to images which tended to turn men away from the path leading to chastity
and purity. Profane pictures serving the pleasures of the eye and especially
the erotic themes celebrating the interests of the flesh were condemned by
arguments which established a causal link between the image and its
behavioural consequences – mediated by the faculty of *imagination*. The
argument was formulated into the following warning by the late sixteenth-
century theologian Johannes Molanus: 'In Pictures One Should Beware of
Anything that Provokes Lust' (*in picturus cavendum esse quidquid as
libidem provocat*; Molanus, 1570; cited in Ginzburg, 1990: 77).

Molanus' work (titled *De Picturis et imaginibus sacris*) was concerned
primarily with the role of sacred images 'in the service to strengthen the
links with the faithful' (Ginzburg, 1990: 79), while the question of the
negative effects of images was related to the aims of controlling the sexual
life of the common people. The latter question was, however, of secondary
importance simply due to the fact that there did not exist (yet) any
substantial sphere of profane images among the common people. The
world of profane images – the other 'iconic circuit', as Ginzburg calls it
(Ginzburg, 1990: 77) – was primarily located within the boundaries of the

aristocracy, in their private collections of paintings. And this is where the other discourse on the nature and effects of representations was constituted, a discourse which only later would evolve into one concerning the questions of the 'beautiful' and the 'aesthetic'.

But in the sixteenth century the discourses within the profane iconic circuit did not yet draw a line between the lower and higher or the erotic and the aesthetic qualities of the images (paintings); not, for example, in Italy where Titian created his erotic paintings illustrating the themes of Ovid's *Metamorphoses*. As Carlo Ginzburg points out, these paintings were made for the aristocracy to be 'consumed' as erotic images provoking sexual responses which were in no way considered as opposed to the experiences of the beautiful or the aesthetic. So, the evaluation of the representations according to the norms of naturalness and truthfulness concerned *both* the potency of the images in evoking erotic fantasies and experiences *and* their ability to represent natural objects, such as the female body. Consequently, there was a curious parallelism of the two iconic circuits – that of the sacred and of the profane images – which lived in more or less harmonious coexistence and which both had a common denominator in the discourses on the positive effects of the representations, the former from a spiritual aspect excluding the bodily one and the latter from a vantage point which does not distinguish the two.

The historical episode described above may be regarded as a marginal case in the contextualization of pornography, but it surely brings up two related issues: (1) the distinction between the erotic and the aesthetic is historically constituted and (2) the intended aims of representations or the corresponding modes of reception are not a sufficient basis for a positive definition of pornography. This implies that pornography is always defined in negative terms as something, which according to a certain code of representation – be it moral or aesthetic – must be excluded. The code prevails, even if it changes in history, removing the 'erotica' of the sixteenth-century Italian aristocracy to the category of legitimate art (the paintings of Titian) and producing ever new definitions of the representable versus the unrepresentable.

However, looking from the broader historical perspective of the Western tradition the issue of obscenity was thematized primarily in terms of *conduct* – and not in terms of *representations* (and their effect) – up to the end of the seventeenth century. This is due to the simple fact that the production and consumption of literary and iconic representations was developing on a more massive scale in those times making it into a concern of the common people.[1]

So, at the turn of the seventeenth century that obscenity is thematized within the realm of representations, manifested in a condensed form in the definition of '*libri obscoeni*' given by Johannes David Schreber (1688) in the late seventeenth century. According to Schreber, obscene literature contains explicit descriptions of sexual acts and organs and, furthermore, its aim is to evoke sexual arousal and pleasure (Glaser, 1974: 8).[2] This is of course a general definition that applies also to contemporary pornography – whether literary or iconic. Nevertheless, to explicate the specificity of modern pornography we have to gain a much more detailed conception of the historical changes and discursive turns setting boundaries to legitimate modes of representation, that is, defining *what* may and may not be represented and *how* it should be done.

The discursive turns may be conceived of as a sequence of separations. First, as a sequence in which the topic of obscene representations or pornography is thematized first in religious, then in moral and juridical and finally in aesthetic and medical (psychological) discourses, following the historical differentiation of the discursive field (ethic, aesthetic, epistemic), but being all the same granted the position of that excluded – as evil, immoral, ugly and/or pathological. Secondly, within the realm of moral-aesthetic discourse, the turns of discourse are structured into a sequence of distinctions which again and repeatedly defines pornography as the excluded Other: the aesthetic versus the erotic (and sensual), erotic art and literature versus pornography up to the more recent distinction of 'soft core' vs. 'hard core' pornography (from both a moral-aesthetic and juridical point of view). Finally, more conspicuously from the beginning of the 1980s onwards, pornography is thematized in a variety of feminist discourses as a gender-political issue, in a way which reduces the older strata of *moral-aesthetic* discourses to the binary opposition male–female, mainly conceived of as a culturally constructed gender distinction involving a repressive relationship.

Erotic versus aesthetic

The change in focus from obscene public conduct, that is, sexual behaviour which should be kept 'off scene' or 'back stage' (Goffman, 1959), to the production and consumption of representations implies a restructuring of the hierarchy of senses, that is, a shift in emphasis from the close or contact senses to the realm of the *imaginary*, which is fed through the distant senses, in particular the eye.

The moral discourses in the era following the Renaissance were not just dealing with the evils of immorality and obscenity but with the dangers of imagination in general. After the Reformation both Catholics and Protestants implemented a crusade against the imagination. It was the very 'mechanism of fantasy' that was considered 'the site of communication between demon and man' (Couliano, 1987: 203). The imaginary world (*mundus imaginalis*) was the dangerous terrain that lured men into the sins of the flesh by seductive images, be they descriptions, depiction or scenes. Thus the pursuit of censoring the fantasy was linked both to the iconoclastic aims of the Protestants and to the Catholic objective of controlling the imagination by means of good images and excluding the evil and corrupting ones. However, these discourses went far beyond the theme of obscenity and included the whole range of condemnable consequences produced by the uncontrolled fantasy – from laziness and other moral deficiencies to different kinds of illness.

Another line of moral discourse was that of moral philosophy. Developing outside the Church it transformed itself gradually into a discourse on the aesthetic. Its origin can be traced to the seventeenth century beginning from the organic unity of the moral, sensual and aesthetic 'goods' and ending up in the disintegration of these dimensions. This is where the revaluation of the hierarchy of senses takes a course which stands in direct opposition to the ecclesiastical ones. The distant senses, especially the eye, are granted superior status being channels which cultivate man into a virtuous being experiencing the world of beauty; from Edmund Burke's (1792 [1757]) sensualist aesthetics, which still emphasized the bodily origins of spiritualized pleasures to the 'pure reflective' aesthetics of the 'critical' Kant (1790) condemning the bodily (and in general 'interested') pleasures to the lower category of the 'agreeable' (see Grimminger, 1986). Here the imagination is given a positive role, provided that (1) the distance to the objects is maintained; (2) the object is experienced, or contemplated, in a mode which is in harmony with the sublimated values of virtue and 'good taste' (Lord Shaftesbury); and (3) that the experience or reception does not involve any desire for a realizing act concerning the object itself.

These three conditions furnish the moral-aesthetic discourses with a distinction into preferable and unpreferable (positive/negative, higher/lower) modes of reception 'at a distance' – whether it be images, text, dramas or music – but not in the same manner as in the Catholic discourse on good and evil images in which the main issue was the regulation of conduct. The moral philosophical discourse relied on the cultivation of man, as a 'natural' growth from inside or by supportive means of education.

While the sensualistic aesthetics of Edmund Burke still maintained a link between the bodily (sensual) pleasures and the 'higher' gratifying feelings towards the beautiful, even if distinguished by the level of refinement (cf. Freud's 'sublimation'), Kantian (reflective) aesthetics defined the realm of the beautiful categorically excluding the 'lower' forms of bodily pleasure – be they erotic or oral. According to Kant 'an object which merely arouses sensual pleasure, such as some drink or food is said to "gratify" (*vergnügen*) a person and is called "agreeable" (*angenehm*)', while 'an object which merely "pleases" (*gefällt*) is called "beautiful" ' (cited in Guyer, 1979: 170). The pure aesthetic attitude and experience is explicitly defined through a negation: maintaining a 'disinterested' and contemplative distance from the object without any desire for realization or reference to bodily pleasures.

Kant's contemporary, Friedrich Schlegel (1794) formulated in most explicit terms that which unambiguously falls outside the aesthetic: 'Physical excitement is the end of all art, lowering it into a tickling of sensuality' (cited in Glaser, 1974: 15). The aesthetic becomes the sphere of spirituality and difference opposing the imprudent, obscene and dissolute.

The principle of pure aesthetics was applied not only to exclude the actual bodily sensations of oral or erotic practices but also to criticize the literal and visual representations which tended to cancel the required distance to the object and thus desublimate the pure experience into an impure and sensual one. Thus, for example, Schopenhauer (1883), following Kant's ideas, dismissed the Dutch paintings of 'culinary' still life in the following terms:

> they err by representing articles of food, which by their deceptive likeness necessarily excite the appetite for the things they represent, and this is just an excitement of the will, which puts an end to all aesthetic contemplation of the object.

And he continues:

> painted fruit is yet admissible, because we may regard it as the further development of the flower, and as a beautiful product of nature in form and colour, without being obliged to think of it as eatable; but unfortunately we often find, represented with deceptive naturalness, prepared and served dishes, oysters, herrings, crabs, bread and butter, wine, and so forth, which is altogether to be condemned.

But the same goes for other bodily attractions too and especially for the erotic ones, which Schopenhauer takes up in the end of his argumentation:

> in historical painting and in sculpture the charming consists in naked figures, whose position, drapery, and general treatment are calculated to excite the passions of the beholder, and thus pure aesthetical contemplation is at once annihilated, and the aim of art is defeated. (Schopenhauer, 1883; cited in Bourdieu, 1984: 487)

Similar arguments concerned with the 'lower' limit of aesthetic experience are not only found in the nineteenth-century discourses which were still based on the concept of the 'beautiful' but also in contemporary discussions, even if in somewhat less categorical mode, focusing on a distinction between actual pornographic efficiency and erotic experiences. This may be exemplified by Bohdan Dziemidok's stance according to which,

> aesthetic satisfaction does not have to exclude erotic experience which can hardly be called disinterested, impersonal or desireless. An *intensive sexual desire* destroys aesthetic experience. This last one, however, may quite harmoniously go together with *erotic fascination*. (Dziemidok, 1986: 143; my italics)

But how are these distinctions justified, the distinctions defining the lower limit of the aesthetic? Is it really possible to argue on behalf of them in purely aesthetic terms or are we, at least implicitly, forced to rely on some moral arguments?

The key term is of course *distance* – in at least two senses of the word. From the sense hierarchical point of view the experiences of the beautiful are then broadened into the aesthetic (cf. Kant's 'sublime'), the distant senses and in particular the eye is given a primary status. The pleasure of the eye makes possible the most purified experiences which exclude any involvement with the actual object of perception. It is the site where the relationship to the object remains at the level of reflection. But this is far from enough. The eye may take over the functions of the mouth – become an organ of voracity (see Mattenklott, 1982: *'die gefrässige Auge'*) – or it may be transformed into an extension of sexual organs, a form of erotic contact which eliminates the distance required. In other words, the distance to the object does not only enable a reflective position but also constitutes the dissolving experience of *fascination* (cf. Blanchot's formulation 'the contact at distance' in his *La Solitude Essentielle*; cited in Mattenklott, 1982: 80).

That which excites – disgust

The distance must be maintained also through a certain orientation, which Edward Bullough (1912) called the 'psychical distance'. Or, as Derrida points out in his deconstructive reading of Kant's *Critique of Judgement*: the judgement (of beauty) is not concerned with the object itself and not even with the relationship between the object and its representation. It is only concerned with the subject's relationship to the object as representation, which, paradoxically, is detached from the object itself – a paradox which Derrida summarizes as follows: 'The purely subjective affect is provoked by what is called beautiful, that which is said to be beautiful· *outside*, in the object and independently of its existence' (Derrida, 1987: 47).

The only positive characterization Kant seems to give to the lower (interested) pleasure of the 'agreeable' kind[3] is that it evokes and involves a *desire* for the object, that is, a *relationship* to the object itself. However, as soon as the focus is turned to the realm of aesthetic experience, the only positive characterization (that is, desire) is transformed into pure negativity – into something that evokes *disgust*.

Now the Kantian system functions entirely according to the principle of negativity or exclusion. But the exclusion is not based on some postulated and explicated aesthetic code (harmony, etc.). It is based on the norm of *distance* which is conceived of as the necessary condition not only for the separation of the object from the subject but for the separation of the *representation* from the object to be contemplated by the subject without any (interested) relation to the object itself. In other words, the loss of distance breaks the rules of representation – necessary for aesthetic reflection and contemplation – and tends to transform the experience into something unrepresentable.

This is the absolute Other, absolute ugliness or absolute negative which can never be assimilated into the Kantian aesthetics, as Derrida (1981b) has pointed out. Kant's system of the aesthetic may include 'negative pleasure', for example in the 'feeling of the sublime' (Derrida, 1981b: 21), but this is still not the absolute Other of the beautiful. 'Negative pleasure' is still pleasure and may still be assimilated to the system. The only kind of ugliness that, according to Kant, 'cannot be [re]presented in conformity with nature without obliterating all aesthetic liking and hence artistic beauty [is] that ugliness which arouses *disgust*' (1987, § 48:180 [1790]). The disgusting – or 'vomit' as Derrida puts it – is something which,

> by limitlessly violating our enjoyment, without granting it any determining limit [. . .] abolishes representative distance – beauty too. [. . .] It irresistibly forces one to consume, but without allowing any chance for idealisation. [. . .] By forcing enjoyment, it suspends the suspense of non-communication, which accompanies pleasure that is bound up with representation [*Vorstellung*]. (Derrida, 1981b: 22)

So, the disgusting (or vomit) is represented as something *forcing* into pleasure – 'insisting' that it be enjoyed (Kant, 1987: 180) – while we strive against it with all our might. And that is why it disgusts. This is a characterization of the loss of distance, of the collapse of the representation back to the object, regressing the aesthetic experience into a sensual one – or a sexual one, which brings us full circle to the main topic.

To summarize, that which *excites* by transforming the representation into a mere stimulus-evoking (bodily/sexual) response – even if by representational means (as in the case of a pornographic representation) – excites *disgust* precisely because of the resistance towards the abolition of the representative distance. Thus, if there is a desire for the object, a desire for realization – be it eating or sexual contact – then there is no aesthetic experience. Accordingly, if there is an aesthetic experience it unambiguously excludes the desire, turning it into disgust. Applying Kant to the pornographic scheme: that which is pressing to 'turn me on' not only 'turns me off' but turns me *against* my own bodily sensation with a response of disgust. The realm of 'sublimated' or distanced (aesthetic) representation is configured into a vertical scale, in which the upper limit is just above the 'sublime' and the lower limit definitely excludes the 'subliminal'.

However, when transferred into the lower register of the sub-representational delights it is redefined simply as the 'agreeable'. Thus the whole point lies in the way in which the boundaries for the representable are defined – and this is surely an historical variable, within certain limits at least (to which I will return below). If Titian's paintings of *naked* women (etc.) were 'consumed' as erotica in sixteenth-century Italy they were later received as aesthetically legitimated *nudes*, a term which was not incorporated into the vocabulary of the arts until the eighteenth century (from the French *nu*), referring to a tradition of a neutralized mode of representation and reception which is something not found outside Europe (cf. Bryson, 1983: 131).

All the arguments dealt with above apply not only to iconic representations but also to the *literary* ones which is the other means by which to gain reflective and aesthetic distance (cf. Grimminger, 1986: 161–2). Then again, the same dangers reside in the literary representations too. They may serve the aim of aesthetic-reflective distancing but also be used in a manner which abolishes the distance and turns words into flesh, as it were. This 'problem' was not only thematized in connection with the *'libri obscoeni'* – which in fact was the main concern of the juridical control of 'obscene publications' well into the present century (Rembar, 1968; Charney, 1981) – but in a much broader perspective concerned with the unreflective and 'culinary' (cf. Jauss, 1970: viii) mode of reception, feeding the imagination with other less cultivating and rather desublimating themes.

The problem of culinary reading surfaced already in late eighteenth century Germany where the expanding 'reading addiction' (*Lese-Sucht*) was equated, for example by Fichte, other ones, such as drug use (Bürger, 1980: 200). Or as Johann Adam Bergk in 1799 noted: 'the majority of readers *devour* the most wretched and tasteless novels with a *voracious appetite* that spoils head and heart. By reading such worthless material people get used to idleness that only the greatest exertion can overcome again' (cited in Woodmansee, 1988: 205; my italics). Nevertheless, even if the arguments against voracious reading used not only addiction but also *masturbation* as its equivalent, the topic of pornography must be kept within the boundaries set by the discursive economy. So, the next question will focus – in a rather un-Kantian manner – on the possible *objects* remaining beneath the lower limit of representation.

The unrepresentable object

The aesthetic distinction between that which is beautiful and that which is not – or that which is defined as 'ugly' in a general exclusive way (Rosenkrantz, 1853) – did not, however, concern itself merely with the unacceptable ways of representation, evoking unacceptable modes of reception, but it also concerned those things that should not be represented at all. And, as it was, this norm was applied, especially to the realm of erotics. Nude bodies may be represented (cf. Schopenhauer and representations of food) if it is done in a way that does not break the principle of pure aesthetic contemplation and – as I would like to add – which does not break the (legitimate) *code of representation*. The code of representation is a principle of Order[4] which determines both the legitimate modes of representation and the boundaries to what may be represented in the first place and what may not.

According to Rosenkrantz (1853: 235–6) the human body and its genital regions are 'holy and beautiful' in their naturalness. They are turned into obscenities only when (re)presented in the explicitness of sexual intercourse both *manifesting* and *provoking* sexual excitement. However, Rosenkrantz applies an *aesthetic* rather than a moral evaluation on the thing represented and focuses especially on the manifestation of male sexual excitement, that is, the erect male member. In Rosenkrantz's view the erect penis gives it an ugly form which is out of proportion with the rest of the body. He proceeds to conclude the argument in the following way: 'everything phallic, even if in some religions considered as sacred, is from an aesthetic point of view (unambiguously) ugly' (Rosenkrantz, 1853: 236).

The phallus – here referring to the erect penis and not to its psychoanalytical (symbolic) meanings – is the thing which does not fit into the aesthetic code of representation: it does not 'stand for' something (as a representation) but simply stands up and against the Order (see note 4). It falls outside or beneath the realm of representation, being one of the two things which should not be made into pictures. The other is the Christian God which is beyond representation as the Order conditioning all representation.[5]

Even if Rosenkrantz's argumentation against phallic representation – or presentness – seems to be purely aesthetic, it nevertheless manifests an interesting parallel with the religious-moral arguments concerning erection presented by Saint Augustine. Michel Foucault explicates Augustine's view of the Edenic scene as follows:

> the famous gesture of Adam covering his genitals with a fig leaf is [. . .] not due to the simple fact that Adam was ashamed of their presence, but to the fact that his sexual organs were moving by themselves without his consent. (Foucault, 1982a: 14)

This is the autonomous movement Augustine called *libido*. According to him,

> sex in erection is the image of man revolting against God. Adam's uncontrolled sex is exactly the same as what he himself has been towards God – a rebel. (Foucault, 1982a: 15)

This constitutes a metaphorical scheme where man's relation to God is equated to the penis' relation to its beholder (the man) – or who is really controlling whom in the second relation, an ambivalence aptly described in Alberto Moravia's novel *Me and Him* (*Io e Lui*; Moravia, 1988). This was also the most outstanding manifestation of the problem of self-control – 'the relationship between one's will and involuntary assertions' (Foucault, 1982a: 14).

The problem of controlling involuntary sexual manifestations and especially their most visible form, the erection, may not have been the most central problem in Paradise but it surely was actualized long before the 'civilizing process' as described by Norbert Elias (1978). As Hans Peter Duerr (1988) notes, in accordance with Augustine's interpretation, the primary concern in the primitive cultures has not been the covering of (male) genitals but their control by binding (etc.) in the social context of non-sexual nature.[6]

And, in a curious way, this is the theme which prevails through all the later stages of civilization, figuring in the moral, juridical, aesthetic and medical argumentation concerning obscene representations up to present-day pornography discourses and to the juridical definition which draws the line between hard core and soft core according to the presence vs. absence of the 'photographed' erection.

At least this was the situation until recently: the editor of the men's magazine *Hustler* pointed out in an interview included in the anti-pornographic film *Not a Love Story* (1981) that the acceptable angle of erection outside the hard core genre was at that time about 45°. What the growing degree of the acceptable angle of erection implies, has surely something to do not only with the 'loosening' of the boundaries for erotic (?) representation but more generally with the fates of the representational in modern society – a theme I shall return to below.

The anti-aesthetics of modernism

The clear dichotomy of erotic and aesthetic was, however, confused by the anti-aesthetic tendencies and principles of modernism (after the mid-nineteenth century). The link between the beautiful – or more broadly that representing 'good taste' – and the aesthetic was fundamentally problema-tized in the traditions of literary and visual arts. The classical principles emphasizing the close relations between the beautiful and the Order were inverted: art begins with the transgression of taboos and norms. The focus shifted from the representational 'middle range' to its upper (sublime) and lower (subliminal) threshold, aiming both beyond and beneath represen-tation – yet, with means of literary and visual representation (which is the unavoidable paradox). The opposition to the rule of representation is actualized in the questioning of both the *how* and *what* of the legitimate code of (aesthetic) representation. In the pictorial arts it is manifested as a rejection of mimetic representation of the reality 'outside' but also as a transgressive move into the mimetic representation of 'forbidden' (unre-presentable) objects of the real. Both of these tendencies are summed up in the reformulation of the aesthetic question, from 'What is beautiful?' to 'What can be said to be art (and literature)?', as Thierry de Duve has noted (cited in Lyotard, 1984: 75).

The idea of transgression did not point only to the aesthetic and moral order but also more profoundly to the basic structures of expression. In literature there was a tendency to break with the traditional narrative novel format and, more generally, to become liberated from the representative character of language. No more orthodox novels with the beginning–middle–end form, no more unilinear narrative structures and no more language sublimating away from sensuality and bodiliness. The last mentioned aspect, which does not of course characterize all modernist tendencies, is especially interesting from the present viewpoint. Here language must find anew its carnal basis, it must demolish the represen-tational absence, and erotic themes suited this purpose very well.

The traditional novel form is broken by repetition and variation, the narrative is destroyed by description (cf. Blanchard, 1980), especially related to erotics. So, it seems, we approach the field of pornographic literature, or at least almost: Gilles Deleuze (1991) calls the 'higher' genre of pornographic literature 'pornology' (or 'theo-pornology') referring to names like de Sade, Sacher-Masoch, Gombrowich, Bataille and Klossowski.[7]

The distinction between pornography and pornology is not, however, identical with that between pornographic vs. erotic literature and art, as the latter genre is always legitimized by reference to some aesthetic criteria which may always be questioned and rejected in the transgressive pursuit of modern anti-aesthetics. So it is not surprising that the aesthetic argument against literary modernism and that against pornography have much in common. Or, as Ian Hunter has pointed out,

> pornography for Marcus, like modernism for Lukács and the eighteenth-century novel for Watts, is both too abstract and too exprimental; at once imprisoned in language and attempting to by-pass it in favour of an immediate connection with (sexual) experience. (Hunter, 1984: 404)[8]

In other words, the argument made by Adorno (among others) that the works of pornography lack the proper narrative structure (beginning–middle–end) applies to the modernistic (experimental) novel by and large (Sontag, 1982: 208), especially from James Joyce's *Ulysses* onwards.

In the visual arts, especially modern painting, the fight against and flight from representation was realized in somewhat different ways. The surrealists – inspired by psychoanalytical discourse – often made sexuality the subject of their work (see Koslow, 1986: 75–83; Williams, 1981) and Salvador Dali even formulated his aesthetic code according to the principle 'picture made flesh'. In Dali's definition the beautiful 'must be edible, otherwise it does not exist' (cited in Mattenklott, 1982: 101) – a stance diametrically opposed to the one presented by Schopenhauer (cf. above). Actually, some of Man Ray's photographic art meets very easily the requirements of hard core in the contemporary sense. Nevertheless, the mainstream of anti-representationalism in the visual arts headed towards the non-representational, non-figurative and abstract – a path which may be characterized by Malevich's interpretation of his own compositions: 'He [. . .] didn't say it was a "picture of a red and a black square" or a *representation* of these figures. He saw it as a direct *presentation* of the figures' (Mitchell, 1989: 357; my italics). However, the other representative relationship remains, that one between the work of art and the artist – the former interceding between the spectator and the creator – and this is done away with in the contemporary 'performance' art which *embodies* the 'work of art' in the artist's presence (or presentness), thus approaching the presentness of the bodily theatre (Thévoz, 1984).

The anti-representational aims of the modern bodily theatre – from Antonin Artaud onwards – may be conceived of as a pursuit of moving from 'acting' to 'non-acting', to marginalize the role of language, to 'carnalize' theatrical acts, to go back to the ritual roots of shared immediate and bodily experience and break the representational distance.

Or, to take another point of reference, it may be seen as a restoration of 'glorious cruelties of the Jacobean theatre' of the early seventeenth century celebrating the 'pre-disciplinary' (Foucault) or 'spectacular' body and

> that unseparated word made flesh which is the principle of its representational practices (practices which cannot, thus, be regarded as *representational* in the strictest sense). A mode of discourse operates here which, basing itself in incarnation, exercises a unitary *presence* of meaning of which the spectacular body is both symbol and instance. (Barker, 1984: 24).

Going back to the ritual origins of theatrical performances (cf. MacAloon, 1984; Schechner, 1988; Schechner and Appel, 1990; V. Turner, 1982) takes us in fact into themes which are not that far away from the pornographic performances called 'live-shows'. The explicit sexual acts of primitive fertility rites and the violence of sacrificial rites to the old Roman theatre in which slaves *really* were mutilated and killed have much in common with the contemporary live-shows: both aim at breaking the code of representation, replacing theatrical acting by 'real action'.

The same applies also to 'actions' of the 1960s and early 1970s – later cultivated into 'performances' – which used explicit sex and violence to fight the Order of Representation and to eliminate the distance between the act/actors and the audience, at least on the experiential level. Pornographic scenes were used to amplify the effects of presentness – from public masturbation and public sexual intercourse to one recorded case of public self-castration, with fatal consequences (Gorsen, 1972).

When specifying the demarcation of representation and presentation (or presentness) into the relation between 'acting' and 'non-acting' we may now enter into a more detailed analysis of the anti-representational logic of hard core pornography. The parallelism of modern bodily theatre (including the genre of performance) and the pornographic live-show allows us to build a bridge with means of the problematization of the notion of 'acting'.

Just acting?

For illustrative reasons let us proceed by comparing a theatrical act – interpreted in a conventional way – to the pornographic live-show. In other words, theatrical acting is here reduced into a 'pure' representational conduct, which is, of course a one-sided interpretation.[9]

An actor in a play uses his body primarily as a tool, as a means of expression (speech, mime, gestures). The actor uses his body as an instrument in a re-presentation: standing *before* the audience (his concrete presence) but at the same time standing *for* something which is absent, that is, his or her 'role' in the play.

Even if a good actor is not 'just acting' or deceiving but should be conceived of as an 'incarnation' of the character represented (Kelsey, 1984: 68), 'really' feeling his or her emotions, it still remains a re-presentation. This becomes evident in the case of second-order acting with multiple audiences aptly described by Bela Balazs. The description is so illuminating that I cannot resist quoting at length:

> Asta Nielsen once played a woman hired to seduce a rich young man. The man who hired her is watching the result from behind a curtain. Knowing that she is under observation, Asta Nielsen feigns love. She does it convincingly: the whole gamut of appropriate emotion is displayed in her face. Nevertheless we are aware, that it is a sham, a mask. But in the course of the scene Asta Nielsen really falls in love with the young man. Her facial expression shows little change; she had been 'registering' love all the time and done it well. How else could she now show that this time she was really in love? Her expression changes only by a scarcely perceptible and yet immediately obvious nuance – and what a few minutes before was a sham is now sincere expression of a deep emotion. Then Asta Nielsen suddenly remembers that she is under observation. The man behind the curtain must not be allowed to read her face and learn that she is no longer feigning but really feeling love. So Asta now pretends to be pretending. Her face shows a new, by this time threefold change. First she feigns love, then she genuinely shows love, and as she is not permitted to be in love in good earnest, her face is lying that she is lying. And we can see all this clearly in her face, over which she has drawn two different masks. At such times an invisible face appears in front of the real one. (Balazs, 1952: 64).

The situation is quite different in the case of a live-show. In the staged sexual act there is something more real than acting – as role-playing. It defies the three-part categorization of acting, the use of language (signification) and (the possibility of) lying. Or as Umberto Eco puts it: 'every time there is a possibility of lying, there is a sign-function' (Eco, 1976: 58).[10] In a live-show the destruction of this trinity is given definite visible form – or becomes flesh – especially in the manifestations of male sexuality: erection and penetration. This is the phallic system which does not fit into the realm of representation: it is presentation, an actual presence of (sufficient) sexual arousal.

On the other hand the female partner is able to lie or act, that is, to use her body – the mime, gestures and vocalization – as a means of expression communicating something intended to the audience. The bodily sounds, 'like moans and sounds of love' may be characterized as 'the linguistic analogues of an erection, or of a nameless pain, or of tears' – in the words of Michel de Certeau (1984: 163) – but being an actor/actress implies a certain linguistic competence which then may be applied also to the bodily register of pre-linguistic vocalization, more or less successfully depending on the competence of 'acting'.

This holds true to the use of the body as a means of expression in general, also to the mimes and gestures, which occupy a double role both as pre- or sub-linguistic manifestations of bodily states (cf. Kristeva's concept of 'gesturality')[11] and as linguistic means of expression signifying the bodily state *in absentia* (cf. Eco, 1976) as an intended message for the other, the audience. And this seems to be (as will be shown further below) one of the central problems in modern hard core pornography: how to create a convincing representation of *female sexual pleasure* in the absence of evidential signs such as the male erection. The 'faking' may be more or less convincing and, on the other hand, the problem may be of greater or lesser importance depending on the audience and its mode of reception (see MacCannell, 1989), but still the mystery remains. This may be exemplified by the discussions surrounding the 'ivory-soap-girl' Marilyn Chambers who turned into a porn star in the early 1970s' (cult) film titled *Behind the Green Door* (1972). The question was: did she *really* have orgasms on-screen or was she *just acting* well (Jordan, 1987)?

In distinction to the female situation, the male part performs a more fundamental and surely more visible ex-pression: something standing and 'pressing out'[12] of his body, something real and authentically present, something with the power of *evidence*. It is not an element in a body-language (sign function) but can be understood as an 'indexical sign' in Peircean sense (see Sebeok, 1990), that is, referring to a sign wherein there is a spatio-temporal or physical connection between the sign vehicle and the entity signified – as in the relation of smoke to fire.[13]

The evidential power in the context of a live-show is focused on erection and penetration. In film/video pornography – especially from the 1970s onwards (cf. Williams, 1989) – it is supplemented, however, with scenes of explicit ejaculation, as the ultimate evidence. But as evidence for *what*? This is the topic I shall now analyse in more detail.

Photography – pornography

The pornographic and erotic *picture* has also had a history since the days of Titian: in private uses, in the 'lower arts' of the people, in carnivalistic contexts such as caricatures, etc. The lower arts of obscene illustrations prior to photography fulfil all the *iconic* requirements of the modern hard core (erection, penetration, etc.), but nevertheless consist of constructed pictures based on the interpretations and illustrative powers of the artist without necessary reference to the authentic. Interpreted retrospectively – and somewhat anachronistically – they are iconic signs of hard core. They still lack the indexical and evidential power which seems to be at the (hard) core of modern pornography.[14]

In the lower arts of pornography the problem of representation was solved at the historical moment photography was invented, that is, in the 1840s. But, of course, in the case of pornography, there was no avant-garde pursuit of transgressing representation in itself. There was just the simple aim to produce 'effective' sexual stimulation by visual means – the efficacy of which was not a central concern as long as there was enough demand for these specialized markets. However, this simple aim of stimulation pointed, curiously enough, in the same direction as the anti-representational aesthetics. So, it is no wonder that Charles Baudelaire stated in his essay on 'The Modern Public and Photography' from the year 1859 that 'pornography is the major function of the new art of photography' (Baudelaire, 1965: 153). This was written in the times of the

invention of the *carte-de-visite* photograph which also initiated the circulation of photo-pornographic pictures (Tagg, 1988: 104) – and, as it was, only
two years after the British 'Obscene Publications Act' was passed.

From its birth photography sought its proper place, both imitating the
representational visual language of the painting (producing a whole genre
of kitsch-like compositions) and making a heavy intervention into the
realm of pornography, straight to hard core. The first photo-pornographic
pictures were painting-like (or theatrical) 'posings' in character – one
understandable reason for this being the long exposure time needed – but
they did contain the same necessary basic elements as the later action-
oriented photographic pictures. Anyway, the technical innovations con-
siderably reducing the exposure time (in the 1880s) permitted a clear shift
from 'staged' compositions towards 'taking pictures' in and of action. The
authentic-documentary character – and thus also the presentness effect – of
the photograph was dramatically reinforced. The emphasis was now on
taking *rather* than *making* a picture. The camera was turned into a weapon,
'shooting' the object and 'capturing' it on the plate.

The uses of photography went far beyond the imitation of painting and
pornographic images, to legal and scientific contexts and later to almost
anything (to the newspapers and to the whole photo-based image industry). Nevertheless, the use of photography as a means of identification in
legal matters – especially as court evidence (Tagg, 1983: 292) – or as a
means of scientific research has a shared common characteristic with the
pornographic applications. In all these cases photography was used as
evidence of reality – of a past presence ('having-been-there'; Barthes,
1977: 44) or of physiognomic features of the insane, as was the case in Dr
Hugh Welch Diamond's 'clinical photography' from 1856 (Tagg, 1983: 293;
1988: 77–81).

In fact, the line between the 'scientific' and the 'pornographic' uses of
photography is not always easily drawn. One of the borderline cases is
C.H. Stratz's study in physical anthropology entitled 'The Beauty of the
Female Body' (*Die Schönheit des weiblichen Körpers*, 1898) which aimed
at detecting the universal 'golden scale' of female beauty by means of a vast
photographic material of naked women from a number of different
cultures. The book went through several printings and surely not only due
to 'scientific' demand. In other words, Stratz's book was obviously located
in the marginal zone of 'scientific pornography' of its time (Johannesson,
1978: 159–65; 1984: 41–50).

But how should the evidential nature of the photograph be conceived?
How should we understand Roland Barthes' formulation according to
which the photograph 'by virtue of its absolutely analogical nature, seems
to constitute a message without a code' (Barthes, 1977: 43) – or his later
statement noting that 'from a phenomenological viewpoint, in the photograph, the power of authentication exceeds the power of representation'
(Barthes, 1981: 89)?

The evidentiality of the photograph is obviously based on the physical (photogenic) link between the object and the image, the 'imprint'. Thus, in Charles S. Peirce's words, photograph is not only an iconic but also an indexical sign:

> Photographs, especially instantaneous photographs, are very instructive, because we know that they are in certain respects exactly like the object they represent. But this resemblance is due to the photographs having been produced under such circumstances that they were physically forced to correspond point by point to nature. In that aspect, then, they belong to the second class of signs, those of physical connection. (Peirce, *Collected Works*, vol. 2.; cited in Mitchell, 1986: 59–60)

The indexical evidentiality of the photograph does not imply that it stands entirely outside the code of representation – as for example W.J.T. Mitchell (1986: 60–1) and E. Ann Kaplan (1985: 27) seem to interpret Barthes' formulation quoted above. It simply means that the indexical link between the object and the picture (taken) grants the photograph a certain in-between position, between (past) presence and its re-presentation – a position which cannot be explained away by reference to 'an ideology of the visible as evidence'[15] (Kaplan, 1985: 27) or to 'a certain mystique' attached to the photograph 'in our culture' (Mitchell, 1986: 61).

Mitchell (1986: 61) backs up his argument by referring to the anthropological evidence according to which the so-called primitive man does not 'see' the photograph as a depiction of reality. In other words, there is a cultural learning process – an internalization of a certain representational code – which transforms the photograph into an intelligible (evidential) representation of reality or past presence. From this vantage point the Western tradition of perspective painting – especially from Alberti onwards – may be regarded as the necessary learning process which makes the contemporary mode of photo-reception possible.

But even this is not a very strong argument against the ambiguous role of the photograph in between the (past) presence and representation. It just points to the fact that one has to learn, that is, to internalize a representational code, which transforms the flat two-dimensional surface (of the photograph as print) into a three-dimensional space 'behind the frame'. Then again, if you take the primitive man to the movies – which is still a photo-based iconic system, even if it involves a more complicated 'illusion of presence' (Williams, 1981: 218) or 'impression of reality' (Baudry, 1986: 314) – you would get responses similar to those the Lumière-brothers received when presenting the film of 'the train arriving at the station' in Paris in the year 1895. The response would be, if not actual panic then, at least, a three-dimensional reception of a live scene.

The point is that even if the cinematic apparatus functions on levels other than the 'photographic message', it is still based on the evidential-indexical characteristics of the photograph. Thus I am prepared to accept the counter-critique Roland Barthes returns to those who regard the photograph as merely a continuation of the Albertian tradition. According to Barthes, this argument is futile: nothing prevents the Photograph from being analogical; but at the same time, Photography's *noeme* has nothing to do with analogy (a feature it shares with all kinds of representations). The realists, of whom I am one and of whom I was already one when I asserted that the Photograph was an image without a code – even if, obviously, certain codes do inflect our reading of it – the realists do not take the photograph for a 'copy' or reality, but for an emanation of *past reality*: a *magic*, not an art. (Barthes, 1981: 88)[16]

Curiously enough, the primitive man, being perhaps unable to 'read' the photograph in a proper (Western) manner, is, however, intuitively aware of its magic powers, its ability to capture the soul in the black box. This is not so far away from the new panoptical uses of photography in the Norwegian highways. The 'big brother's' eye, the camera, will automatically take an identifiable (register plate and face) photo of the speeding driver, who will then be tracked down and fined, automatically.

This exemplifies photographic evidentiality as an indexical transfer which in photo-pornography is supplemented with the evidential aspects of the act, the erection (etc.) as an indexical sign of (the presence) of sexual excitement.

The photo-pornographic effect

The double indexicality of photo-based pornography aims at provoking a receiver's response which is, in a sense, symmetrical to that performed by the 'sender'. This seems to apply primarily to the ideal- or stereotypic porn-consumer, the lone male spectator (masturbator). But, as has been noted (Brown, 1991: 115) the audience is not that homogeneous and the expanding markets for video-pornography actually point to a change in the structure of demand, that is, towards private 'couples'-consumption, probably as an occasional ingredient in erotic practices.[17] This forces us to take a closer look at the modes in which a photo-pornographic effect is constituted and to the types of audience they appear to presuppose. The question is: how to characterize the relationship between the spectator and the photograph depicting sexual organs and acts?

As it appears, the relationship is in its simplest form that of *stimulus and response* – with the precondition that the pornographic effect 'works' as intended. Accordingly, it might be presumed that this is what the pornographic emphasis on (non-representational) presentness aims to strengthen, relying on, what could be called, *indexical transmission*: first, by attempting to give evidence of real and authentic sexual excitement in the performance, and then using the evidential status of the iconic-indexical photograph (Barthes' 'having-been-there') and, hopefully, resulting in a symmetrical indexical or performative effect in the spectator, that is, sexual excitement accompanied with all its indexical signs. But the constellation appears to be of a more complicated nature.

In this *ideal* case the relationship is that of plain transmission (of the stimulus) containing no moments of transformation: the 'same' is transferred from the scene (sender) to the spectator (receiver), corresponding to the technical (or information-theoretical) concept of communication (signal transported through a channel) in distinction to the semiotic model including the moments of transformation (encoding–decoding and the different processes of signification, inference and interpretation). In other words, the ideal(ized) case of stimulus transmission is close to a situation of tacit stimulation (tickling someone etc.). The only difference is that the tacit is replaced by visual means of stimulation. The difference is, however, a significant one.

It implies a rejection of a plain stimulus–response model in favour of representational mediation. In Freudian terms, the stimulus is not received at the level of 'organ pleasure' but implies a mediation (the eye) which necessarily involves some mode of representation. It could be conceived of as something hardly more than mere mimetism which is the other form of 'primary identification' besides actual (oral) incorporation (cf. Fenichel, 1982: 36–7). But even here the mimetic relation involves a representation, a (primary) identification with the desired other (Freud), with the object of the other's desire (Girard, 1977) or the ambiguous unity of the two (Lacan).[18] What this means is that mimetism is not a transmission of the same (such as a contagious yawn) but involves a moment of transformation constituting the object (of desire) as a representation. And this is all that can be said at this stage.

Yet, stimulation by visual means is not to be identified with the 'higher' levels of representational communication. It remains in the liminal space between these two poles. It is a mode of transmission which is located between the *signal-function* – thematized by Thomas Sebeok's (1971) 'zoosemiotic' studies in which the olfactory and visual signals function according to the same principle – and the (semiotic) *sign-function*.

Then again, the transmission mechanism of pornographic (re)presentation maintains fairly simple structure if the spectator is reduced into an ideal type of the 'pure' voyeur or scopophilic. The voyeur's sexual excitement derives primarily – in the idealized case, merely – from his position as a witness to the other's sexual intimacy: being present but at the same time excluded (cf. the 'primal scene': realized or imaginary). He (she) does not necessarily need any evidence of the sexual pleasure of the performers. He is satisfied with the *ocular penetration* he exercises, possibly supplemented by masturbation. Hence, the mode of transmission is still more basic than that which is hardly above the tacit stimulus–response case: it is simply a *transfer* of the voyeur to the (primal) scene with evidential means of indexicality, both in the act and in the photographic transmission (the latter being the additional element distinguishing photographic porn-consumption from the actual performance in front of an audience). In other words, the ocular penetration is not necessarily linked to a 'substitute' sexual penetration in an imaginary identification with the performed act.

But the pure voyeur-type may be less common among the erotica

consumers (in a broad sense) than could be expected on the basis of the
hard core supply. And it may be even argued, that the pure voyeur seeking
sexual excitement only in the experience of illegitimate presence is actually
an ideal type which does not exist in reality (see Fenichel, 1982 [1946]: 347–
8). The spectators are certainly also involved in an identificatory relationship to the performance seeking for 'mimetic excitement' (to use Leo
Bersani's term in a somewhat different sense; see Bersani and Dutoit,
1985). And this is where both the presentness and representation of sexual
pleasure have a crucial role. It may also be said that this is what the
conventional hard core really seems to aim at, desperately, one might add.
The task appears to be really a hard one but not because of the general
reasons of communicability. Not only is it because there is a lack of
competence in creating 'works of pornography' that really work but it is
also due to the contradictions built into the double target of pornography:
to please the (ideal) pure voyeur by evidential presentness on the one
hand, and supply material for the mimetic excitement by both evidential
and representational means on the other hand. As I try to show in the
following, the latter (sub)duality – to communicate and evoke sexual
pleasure evidentially and representationally – is the other inner contradiction of pornography leading to problems of 'efficacy'.

From the *receiver's* point of view the counter-effectiveness of hard core
pornography may of course be explained also on other grounds, especially
by reference to the too explicit, too intruding and too insistent mode of
(re)presentation. In other words, as something which rudely 'forces' us to
pleasure, which is reduced to (almost) plain immediate stimulation, and
thus excites – disgust. This is a common argument which is easily justified
not only by puritan moralists but also by those who make a distinction
between the positive pole of eroticism in art or even 'erotic art' (and
literature) and the negative pole of pornography.

But, even if the arguments are well grounded – for example from D.H.
Lawrence[19] to Roland Barthes[20] – they are still based on the Kantian
'exciting-therefore-disgusting' scheme. That is, they emphasize the necessity of some aspect of *distance* – hidden, hinted, indirect, mediated,
symbolized, etc. – even if allowing it to be reduced to the minimum of
erotic feelings, fantasies and tensions.

All this does not, however, apply to the case of mimetic excitement
which, by definition, presupposes the abolition of that distance. And thus
the reasons for a (possible) counter-effect must be sought elsewhere –
according to my suggestion, from the contradiction between the dimensions of evidential presentness and representation.

Looking from the *sender* point of view (pornographic production), the
above contradiction could be conceived of as an outcome of the desperate
pursuit of pleasing two antagonistic audiences, the pure voyeurs and those
seeking mimetic excitement. That is, to supply the former with evidential
presentness and the latter with convincing representations of sexual
pleasure. But, as noted earlier, this is hardly the case.

The dilemma seems to be located in the 'porno-logic' which places these two dimensions along a unilinear continuum: the amplification of evidential presentness is supposed to strengthen also the transmission of 'excitement' even if the latter is always bound to some mode of representation. Thus, there is a tendency to invert the effect into counterproductive (for the latter), as exemplified in an articulated way in detailed organ/act close-ups tending to replace the hot look of mimetic excitement by a cold one resembling the 'clinical gaze' described by Foucault (1973). Then again, the inversion does not apply to the spectator types which gain pleasure in an ever more complete control of the object, by seeing (*scopophilia*) and knowing (*epistemophilia*) – both linked to the 'instinct for mastery (sadism)', according to Freud (1976: 371).

The analysis developed above is specifically focused on the photopornographic hard core which involves the combination of explicit act and organ exposures. Thus I am not concerned with, say, the sub-genre of (usually) female 'posings' for (usually) male gazes, which seems to be the basis for E. Ann Kaplan's (1985) analysis. Although the voyeuristic look – which Kaplan unproblematically identifies with the 'male gaze' (Kaplan, 1985: 14–15) – is found also in the posing genre, the mechanism of looking functions primarily according to a simpler principle. This is exemplified by the (almost) systematic use of the 'seductive' counter-look of the model which not only reveals the voyeur but invites him (his look) into an imagined contact (intercourse). Hence, the one invited by the counter-look ceases to be an illegitimate voyeur and turns into an imaginary partner. Consequently, the weak presentness effect – lacking the indexical signs of the male part (object) – is transformed into mere fantasy, ignited by the image.

The imaginary dimension is, however, actualized also in the hard core photographic genre as soon as it is serialized, narrativized and especially when it is turned into a 'motion picture' – as film (and its later technical variant, video). This is where the basic contradiction of evidentiality and representation acquire new forms.

The motion (of) pictures

Film is surely something more than a moving photograph. Nevertheless it should be emphasized that a movie is still based on the 'photographic referent', even if 'this referent shifts' and 'does not make a claim in favour of its reality, it does not protest its former existence' (Barthes, 1981: 89). According to Barthes, the cinema, 'particularly the fictional cinema', participates in the 'domestication of photography' (Barthes, 1981: 117) by constantly weakening its *noeme* ('that-has-been'), or its evidential effect of (past) presence: 'film can no longer be seen as animated photographs: the *having-been-there* gives way before a *being-there* of the thing' (Barthes, 1977: 45). The cinematic experience of *being-there* – the 'illusion of presence' (Williams, 1981: 218) or the 'impression of reality' (Baudry, 1986: 314; Metz, 1983: 118) – is actually the opposite of the evidential effect of photography, but, nevertheless, it simultaneously builds on the photographic referent.[21]

In a (fictional) film the 'photo-realism' is harnessed in the service of the imaginary order, the 'more-than-real' of the hallucinatory dream world (Baudry, 1986: 314). The perception and the representation melt into one producing 'artificial psychosis without offering the dreamer the possibility of exercising any kind of immediate control' (Baudry, 1986: 315).

Then again, this is exactly what the hard core pornographic film struggles against with its insistence on the primacy of the evidential presentness. The problem is not actualized in the earlier 'stag films', consisting simply of a number of more or less disconnected (documented) sexual acts (cf. Williams, 1989: 58–92). The problem does not surface until pornography enters feature-length film narration, from the 1970s onwards (Williams, 1989: 93ff.).

Now, the hard core genre confronts new challenges which concern both the narrativity and the diegesis of the cinematic representation – and its reception. It has to accommodate somehow to the cinematic apparatus while at the same time accumulating the evidential effect by emphasizing the visibility of ejaculation. In a sense, the move towards the higher levels of representational transmission (or communiction) is balanced and/or counteracted by a move towards stronger evidential presentness. What does this paradoxical double move imply?

The problem of narrativity is actually not the most crucial one. The feature-length hard core film may be structured into a frame story which guides the spectator from one 'act-episode' to the next. Even if the act-episodes are conceived of as ruptures in the narrative continuum, the structure of the film as a whole is not that far away from the 'musical song-and-dance numbers' which 'break the flow of the diegesis' in the genre of musical-films (Mulvey, 1986: 203; cf. Williams, 1989: 123–4).[22] Only now, the interrupting act-episodes are not realized as a move from one fictional register to another but as a move to a register which, due to its evidential effect of presentness, opposes the representational logic of the fictional narrative.

This implies that the identificatory mechanism of cinematic experience – both as (narrative) character identification and as (diegetic) 'identification with the camera' (Metz, 1983: 49–51) – lacks a continuity in the scale of the film as a whole. Thus, the spectator, being a voyeur and/or seeking 'mimetic excitement', is bound to return to the frame-story structure, just anticipating the next act-episode to be consumed.

This mode of anticipation is something other than what Barthes (1977: 10) refers to when equating 'the pleasure of corporeal striptease' to the 'narrative suspense', both characterized by 'gradual unveiling'.[23] The pornographic frame-story anticipation functions more like a repetition of the same, even if involving a certain degree of variation. The structure of act-episodes within the frame-story also differs from the function of descriptive sequences in literary representation which also break and suspend the narrative flow, producing an effect which Bersani (Bersani and Dutoit, 1985) compares with the accumulation and relation of sexual excitement. According to Bersani, these sequences are the chaotic elements which dynamicize the narrative order and intensify the 'mimetic excitement' (Bersani and Dutoit, 1985: 38). This is a strategy implemented also in literary eroticism, including the 'pornology' from de Sade to Klossowski (see Deleuze, 1991: see also Blanchard, 1980), but it does not apply to cinematic hard core. The registers of evidential presentness and narrative/ diegetic representation just cannot be linked together complementarily, that is, in a way which would strengthen both effects reciprocally.

Be that as it may, this does not seem to bother the producers of hard core films – at least no more than the occasional breaking the rule of actor's counter-look-prohibition, established in Hollywood in the 1910s. In other words, there is no explicit aim to uphold the 'diegetic process' by avoiding revealing the spectator/voyeur through a counter-look from the screen – the function of which (absence) Noël Burch characterizes as follows:

> in order to increase the cine-spectator's sense of being-there, it was necessary to eliminate the camera from the (apparent) consciousness of the actors; they had ostensibly to ignore it. For the spectator to receive as directed at him/her a gaze at the camera had become tantamount to the hidden voyeur's shock when his/her gaze is unmasked and returned. (Burch, 1982: 22)

The ambivalence concerning the counter-look is just another manifestation of the contradiction of the evidential presentness versus representation: the counter-look reveals the voyeur but also confirms his/her photo-indexically mediated presence. Furthermore, by breaking the imaginary identification with the performers or their 'part objects' and with (the eye of) the camera, thereby revealing the presence of the camera itself, the spectator is placed right behind the camera, and enters into a copresence with it. In other words, the spectator/voyeur takes the place of the cameraman who is really there when the act takes place.[24]

The spectator's identification with the one *behind* the camera excludes the other two modes of identification – the (narrative) identification with whatever is *in front of* the camera and the (diegetic) identification with the camera *itself*. Then again, precisely these two modes of identification are crucial for the spectator seeking mimetic excitement, being the other type of porn-consumer which the pornographic apparatus also attempts to titillate. Consequently, the producers of the contemporary feature-length hard core films by and large[25] apply the rule of prohibited counter-look – not because of conscious audience targeting but simply due to an intuitive accommodation to the general code of film fiction ('this is how these kinds of films are done').

However, the acceptance of the rule prohibiting the counter-look does not solve the basic contradiction of evidential presentness and representation. The structure of a feature-length hard core (fiction) film is necessarily reduced into a frame-story of secondary importance in relation to the reiterated act-episodes – unless the act-episode is writ large, into a full-length film. This would imply a structure reminiscent of Barthes' idea of the analogy of striptease and narrative suspense, only now replacing striptease with a suspended or prolonged progress of sexual act(s), until 'the end' – which could hardly be called 'happy' in the conventional sense. The other difference, compared to Barthes' scheme, is that the focus is now on the audience seeking mimetic excitement by means of some identificatory mechanism and not just longing to see everything – the body and story – uncovered.

This does not mean that the act-episode would be prolonged to the scale of one realized sexual act, from everything preceding and preparing it until the orgasmic climax in all its evidential explicitness. This would be something like a classical *film noir* charged with erotic tensions and then supplemented with what would be more properly characterized as an anti-climax, an end which would be a collapse of the whole story.[26] However, it is that there is a progress which is not just a repetition but also an accumulation towards an orgiastic end – in somewhat similar manner to the 'apocalyptic narratives (such as the Book of Revelation)' characterized by Leo Bersani as stories which, 'accumulate climaxes in addition to develop-ing toward them; to a certain extent, they de-emphasize beginnings and middles and allow the entire narrative space to become a repetition of climatic moments' (Bersani and Dutoit, 1985: 51).

What Bersani calls 'narrative space' comes very close to the concept of diegesis, primarily used in the context of fictional film – both as a representation and an experience. And actually Hans-Thies Lehmann, in his interesting article on cinema as 'spatiality-factory', uses the expression 'mythical-spatial experience of the film' (Lehmann, 1983: 580–9) when referring to the diegetic order of the film. Thus diegesis may be conceived of as spatiality which absorbs into itself the temporality of the narrative, enduring breaks in the latter (by spectacles) without collapse.

So, is it possible to imagine a hard core pornographic fictional film structured like an 'apocalyptic narrative' filling up the film's experiential 'mythical space'? At least it would avoid the clumsy frame story structure and a mere repetition of the (almost) same, in the form of the act-episodes. It would be structured in a way reminiscent of what I would call a *ritual scheme* rather than a narrative.

And, as it appears, the classical hard core film *Behind the Green Door* (dir. Art and Jim Mitchell, 1972) is more or less successfully structured according to these principles, in distinction to the other hard core cult film, *Deep Throat* (dir. G. Damiano, 1972) which leans on a more conventional narrative structure. In *Behind the Green Door* the frame story (two men telling about their erotic experiences to a third) is marginalized into a prologue and an epilogue while the whole sequence of events is built into a continuous ritual scene 'behind the green door' supplemented with an additional effect of audience doubling: those watching the live-show (the ritual) assimilated to those watching the film. The sexual acts are accumulated according to a ritual logic in which the female sacrificial 'victim' (object) is transformed into an active subject of sexual desire and pleasure, thus, if not inverting then at least turning the subject/object, active/passive, etc. relationship into an ambivalence ('who's eating whom?'). The ritual scene also corresponds to the logic of the rite of passage transferring the initiated into the realm of complete and unbound sexual femininity.

I am not, of course, insisting that the film *Behind the Green Door* represents a hard core film that 'works', especially among the audience of 'mimetic excitement', male and/or female. What I am arguing, however, is that this is a structure which could possibly function in accordance with identificatory processes which are located beneath the 'identificatory pleasure' of empathizing 'with a character' (Lehmann, 1983: 578) but simultaneously maintaining the basic identification with the camera – the spectator as 'all-seeing' (Metz, 1983) but also 'only-seeing' (Lehmann, 1983: 582) – which is crucial to the diegetic order.

In other words, there is a lower level of identification – of 'psychotic' nature fitting into the 'artificial psychosis' (Baudry, 1986: 314; cf. also Guattari, 1977: 82–99) offered by the cinema – which ranges from non-specific character identification[27] (here especially the transgression of the male/female distinction) to 'part object' identification (not only sexual organs but bodily fragments in general) up to a magic-animistic confusion of live beings and things (Lehmann, 1983: 581). And this is precisely the level of transmission (or communication) in which the 'mimetic excitement' resides – presupposing, however, one crucial condition: all this is possible only if the ritual structure (in the case of full-length film fiction) or the act story (separately experienced) involves a *convincing representation of sexual pleasure or excitement* triggering the mimetic process. And this is where we again encounter the basic contradiction between evidential presentness and representation.

The female mystery

The basic problem can be formulated as follows: how to produce a convincing and effective representation of *female* sexual pleasure, which, it seems, plays a primary role both in male and female mimetic (sexual) excitement. And why female pleasure?

To be sure, the portrayal of female sexual pleasure is a problem in the pursuit of evidential presentness due to the lack of obvious indexical signs. Then again, the problem is located in the realm of representation and not in evidential presentness. So, in a sense, there exists a division of (pornographic) labour in which the burden of *representation* of sexual pleasure lies on the female part while the *evidential* burden lies on the male part.

What this implies is that the problem of the representation of female sexual pleasure does not derive from the lack of evidential (indexical) signs but is crucial in itself. It is crucial due to the central role that female sexual pleasure has in the representation of sexual pleasure *in general*. This may be related to the analogous situation of the female performer experiencing in an absorbing mode the sexual act, on the one hand, and the spectator on the other: both are receiving and incorporating the experience. This does not imply a passive stance, in simple terms, not at least in the case of the female performer, who, nevertheless, occupies the receptive position which is expected to be turned into certain expressions of response, that is, of sexual pleasure.

But even this does not take us far enough. Nor is it enough to refer to the cultural fact which gives the woman a primary position in representing sexuality. It should also be noted that, from a psychoanalytical vantage point, woman as mother is undoubtedly the first object, moreover the first sexual object for both male and female. So, if the mode of transmission (the effect) involved in 'mimetic excitement' is somewhere close the level of primary identification, it is no wonder that the representation of female sexual pleasure tends to be equated with sexual pleasure in general, and for both sexes.

Again, all this is of less importance in the case of the pure voyeur who is happy with the evidential effects. It is, however, of central importance to the audience, female or male, seeking mimetic excitement. Nevertheless, as noted above, the problem of the pornographic apparatus is not in the pursuit of pleasing two different audiences, but in the one-dimensional conception which identifies the evidential and representational into one and the same thing. The accumulation of evidential effectiveness is expected to strengthen the representational effect – female sexual pleasure – which again is reduced to a simple *response* to the former. This means, that, in most cases, the representation of female sexual pleasure is not thematized in itself at all. So, the evidential signs are harnessed in the service of representation after all: it is supposed to evince the sexual pleasure of the act in general delegating the task to the male partner who, however, merely gives the evidence and hence falls outside the regime of representation.

This is not to say, however, that the pornographic apparatus would not be concerned with the quality of the female performance. Of course convincing acts are preferred to less convincing ones. But still the logic prevails, according to the following lines: the female pleasure cannot be subsumed to the evidential scheme, and thus it is always necessarily represented or 'acted' – regardless of whether it is 'real' of 'faked' (cf. MacCannell, 1989). So, the evidential burden of sexual pleasure is placed primarily on the male part – and his part object which 'proves', as it were, the fulfilment of real (present) sexual pleasure by the climax of ejaculation – called 'money shot' in the professional jargon.

At first sight this appears to be an unproblematic indexical case based on the equation: erection + ejaculation = the fulfilment of sexual pleasure (itself an oversimplification). But, on the other hand, it is given the status of a representation – standing for the whole and shared sexual pleasure of the act. And this is precisely where the basic contradiction is realized: the evidential force of presentness tends to destroy its status as a representation. Moreover, the result is a paradoxical inversion in which the evidentiality is finally transformed into a super sign or *representation of* mere *presence*. This is the paradoxical outcome which appears to be in accordance with Jean Baudrillard's formulation: 'if there is fantasy in pornography, it is not of sex, but of the real' (Baudrillard, 1990: 29).

Epilogue

The paradox is, however, that on a larger scale the 'fantasy of the real' turns into a mechanism promoting that which Baudrillard has called 'hyperreality' (for example Baudrillard, 1983). This is aptly exemplified by the genre of documentary 'media-events' offered particularly by TV-news and other documentaries.

The reporters and cameramen 'being there' when it all happens – ideally as a real-time broadcast, such as the War in the Gulf spectacularized by CNN – are primarily concerned with the evidential (re)presentation of disasters, catastrophes, violence and, in the last instance, death. Accordingly, the evidential climax of the catastrophic news reportage is not in the scene after the 'act' (collapsed buildings, crashed planes, dead bodies, etc.) but in the very 'death act' itself, such as the repeatedly shown sequence from the Vietnam War in which a Vietcong guerrilla kills his prisoner in the street by a shot in the head. Here the 'death act' has a role corresponding to the 'sexual act' in hard core pornography: both offer evidence of ultimate realness.[28]

The same applies also to documentaries such as *Cops* in the USA, where the camera follows the 'police-work' into authentic, more or less violent situations. Or, to take a more spectacular example, there is a genre of disaster-aesthetics, in which the most spectacular accidents – including fatal ones – which have taken place in the motor sports, are serialized into a repetitive sequence, reminiscent of the structure of pornographic films (for example the serial *Havoc 5*).

The pornographic pursuit of evidential explicitness – ending up in the representation of presence – is repeated, and even multiplied, in these documentary genres. The elimination of the interpretative and even representational distance (cf. Falk, 1988a) aiming at the presentness-effect ('Look! This is *really* happening!') turns the media-event, in the last instance, into a spectacle cancelling the difference between (authentic) presence and (fictional) representation in reducing it into mere (special) effect – s(t)imulation.

Notes

1. Chandra Mukerji (1983) has made an interesting study of the rise of mass production and consumption related to its early forms of printed (graphic) images. This was also the basis for the expansion of the obscene pictorial sphere, later followed by the 'mechanical reproduction' (see Benjamin, 1969a) of photographs.

2. From a juridical point of view the thematization of obscenity in representations is a much more recent phenomenon. As Anette Kuhn (1982: 120) notes, it was not until the 'Obscene Publications Act', passed in Britain in 1857, that the link between obscenity and representations was formulated in juridical terms.

3. I am here focusing – according to the topic – on the lower limit of the aesthetic and the bodily experiences beneath it and thus disregarding the other form of interested delight, that which is based on 'respect' and relates to (moral) 'good' (cf. Guyer, 1979: 172).

4. In the words of Karl Wilhelm Ramler (1774): *'Der Gute Geschmack ist eine zur Gewohnheit gewordene Liebe zur Ordnung'* (cited in Grimminger, 1986: 135).

5. Developing the relation of these two unrepresentable beings some steps further, in a Lacanian manner, would perhaps reveal a certain kind of identity between the Phallus and the Law of 'the name-of-the-father' (in Heaven). Nevertheless, already Hegel – Rosenkrantz's primary source – pointed to an interesting relationship between the Phallus and God in his 'Aesthetics'. Hegel takes the Hindu creation myth, which describes in explicit (porno-graphic?) terms how Shiva 'spills his seed on the earth', as an example of inadequacy of 'unconscious symbolism' and contrasts it with 'genuine symbolism' that can occur only when 'the meaning becomes *free* for itself from the immediate sensuous form' (*Ästhetik*; cited in Krell, 1984: 123). This liberation of meaning is possible, according to Hegel, 'only if the sensuous and natural are seen as *negative in themselves*, as that which is to be cancelled and surpassed' (cited in Krell, 1984: 123). And this is exactly what is found in the 'genuine symbolism' originating in the sacred poetry of the Hebrews, where the 'unity of spirit and nature' is not represented as an external – genital – relation. Shiva's phallus is replaced by God the creator and the semen by God's word – 'the purest, altogether bodiless, ethereal externalization' (Krell, 1984: 123). Thus, while emphasizing the difference between the unconscious symbolism and the genuine one (the Order of representation) Hegel is also establishing an identity between Phallus and God – both falling outside (beneath/beyond) representation.

6. An additional proof of the 'autonomy' of man's visible libido derives from the traditional knowledge of all those cultures which have used hanging as death sentence. The scene of an ejaculating victim is not only found in de Sade's illustrated phantasies but in the actual reality of the gallows. The phallus outlasting, for some moments at least, its owner (cf. Duerr, 1988: 271–5). This is a theme inbuilt in Nagisha Oshima's film *The Realm of Senses* (*Ai No Corrida*, 1975), in the dramatic love scene in which the woman strangles her lover to death during the ultimate sexual intercourse. Oshima's film is interesting also from a more general point of view, that is, as an application of pornographic explicitness in a non-pornographic genre, as it were (cf. Oshima, 1981: 73–81).

7. The pornology theme was particularly topical in the French literary discussions around Pierre Klossowski's work 'The Laws of Hospitality' at the beginning of the 1960s (see Klossowski et al., 1979). Many of those later labelled 'post-structuralist' were searching for a 'non-discursive language' (Foucault, 1977: 29–52) that would break the spell of represen-tation.

8. Ian Hunter refers here to Steven Marcus' book about *The Other Victorians* (1964) dealing with the pornographic literature of the Victorian era, to Ian Watt's *'The Rise of the Novel'* (1957) and Georg Lukács' article titled 'Realism in the Balance' 1977).

9. For example R. Bruce Kelsey characterizes the problematical character of acting as representation in the following way:

> An actor does not merely stand in for the character: he must revitalize the dead letter of the
> script and invest himself with the emotions, ideas, and movements of the character to

whatever extent his own sensibilities, the director's plan for the production, and the play's style permit. (Kelsey, 1984: 67).

10. Eco formulated the idea in more detail in another context:

A sign is [. . .] something [. . .] which stands in the place of something which is absent, which could not even exist, or at least not be present anywhere at the time at which I use the sign. This means that the fundamental characteristic of the sign is that I can use it to lie. So that everything that is a sign that can be used to LIE (since everything that serves to tell a lie can also be used, in the right circumstances, to tell the truth). (Eco, 1975: 12)

11. According to Kristeva, 'gesturality, more than phonetic discourse or visual image, can be studied as an activity, in the sense of *spending*, of productivity anterior to the product, and so anterior to *representation* as a phenomenon of significance in the circuit of communication' (Kristeva, 1978: 267). Then again, the linguistic or representational system is able to assimilate these non-signs into the sign-function, turning them into potential 'lies'.

12. Freud (when dealing with the symbolism of dreams) points 'to the remarkable characteristic of the male organ which enables it to rise up in defiance of the laws of gravity' (Freud, 1976: 188). Later it will be discovered that the phallic 'standing up against' has many other meanings besides that of a resistance of gravity.

13. These are the two modes of bodily externalization (vs. internalization): in the first the body is used as a medium of symbolic expression distinguished from the latter which involves a pre-symbolic physical expression entering into the realm of the symbolic (or signification) only post hoc (see Chapter 3).

14. This is what Kendall L. Walton refers to when stating that 'photographic pornography is more potent than the painted variety' (Walton, 1984: 247; Roskill and Carrier, 1983: 101–104).

15. Etymologically this is almost a tautology: 'evidence' derives from the Latin word '*videre*' or 'to see'. This may of course be interpreted as an evidence of our over-visual culture, in which 'seeing has become a cultural form of believing' (Tomas, 1988: 62). Then again, the ultimate proof of actual presence is gained by touch: if one does not believe one's eyes, one has to touch it, to make sure that it is not a ghost or hallucination. As Dietmar Kamper (1984) points out, the touch is the ultimate proof of presence, while the eye may always be deceived (*trompe-l'œil*).

16. The *noeme* of the photograph, the experience of 'that-has-been', is based on the photographic *trace* in a much more fundamental and physical sense than what the analogy refers to. It actualizes the relation to death – just as a live mask always is transformed into a death mask, as an imprint of that which has been.

17. The rise of the 'feminine' pornography (Candide Royalle and others) and the feminist discourse linked to it also exemplifies a trend towards more heterogeneous consumption patterns of pornography.

18. Lacan's *le désir de l'Autre* maintains the double sense of 'the desire for the Other' and 'the Other's desire' (Benvenuto and Kennedy, 1986: 130).

19. D.H. Lawrence – himself a victim of pornographic accusations – characterized the lower genre as follows:

Pornography is the attempt to insult sex, to do dirt on it. This is unpardonable. Take the very lowest instance, the picture post-card sold underhand, by the underworld, in most cities. What I have seen of them have been of an ugliness to make you cry . . . (Lawrence, 1929; cited in Charney, 1981: 1–2)

20. Barthes distinguishes the pornographic photograph from the erotic one as follows:

Pornography ordinarily represents the sexual organs, making them into motionless object (a fetish), flattered like an idol that does not leave its niche; for me, there is no *punctum* in the pornographic image. [. . .] The erotic photography [. . .] does not make the sexual organs into a central object; it may very well not show them at all; it takes the spectator outside its frame, and it is there that I animate this photograph and that it animates me. (Barthes, 1981: 58–9)

Or as Barthes also notes, the 'erotic photograph' is 'a pornographic one that has been disturbed, fissured' (Barthes, 1981: 41).

21. An animation film, however spectacular it may be, captures the spectator primarily by narrative magnetism, but the 'diegesis' (Souriau, 1953: 5–10; Metz, 1983: 145) of the film, assimilating the narrativity into itself, is realized to the full extent only when based on the photographic referent – however fictional the film may be.

22. The flow of diegesis does in fact allow a considerable degree of narrative breaks, or the combination of 'spectacle and narrative' which is a common feature of the 'mainstream film' (Mulvey, 1986: 203). The tolerance towards narrative ruptures increases along with the increased strength of the 'diegetic effect', as Noël Burch (1982) puts it.

23. Or as Barthes adds: 'the entire excitation takes refuge in the *hope* of seeing the sexual organ (schoolboy's dream) or in knowing the end of the story (novelistic satisfaction)' (Barthes, 1977: 10).

24. This is a constellation exploited – in an ironical mode, perhaps – in the hard core film *WPINK-TV – It's red hot* (dir. M. Kidder, 1984). It starts with a scene in which the naked woman, looking straight to the camera, poses in an amateurish manner. The next scene 'reveals' the camera, and the cameraman who is the male partner supplementing his and her private erotica-collection. The doubling of the camera – into that appearing inside the frame and that which frames – functions as an ironical reference to the voyeur/cameraman identification, leaving the former behind the camera while the exposed cameraman turns into a performer in the act. The ironic play with the camera doubling becomes manifest in the female partner's (exhibitionist) comment: 'something in that camera makes me so horny'. The question is of course: *which* camera and *which* man behind the camera.

25. However, the ambivalence prevails, manifested in versions applying both principles. In the *WPINK-TV* film (mentioned above) the duality is solved by structuring the counter-look sequences into TV-performances in distinction to the 'back-stage' sequences where the counter-look is avoided. But the dual strategy may also be used without any structural grounds, as is done for example in the film '*The Story of Marilyn*' (dir. J. Benezerat, 1986). In the amateurish stag films, preceding and partly paralleling the feature-length films, the focus of the performers' eyes is usually purely contingent and lacking any rules – a feature, which makes these hard core films, in a certain way, more 'authentic' and less acted.

26. The classical Hollywood *films noirs* of the 1940s, especially those based on James M. Cain's stories, accumulate the illicit eroticism by means of the indirect and non-explicit: 'the sexuality which could not be explicitly shown was implied through looks, through the delirious visual style, through metaphorical dialogue . . .' (Krutnik, 1982: 43). In distinction to the classical genre, the 1980s Cain film-versions (*The Postman Always Rings Twice*, 1981; *Body Heat*, 1982) apply a much more explicit erotic register in which the erotic scenes break the narrative flow by 'spectacles' (Krutnik, 1982: 44). This is characterized by Judith Williamson (1986: 177) as a contradiction of the aim 'to show more and more, while still holding it up as a great naughty secret'. Nevertheless, these spectacles, even if disrupting the narrative flow, do not break the order of diegesis (cf. Mulvey, 1986), not even in the extreme case where the explicit is just beyond the frame and re-presented to the spectator via the eyes (mirror) of the male partner, as is done in a scene in the film *Body Heat* (1982). The out-of-frame presentness is the ultimate limit that the diegetic order may tolerate.

27. The so-called Carpenter-effect (Hickethier, 1980: 80) referring to uncontrolled facial mimetism (especially in the case of children) mirroring in an unspecific manner the mimics on the screen is located on the borderline of the representational and the sub- or pre-representational. Thus, the identificatory process involved in 'mimetic excitement' presupposing representational mediation must reside somewhere above this lower limit but surely

beneath the relatively stable character identification of narrativity – in the extreme case as hero-identification involving an ego-ideal projection (cf. Chasseguet-Smirgel, 1985).

28. Furthermore, there is a marginal genre of pornographic film in which these two evidential themes are actually combined, namely in the so-called 'snuff-movies', some of which were found to be evidences for actual mutilation and/or killing (cf. Seesslen, 1990: 270–3).

REFERENCES

Abrahams, R. (1984) 'Equal Opportunity Eating: A Structural Excursus on Things of the Mouth', in: L. Brown and K. Mussell (eds), *Ethnic and Regional Foodways*. Knoxville, TN: University of Tennessee. pp. 19–36.

Appadurai, Arjun (ed.) (1986) *The Social Life of Things*. Cambridge: Cambridge University Press.

Apple, Rima D. (1986) ' "Advertised by our loving friends." The Infant Formula Industry and the Creation of New Pharmaceutical Markets, 1870–1910', *Journal of the History of Medicine and Allied Sciences* 41(1): 3–23.

Aronson, Naomi (1982) 'Social Definitions of Entitlement: Food Needs 1885–1920', *Media, Culture and Society* 4(1): 51–61.

Attali, Jacques (1981) *Die kannibalistische Ordnung*. Frankfurt am Main: Campus Verlag.

Austin, J.L. (1975) *How to Do Things With Words*. Cambridge, MA: Harvard University Press.

Bailey, Peter (1978) *Leisure and Class in Victorian England*. London: Routledge & Kegan Paul.

Bakhtin, Mikhail (1968) *Rabelais and his World*. Cambridge, MA: MIT Press.

Balazs, Bela (1952) *Theory of the Film*. London: Dennis Dobson.

Balint, Michael (1959) *Thrills and Regressions*. London: Hogarth Press.

Banta, Martha (1983) 'Medical Therapies and Body Politic', in Jack Salzman (ed.) *Prospects. The Annual of American Cultural Studies*. New York: Cambridge University Press, pp. 59–128.

Barker, Francis (1984) *The Tremulous Private Body*. London: Methuen.

Barnhart, R.K. (ed.) (1988) *The Barnhart Dictionary of Etymology*. New York: Wilson.

Barrett, Michèle et al. (eds) (1979) *Ideology and Cultural Production*. London: Croom Helm.

Barthes, Roland (1977) *Image, Music, Text. Selected Essays*. New York: Fontana.

Barthes, Roland (1981) *Camera Lucida*. New York: Hill & Wang.

Barthes, Roland (1982 [1970]) *Empire of Signs*. New York: Hill & Wang.

Bataille, Georges (1962 [1957]) *Death and Sensuality. A Study of Eroticism and the Taboo*. New York: Walker & Co.

Bataille, Georges (1975 [1933, 1949]) 'Der Begriff der Verausgabung', in: G. Bataille, *Das theoretische Werk, Bd. I*. München: Rogner & Bernhard.

Bataille, Georges (1981) *Die Tränen der Eros*. München: Matthes & Seitz.

Baudelaire, Charles (1965) 'The Salon of 1859 (2). The Modern Public and Photography', in Charles Baudelaire, *Art in Paris 1845–1862. Salons and Other Exhibitions*. London: Phaidon.

Baudrillard, Jean (1975) *The Mirror of Production*. New York: Telos Press.

Baudrillard, Jean (1981) *For a Critique of the Political Economy of the Sign*. St Louis: Telos Press.

Baudrillard, Jean (1982) *Der symbolische Tausch und der Tod*. München: Matthes & Seitz. (English edition: [1993] *Symbolic Exchange and Death*. London: Sage Publications & TCS.)

Baudrillard, Jean (1983) *Simulations*. New York: Semiotext(e).

Baudrillard, Jean (1990) *Seduction*. London: Macmillan.

Baudry, Jean-Louis (1986) 'The Apparatus: Metapsychological Approaches to the Impression of Reality in Cinema', in Philip Rosen (ed.), *Narrative, Apparatus, Ideology*. New York: Columbia University Press. pp. 299–318.

Bauman, Zygmunt (1971) 'Semiotics and the Function of Culture', in Julia Kristeva et al. (eds), *Essays in Semiotics*. The Hague/Paris: Mouton. pp. 279–91.

Bauman, Zygmunt (1990) 'Communism: A Post-Mortem', *Praxis International* 10(3/4): 185–92.

Beard, George M. (1869) 'Neurasthenia, or Nervous Exhaustion', *Boston Medical and Surgical Journal* 80: 245–59.

Beard, George M. (1881) *American Nervousness*. New York: G.P. Putnam's & Sons.

Beecher, Jonathan (1986) *Charles Fourier*. Berkeley: University of California Press.

Bell, Daniel (1976) *The Cultural Conditions of Capitalism*. London: Heinemann.

Bellah, Robert et al. (1985) *Habits of the Heart*. New York: Harper & Row.

Benjamin, Walter (1969a) *Walter Benjamin: Illuminations*, edited by Hanna Arendt. New York: Schocken Books.

Benjamin, Walter (1969b) 'The Work of Art in the Age of Mechanical Reproduction', in Hanna Arendt (ed.), *Walter Benjamin: Illuminations. Essays and Reflections*. New York: Schocken Books

Bentham, Jeremy (1789) *Principles of Morals and Legislation*. London.

Benvenuto, Bice and Kennedy, Roger (1986) *The Works of Jacques Lacan. An Introduction*. London: Free Association Books.

Bersani, Leo (1990) *The Culture of Redemption*. Cambridge, MA: Harvard University Press.

Bersani, Leo and Dutoit, Ulysse (1985) *The Forms of Violence. Narrative in Assyrian Art and Modern Culture*. New York: Schocken Books.

Birken, Lawrence (1988) *Consuming Desire. Sexual Science and the Emergence of a Culture of Abundance, 1871–1914*. Ithaca: Cornell University Press.

Blanchard, Marc Eli (1980) *Description: Sign, Self, Desire*. New York: Mouton Publishers.

Blanchot, Maurice (1977) *La Solitude Essentielle*. Paris: Gallimard.

Blanck, Rubin and Blanck, Gertrude (1986) *Beyond Ego-Psychology*. New York: Columbia University Press.

Blau, Peter M. (1964) *Exchange and Power in Social Life*. New York: John Wiley & Sons.

Bongard, Willi (1964) *Fetische des Konsums*. Hamburg: Nannen-Verlag.

Bonnet, Jean-Claude (1979) 'The Culinary System in the "Encyclopédie" ', in Robert Forster and Orest Ranum (eds), *Food and Drink in History*. Baltimore: The Johns Hopkins University Press. pp. 139–65.

Boorstin, Daniel (1962) *The Image*. New York: Atheneum.

Boorstin, Daniel (1973) *The Americans: The Democratic Experience*. New York: Random House.

Bottomley, Frank (1979) *Attitudes to the Body in Western Christendom*. London: Lepus Books.

Bourdieu, Pierre (1977) *An Outline of a Theory of Practice*. Cambridge: Cambridge University Press.

Bourdieu, Pierre (1984) *Distinction. A Social Critique of the Judgement of Taste*. Cambridge, MA: Harvard University Press.

Boyd, Robert and Richerson, Peter J. (1985) *Culture and the Evolutionary Process*. Chicago: The University of Chicago Press.

Boyden, Stephen (1987) *Western Civilization in Biological Perspective. Patterns in Biohistory*. Oxford: Clarendon Press.

Brain, Robert (1979) *The Decorated Body*. New York: Harper & Row.

Brantlinger, Patrick (1983) *Bread and Circuses*. Ithaca: Cornell University Press.

Braudel, Fernand (1973) *Capitalism and Material Life 1400–1800*. Suffolk: Fontana/Collins.

Brewer, John and Porter, Roy (eds) (1993) *Consumption and the World of Goods*. London: Routledge.

Brigham, Jerry C. and Kenyon, Karlie K. (1976) 'HADACOL -The Last Great Medicine Show', *Journal of Popular Culture* 10(3): 520–33.

Brillat-Savarin, Jean Anthêlme (1971 [1824]) *The Physiology of Taste*. New York: Alfred A. Knopf.

Brittan, Arthur (1977) *The Privatized World*. London: Routledge & Kegan Paul.

Brock, J.F. (1963) 'Sophisticated Diets and Man's Health', in G. Wolstenholme (ed.), *Man and His Future*. London: Churchill.

Brown, Beverley (1991) 'Review of Linda Williams' "Hard Core" (1989)', *Screen* 32(1): 114–19.

Brown, Norman O. (1966) *Love's Body*. New York: Vintage Books.

Brown, Richard H. (1987) *Society as Text*. Chicago: The University of Chicago Press.

Bryson, Norman (1983) *Vision and Painting*. London: Macmillan.

Bullough, Edward (1912) ' "Psychical Distance" as a Factor in Art and Aesthetic Principle', *British Journal of Psychology* 5.

Burch, Noël (1982) 'Narrative/Diegesis – Thresholds, Limits', *Screen* 23(2): 16–33.

Bürger, Christa (1980) 'Literarischer Markt und Öffentlichkeit am Ausgang des 18. Jahrhunderts in Deutschland', in Christa Bürger et al. (eds), *Aufklärung und literarische Öffentlichkeit*. Frankfurt am Main: Suhrkamp. pp. 162–212.

Burke, Edmund (1792 [1757]) *A Philosophical Inquiry into the Origin of Ideas of the Sublime and Beautiful*. London: Basil.

Burke, Peter (1988) 'The Uses of Literacy in Early Modern Italy', in Peter Burke and Roy Porter (eds), *The Social History of Language*. Cambridge: Cambridge University Press.

Burke, Peter (1993) *The Art of Conversation*. Cambridge: Polity Press.

Burton, Robert (1660 [1621]) *The Anatomy of Melancholy*. London.

Caillois, Roger (1959) *Man and the Sacred*. Glencoe, Ill.: The Free Press.

Campbell, Colin (1983) 'Romanticism and the Consumer Ethic', *Sociological Analysis* 44(4): 279–95.

Campbell, Colin (1987) *The Romantic Ethic and the Spirit of Modern Consumerism*. Oxford: Basil Blackwell.

Campbell, Colin (1990) 'Character and Consumption. An Historical Action Theory Approach to the Understanding of Consumer Behaviour', *Culture and History* 7: 37–48.

Camporesi, Piero (1989) *Bread of Dreams: Food and Fantasy in Early Modern Europe*. Cambridge: Polity Press.

Canetti, Elias (1991) 'On the Psychology of Eating', in Elias Canetti, *Crowds and Power*. New York: The Noonday Press. pp. 219–24 .

Carrier, James (1990) 'Reconciling Commodities and Personal Relations in Industrial Society', *Theory and Society* 19(5): 579–98.

Carson, Gerald (1959) *Cornflake Crusade*. London: Victor Gollancz.

Certeau, Michel de (1984) *The Practice of Everyday Life*. Berkeley: University of California Press.

Charney, Maurice (1981) *Sexual Fiction*. New York: Methuen.

Chasseguet-Smirgel, Janine (1985) *The Ego Ideal*. London: Free Association Books.

Cheyne, George (1991 [1733]) *The English Malady* (facsimile). London: Tavistock/ Routledge.

Cohen, Stanley and Taylor, Laurie (1976) *Escape Attempts*. London: Allen Lane.

Couffignal, Huguette (1970) *La Cuisine des pauvres*. Paris: Robert Morel Éditeur.

Couliano, Ioan P. (1987) *Eros and Magic in the Renaissance*. Chicago: The University of Chicago Press.

Culler, Jonathan (1979) 'Derrida', in John Sturrock (ed.), *Structuralism and Since*. Oxford: Oxford University Press. pp. 154–80.

Cunningham, Hugh (1980) *Leisure in the Industrial Revolution, 1780–1880*. London: Croom Helm.

Debord, Guy (1977) *Society of the Spectacle*. Detroit: Black and Red.

Deleuze, Gilles (1991) 'Coldness and Cruelty (introduction to von Sacher-Masoch's "Venus in Furs")', in G. Deleuze and L. von Sacher-Masoch, *Masochism*. New York: Zone Books.

Deleuze, Gilles and Guattari, Felix (1983) *Anti-Oedipus*. Minneapolis: University of Minnesota Press.

Derrida, Jacques (1976) *Of Grammatology*. Baltimore: The Johns Hopkins University Press.

Derrida, Jacques (1981a) *Dissemination*. Chicago: The University of Chicago Press.

Derrida, Jacques (1981b) 'Economimesis', *Diacritics* 11(1): 3–25.

Derrida, Jacques (1981c) *Positions*. Chicago: The University of Chicago Press.

Derrida, Jacques (1986) 'The Anglish Words of Nicholas Abraham and Maria Torok (Foreword)', Nicholas Abraham and Maria Torok: *The Wolf Man's Magic Word*. Minneapolis: Minnesota University Press.

Derrida, Jacques (1987) *The Truth in Painting*. Chicago: The University of Chicago Press.

Derrida, Jacques (1991) ' "Eating Well", or the Calculation of the Subject: An Interview with Jacques Derrida', in Eduardo Cadava et al. (eds), *Who Comes After the Subject?* London: Routledge. pp. 96–119.

Detienne, Marcel (1977) *Dionysos Slain*. Baltimore: The Johns Hopkins University Press.

Detienne, Marcel and Svenbro, Jesper (1989) 'The Feast of the Wolves, or the Impossible City', in Marcel Detienne and Jean-Pierre Vernant (eds), *The Cuisine of Sacrifice Among the Greeks*. Chigago: The University of Chigago Press. pp. 148–63.

Dichter, Ernest (1960) *The Strategy of Desire*. London: T.V. Boardman & Co. Ltd.

Dobb, Maurice (1973) *Theories of Value and Distribution since Adam Smith*. Cambridge: Cambridge University Press

Douglas, Mary (1988 [1966]) *Purity and Danger*. London: Routledge.

Douglas, Mary and Isherwood, Baron (1980) *The World of Goods*. Harmondsworth: Penguin.

Duerr, Hans Peter (1988) *Naktheit und Scham. Der Mythos vom Zivilisationsprozess*. Frankfurt am Main: Suhrkamp.

Durkheim, Emile (1951 [1897]) *Suicide*. New York: The Free Press.

Durkheim, Emile (1954 [1912]) *The Elementary Forms of the Religious Life*. London: Allen & Unwin Ltd.

Dziemidok, Bohdan (1986) 'Controversy about Aesthetic Attitude', in Michael Mitias (ed.), *Possibility of Aesthetic Experience*. Dordrecht: Martinus Nijhoff

Eckert, Charles (1978) 'The Carole Lombard in Macy's Window', *Quarterly Review of Film Studies* 1: 1–21.

Eco, Umberto (1975) 'Looking for a Logic of Culture', in Thomas A. Sebeok (ed.), *The Tell-Tale Sign*. Lisse: Peter de Ridder Press.

Eco, Umberto (1976) *A Theory of Semiotics*. Bloomington: Indiana University Press.

Eco, Umberto (1979) *The Role of the Reader*. Bloomington: Indiana University Press.

Elias, Norbert (1969 [1939]) *Über den Prozess der Zivilisation. Wandlungen der Gessellschaft*. Bern: Verlag Francke AG.

Elias, Norbert (1978 [1939]) *The History of Manners. The Civilizing Process*. Oxford: Basil Blackwell.

Elias, Norbert (1982 [1939]) *Power and Civility. The Civilizing Process*. Oxford: Basil Blackwell.

Enzensberger, Hans Magnus (1974) *The Consciousness Industry*. New York: Seabury.

Erikson, Erik H. (1959) 'Identity and the Life Cycle', *Psychological Issues* 1(1).

Ewen, Stuart (1976) *Captains of Consciousness. Advertising and the Social Roots of the Consumer Culture*. New York: McGraw-Hill Book Co.

Falk, Pasi (1979a) 'Palkkatyömuodon kehkeytyminen ja työläisten alkoholinkäytto 1800-luvun Englannissa (The Coming of Wage Labour and the Drinking Habits of the Working Class in 19th century England)', *Sosiaalipolitiikka* 4: 189–204.

Falk, Pasi (1979b) 'Subjektiviteetin historiallinen ulottuvuus (The Historical Dimension of Subjectivity)', in Tuomas Takala (ed.), *Keskustelua 'pääomalogiikasta' ja kapitalismin tutkimisesta*. Tampere: Tampere University.

Falk, Pasi (1982) 'Tavarametafysiikkaa' (Commodity Metaphysics), *Tiedotustutkimus* 5(3): 78–84.

Falk, Pasi (1983) *Humalan historia (The History of Intoxication)*. Helsinki: University of Helsinki, licenciate thesis.

Falk, Pasi (1987) 'Makean mysteeri (The Mystery of Sweetness)', *Sokeri Elämässä* 4(3): 6–8.

Falk, Pasi (1988a) 'The Past to Come', *Economy and Society* 17(3): 375–94.

Falk, Pasi (1988b) 'Tabacum – Original', *Terveys 2000* 3(6): 38–9.

Falk, Pasi (1990) 'Modernin hedonistin paradoksi (The Paradox of the Modern Hedonist)', *Sosiologia* 27(2): 108–24.

Falk, Pasi (1991) 'Coke is it!', *Cambridge Anthropology* 15(1): 46–55.

Falk, Pasi and Gronow, Jukka (1985) 'Ravintotiede ja ruokahalun disiplinointi (Nutrition Science and the Disciplining of Appetite)', *Tiede & Edistys* 10(1): 47–53.

Featherstone, Mike (1991) *Consumer Culture and Postmodernism*. London: Sage Publications.

Fenichel, Otto (1982 [1946]) *The Psychoanalytic Theory of Neurosis*. London: Routledge & Kegan Paul.

Ferenczi, Sandor (1926 [1909] 'Introjection and Transference', *Ferenczi, S., First Contributions to Psycho-Analysis*. London: Hogarth Press.

Finkelstein, Joanne (1989) *Dining Out*. Oxford: Basil Blackwell.

Fischler, Claude (1980) 'Food Habits, Social Change and the Nature/Culture Dilemma', *Social Science Information* 19(6): 937–53.

Fischler, Claude (1988) 'Food, Self and Identity', *Social Science Information* 27(2): 275–92.

Flandrin, Jean-Louis and Hyman, Philip (1986) 'Regional Tastes and Cuisines. Problems, Documents, and Discourses on Food in the Southern France in the 16th and 17th Centuries', *Food and Foodways* Sample Issue: 1–31.

Foucault, Michel (1965) *Madness and Civilization*. New York: Pantheon.

Foucault, Michel (1973) *The Order of Things*. New York: Vintage Books.

Foucault, Michel (1976) *The Birth of the Clinic. An Archaeology of Medical Perception*. London: Tavistock Publications.

Foucault, Michel (1977) 'A Preface to Transgression', in Donald Bouchard (ed.), *Language, Counter-Memory, Practice. Selected Essays and Interviews*. Ithaca: Cornell University Press.

Foucault, Michel (1979) *Discipline and Punishment. The Birth of the Prison*. Harmondsworth: Penguin Books.

Foucault, Michel (1981) *The History of Sexuality: Introduction*. Harmondsworth: Penguin Books.

Foucault, Michel (1982a) 'Sexuality and Solitude', in *Humanities in Review, Vol. 1*. New York: Cambridge University Press.

Foucault, Michel (1982b) 'The Subject and Power (Afterword)', Hubert Dreyfus and Paul Rabinow (eds), *Michel Foucault: Beyond Structuralism and Hermeneutics*. Chicago: The University of Chicago Press.

Foucault, Michel (1987) *The Use of Pleasure*. Harmondsworth: Penguin Books.

Foucault, Michel (1988a) 'The Battle for Chastity', in Lawrence Kritzman (ed.), *Michel Foucault – Politics, Philosophy and Culture*. New York: Routledge.

Foucault, Michel (1988b) *The Care of the Self*. Harmondsworth: Allen Lane/Penguin.

Fraser, Nancy (1983) 'Foucault's Body-Language: A Post-Humanist Political Rhetoric?', *Salmagundi* 61: 55–70.

Fraser, W. Hamish (1981) *The Coming of the Mass Market, 1850–1914*. London: Archon.

Frazer, J.G. (1983 [1922]) *The Golden Bough*. London: Macmillan.

Freud, Sigmund (1976) *Introductory Lectures on Psychoanalysis*. Harmondsworth: Penguin Books.

Freud, Sigmund (1977) *New Introductory Lectures on Psychoanalysis*. Harmondsworth: Penguin Books.

Freud, Sigmund (1984) *On Metapsychology*. Harmondsworth: Penguin.

Friedman, Jonathan (1983) 'Civilisation Cycles and the History of Primitivism', *Social Analysis* 14: 31–52.

Fromm, Erich (1955) *The Sane Society*. New York: Harvester.

Frosh, Stephen (1991) *Identity Crisis*. London: Macmillan.

Gans, Eric (1981) *The Origin of Language*. Berkeley: University of California Press.

Gebauer, Gunter (1982) 'Ausdruck und Einbildung. Zur symbolischen Funktion des

Körpers', in Dietmar Kamper and Christoph Wulf (eds), *Die Wiederkehr des Körpers*. Frankfurt am Main: Suhrkamp Verlag. pp. 313–29.

Ginzburg, Carlo (1990) *Myths, Emblems, Clues*. London: Hutchinson Radius.

Girard, René (1977) *Violence and the Sacred*. Baltimore: The Johns Hopkins University Press.

Girard, René (1987) *Things Hidden Since the Foundation of the World*. London: Athlone.

Glaser, Horst A. (1974) 'Libri Obscoeni', in Horst A. Glaser (ed.), *Wollüstige Phantasie*. Karl Hanser Verlag.

Goffman, Erving (1959) *The Presentation of Self in Everyday Life*. New York: Anchor Books.

Goffman, Erving (1967) *Interaction Ritual. Essays on Face-to-Face Behaviour*. New York: Allen Lane and Penguin.

Goffman, Erving (1970) *Stigma*. Harmondsworth: Penguin Books.

Goody, Jack (1982) *Cooking, Cuisine and Class. A Study in Comparative Sociology*. Cambridge: Cambridge University Press.

Gorsen, Peter (1972) *Sexualästhetik*. Hamburg: Rowohlt.

Goux, Jean-Joseph (1990) *Symbolic Economies*. Ithaca: Cornell University Press.

Gowans, Alan (1980) 'Ritual Illustration Functioning as Substitute Imagery: Pornography', in Ray B. Browne (ed.), *Rituals and Ceremonies in Popular Culture*. Ohio: Bowling Green University Popular Press.

Gregory, C.A. (1982) *Gifts and Commodities*. New York: The Academic Press.

Grimes, Ronald L. (1982) *Beginnings in Ritual Studies*. New York: University Press of America.

Grimminger, Rolf (1986) *Die Ordnung, das Chaos und die Kunst*. Frankfurt am Main: Suhrkamp.

Guattari, Félix (1977) *Mikro-Politik des Wunsches*. Berlin: Merve Verlag.

Gurevitch, Z.D. (1990) 'The Dialogic Connection and the Ethics of Dialogue', *British Journal of Sociology* 41(2): 181–96.

Guyer, Paul (1979) *Kant and the Claims of Taste*. Cambridge, MA: Harvard University Press.

Hall, Edward T. (1966) *The Hidden Dimension*. New York: Doubleday & Co.

Harpham, Geoffrey G. (1987) *The Ascetic Imperative in Culture and Criticism*. Chicago: The University of Chicago Press.

Harris, Marvin (1986) *Good to Eat. Riddles of Food and Culture*. London: Allen & Unwin.

Hartley, David (1749) *Observations on Man*. London.

Harvey, Irene E. (1986) *Derrida and the Economy of Différance*. Bloomington: Indiana University Press.

Haug, Wolfgang F. (1980) *Warenästhetik und kapitalistische Massenkultur. Systematische Einführung in die Warenästhetik*. Berlin: Argument Verlag.

Hayes, Carlton J.H. (1941) *A Generation of Materialism, 1871–1900*. New York: Harper & Bros. Publishers.

Heinisch, Bridget Ann (1976) *Fast and Feast*. University Park: The Pennsylvania State University Press.

Hénaff, Marcel (1992) 'The Cannibalistic City: Rousseau, Large Numbers, and the Abuse of the Social Bond', *SubStance* 21(1): 3–23.

Hess, John L. and Hess, Karen (1989) *The Taste of America*. South Carolina: The University of South Carolina Press.

Hickethier, Knut (1980) 'Kinowahrnehmung – Kinorezeption – Film im Kopf', *Ästhetik und Kommunikation* 42: 75–90.

Hirsch, Fred (1975) *The Social Limits of Growth*. Cambridge: Cambridge University Press.

Hirschman, Albert O. (1977) *The Passions and the Interests*. Princeton: Princeton University Press.

Hirschman, Albert O. (1982) *Shifting Involvements*. Princeton: Princeton University Press.

Hohmans, George C. (1958) 'Social Behavior as Exchange', *American Journal of Sociology* 62: 597–606.

Hohmans, George C. (1961) *Social Behavior*. New York: Harcourt, Brace & World.

Holbrook, Stewart H. (1959) *The Golden Age of Quackery*. New York: The Macmillan Company.

Horkheimer, Max and Adorno, Theodor W. (1972 [1944]) *Dialectic of Enlightenment*. New York: Seabury.

Horney, Karen (1937) *The Neurotic Personality of our Time*. New York: W.W. Norton & Co.

Howes, David and Lalonde, Marc (1991) 'The History of Sensibilities', *Dialectical Anthropology* 16(2): 125–35.

Hugh-Jones, Stephen (1988) *The Palm and the Pleiades. Initiation and Cosmology in Northwest Amazonia*. Cambridge: Cambridge University Press.

Humphrey, Caroline and Hugh-Jones, Stephen (eds) (1992) *Barter, Exchange and Value*. Cambridge: Cambridge University Press.

Hunter, Ian (1984) 'After Representation', *Economy and Society* 13(4): 397–430.

Hyde, Lewis (1983) *The Gift. Imagination and Erotic Life of Property*. New York: Vintage Books, Random House.

Jackson Lears, T.J. (1981) *No Place of Grace*. New York: Pantheon Books.

Jackson Lears, T.J. (1983) 'From Salvation to Self-Realization', in R.W. Fox and T.J. Jackson Lears (eds), *The Culture of Consumption*. New York: Pantheon Books. pp. 1–38.

Jackson Lears, T.J. (1984) *Some Versions of Fantasy. Toward a Cultural History of American Advertising, 1880–1930*. New York: Cambridge University Press.

Jacobs, M. (1969) 'Metabletics of Loneliness', *Social Research* 36: 606–39.

Jauss, Hans Robert (1970) *Literaturgeschichte als Provokation*. Frankfurt am Main: Suhrkamp.

Jay, Martin (1973) *The Dialectical Imagination*. Boston: Little, Brown & Company.

Jevons, W. Stanley (1970 [1871]) *The Theory of Political Economy*. Harmondsworth: Penguin Books.

Johannesson, Lena (1978) *Den Massproducerade Bilden*. Stockholm: AWE/Geber.

Johannesson, Lena (1984) 'Pictures as News, News as Pictures', in D. Jonsson et al. (eds), *Visual Paraphrases*. Uppsala: Almqvist & Wiksell.

Johnson, Mark (1987) *The Body in the Mind*. Chicago: The University of Chicago Press.

Jones, Olive R. (1981) 'Essence of Peppermint. A History of the Medicine and its Bottle', *Historical Archaeology* 15(2): 1–33.

Jordan, Pat (1987) 'Inside Marilyn Chambers', *Gentlemen's Quarterly*.

Kamper, Dietmar (1984) 'Die Transzendenz der Sinne und die Paradoxie des Sinns', in Dietmar Kamper and Christoph Wulf (eds), *Das Schwinden der Sinne*. Frankfurt am Main: Suhrkamp.

Kamper, Dietmar and Wulf, Christoph (1982) 'Die Parabel der Wiederkehr', in Dietmar Kamper and Christoph Wulf (eds), *Die Wiederkehr des Körpers*. Frankfurt am Main: Suhrkamp Verlag. pp. 9–21.

Kant, Immanuel (1820 [1798]) *Anthropologie in pragmatischer Hinsicht*. Königsberg.

Kant, Immanuel (1987 [1790]) *Critique of Judgement*. Indianapolis: Hackett Publ. Co.

Kaplan, E. Ann (1985) *Women and Film*. New York: Methuen.

Kelsey, R. Bruce (1984) 'The Actor's Representation: Gesture, Play, and Language', *Philosophy and Literature* 8(1): 67–74.

Kendrick, Walter (1987) *The Secret Museum*. New York: Viking.

Kernberg, Otto (1970) 'Factors in the Psychoanalytic Treatment of Narcissistic Personalities', in A. Morrison (ed.), *Essential Papers on Narcissism*. New York: New York University Press.

Kilgour, Maggie (1990) *From Communion to Cannibalism*. Princeton: Princeton University Press.

Kitson, Henry Dexter (1921) *The Mind of the Buyer. A Psychology of Selling*. New York: Macmillan.

Kittler, Friedrich A. (1990) *Discourse Networks 1800/1900*. Stanford: Stanford University Press.

Klaukka, Timo (1989) *Lääkkeiden käyttö ja käyttäjät Suomessa* (Use and Users of Medicines in Finland) Helsinki: Kansaneläkelaitos.

Klein, Melanie (1932) *The Psycho-Analysis of Children*. London: Hogarth Press.

Kleinspehn, Thomas (1987) *Warum sind wir so unersättlich?* Frankfurt am Main: Suhrkamp.

Klossowski, Piere et al. (1979) *Sprachen des Körpers*. Berlin: Merve Verlag.

Knauft, Bruce M. (1989) 'Bodily Images in Melanesia', in M. Feher (ed.), *Fragments for a History of the Human Body*, Vol 3. New York: Zone Books.

Kopytoff, Igor (1986) 'The Cultural Biography of Things: Commoditization as Process', in Arjun Appadurai (ed.), *The Social Life of Things. Commodities in Cultural Perspective*. Cambridge: Cambridge University Press. pp. 64–91.

Koslow, Francine A. (1986) 'Sex in Surrealist Art', in Donald Palumbo (ed.), *Eros in the Mind's Eye*. New York: Greenwood Press.

Kovel, Joel (1981) *The Age of Desire*. New York: Pantheon Books.

Krell, David F. (1984) 'Pitch: Genitality/Excrementality – From Hegel to Crazy Jane', *Boundary* 2: 113–41.

Kristeva, Julia (1978) 'Gesture: Practice or Communication?', in Ted Polhemus (ed.), *Social Aspects of the Human Body*. Harmondsworth: Penguin Books. pp. 264–84.

Kristeva, Julia (1982) *Powers of Horror. An Essay on Abjection*. New York: Columbia University Press.

Kroeber-Riel, Werner (1984) 'Effects of Emotional Pictorial Elements in Ads Analyzed by means of Eye Movement Monitoring', in T. Kinnear (ed.), *Advances in Consumer Research*. Greenwich, CN. JAI Press.

Kroeber-Riel, Werner (1993) *Bild Kommunikation. Imagerystrategien für die Werbung*. München: Verlag Franz Vahlen.

Krovoza, Alfred (1976) *Produktion und Sozialisation*. Frankfurt am Main: EVA.

Krutnik, Frank (1982) 'Desire, Transgression and James M. Cain', *Screen* 23(1): 31–44.

Kuhn, Anette (1982) *Women's Pictures: Feminism and Cinema*. London: Routledge & Kegan Paul.

Kutcher, Louis (1983) 'The American Sport Event as Carnival', *Journal of Popular Culture* 16: 34–41.

Lacan, Jacques (1968) *The Language of the Self*. Baltimore: The Johns Hopkins University Press.

Lacan, Jacques (1977) *Ecrits*. New York: W.W. Norton.

Lasch, Christopher (1980) *The Culture of Narcissism*. London: Abacus.

Lasch, Christopher (1985) *The Minimal Self*. London: Picador.

Lauderdale, Earl of (1804) *An Inquiry into the Nature and Origin of Public Wealth*. Edinburgh.

Leach, Edmund (1961) *Rethinking Anthropology*. Cambridge: Cambridge University Press.

Leach, Edmund (1964) 'Anthropological Aspects of Language. Animal Categories and Verbal Abuse', in Eric H. Lenneberg (ed.), *New Directions in the Study of Language*. Cambridge, MA: MIT Press. pp. 30–62.

Leder, Drew (1990) *The Absent Body*. Chicago: The University of Chicago Press.

Lefebvre, Henri (1971) *Everyday Life in the Modern World*. New York: Harper & Row.

Lehmann, Hans-Thies (1983) 'Die Raumfabrik. Mythos im kino und Kinomythos', in Karl Heinz Bohrer (ed.), *Mythos und Moderne*. Frankfurt am Main: Suhrkamp. pp. 572–609.

Leiss, William, Kline, Stephen and Jhally, Sut (1986) *Social Communication in Advertising*. Toronto: Methuen.

Lepenies, Wolf (1972) *Melancholie und Gesellschaft*. Frankfurt am Main: Suhrkamp.

Levenstein, Harvey (1988) *Revolution at the Table*. New York: Oxford University Press.

Lévi-Strauss, Claude (1963) *Totemism*. Boston: Bacon Press.

Lévi-Strauss, Claude (1965) 'Le Triangle culinaire', *L'Arc* 26: 19–29.

Lévi-Strauss, Claude (1966) *The Savage Mind*. Chicago: The University of Chicago Press.

Lévi-Strauss, Claude (1967 [1958]) *Structural Anthropology*. Garden City, NY: Doubleday.

Lévi-Strauss, Claude (1981) *The Naked Man. Introduction to a Science of Mythology*, Vol. 4. New York: Harper & Row.

Lévi-Strauss, Claude (1987) *Anthropology and Myth. Lectures 1951–82*. Oxford: Basil Blackwell.

Lewin, Louis (1920) *Die Gifte in der Weltgeschichte*. Berlin: Springer Verlag.

Lewin, Louis (1927) *Phantastica*. Berlin: George Stilke Verlag.

Lewis, Gilbert (1988) *Day of Shining Red*. Cambridge: Cambridge University Press.

Lloyd, G.E.R. (1986) *Science, Folklore and Ideology*. Cambridge: Cambridge University Press.

Lowe, Donald M. (1982) *History of Bourgeois Perception*. Brighton: The Harvester Press.

Lukács, Georg (1977) 'Realism in the Balance', in Ernst Bloch et al. (eds), *Aesthetics and Politics*. London: New Left Books.

Lumsden, C. and Wilson, E. O. (1981) *Genes, Mind, and Culture*. Cambridge, MA: Harvard University Press.

Lyotard, Jean-François (1978 [1971]) *Intensitäten*. Berlin: Merve.

Lyotard, Jean-François (1984) *The Postmodern Condition*. Minneapolis: University of Minnesota Press.

MacAloon, John J. (ed.) (1984) *Rite, Drama, Festival, Spectacle*. Philadelphia: Institute for the Study of Human Issues.

MacCannell, Dean (1989) 'Faking it: Comment on Face-work in Pornography', *American Journal of Semiotics* 6(4): 153–74.

MacClancy, Jeremy (1992) *Consuming Culture*. London: Chapmans.

McCracken, Grant (1988) *Culture and Consumption*. Bloomington: Indiana University Press.

MacDonogh, Giles (1987) *A Palate in Revolution. Grimod de La Reynière and the Almanach des Gourmands*. London: Robin Clark.

McDougall, Joyce (1986) *Theatres of the Mind*. London: Free Association Books.

McKendrick, Neil et al. (1982) *The Birth of a Consumer Society*. Bloomington: Indiana University Press.

Malcolmson, Robert W. (1973) *Popular Recreations in English Society 1700–1850*. Cambridge: Cambridge University Press.

Malthus, Thomas R. (1820) *Principles of Political Economy*. London.

Mandeville, Bernard (1970 [1714]) *The Fable of the Bees*. Harmondsworth: Penguin Books.

Marchand, Roland (1986) *Advertising the American Dream*. Berkeley: University of California Press.

Marcus, Steven (1964) *The Other Victorians. A Study of Sexuality and Pornography in Mid-Nineteenth-Century England*. New York: Meridian.

Marquette, Arthur (1967) *Brands, Trademarks and Good Will. The Story of the Quaker Oats Company*. New York: McGraw-Hill Book Co.

Marriott, McKim (1976) 'Hindu Transactions', in B. Kapferer (ed.), *Transaction and Meaning*. Philadelphia: Institute for the Study of Human Issues.

Marx, Karl (1973) *Grundrisse*. Harmondsworth: Penguin Books.

Marx, Karl (1976) 'The 1844 Manuscripts', in Karl Marx and Frederick Engels, *Collected Works*. London: Lawrence & Wishart.

Maslow, A.H. (1973) *The Farther Reaches of Human Nature*. Harmondsworth: Penguin Books.

Mattenklott, Gert (1982) *Der übersinnliche Leib*. Hamburg: Rowohlt.

Mauss, Marcel (1967 [1925]) *The Gift. Forms and Functions of Exchange in Archaic Societies*. New York: Harvester.

Mauss, Marcel (1989 [1938]) 'A Category of the Human Mind: The Notion of Person: The Notion of Self', in Michael Carrithers et al. (eds), *The Category of the Person*. Cambridge: Cambridge University Press.

Mayne, Judith (1988) *Private Novels, Public Films*. Athens, GA: The University of Georgia Press.

Mead, George H. (1934) *Mind, Self and Society*. Chicago: University of Chicago Press.

Meigs, Anna (1984) *Food, Sex, and Pollution*. New Brunswick: Rutgers University Press.

Meigs, Anna (1988) 'Food as Cultural Construction', *Food and Foodways* 2: 341–57.

Menger, Carl (1871) *Grundsätze der Ökonomie*. Berlin.

Mennell, Stephen (1985) *All Manners of Food*. Oxford: Basil Blackwell.

Merleau-Ponty, Maurice (1964) 'Eye and Mind', in James M. Edie (ed.), *The Primacy of Perception and Other Essays*. Evanston: Northwestern University Press.

Merleau-Ponty, Maurice (1981) *Phenomenology of Perception*. London: Routledge.

Metz, Christian (1983) *Psychoanalysis and Cinema. The Imaginary Signifier*. London: Macmillan.

Miller, Daniel (1987) *Material Culture and Mass Consumption*. Oxford: Basil Blackwell.

Mitchell, W.J.T. (1986) *Iconology. Image, Text, Ideology*. Chicago: The University of Chicago Press.

Mitchell, W.J.T. (1989) 'Ut Pictura Theoria. Abstract Painting and the Repression of Language', *Critical Inquiry* 15: 348–71.

Monro, D.H. (ed.) (1972) *A Guide to the British Moralists*. London: Fontana.

Moravia, Alberto (1988) *Io e Lui*. Milano: Pompiani.

Mukerji, Chandra (1983) *From Graven Images*. New York: Columbia University Press.

Mulvey, Laura (1986) 'Visual Pleasure and Narrative Cinema', in Philip Rosen (ed.), *Narrative, Apparatus, Ideology*. New York: Columbia University Press.

Nef, John U. (1958) *Cultural Foundations of Industrial Civilization*. Cambridge: Cambridge University Press.

Nitzschke, Bernd (1974) *Die Zerstörung der Sinnlichkeit*. München: Kindler Verlag.

Nora, Pierre (1983) 'Monster Events', *Discourse* 5: 5–20.

O'Neill, John (1989) *The Communicative Body*. Evanston: Northwestern University Press.

Ong, Walter (1967) *The Presence of the Word*. New Haven: Yale University Press.

Orléan, André (1988) 'Money and Mimetic Speculation', in Paul Dumouchel (ed.), *Violence and Truth*. London: Athlone Press. pp. 101–12.

Oshima, Nagisa (1981) 'Experimentelle Theorie des pornographischen Films', *Ästhetik und Kommunikation*. Sonderheft : 73 81.

Osterloh, Karl-Heinz (1976) 'Die Entstehung der wetlichen Industriegesellschaft und die Revolution der Interaktionsweisen', *Archiv für Kulturgeschichte* 58. 340–70.

Ozouf, Mona (1975) 'Space and Time in the Festivals of the French Revolution', *Comparative Studies in Society and History* 17: 372–84.

Packard, Vance (1979 [1957]) *The Hidden Persuaders*. Harmondsworth: Penguin.

Parin, Paul (1978) *Der Widerspruch im Subjekt*. Frankfurt am Main: Syndikat.

Parry, Jonathan (1986) 'The Gift, The Indian Gift and the "Indian Gift" ', *Man* 21(3): 453–73.

Patten, Simon Nelson (1968 [1907]) *The New Basis of Civilization*. Cambridge, MA: John Harvard Library.

Petersen, William J. (1969) 'Devils, Drugs, and Doctors. Patent Medicine Advertising Cards', *Palimpsest* 50(6): 317–31.

Pohrt, Wolfgang (1976) *Theorie des Gebrauchswerts*. Frankfurt am Main: Syndikat.

Polanyi, Karl (1957) *The Great Transformation*. Boston: Beacon Press.

Pope, Daniel (1983) *The Making of Modern Advertising*. New York: Basic Books.

Porter, Roy (1989) *Health for Sale*. Manchester: Manchester University Press.

Porter, Roy (1991 [1733]) 'Introduction', *George Cheyne: The English Malady* (facsimile). London: Tavistock/Routledge. pp. ix-li.

Poster, Mark (1990) 'Words without Things: The Mode of Information', *October* 53: 63–77.

Rajaniemi, Pirjo (1992) *Conceptualization of Product Involvement as a Property of a Cognitive Structure*. Vaasa: University of Vaasa.

Rath, Claus-Dieter (1984) *Reste der Tafelrunde. Das Abenteuer der Esskultur*. Hamburg: Rowohlt.

Raulff, Ulrich (1982) 'Chemie des Ekels und des Genusses', in Dietmar Kamper and Christoph Wulf (eds), *Die Wiederkehr des Körpers*. Frankfurt am Main: Suhrkamp. pp. 241–58

Rembar, Charles (1968) *The End of Obscenity*. New York: Random House.

Revel, Jean-François (1982) *Erlesene Mahlzeiten. Mitteilungen aus der Geschichte der Kochkunst*. Frankfurt am Main: Propyläen/Ullstein.

Ricardo, David (1971 [1821]) *Principles of Political Economy*. Harmondsworth: Penguin Books.

Richards, Thomas (1990) *The Commodity Culture in Victorian England. Advertising and Spectacle, 1851–1914*. Stanford: Stanford University Press.

Rieff, Philip (1966) *The Triumph of the Therapeutic*. New York: Harper & Row.

Riesman, David (1955) *The Lonely Crowd*. New Haven: Yale University Press.

Robinson, Joan (1970) *Economic Philosophy*. Harmondsworth: Penguin Books.

Roland, Alan (1988) *In Search of the Self in India and Japan*. Princeton, NJ: Princeton University Press.

Rosenkranz, Karl (1853) *Aesthetik des Hässlichen*. Königsberg: Verlag der Gebrüder Bornträger.

Roskill, Mark and Carrier, David (1983) *Truth and Falsehood in Visual Images*. Amherst: The University of Massachusetts Press.

Rozin, Paul (1982) 'Human Food Selection. The Interaction of Biology, Culture and Individual Experience', in L.M. Barker (ed.), *The Psychobiology of Human Food Selection*. Chichester: Ellis Horwood. pp. 225–54.

Rutschky, Michael (1980) *Erfahrungshunger*. Köln: Kiepenheuer & Witsch.

Sahlins, Marshall (1972) *Stone Age Economics*. Chicago: Aldine-Atherton.

Sahlins, Marshall (1976) *Culture and Practical Reason*. Chicago: The University of Chicago Press.

Sahlins, Marshall (1983) 'Other Times, Other Customs: The Anthropology of History', *American Anthropologist* 85(3): 517–44.

Sahlins, Marshall (1985) *Islands of History*. Chicago: The University of Chicago Press.

Sanday, Peggy Reeves (1986) *Divine Hunger*. Cambridge: Cambridge University Press.

Sartre, Jean-Paul (1966) *Being and Nothingness*. New York: Washington Square Press.

Schaper, Eva (1987) 'The Pleasures of Taste', in Eva Schaper (ed.), *Pleasure, Preference and Value*. Cambridge: Cambridge University Press.

Schechner, Richard (1988) *Performance Theory*. New York: Routledge.

Schechner, R. and Appel, W. (eds) (1990) *By Means of Performance*. Cambridge: Cambridge University Press.

Schlereth, Thomas J. (1982) 'Material Culture Studies in America, 1876–1976', in T.J. Schlereth (ed.), *Material Culture Studies in America*. Nashville: The American Association for State and Local History.

Schopenhauer, Arthur (1883) *The World as Will and Idea, Vol. 1*. London: Routledge & Kegan Paul.

Schudson, Michael (1986) *Advertising. The Uneasy Persuasion*. New York: Basic Books.

Schulze, Gerhard (1992) *Die ErlebnisGesellschaft. Kultursoziologie der Gegenwart*. Frankfurt am Main: Campus Verlag.

Scitovsky, Tibor (1976) *The Joyless Economy*. New York: Oxford University Press.

Sebeok, Thomas A. (1971) 'On Chemical Signs', in Julia Kristeva et al. (eds.), *Essays in Semiotics*. Paris/Hague: Mouton.

Sebeok, Thomas A. (1990) 'Indexicality', *American Journal of Semiotics* 7(4): 7–28.

Seesslen, Georg (1990) *Der pornographische Film*. Berlin: Ullstein.

Sekora, John (1977) *Luxury. The Concept in Western Thought. Eden to Smollett*. Baltimore: The Johns Hopkins University Press.

Senior, Nassau (1836) *Outline of Political Economy*. London.

Sennett, Richard (1978) *The Fall of Public Man*. New York: Vintage Books.

Shaftesbury, Earl of (1699) *Characteristicks of Men, Manners, Opinions, Times*, Vol. 1.

Simmel, Georg (1950 [1912]) 'Sociability', in Kurt H. Wolff (ed.), *The Sociology of Georg Simmel*. New York: The Free Press. pp. 40–57 .

Simmel, Georg (1958 [1908]) *Soziologie*. Berlin: Duncker & Humblot.

Simmel, Georg (1984 [1910]) 'Soziologie der Mahlzeit', in Georg Simmel, *Das Individuum und die Freiheit*. Berlin: Wagenbach. pp. 205–11.

Smith, Adam (1970 [1776]) *The Wealth of Nations*. Harmondsworth: Penguin Books.

Sombart, Werner (1922 [1912]) *Luxus und Kapitalismus*. München: Duncker & Humblot.

Sontag, Susan (1982) 'The Pornographic Imagination', in *A Susan Sontag Reader*. Harmondsworth: Penguin Books.

Souriau, Etienne (1953) 'Préface', in Etienne Souriau, *L'Univers filmique*. Paris: Flammarion.

Sperber, Dan (1975) *Rethinking Symbolism*. Cambridge: Cambridge University Press.

Spitz, R.A. (1965) *The First Years of Life*. New York: International Universities Press.

Springborg, Patricia (1981) *The Problem of Human Needs and the Critique of Civilisation*. London: George Allen & Unwin.

Sraffa, Piero (1960) *Production of Commodities by Means of Commodities*. Cambridge: Cambridge University Press.

Starobinski, Jean (1982) 'A Short History of Body Consciousness', *Humanities in Review, Vol. 1*. New York: Cambridge University Press.

Starobinski, Jean (1993) 'Medizin und Antimedizin', *Freibeuter* 57: 3–18.

Steiner, Jacob E. (1977) 'Facial Expressions of the Neonate Infant Indicating the Hedonics of Food-related Chemical Stimuli', in J.M. Weiffenbach (ed.), *The Genesis of Sweet Preference*. Bethesda, MA: US Department of Health, Education and Welfare. pp. 173–89.

Stewart, Susan (1984) *On Longing*. Baltimore: The Johns Hopkins University Press.

Stewart, Susan (1988) 'The Marquis de Meese', *Critical Inquiry* 15(1): 162–92.

Stjernfelt, Frederik (1987) 'En dift af jeg ved ikke hvad', *Hug!* 10(48): 39–46.

Strathern, Andrew (1982) 'Witchcraft, Greed, Cannibalism and Death', in Maurice Bloch and J. Parry (eds), *Death and Regeneration of Life*. Cambridge: Cambridge University Press. pp. 111–33.

Strong, L.A.G. (1954) *The Story of Sugar*. London: George Weidenfeld & Nicolson.

Stukeley, William (1722) *Of the Spleen*. London.

Styles, John (1993) 'Manufacturing, Consumption and Design in Eighteenth-century England', in John Brewer and Roy Porter (eds), *Consumption and the World of Goods*. London: Routledge. pp. 527–54.

Summers, David (1990) *The Judgement of Sense*. Cambridge: Cambridge University Press.

Susman, Warren I. (1984) *Culture as History*. New York: Pantheon Books.

Swingewood, Alan (1977) *The Myth of Mass Culture*. London: 'Macmillan.

Tagg, John (1983) 'Power and Photography', in Tony Bennett et al. (eds), *Culture, Ideology and Social Process*. London: The Open University.

Tagg, John (1988) *The Burden of Representation*. London: Macmillan

Tarde, Gabriel (1962 [1890]) *The Laws of Imitation*. Clouchester, MA: Peter Smith.

Taylor, Charles (1989) *Sources of the Self*. Cambridge, MA: Harvard University Press.

Thévoz, Michel (1984) *The Painted Body*. New York: Rizzioli International Publications, Inc.

Thomas, Keith (1977) 'The Place of Laughter in Tudor and Stuart England', *Times Literary Supplement* 21 January: 77–81.

Thompson, E. P. (1967) 'Time. Work-discipline and the Industrial Capitalism' *Past & Present* 38: 56–97.

Thompson, Michael (1979) *Rubbish Theory*. Oxford: Oxford University Press.

Thorne, Stuart (1986) *The History of Food Preservation*. London: Parthenon Publishing.

Thurn, Hans Peter (1980) *Der Mensch im Alltag*. Stuttgart: Ferdinand Enke.

Tomas, David (1988) 'From the Photograph to Postphotographic Practice. Toward a Postoptical Ecology of the Eye', *SubStance* 55: 59–68.

Turnbull, Colin (1984) *The Mountain People*. London: Triad Paladin.

Turner, Bryan S. (1982) 'The Government of the Body: Medical Regimens and the Rationalization of Diet', *British Journal of Sociology* 33: 254–69.

Turner, Bryan S. (1984) *The Body and Society*. Oxford: Basil Blackwell.

Turner, Bryan S. (1991) 'Recent Developments in the Theory of the Body', in Mike Featherstone et al. (eds), *The Body*. London: Sage Publications. pp. 1–35.

Turner, Victor (1969) *The Ritual Process. Structure and Anti-Structure*. London: Routledge & Kegan Paul.

Turner, Victor (1982) *From Ritual to Theatre*. New York: Performing Arts Journal Publications.

Tyler, Stephen A. (1987) *The Unspeakable*. Madison: The University of Wisconsin Press.

Urban, Greg (1981) 'The Semiotics of Tabooed Food. The Shokleng Case', *Social Science Information* 20(3): 475–507.

Valeri, Valerio (1985) *Kingship and Sacrifice*. Chicago: The University of Chicago Press.

van den Berg, J.H. (1960) *Metabletica – Über die Wandlung des Menschen*. Götingen: Vandenhoeck & Ruprecht.

van den Berg, J.H. (1974) *Divided Existence and Complex Society*. Pittsburgh: Duquesne University Press.

van Gennep, Arnold (1960 [1909]) *The Rites of Passage*. London: Routledge & Kegan Paul.

Veblen, Thorstein (1970 [1899]) *The Theory of the Leisure Class*. London: Unwin Books.

Vernant, Jean-Pierre (1989) 'Food in the Countries of Sun', in Marcel Detienne and Jean-Pierre Vernant (eds), *The Cuisine of Sacrifice among the Greeks*. Chicago: The University of Chicago Press. pp. 164–9.

Walens, Stanley (1981) *Feasting with Cannibals*. Princeton: Princeton University Press.

Walras, Léon (1954 [1874]) *Elements of Pure Economics*. London.

Walton, Kendall L. (1984) 'Transparent Pictures. On the Nature of Photographic Realism', *Critical Inquiry* 11(2): 246–77.

Watt, Ian (1957) *The Rise of the Novel. Studies in Defoe, Richardson and Fielding*. London: Chatto & Windus.

Weber, Max (1947 [1904–5]) 'Die protestantische Ethik und der Geist des Kapitalismus', in Max Weber, *Gesammelte Aufsätze zur Religionssoziologie*. Tübingen: Verlag von J.C.B. Mohr/Paul Siebeck.

Wellbery, David E. (1990) 'Foreword', in Friedrich A. Kittler, *Discourse Networks 1800/1900*. Stanford: Stanford University Press. pp. vii-xxxiii.

Werlen, Iwar (1984) *Ritual und Sprache*. Tübingen: Gunter Narr Verlag.

Wernick, Andrew (1991) *Promotional Culture. Advertising, Ideology and Symbolic Expression*. London: Sage Publications.

Wiegelmann, Gnter (1967) *Alltags-und Festspeisen. Wandel und Gegenwärtige Stellung*. Marburg: N.G. Elwert Verlag.

Wilbert, Johannes (1987) *Tobacco and Shamanism in South America*. New Haven: Yale University Press.

Wilden, Anthony (1987) *The Rules are No Game*. London: Routledge & Kegan Paul.

Williams, Linda (1981) *Figures of Desire*. Chicago: University of Illinois Press.

Williams, Linda (1989) *Hard Core. Power, Pleasure, and the Frenzy of the Visible*. Berkeley: University of California Press.

Williams, Rosalind (1982) *Dream Worlds. Mass Consumption in Late Nineteenth-Century France*. Berkeley: University of California Press.

Williamson, Judith (1978) *Decoding Advertisements. Ideology and Meaning in Advertising*. London: Marion Boyars.

Williamson, Judith (1986) *Consuming Passions*. London: Marion Boyars.

Willis, Susan (1993) *A Primer for Daily Life*. London: Routledge.

Wills, Gary (1989) 'Message in the Deodorant Bottle: Inventing Time', *Critical Inquiry* 15(3): 497–509.

Wimmer, Michael (1984) 'Verstimmte Ohren und unerhörte Stimmen', in Dietmar Kamper and Christoph Wulf (eds), *Das Schwinden der Sinne*. Frankfurt am Main: Suhrkamp.

Woodmansee, Martha (1988) 'Toward a Genealogy of the Aesthetic: The German Reading Debate of the 1790s', *Cultural Critique* 11: 203–21.

Wouters, Cas (1977) 'Informalisierung und der Prozess der Zivilisation', in Peter Gleichmann et al. (eds), *Materialien zu Norbert Elias' Zivilisationstheorie*. Frankfurt am Main: Suhrkamp. pp. 279–98.

Wright, A. (1991) 'Early Advertising and Media', *Pharmaceutical Historian* 21(1): 6–8.

Young, James Harvey (1961) *The Toadstool Millionaires. A Social History of Patent Medicines in America before Federal Regulation*. Princeton: Princeton University Press.

Young, James Harvey (1967) *The Medical Messiahs. A Social History of Health Quackery in Twentieth-Century America*. Princeton: Princeton University Press.

zur Lippe, Rudolf (1978) *Am eigenen Leibe*. Frankfurt am Main: Syndikat.

zur Lippe, Rudolf (1979) *Naturbeherrschung am Menschen*. Frankfurt am Main: Syndikat.

NAME INDEX

SUBJECT INDEX

abject (Kristeva) 150n
abstinence 110, 146n
abundance 28, 95, 146n
acting, theatrical 199, 214–15n
actions, and performances 199
addition 98
advertisement: announcement and 151, 158;
  Benetton 180, 182; experiential goods as 157,
  179; guarantee, rhetorical in 174; patent
  medicines 156, 162–7, 173–4
advertising 116, 127, 147n, 148n: modern 151–85;
  before-after scheme 169; credibility in 178;
  dimensions of change 156–7; ethics of 167;
  impressionistic principle of (Johnson) 154,
  185n; irreferentiality in 176; Jubilee advertising
  94; negative register in 183n; positive register
  in 165–73; positive representations in 155;
  psychology of 153, 177; rational arguments in
  154; religious conversion and 163–4; rhetorical
  turn in 167; self-reflective 183n; truthfulness of
  178
aesthetics: aesthetic experience, lower limit of
  192; aesthetic man 109, 110, 112; anti-aesthetics
  in modernism 197; anti-representationalism in
  modern art 198; eroticism and 190; reflective
  111, 191–6; sensualistic 111, 191
alimentary code 13, see also food categorizations
alimentary communion (Durkheim) 70
always already (Derrida) 130
announcement, and advertisement 151, 158
anthro(to)pology 12–40 passim, see also
  topographical scheme
anti-aesthetics, modernism and 197
appetite 28
asceticism 47, 50, 110, 111, 112, 139, 150n
assimilative body (O'Neill) 27

beauty 111, 112, 192
binary opposition 16, see also edible/inedible;
  inside/outside
bodily control 13
bodily ego (Freud) 3, see also body, self and
bodily pleasures 56
bodily theatre, modern 198
bodily sovereignty 13
body: ambiguous role of 1–3; boundaries of 87;
  concept of 45–6, 52; corporeality and 8n, 57,
  61; cultivated 3; disciplined 3, 48–9;
  experiential aspect of 2; ex-pressions of 7, 14,
  32; grotesque body (Bakhtin) 25; historicity of
  2, 45–67; means of expression as 54, 199–200;

mind and 1; self and 3–8 passim 10, 12, 14–15,
  17, 19–28 passim, 32, 136, 150n; sensory 2, 7,
  11, 12, 40n; sensory apertures of 3; sensual 2,
  7, 10, 56, 57, 58, 191; soul and 46–7; speaking
  42n; surface of 12; tool as 49–51
brand, product 159
British moralists 111–12

cannibalism 74, 75, 91n, see also eater/food
  ambiguity
Carpenter-effect 216n
character vs. personality (Susman) 36
cinematic experience 207–9
civilizing process (Elias) 26, 53, 114, 116
classical political economy 99–102
collector 141–2
communication 43–4n: communion and 25, 36;
  individualizing mode of 160; mass
  communication 152; transmission and 204–12
  passim
communicative body (O'Neill) 27
communion 20, 25, 36, see also alimentary
  communion; eating-community
community 21, 136, 150n; see also eating-
  community
consciousness industry (Enzensberger) 116
conspicuous consumption 38, 121, 147n
constitution of the subject 19
consumer: economic factor as 106; of erotica 206;
  consumer society 93, Janus-faced 94, 152-3;
  subject of desire as 138
consumerism, mental basis of 38
consumption: concept of 93–7, 106, 145n;
  distinctive logic of 133, 137, 144; experience as
  156, 169; instrumental consumption 128;
  introjective logic of 132, 138, 144; non-
  consumption and 112; self-consumption as 100,
  112, 139; market economy of 107; mass
  consumption 116; modern consumption 7, 93,
  94; objects of 107, oral consumption 14–31,
  68–91, 167; private 100, 102; unproductive 102
control: collective boundaries of 21; individual
  boundaries of, see self-control; symbolic and
  practical 77
conversation 33, 43n
cooking 70, 71
corporeality 2, 8n, 55, 61; dimensions of 26, 62–5;
  post-structuralism on 4
cosmological schemes 1; oral cosmologies 24
counter-look-prohibition, in film 209
critical theory 116